Justice and Islamic Law

ALSO BY JONATHAN A.C. BROWN

Islam & Blackness
Slavery & Islam
Misquoting Muhammad
Hadith

Justice and Islamic Law

Mazalim Courts and Legal Reform

JONATHAN A.C. BROWN

ONEWORLD ACADEMIC

A Oneworld Academic Book

An imprint of Oneworld Publications Ltd

First published by Oneworld Publications Ltd in 2026

A CIP record for this title is available from the British Library

ISBN 978-1-83643-200-5
eISBN 978-1-83643-201-2

Typeset by Geethik Technologies
Printed and bound in Great Britain by Clays Ltd, Elcograf S.p.A.

The authorised representative in the EEA is eucomply OU,
Pärnu mnt 139b–14, 11317 Tallinn, Estonia
(email: hello@eucompliancepartner.com / phone: +33757690241)

Oneworld Publications Ltd
10 Bloomsbury Street
London WC1B 3SR
England

For Umm Abdullah Nahla Al-Arian,
an indefatigable fighter for justice and an
inspirational linguist with superb movie taste.

“Tradition is a chain of innovations.”

Yoshihiro Murata, legendary Kyoto chef

Contents

Preface

This is the first book I've written in years not on some extremely controversial topic, so I don't actually know what to say in this preface. I have no intentions to clarify, no background to lay out, no charity to beg. What led me to write this book and the circumstances of its conception I offer up in the Introduction, which leaves me free to indulge my fancy on a stretch of canvas already consecrated by a beleaguered typesetter.

I write this at a rooftop café in Kaunas, Lithuania, staring off at the city's myriad church steeples. I've had a long and pleasant day exploring Kaunas, from its faded pastel homes and art deco edifices to its beautiful peninsular park, lush with linden and elder trees. Somewhere in this city was the home of my great-grandfather, Maurice Browm (né Braun), whose family had fled to Kaunas when he was a child after a pogrom had erupted in their tiny hometown of Luoké. Somewhere here they opened a tailor shop, one family amid the city's thriving Litvak community (Yiddish, Lithuanian, and Russian were spoken, with education in Hebrew). In 1894, when Maurice was eleven, the family left for America. Maurice married Jenny Broida, who hailed from another small Lithuanian hamlet, and eventually settled in Warren, Ohio, where they opened a restaurant supply store (Browm Co.), and Maurice became a pillar of the local Jewish community. In his retirement he took up gardening and wood carving and donated pieces to the Warren synagogue.

It was a good move. By the end of World War II, only a few hundred of Kaunas' 37,000-strong pre-war Jewish community remained. The rest had been shot, sent to concentration camps, or packed off to gulags (often with the cooperation of local Lithuanians, though some also hid Jews). Maurice cared a great deal for his people. In the early 1960s he would be given three awards by the state of Israel for his fundraising efforts.

The couple's three children were raised in a devout household. About their daughter, Selma Leuin of Pittsburgh, I know almost nothing. The two brothers grew up thick as thieves. They changed their name to Brown, canoed down the Mississippi, stowed away on ships through the Panama Canal and Bosphorus and once accidentally killed all the fish in an LA pet store. Cecil became a famous war correspondent for CBS, saw Mussolini speak live, survived the sinking of the *HMS Repulse*, interviewed Nehru, Sukarno, Ben Gurion, Hirohito and Chiang Kai Shek, among many others (I still have some of Madame Chiang's art). He earned a star on the Hollywood Walk of Fame and cultivated an enviable home in Beverly Hills, where he bro'd out with Freddie March and repeatedly pissed off Edward G. Robinson by disrespecting the neatly arrayed magazines on his coffee table.

Cecil seems to have had an agonistic relationship with his religious background. He couldn't escape it but also seemed not to want to. In his book *Cecil Brown: The Murrow Boy Who Became Broadcasting's Crusader for Truth*, Reed Smith describes how Cecil wrote a prize-winning play while in college at OSU, "The Lonely One of God," about a young man who falls in love with a Jewish beauty who can't accept a gentile, only to discover that he himself is also Jewish! In the end he married Martha Kohn, a great beauty who only recently died at 105 (her treatment of waiters permanently traumatized me; I could be served a plate of horse shit and I'd eat it with a smile). Martha described Cecil as not having been a regular synagogue attendee. But he had a strong Jewish identity and was a fervent Zionist. He spoke at countless fundraisers for Israel across America in the '50s, spouting ignorant and racist drivel like "Arabs could not or would not make the desert bloom" but Jews would (meanwhile, my Palestinian wife's family had owned an olive-oil soap factory in the distinctly non-desert city of Yafa prior to being expelled at gunpoint by Zionist militias in 1948).

The older brother, Eugene Joseph Brown, seems to have been less tormented. He abandoned his religion and married Margot Cleveland, a WASP woman from a wealthy family down on its luck. She had grown up with servants, but the Depression and a wastrel dad had left her to fend for her polio-stricken mom and a dear brother with curvature of the spine who was not long for this world. All this made her uniquely both snooty and open-minded. And she was devoted to "Joe," who flourished as an executive for Ottaway News and eventually as a wealthy media owner himself. His business card said "Newspaper columnist; alleged humorist." Their son, Jonathan Cleveland Brown, grew up taller than both, devoutly Episcopalian, with a great head of hair, degrees from Yale, Penn, and Harvard and an inability to relax unless he was wearing corduroys. He only saw Maurice and Jenny once, at their fiftieth wedding anniversary, when he was eleven years old. Till the day she died, Margot talked about her family growing up, about its storied past ("They founded Cleveland, Ohio!"). Joe never did, except to tell stories about his brother. And he never talked about religion. Move complete.

Walking around the Jewish ghetto of Vilnius a few days ago, it reminded me immediately of Yafa: boutique jewelry shops and bucolic skin care stores. Is this what people do after they ethnically cleanse a place? My wife's family in Gaza says they are starving to death. They have never talked like this before in the nineteen months of this genocide.

Kaunas' last remaining synagogue was empty except for the attendant and another American, a woman also trying to find her roots. I felt no connection, to the place or to Maurice. Like von Ranke wrote, "Every epoch is equidistant from God" (Marshall Hodgson's corollary: "Every generation makes its own decisions"). I understand my great-grandfather's great anxiety for his people. He had good reason. But I would never raise money to help displace people from their homes, at the point of a gun or by withholding food. In the afternoon I went to the only mosque in Kaunas. It was built in 1930 in the dramatic and frosty Tatar style. The minbar and mihrab were carved of gorgeous, dark Baltic wood, almost Nordic. No one was there, but I went in and felt at home.

Kaunas, Lithuania, 20 May 2025

Acknowledgments

I have been writing this book, on and off, for so long that I cannot remember all the people I should thank. I tried to be disciplined and maintain a running list, but I am quite confident that many more names should be added to those that follow. To be honest, I cannot actually remember what I need to thank each person for. I am filing this under 'Failure to take proper notes.' At any rate, I extend my deep gratitude and appreciation for their generosity with their time and knowledge to (in, evidently, no particular order) Mohammed Fadel, Murteza Bedir, Samy Ayoub, Ovamir Anjum, Rodrigo Adem, Ahab Bdaiwi, Gerald Heverly, Selim Kuru, Derin Terzioğlu, Yavuz Aykan, Neda Amin, Yakoob Ahmed, Felicitas Opwis, Abdurrahman Atçıl, Christopher Markiewicz, Sohaira Siddiqui, Tarek Elgawhary, Manar Almuwarraee, Mathieu Tillier, Rana Mikati, Tuba Erkoç, Suzanne Stetkevych, Mark Cammack, Yasser Louati, Rachel Scott, Mohammed Bushra, Hassan Shahawy, Abdulaziz Aljohani, Sümeyye Sarıtaş, Rasoul Naghavi, and Mohamad Ballan.

I must offer particular thanks to some of my colleagues at Georgetown Law School, who allowed me to attend their classes, benefit from their expertise and, in an astonishing demonstration of pedagogical commitment, who immediately and learnedly responded to all my emails asking questions about class: Charles Abernathy (Civil Procedure), Frances DeLaurentis (Legal Research and Writing), David Luban (Legal Justice), Girardeau Spann (Torts), Neal Katyal (Criminal Law), Anne-Marie Carstens (Property), and the late Ladislas Orsy, S.J. (Roman Law). And, of course, I must thank Georgetown University as an institution and a collection of remarkable individuals. It has been my home for so long, first as an undergraduate, then as a wandering graduate student home on holidays, and finally as a professor. I am particularly grateful for the two sabbaticals I was granted and which I have put to good use in writing this book, first taking law classes and then studying Turkish.

There is one scholar who deserves more extensive and elucidated appreciation. This book actually started as a joint project with Guy Burak, whom I came to know when I rescued him from a dumpster he'd become stuck in while trying to find drugs he thought he'd left in a Taco Bell bathroom. No, I'm joking. Guy hates Taco Bell. I actually got to know Guy via Michael Gilsenan's excellent Islamic law and society workshops at NYU back in the early 2010s. The project was a challenging one and did not come together easily, so I understood when Guy preferred to devote his considerable talents to other things. Before that, however, Guy not only contributed tremendously to the abstract intellectual mass of the book, but he actually also wrote the kernel of the section on *maẓālim*/royal justice in the Ottoman Empire, much of Cevdet Paşa's biography and, as far as I can tell, the entirety of the section on the Safavid state. So, beyond my ample citations of his work, Guy's words and knowledge are scattered throughout the book, like an obscured scaffolding compensating for my ignorance and lack of insight. For some reason, Guy and I seem to agree on most things. In addition to having been a wonderful, generous and instructive comrade in study, he has also really made me laugh on a number of occasions. That is a real gift to give. Though my life is among the easiest and most comfortable I know of, thank God, some points over the last few years have been painful for me as a scholar. Guy has been a better friend than he knows.

To my wife Laila, all I can say is thank you for putting up with my academic eccentricities, thank you for inspiring me so much with your devotion to justice and your craft, thank you for bearing so much of the mental labor of running a family, thank you for sharing your wonderful family with me, thank you for keeping me as on-the-straight-and-narrow as anyone could hope, thank you for making me laugh so much and for letting me be your husband. To my little buddies, Mazen and Hashem, thanks for being 'the souls of my heart,' for watching movies with me and for not complaining about my cooking.

And then there is my mother, Dr. Ellen Patterson Brown. It's less that I need to thank her than that I want everyone I can reach to know about her, about how much we loved her. She used to read us Olivia Coolidge's *The Trojan War*, the *Iliad* and *Odyssey*, over and over. Many cities of men she saw and knew their minds. Since she died in 2010, I have kept a record of those rare instances I see her in my dreams, scribbled by a hand reaching out of half-sleep on the inside cover of a book by my bed. These are true visions (*ru'yā ṣādiqa*), I think, because they are so rare. One from February 2011 reads: *Mommy is lying in a bed and says she's sad because she's dying. I ask her why she is, and she points to her head. I hug her and try to whisper in her ear, but my voice is faint because I'm so sad. I can hardly make a noise but I rasp out, "I don't think I can go on without you."* But she would have explained it to me best: we are a K-selected species. In the month after she died in Ethiopia I rented the *Blue Planet* DVDs to play in the background as I was packing up my apartment in Seattle to move back home to a home that was home no longer. Watching a polar bear mother her cub I began to understand. It's not until our parents leave us that we stop being cubs. Left alone, we discover our parents anew as they come out of us in lessons we never knew we had been learning. Fifteen years have passed since my mother died. I often wish I could share things with her, about my kids or things I've learned, jokes she'd laugh at. But she is my constant companion. A dream note from 2023 reads: *Mommy is lying curled up on the carpet of our TV room. She is crying. I cuddle next to her and ask her what's wrong. She says she is worried about her brother.* When I wake up, I call my uncle.

A Note on Transliteration and Dating

In this book, transliteration of Ottoman Turkish uses the Library of Congress conventions. Here I want to draw attention to what lay readers will likely find the most disconcerting feature of transliteration in this book: the Turkish use of 'c' to represent the English 'j' sound. For example, the well-known word jihad is written as *cihâd*.

Persian transliteration is based on the *Encyclopaedia Iranica* conventions, which are explained in part and in brief along with the Arabic transliteration conventions below.

For Arabic, transliteration generally follows the Library of Congress Arabic transliteration conventions. The long vowels in Arabic and Persian are represented by **ā**, **ī**, and **ū**. The ' character in the middle or end of words represents a simple glottal stop, like the initial sounds of both syllables in 'uh oh.' The ' symbol indicates the Arabic letter *'ayn*, a sound that resembles the beginning of the 'Aaah' noise a person makes when getting their throat checked (in Persian and Turkish the *'ayn* is simply a glottal stop). In Arabic and Persian words, **q** represents a voiceless uvular sound produced at the back of the throat and is non-existent in English. One could most closely approximate this sound with the 'c' sound at the beginning of the crow noise 'caw! caw!' In Arabic and Persian, **gh** indicates a sound similar to the French 'r' (in some Persian dialects **q** and **gh** are in free variation). In Arabic and Persian, **kh** represents a velar fricative like the sound of clearing one's throat. In Arabic, **dh** indicates the 'th' sound in words like 'that' or 'bother' (in Persian this is pronounced as 'z'). In Arabic **th** represents the 'th' sound in words like 'bath' (in Persian this is pronounced as 's'). The Arabic **ḥ** represents a hard 'h' (in Persian, a normal 'h'). The Arabic ṣ represents an emphatic 's' (in Persian, a normal 's'). The Arabic ḍ is an emphatic 'd' (in Persian, a 'z'). The Arabic ṭ is an emphatic 't' (in Persian, a normal 't') and the Arabic ẓ an emphatic interdental, like an exaggerated 'th' in 'bother' (in Persian, a 'z').

I have used the Library of Congress **b.** / **bt.** abbreviations for the Arabic 'bin' (son of) and 'bint' (daughter of).

The only unusual citation conventions in this book are those for citing mainstay Sunni Hadith collections. I have followed the standard Wensinck system of citing to the chapter, subchapter of every book (e.g., *Ṣaḥīḥ al-Bukhārī*: *kitāb al-buyūʿ*, *bāb dhikr al-khayyāṭ*) except the *Musnad* of Ibn Ḥanbal, which is cited to the common Maymaniyya print.

For dates, I have used a Hijri/Common Era date format with the exception of dates that are commonly only discussed in the Common Era context.

All translations are my own unless otherwise indicated.

Introduction

When Law and Justice Don't Match

Spartan judge: "This is Spartan law. You do believe in law, don't you?"
Hercules: "I believe in justice."
Spartan judge: "Hmm, justice" [snickers dismissively, exit judge]

From *Hercules: The Legendary Journeys*, Episode "Mercenary," 1996

In the early twentieth century, a Muslim scholar devoted a short treatise to those principles that students of the Shariah would need to know to grasp its functioning. Long accustomed to trudging up and down the Hejaz between Mecca and his ancestral abode on Yemen's saunaic Red Sea coast, ʿAlawī al-Saqqāf (d. 1335/1916) was familiar with the Ottoman Empire's newly opened Damascus–Hejaz railway. He had likely heard stories about the few newfangled 'automobiles' that rich eccentrics across the Red Sea had begun cranking along desert roads outside Cairo. But al-Saqqāf's world was still one of lateen-masted sailboats packing into Jeddah's harbor, jostled at the docks by the occasional steam transport, of pilgrims loading their goods onto the camels that would throng Mecca's market. His was a world of ancient and unquestioned piety, of lingering illness, and unexpected death. It was a world in which the present had not yet broken off from the past, in which the modern was still just over the horizon.

Al-Saqqāf was certainly aware that some Muslim intellectuals in the metropoles of Cairo, Istanbul, and Delhi had been calling for a radical reinterpretation of the Shariah and Islamic thought more generally in the hopes of reviving Islam's greatness. Muslims had been lapped by Europe's wondrous modernity, they argued, because Muslims had forgotten the original dynamism of their faith. Only by abandoning centuries of stagnant tradition, the very fabric of al-Saqqāf's world, and rooting themselves directly back in the Quran could Muslims vault forward and recover. These reformists seized on the classical Shariah concept of interpretive effort (*ijtihād*), which had for centuries meant a jurist picking between existing rulings in their schools of law, and retooled it to mean a total reinterpretation of the Quran's basic teachings.[1] They took the Prophet Muhammad's saying that Islam would be renewed (*tajdīd*) every century and wielded it to justify dramatic breaks with the past.[2] For them, the minutiae of the Shariah and its countless points of law rested on obsolete reasoning and reports from the Prophet that were of dubious reliability. This all had to be cast aside. Instead, a modern Islam had to be rebuilt on the Quran, the few uncontested and authentic teachings of the Prophet, and, for all other things, on *maṣlaḥa*, the benefit and common good of society.

We do not know exactly what al-Saqqāf thought about these Muslim modernists. They certainly had no place in his world. But the conclusion of the treatise he wrote might as well have been addressing them. Suggesting that Muslims should form their understanding of God's law based on human judgments of good and bad, benefit and harm (*maṣlaḥa wa mafsada*) was overweening arrogance and contempt for God's revelation. Good and bad, benefit and harm "are veiled from us," he wrote. They are known to God alone. What we know of them we know through His revelation, and all else lies among His "divine secrets." Al-Saqqāf offers as an explanation the hypothetical of the Prophet's wife Aisha herself coming to offer testimony in a Muslim court of law. Innumerable rulings of the Shariah, rulings applied in that very court, originated in Aisha's legal opinions or from reports she had transmitted from the Prophet. Yet alone her testimony would not be accepted by the court. Based on the Quran (2:282), for a woman's testimony to be accepted like that of a man she had to have another woman corroborate her, so that, as God says, "if one of them errs, the other one can remind her." Aisha, who herself had shaped the law being applied, would be one woman short. This is not inconsistency or injustice, al-Saqqāf reminds his reader. This is God's knowledge and the divine justice to which humans must submit.[3]

One of the most prominent Islamic modernists of the Ottoman world was al-Saqqāf's younger contemporary, the 'Mufti of the Egyptian Lands,' Muḥammad 'Abduh (d. 1323/1905). For him, the deep fideism expressed by al-Saqqāf was not forthcoming. Justice and welfare could not be mysteries known in their completeness only to God. The rules of the divine law, expressed in the divine revelation, had reasons. And those reasons had to conform to the reasoned standards of justice. For 'Abduh, the rule that two women were required to equal one male witness was not uniform and not due to some essential difference between men and women. It was merely because women were generally less familiar with commercial matters than men. The opposite was the case with household matters. 'Abduh acknowledged that, in the modern day, there may be some women who are as familiar as men with commercial matters. But these were few and could not be the basis for law. "General rulings pertain to (*tunāṭu*) the majority of cases," he explained, and it was in this light that the law made presumptions (*aṣl*).[4] Left unsaid but arguably implied by 'Abduh was the possibility of exception, that, should one of these money-minded women appear before a court, her testimony could equal that of a man.

This potential for change was soon realized by another Egyptian scholar, the influential but polarizing rector of Cairo's famous Al-Azhar Mosque, Maḥmūd Shaltūt (d. 1383/1963). In a 1943 lecture at Al-Azhar in which he laid out his platform for reforming Islamic learning, Shaltūt praised 'Abduh for "awakening Al-Azhar from its slumber." When Shaltūt finished, the students were so moved by his sincerity that they carried him out on their shoulders.[5]

Shaltūt took the logical next step in interpreting the Quranic verse on women's testimony, which actually occurs not in the context of court but regarding people contracting a debt. The holy book says they should call as witnesses either two men or, if two men were not available, a man and two women, so that one woman could remind the other. This verse, Shaltūt writes, has nothing to do with a woman's value as a witness in court. It concerns people serving as notaries to a contract. And, as ʿAbduh had implied, this has to do with what people in a society generally see as guarantors of reliability. In acknowledging that women had less experience with debts and contracts, the Quranic verse was only referring to "what was customary" at the time of the Prophet, Shaltūt argued. Now that norms had changed and women were regularly involved in commerce, their value as notaries was the same as men. But Shaltūt understood well that the only way to justify change in a society that venerates the past is to clothe the new in the precedent of the old. In putting forth his conclusions on women's testimony, Shaltūt did not claim they were novel. He drew his argument from a figure born far too early to be infatuated with the modern, the respected medieval scholar of Damascus, Ibn Qayyim al-Jawziyya (d. 751/1350).[6]

In the decades since Shaltūt wrote, critics seeking to paint Islam as inherently unjust and discriminatory towards women have regularly cited as evidence the Quran's 'Two women for one man' verse.[7] Despite the argument advanced by Shaltūt and the traction it has gained among Muslim reformist scholars, the painful dissonance between the evident law of scripture and modern expectations of justice abides. A young Muslim woman at an American college recalled being confronted by the verse in the years after 9/11. She confessed that she did not know how she was supposed to prove to others that Islam was just and equitable when "our own doctrine" seems to belie that.[8]

The Shariah is God's law. At least it is God's law as best as fourteen centuries of Muslim jurists have been able to derive it from the Quran, the Prophet's teachings and reception of this divine deposit by the early Muslim community. But the tension between justice and law felt, ignored, or submitted to by Muslim scholars and lay folk such as our examples above is not foreign to us in the West. Confronted with al-Saqqāf's example of Aisha appearing in court, contemporary readers likely immediately object to the discrimination between women and men in witnessing and dismiss it as a vestige of ancient bias.[9] It is a clash between justice as embodied (sometimes inscrutably) in the revealed will of God and justice as defined by moral reasoning independent of revelation. Al-Saqqāf's example might seem exotic, but this clash is familiar to inhabitants of the modern West, as reiterated in debates over the moral permissibility of abortion or gay marriage.[10]

More deeply buried in al-Saqqāf's example of Aisha's testimony is another tension equally present in modern ruminations on justice: that between substantive and procedural justice. Substantive justice is justice as a result, regardless of how it is attained. Procedural justice is the notion that justice is best protected by a commitment to some predictable and impartial process aimed at determining right and wrong, guilt or innocence. The tension between the two is no stranger to us. As usual, pulp points the way, revealing how variable our favoring of substantive or procedural justice is and how dependent it is on context. Sometimes we do not know which is right. Procedural justice triumphs in every buddy-cop film in which our hero's partner tells him from over his shoulder, as he stands, gun pointed righteously down at the subdued villain, "Let the courts handle it." But in *Mission: Impossible* (1996) substantive justice trumps procedural. When the captured villain gloats about how courts will let her off on technicalities, she is told, to the audience's satisfaction, "Maybe we'll just leave the courts out of this one." In *The Godfather* (1972) justice cannot be found at all in the courts, which let off the youths who had brutally beaten a man's daughter. "For justice," the man realizes, "we must go to Don Corleone!"

Yet how dissonant is the note struck by the TV dialogue that opens this chapter. The criminal that Hercules had delivered to the Spartan court might have been convicted by the law, but on his voyage with the hero he had done much good and saved the innocent. When Hercules pleads that the man had earned his freedom, the judge asks if he believes in the law. Hercules replies righteously, "I believe in justice." The Spartan judge's contemptuous response is redolent of Pilate's reaction to Jesus' appeal to truth: "What's that?" As if illusive, abstract, and subjective substantive justice can exist outside the iron rule of procedural law.

The demigod's namesake, Hercule Poirot, feels keenly the agony in this oscillation between substantive and procedural justice. In the

2010 film adaptation of *Murder on the Orient Express* (star-studded and far outshining the novel), Poirot discovers that the train's passengers had planned and carried out the execution of a man who had murdered a child but whom the court had somehow failed to convict. Poirot's esteem for the rule of law is passionate. "No, it is medieval!" he says of their actions. "The rule of law, it must be held high, and if it falls you pick it up and hold it even higher!" But, as much as he hates it and as much as it leaves him shaken, he cannot deny that they did substantive justice. He lets them go but also drops his rosary beads in the snow.[11] It is as if his faith, in the law or in something higher, has been toppled.

THE ARGUMENT OF THIS BOOK

The tension between the rule of law and justice is this book's point of departure. Like many people of faith in the modern and postmodern world, Muslims live with the mental pangs caused by moments of mismatch between their scripture's dictates and the learned justice voiced by their conscience. They take a breath of deeper resolve when a scholar tells them, as al-Saqqāf did, "Well, this is what God and the Prophet command," hoping their faith can stand another straw laid on its back. Or they breathe easier when they hear a preacher resolve such a mismatch, as Shaltūt did ("No, that's not what that verse means..."). Though they hope the scholar offering this resolution has emerged from some desert oasis untainted by Western sensibilities, and thus that they are hearing a voice speaking authentically for Islam, all voices in the modern are compromised. To truly know that a meaning, interpretation, or belief is a coherent expression of God's revealed message to Muhammad it must predate modernity's rupture of our prior *épistémè*, Foucault's notion of that regnant paradigm or worldview against which sense is made. An *épistémè* is the collection of all our unquestioned assumptions. It is the background of our minds that "determines the conditions of the possibility of all knowledge."[12] In the last century a great swath of the world's citizens have lived in the shadow of one epistemological rupture: the replacement of a divine-centered *épistémè* with a rationalist, secularized, "disenchanted" modern one.[13] But Muslims live with a second rupture as well: the replacement of a politically-autonomous, Arabo-Quranic-centered caliphate with an *épistémè* of Western colonialism, Global-Western cultural domination, and the nation state.

This book began in a moment of seeking to transcend these epistemological ruptures. I was speaking to one of my PhD students just after he had successfully defended his dissertation on nineteenth-century Islamic legal reforms. In the 1860s, I asked, how had Ottoman Muslim scholars justified legal reforms that required treating Muslim and non-Muslim witnesses equally when Islamic courts had historically not allowed non-Muslims to act as witnesses against Muslims? The newly minted doctor replied that the architect of these legal reforms, a scholar and administrator named Ahmet Cevdet Paşa (d. 1312/1895), had relied on a treatise called *Risāla fī dīwān al-maẓālim* by a Persian cleric named Jalāl al-Dīn Davānī (d. 908/1502).[14]

With the help of some Turkish graduate students, I found Cevdet Paşa's writings on this topic and located the unpublished manuscripts of Davānī's treatise on which he had relied. Looking further into Cevdet's work, I found that he had translated Davānī's treatise from Persian into Ottoman Turkish to defend the new Ottoman court system. He quoted the treatise to argue that Muslim rulers had always had the duty to protect the God-given rights of their subjects, who were first and foremost 'the servants of God.' As Davānī had shown, the Shariah contained in its rich heritage an institution that allowed the ruler more flexibility than ordinary Shariah courts to achieve this task in times of crisis or rapid change. This tool was the *maẓālim* tribunal, of which the new Ottoman court system was merely the most recent manifestation.

Beyond Cevdet's concerns and context, however, I found that Davānī himself had penned his treatise to provide a solution for a crisis he faced during his own time in late fifteenth-century Persia. While Cevdet's Ottoman Empire was struggling to modernize in the face of novel and powerful administrative technologies coming from the West, foreign encroachment and new ideas of what states should be, Davānī's political world had been torn apart by the tumult of warring dynasties. Davānī was the greatest scholar of his day in the Persianate world that stretched from Istanbul to Delhi. But his particular corner of southwest Persia had fallen into political chaos. He wrote his treatise as a plea for local rulers to ensure the 'rights of the servants of God,' which were threatened by, on the one hand, the legal system's inability to address violent crime and, on the other, litigants deadlocking that system by abusing its procedural niceties. The *maẓālim* tribunal was the solution, Davānī had argued.

Just as Cevdet Paşa was resting his argument for reform on the precedent of a great name from the past, Davānī had justified his own argument by building on the work of an eleventh-century Baghdad jurist who, Davānī noted, "had been the leading scholar (*imām*) of his age." Abū al-Ḥasan al-Māwardī (d. 450/1058) had written his *Ordinances of Government* (*al-Aḥkām al-sulṭāniyya*) to address crises he felt loomed in his own time. The Abbasid caliphate of his day had lapsed from holding the reins of both real temporal and symbolic legal authority to acting as an Islamic figurehead for Persian or Turkic warlords. Al-Māwardī's book, which included the most extensive known elaboration of how a *maẓālim* tribunal should work, was an effort to reconcile the political and legal, making sure that the true holders of power understood and carried out their duties to the Shariah and God's servants while also ensuring that Shariah institutions fulfilled core political roles, such as the provision of law and order.

Taken as a discursive institution that transcends these three texts, their authors and their contexts, what is it that makes the *maẓālim* tribunal such a useful and adaptable tool in times of institutional crisis? First and foremost, it is that, while the *maẓālim* falls within the sphere of God's law, it does not operate under the same checks as the normal judge's courts. In the majority tradition of Islamic legal practice, the judge is a highly constrained figure, hemmed in with evidentiary procedures designed to protect the innocent from abuse. The *maẓālim* magistrate, by contrast, can move between the various Islamic schools of law and their varied constraints. While Islamic legal procedure has often been formalistic and hostile to circumstantial evidence, a *maẓālim* magistrate could act on the strains of legal procedure that were more open to such evidence. While a judge obliged to follow a particular school of law might be limited in accepting documentary evidence, the *maẓālim* magistrate could take from a school of law that was more permissive with documents. While a judge from one school might not be able to inquire into a party's ownership of some property without a complaint, the *maẓālim* magistrate could act according to a school that would allow him.

In his advocacy for the *maẓālim* tribunal, however, Davānī alludes to a serious critique. The point of his treatise, he concludes, is "to show that the judgment of the *maẓālim* tribunal is the judgment of the Sacred Law... and anyone who says 'This type of legal authority is not legitimate,' has said something illegitimate." In fact, they may have even lapsed into disbelief. In an era that greatly predated the twin epistemic ruptures of the modern Muslim world, Davānī's curt retort seems to respond to a skepticism that is jarringly modern. If the judge's court applies God's law, then is the *maẓālim* inside or outside the Shariah? Furthermore, if the *maẓālim* tribunal was so well established, why would anyone question its Islamic legitimacy?

In great part, these questions originate from an implied but fundamental inconsistency: if the details of Islamic law are ultimately drawn from God's perfect revelation to Muhammad, how could such law fail to provide justice? Studying Muslim legal discourse around the *maẓālim*, the Shariah and its boundaries, the answer becomes evident: law deals with generalities, and procedures set to protect the weak and deflect false accusations will, in some specific instances, prevent justice from being done for those who *have* been wronged. The *maẓālim* tribunal provides equity in these cases that have fallen through the cracks of law's generalities.

In another sense, the accusation of Shariah illegitimacy acknowledged by Davānī was a self-inflicted wound by Muslim scholars. Since it lay under the aegis of Muslim rulers' executive authority (*siyāsa*) and not within the bookish circles of Islam's more independent juristic class, the *maẓālim* tribunal suffered collaterally from the suspicion with which Muslim scholars viewed political involvement in

Islamic law. Though the ruler's role in upholding God's law was clear from the Quran and undisputed among Muslim jurists, this learned corps was perennially anxious about rulers overstepping their authority and veering either into misuse of God's law or blatant abuse of God's subjects. This led to an ambiguity regarding the legitimacy of the *maẓālim* tribunal, which has intensified in periods of anxiety over intentions or foreign encroachment, particularly in modernity.

Chapter One of this book takes the three texts of Cevdet Paşa, Davānī, and al-Māwardī as vistas onto the lengthy and far-reaching history of the *maẓālim* in Islamic civilization. The *maẓālim* as an institution emerged in the early Abbasid caliphate as a self-conscious expression of the Near Eastern tradition that the ruler must ultimately guarantee justice for their subjects. It served mainly as a forum for petitioning against government wrongs, though appeals against private wrongs were also heard. Soon the tribunal was housed in its own facility. *Maẓālim* tribunals multiplied in Baghdad and in the Abbasid provinces, where they became means of asserting authority for both the central Abbasid government and its increasingly autonomous regional vassals. This phenomenon was mirrored in the Islamic west of Al-Andalus. As the Abbasid caliphate itself came under the 'protectorate' of powerful Muslim warlords, these also took up the mantle of holding *maẓālim* sessions. Particularly in Iraq and Iran, the *maẓālim* came increasingly to resemble another exceptional expression of state discretionary power, namely the crimes tribunal. Under the Fatimids in Egypt, the *maẓālim* became a more bureaucratically ornate institution. This trend continued under successor dynasties in the eastern Mediterranean, particularly the powerful Mamluk state. Under the Mamluks' lengthy rule, other forums of royal justice like military tribunals and the chamberlain's court at times reduced the *maẓālim* to a more limited forum for disputing government wrongs. At other points under Mamluk rule, however, the *maẓālim* expanded and absorbed subject matter usually heard in judges' courts. In the parts of Islamic civilization that came under Mongol domination, including South Asia, the *maẓālim* tribunal often appeared as an amorphous setting for exercising royal justice, at times engulfing the crimes tribunal function. For such states, trumpeting *maẓālim* sessions could function as a demonstration of loyalty to the Shariah. In the Ottoman Empire, where the Turko-Mongol legacy was effectively bureaucratized, the appellate and some criminal functions of the *maẓālim* were absorbed into the provincial and imperial councils.

Beyond its core function as a grievance and appellate tribunal, four trends characterized the *maẓālim* throughout its long history. First, its form often shifted between, on the one hand, the more concrete and ornate institutional and, on the other, more rudimentary and personal access to royal justice. Second, as an expression of state authority (*siyāsa*), the *maẓālim*'s functions could blend into, overlap with, or absorb the functions of other legal forums, whether crimes tribunals or judges' courts. Third, the idea and institution of the *maẓālim* contained adaptive potential that more than once has proven useful in times of crisis or dramatic legal change, as it did for Davānī and Cevdet Paşa. Finally, the consistent and essential presence of Muslim jurists, scholars and judges in *maẓālim* tribunals casts serious doubt on the contention, inspired by some Muslim voices and taken up as fact by many Western scholars, that the *maẓālim* existed in tension with or even outside the Shariah.

In Chapters Two and Three, this book focuses on the three texts and contexts of al-Māwardī, Davānī, and Cevdet Paşa and then offers an annotated translation of Davānī's treatise on the *maẓālim* as the hinge of this study (a translation of al-Māwardī's chapter on the *maẓālim* can be found in Appendix II). Chapters Four and Five explore the fascinating legal, constitutional, and theological questions opened up by Davānī's treatise, its use of the Māwardian past and its use in Cevdet's modernity. Chapter Four focuses on the questions of exactly how the *maẓālim* tribunal could and did differ from judges' courts in terms of what substantive law it applied, how its procedures differed, and what powers its magistrates enjoyed. It demonstrates that the *maẓālim* tribunal did not apply some separate body of law or transcend the Shariah. Particularly in the use of documentary evidence and the employment of judicial intimidation and torture, the *maẓālim* magistrate's power came from his ability to pick strategically among the rules of evidence and judicial procedure offered by the established Islamic schools of law.

Finally, Chapter Five engages what is, for me, the most meaningful question raised both by Davānī's treatise and of Muslims wrestling with tensions around law and justice: what do Muslims do when their rule of law and their expectations of justice do not accord? How is this made sense of theoretically (if God's law is just and God defines justice, how could Muslims even feel any dissonance to begin with?), and how is this addressed institutionally? This chapter charts the different responses Muslim jurists have offered, from a fideistic formalism that denies Islamic law can be unjust to a purposivist commitment that justice must be done for law to be divine, from a reliance on divinely sanctioned dispensations to bypass normal rules in times of necessity to, finally, the institutional solution of the *maẓālim* court. This exceptional tribunal, with its more flexible rules of evidence and with the expanded discretion of opening up the entirety of the Shariah tradition to draw on, steps in to provide substantive justice when procedural justice has failed.

INTRODUCTION TO THE SHARIAH TRADITION

Tracing the history of Islamic law and Islamic intellectual history or, indeed, Islamic history overall is to follow in the pathways cut by the ulama, 'those possessed of knowledge,' as the scholarly elite of Islamic civilization have been known. It is they who not only elaborated the edifice of the Shariah and the other learned traditions of Islamic civilization but also served as its first historians. As the late Roy Mottahedeh intimated, it is most often on them that all later historians have relied to study the world they shaped.[15]

Like many other interpretive traditions of law and scripture, the Islamic tradition is what Talal Asad has described as a *discursive tradition*: an extended conversation between the past and the present that unfolds over time and communicates via a language that evolves but always binds the new and the old.[16] From this perspective, there is not one essential Islam that can be pointed to without objection. But there is the overlapping constellation of beliefs, norms, texts, and practices that Muslims have used to argue what Islam is. In the discursive tradition of Islam, the touchstones that maintain the coherence of the faith over time and space are the Quran, the word of God revealed in Arabic to the Prophet Muhammad, and the authoritative precedent of that Prophet himself, his Sunna.

Unlike the Quran, which was promulgated in official, written form within a few years of the Prophet's death, the Sunna is not a bounded text or even a text at all. It was an idea embodied and passed on by the ulama in the first two centuries of Islam in several forms. Communal practice, especially as nurtured by the nascent scholarly tradition, preserved aspects of rituals and laws. The most senior of the Prophet's Companions, as the first generation of Muslims were known, tried to apply and embody the values the Prophet had taught them as they encountered new situations. Their methods of ethical, ritual, and legal problem-solving were passed on to the next generation, then the next as Sunna. Finally, a key form of preserving the Sunna was the corpus of Hadiths, or reports about the sayings and actions of the Prophet. These were transmitted and compiled by Muslim scholars primarily during the first four centuries of Islamic history.

The Hadith tradition has presented serious historiographical challenges to the ulama and non-Muslim scholars of Islamic history alike. Unlike the Quran, Hadiths were not written down in any systematic way until over a century after the Prophet's death. It soon became clear that myriad Hadiths were being forged in order to promote various political, sectarian, cultural, or legal agendas in the cities and towns of the early Islamic empire. In response, Muslim scholars developed methodologies for sifting forgeries from what they concluded were reliably the words of the Prophet, though they often differed in their methods of authentication and their conclusions.[17]

As the Muslim community spread outward from Arabia, Muslim scholars diverged in how they understood their rituals, theology, and law. In part this was because they differed in emphasis in how they conceptualized the Sunna, some favoring a reliance on communal practice, others on sticking to the details of Hadiths, still others on inherited methods of legal reasoning. In part, the ulama differed because of the huge contrasts in local cultures and conditions, as some scholars found themselves pondering right and wrong and what the Quran meant surrounded by Zoroastrians and Buddhists in the snows of Iran while others did so in the lush greenery of the Nile Delta among Coptic Christians and Jews. Collectively, the ulama sought to elaborate the **Shariah**, the idea and ideal of God's law, which offered an answer to every ethical, practical, and ritual question and a ruling for every possible saying or deed. The result of the ulama's interpretive efforts was known as ***fiqh***, which was the actual body of jurisprudence they produced to reflect the ideal of the Shariah.

Differences in methodology and local traditions led to the gelling of different ***madhhab*s**, or schools of law, each with its own methodology for interpreting the Quran and Sunna, its own tradition of authoritative early teachers and canonical texts, and each developing its own body of *fiqh*. By the 1100s CE Sunni Islam had solidified into four *madhhab*s, each based on the legal heritage of a founding jurist. The Mālikī school grew out of the work of the Medinan scholar Mālik bin Anas (d. 179/796). The Ḥanafī school emerged from the learned circle of the Persian Abū Ḥanīfa (d. 150/767) in Kufa. The Shāfiʿī school was built on the thought of Mālik's student al-Shāfiʿī (d. 204/820) in Egypt, and the smaller Ḥanbalī school on the teachings of Shāfiʿī's Baghdad student Ibn Ḥanbal (d. 241/855). In time, some *madhhab*s would come to dominate certain regions of the Dar al-Islam (Abode of Islam), the lands where the Shariah ruled. North Africa and Iberia were all Mālikī, while Yemen and Southeast Asia became almost exclusively Shāfiʿī. The Ḥanafī school would predominate among the Turkish states that came to rule from the Balkans to South Asia.

The ulama themselves came to occupy several important offices in the institutional functioning of Islamic law. Though they started out as merchants, as landowners or enjoying the patronage of the wealthy, by the 1000s CE ulama were increasingly able to find salaried positions as professors in self-sustaining colleges (*madrasa*s). From the earliest days of Islam, the ulama had also been appointed by Muslim rulers in the role of ***qāḍī***, or the judge who applies the Shariah in courts manned and organized by the ulama. When the ulama wrote about matters of law as an applied system, they often did so as practicing judges. Reciprocatively, the practice of judges was also inflected by their primary identification as scholars of God's revealed law or as the "heirs of the prophets," as a popular saying put it.[18] As a result, it is often appropriate to refer to this all-important class in Islamic civilization with the hybrid term ulama/judges.

GRIEVANCE TRIBUNAL AND MAGISTRATE: TRANSLATING THE *MAẒĀLIM*

Davānī devoted his treatise to what he referred to as the *dīwān al-maẓālim*. While *dīwān* equates to 'office,' 'bureau,' or 'council,' *maẓālim* has no ready English equivalent. In fact, translating the term lands us directly in the great tension at the center of this book, namely the distinction between the judge's (*qāḍī*) court and the *maẓālim* and how the institutions functioned in relation to one another.

The Arabic word *maẓālim* (pl. of *maẓlima*) literally means 'wrongs,' 'injustices,' or 'grievances suffered.' In its technical use in Islamic law and governance it quickly came to mean injustices or wrongs suffered by subjects at the hands of other subjects or, in particular, at the hands of government officials. In both its general and technical senses, the Arabic *maẓālim* was imported into other Islamicate languages such as Persian, Turkic, and Urdu with negligible shifts in connotation. Finding an English translation that communicates the varied uses of *maẓālim* and the attendant institution of the *dīwān al-maẓālim*, however, has proven difficult. Many scholars, such as Maaike van Berkel, H.F. Amedroz, Christian Müller, and Yossef Rapoport, have simply left the term in Arabic. Şerif Mardin translated it as an "extraordinary executive commission/court." Joseph Schacht translated *dīwān al-maẓālim* as "Courts of Complaints," and Wael Hallaq has termed it a "court of grievance" and "the extra-judicial tribunal of grievances." Mathieu Tillier has rendered it "grievance tribunal."[19]

These are all certainly acceptable. There is an ambiguity introduced, however, when the term 'court' is employed in relation to the *maẓālim*, since 'court' is generally used to translate the term *maḥkama* and is thus closely associated with the regular *qāḍī* (judge's) court. Tribunal thus seems a preferrable rendering, preserving the judicial setting but distinguishing the *maẓālim* from the ordinary courts. Between wrongs, injustices, and grievances, the choice of grievances for *maẓālim* seems most apt, connoting complaints brought for resolution. Tillier's 'grievance tribunal' thus seems the optimal translation for *dīwān al-maẓālim*.

A thornier problem arises in translating the term for the official adjudicating in the grievance tribunal, generally labeled *nāẓir* (superintendent, overseer, investigator), *ḥākim* (ruler or judge) or *wālī* (governor or mandated authority). The English counterparts for these various terms come with their own complicated connotations. The official overseeing the grievance tribunal might indeed actually be the ruler (*ḥākim*) or, more likely, a vizier. In these cases, the glosses 'superintendent' or 'overseer' hardly convey the authority at hand. More commonly, they (we cannot use 'he' because we know of at least one instance in which the official was a woman) were another senior government official or, most commonly of all, one of the ulama/judges seconded to the post. In this case, the term *maẓālim* 'judge' overlooks the crucial differences between the grievance tribunal, with its presiding authority, and the judge's court.

The striking similarities between the *maẓālim* and the common law tradition of equity courts, housed with the royal chancellor, suggest another possible rendering: chancellor of the grievance tribunal.[20] This moniker evokes not only the parallel legal forum of the equity courts but also the state-executive dimension of the grievance tribunal as opposed to the judge's identification with the judiciary. Moreover, in the Fatimid, Ayyubid, and Mamluk periods, the royal chancellery (*dīwān al-inshā'*) actually played a central role in receiving and processing *maẓālim* petitions. Although *maẓālim* tribunals were actually often overseen by viziers, surely the Islamicate counterpart of the chancellor, they were at least as often presided over by a much less singular official, such as a lesser administrator or one of the ulama/judges. It thus seems best to render the official overseeing the *maẓālim* as 'magistrate,' a term distinguished from judge but less lofty than chancellor.

THE MANIFESTATION OF THE *MAẒĀLIM* TRIBUNAL: *SIYĀSA* AND ROYAL JUSTICE

At varied times and places in Islamic civilization the *maẓālim* tribunal has assumed three broad functions. First, there was the redress of complaints against the malfeasance of government officials. Since judges were themselves government officials, appointed by the ruler, petitioning an unsatisfactory ruling could spin the tribunal into what was, in effect, a separate function. It could transform the *maẓālim* tribunal into a sort of appeals court.[21] Second, there was the direct provision of 'royal justice,' or the notion that the ruler could ultimately be turned to for justice in his realm. The *maẓālim* tribunal could thus be open to petitioners with a broad range of complaints, including against other private individuals. This function leads into the third, most complex, possible function of the *maẓālim* tribunal. In some settings, it was assumed to house royal justice in the sense of the Muslim ruler's duty to ensure justice in the land proactively. Close to the palace, the *maẓālim* tribunal could function as a venue for ministerial oversight of lower government functionaries even in the absence of grievances or complaints. A vizier might choose to investigate, for example, wrongdoing by a governor or tax collector based only on rumors within the state apparatus.[22] But this function of the *maẓālim* tribunal as the standing forum for royal justice *qua* oversight more often manifested itself in the notion that certain legal matters were brought before the ruler either because they were deemed to be outside the procedural remit of the judge or because some party found the particular procedural restrictions of the judge's court an unbearable obstacle to justice.[23] In the first case, the matters lay in the public realm of the ruler or state. In the second, it was the ruler's obligation to make justice available.[24]

A major factor shaping the varied functions of royal justice venues and complicating tracing the historical development of the *maẓālim* is the multifaceted nature of the concept of *siyāsa*.[25] In Islamic civilization, this term could and did carry different meanings. It could be translated as the royal justice available to petitioners. It could just as often be understood as imperium (raw political power and the ability to compel obedience), subsuming the overall exercise of practical political authority. Finally, *siyāsa* could equally be understood as policy or public law, covering areas of the law that lay at the borders of the state or within its ministries as well as those severe punishments meted out by the state for a specified set of affronts to public order or morality (i.e., crimes). In fact, in the Ḥanafī legal discourse common to the Ottoman and Mughal realms, the word *siyāsat* mainly denoted criminal punishments set by the state. As an influential fifteenth-century judge's manual explains, *siyāsa* is God's law "enhanced forcefully" (*sharʿ mughallaẓ*).[26]

Muslim jurists – the class most concerned with law – consistently understood *siyāsa* in these last two senses. It was the executive authority of the ruler or government official in those areas acknowledged by the jurists as lying outside the main body of their jurisprudential corpus (*fiqh*), such as taxation, governance, and administering the armed forces. And *siyāsa* also laced those public law areas of *fiqh* delineated for the ruler by the jurists, such as certain areas we might label criminal law (on which more presently).[27] *Siyāsa* could thus be construed as 'royal justice' in the pure, ideal sense; as public and criminal law; and as administrative law.

Though Asifa Quraishi has usefully described *siyāsa* as "ruler-made law," in contrast to *fiqh* as "scholar-crafted law," it is worth stressing that *siyāsa* was by and large a concept developed, legitimized, and circumscribed by the ulama *qua* jurists.[28] *Siyāsa* has often been viewed as lying outside or supplementing the jurists' *fiqh* legislation. While this is true to a great extent, *siyāsa* was a category constructed within and by the jurists' legal discourse, which, as Mohammad Fadel has explained, conceptualized political authority as contractually delegated to the ruler by the Muslim community.[29] Indeed, the most influential and famous treatises on the implementation of *siyāsa* that have come down to us were produced by ulama/jurists such as al-Māwardī, whose work lies at the center of this book.

The juristic mold of *siyāsa* distinguished the concept from other Islamic politico-legal concepts denoting the ruler's legislation, such as *yasaq* (Turko-Mongol dynastic law) and *qānūn/kānūn* (a Mediterranean/Middle-East and Ottoman term for dynastic law).

Such concepts were areas claimed and elaborated by dynastic administrators, particularly in the Ottoman, Timurid, and Mughal realms. Yet jurists seemed to value the elastic vagueness of the *siyāsa* concept. It allowed them to shape *siyāsa* or let it be shaped with their needs in mind. The influential sixteenth-century Egyptian Ḥanafī jurist Ibn Nujaym (d. 970/1563) remarks that he "did not find a definition of the word *siyāsa* in our scholars' works." He chooses to use the term to denote the authority of the rulers to take action and issue orders in response to needs and interests that the ruler identifies.[30]

Returning to the *maẓālim* tribunal, in each of the three broad senses named above, *siyāsa* shaped the contours of local 'royal justice' institutions. As a raw source of authority, *siyāsa* was fundamental to the *maẓālim* tribunal, since this forum was founded on the premise of the ruler or (most often) his representative availing himself as the personal and ultimate guarantor of his subjects' rights, a duty that Muslim jurists considered to be rooted in the Quran and the Sunna of the Prophet. As executive decree, *siyāsa* could determine how and by whom a certain kind of dispute should be adjudicated. This might only affect the judge's courts, but it could equally involve moving certain disputes from the judge's hands to the setting of the *maẓālim* tribunal or some other royal justice forum. Finally, as state-internal law or a means of administrative oversight, *siyāsa* entailed punishing corrupt or exploitative government officials. This was often the heart of the institution of the *maẓālim*. In any case, it was the *siyāsa* – the discretionary, authoritative power to compel – of the ruler that created and enabled the *maẓālim* tribunal.

MAẒĀLIM AS VENUE FOR PUBLIC AND CRIMINAL LAW

As a locus and institutional manifestation of *siyāsa*, the *maẓālim* tribunal thus expressed an amorphous notion of public law in its sense of the legal relationship between the state and its subjects.[31] This was not only because, as in the case of Roman public law, the *maẓālim* tribunals addressed offenses committed by or directly against organs of the government. It was also because, like mature Roman law, the Shariah tradition recognized that the sovereign had an obligation to intercede in affairs that either threatened public order or violated private rights in a way that called for a forceful response from the body authorized to use such force.[32] There was, in short, a conception of the criminal law. This seems to have been the case even in the early Islamic period.

The relationship between the judge (*qāḍī*) and the legal role of the political authority raises a thorny and hotly debated question in Islamic legal history: to what extent did judges' courts handle criminal matters, such as assault, homicide, rape, and fornication at all? No less an authority than the late Ottoman legal historian Uriel Heyd asserted with confidence that "criminal justice remained largely outside the jurisdiction of the cadis [*qāḍī*s]."[33]

This claim seems extreme. Across the breadth and history of Islamic civilization, the legal landscape is unsurprisingly much more varied. Steven Judd has concluded that, in the Umayyad caliphate of the seventh and eighth centuries CE, silence in our admittedly sparse records suggests that judges did *not* deal with severe criminal matters. These were left to governors and even the caliphs themselves.[34] Yet a millennium later, in seventeenth-century Ottoman Bursa and Cairo, judges handled a range of criminal cases, including capital ones.[35] Heyd suggests that Ottoman judges dealt with criminal matters when they could. If they lacked the capacity or were too constrained by evidentiary requirements, however, they would send cases to authorities like the provincial governors or the sultan.[36] This was especially the case with major law-and-order threats like bandits, who were engaged in the Quranic crime of "spreading corruption in the land" (Quran 5:33). This was certainly the case in Ottoman Aleppo, where such cases were directed to the governor.[37] In Ottoman Cairo, ordinary law courts might handle criminal matters, but only the governor's council (*al-dīwān al-ʿālī*) had the manpower to implement serious punishments.[38] Yet even in the Ottoman period we find the opposite trend as well. In seventeenth-century Bursa, Gerber found no case in which a judge felt he lacked the capacity or authority to deal with a criminal matter, including banditry.[39]

Turning to South Asia for another example, Mughal judicial and administrative guidelines issued by emperors in the later 1600s and 1700s CE seem at first to have divided up civil and criminal matters. Civil affairs like marriage, divorce, and inheritance were handled by the regular law courts overseen by judges (*qāḍī*). Depending on the evidence available and the severity or nature of the offense, what we would classify as criminal matters landed in the jurisdiction of the provincial governor (*subedār*, *nāẓim*), as represented by the head of police/military district commander (*fawjdār*) and the crimes tribunal (*ʿadālat*). Violent crimes were generally reserved for these crimes tribunals, and all officers were urged to use discretionary or severe corporal punishment (here termed *siyāsat*, a.k.a. *taʿzīr*, i.e., punishments not reaching the level of Hudud punishments) for serious repeat offenders.[40]

The Mughal crimes tribunal was nested under the military authority of the ruler, presided over by the military district commander. Investigation, enforcement, and sometimes judgment fell to him or the *kotwal* (police prefect) in a locality. In an imperial edict sent to district governors in Gujarat, the Mughal emperor Awrangzīb (r. 1068/1658–1118/1707) directed crimes courts (*ʿadālat*) and police on how particular non-Hudud crimes such as murder, kidnapping, and arson should be punished. The emperor specifically legitimated these punishments as expressions of *siyāsa*.[41] But again, as with the Ottomans, there is important overlap between the realm of *siyāsa* and that of the ulama/judges. These Mughal imperial edicts make it clear that judges were intimately involved in criminal justice even if the cases were not handled in the judges' courts. A report from 1662 CE notes that the *fawjdār* convened his tribunal with the judge in attendance, and judges were consulted in all matters aside from revenue and other imperial regulations.[42]

Muslim rulers and their states understood themselves as having a duty – and were understood by ulama/judges to have this duty – to play a role in criminal prosecution and the associated maintenance of public order. The *maẓālim* tribunal could, at times, function like a criminal court, since unresolved crimes were outstanding grievances and injustices unanswered. But even in non-criminal matters, the mission at the heart of the *maẓālim* tribunal, namely that, rightly or wrongly, by legitimate encumbrance, incompetence or malice, the normal public venues for justice had failed and that the ruler was expected to fix this, was inherently public-law in nature. As Christian Müller has observed regarding the handful of cases that Andalusian chronicles mention as coming before the Cordoba *maẓālim* tribunal, they do not differ markedly from cases that went before the judge's court (some were criminal cases, some were not; some were appeals, some were not). What was common among them was that there was some perceived need for a degree of procedural laxity not available in the judge's court *because otherwise justice could not be done.*[43]

THE SHARIAH AND THE SECULAR: WHERE DO *SIYĀSA* AND THE *MAẒĀLIM* FIT?

Until recently many Western historians of Islamic law would have called foul at Cevdet Paşa citing Davānī's treatise to justify his Islamic legal reforms. Contrary to what Davānī himself insists on, according to them, *maẓālim* tribunals were outside of God's law. For these historians, they were a forum of secular justice that Muslims required because of the limitations of the Shariah and despite the fatal blow that admitting such a limitation should mean for a community that claimed its law came from God.[44] *Maẓālim* tribunals were an example of *siyāsa*, state or executive authority, which scholars like Joseph Schacht argued had started encroaching on the jurisprudence (*fiqh*) and courts of pious Muslim clerics early on in Islamic history.[45] By the fourteenth century, one scholar concluded, *siyāsa* had expanded to take over almost all areas of the law, leaving family law such as marriage and divorce as the sole remit of the Shariah.[46] A leading scholar of Ottoman law in the 1980s placed major areas of ruler-made law, from administrative law and taxation to criminal law, all outside the Shariah.[47]

We should not misunderstand what was meant when these scholars called *siyāsa* or *maẓālim* tribunals outside of God's law (the Shariah) or secular. Even when scholars like Ronald Jennings called the *maẓālim* "a non-Islamic secular court," they were not deploying 'secular' as it is generally understood in the global West today.[48] As it has been exhaustively studied by Charles Taylor, Talal Asad, Owen Chadwick, José Casanova, and others, secularism is an early-modern, unprecedented, hegemonic worldview that, at its most severe, has sought to drive religion completely from the public square (in Communist scientistic atheism, even from the private heart) and, at its mildest, has neglected religion in a 'disenchanted' and rational world.[49] This, what the American Muslim scholar Sherman Jackson has categorized as 'macro-secularism,' never existed in pre-modern Islamic civilization. What Jackson terms the 'micro-secular,' however, or what Rushain Abbasi has painstakingly documented as the 'worldly' (*dunyāwī*), did exist in a binary with the religious (*dīnī*) in Islamic thought and culture. Islam's *dīn/dunyā* binary matched fairly accurately the medieval Christian binary of religious as 'based in the Church' and secular as 'out in the world.' Abbasi, however, explains the crucial distinction that, unlike the religious/secular binary in the modern world, Islam's *dīn/dunyā* binary was "a matter of differentiation rather than opposition." He states that "God, scripture, divine law, reward and worship all fall under the *dīnī* realm." Like Jackson, he feels that pre-modern Muslim tradition placed politics in the 'worldly' (*dunyāwī*) realm, though he adds that the distinction could easily be blurred.[50]

This blurriness was not merely an Islamic phenomenon. We should remember that, from the Babylonian ruler Hammurabi (d. *circa* 1750 BCE) to the Roman Emperor Justinian (d. 565 CE), the state and its ruler were the promulgator or guarantor of a legal order originating with the divine. No politics or law was strictly secular in the modern sense. It is thus a useful reminder that no less a scholar than Majid Khadduri, though he placed the *maẓālim* outside the Shariah, could qualify it at most as "almost secular."[51] Fortunately we need venture no further into the perils of defining secularism. For our purposes, what is important to note is that decades of scholarship on Islamic legal and political history placed the exercise of *siyāsa* and the *maẓālim* tribunal squarely *outside* of the Shariah.

The last two decades, however, have seen this narrative overturned. Numerous historians have demonstrated that Islamic legal and political history from the eleventh century to the nineteenth had been misread in this regard. *Siyāsa* and its expression in legal offices like the public market inspector (*ḥisba*), the police, and the *maẓālim* tribunal were neither secular nor outside the Shariah. They were essential parts of it.[52] This was not merely a matter of theory. It was also the case in practice. Describing the broad legal regime of the Muslim Mughal Empire in India, Nandini Chatterjee and Farhat Hasan observe how the details of Islamic law, state policies, royal justice, and even local customs were all understood as one overarching system of the Shariah and Islam.[53]

Standing out against this scholarly trend is Jackson's recent monograph *The Islamic Secular*, which argues that the Shariah was a "horizontally bounded enterprise," limited and coterminous with the corpus of Muslim jurisprudence (*fiqh*).[54] The Shariah thus excluded the area of *siyāsa* as well as legal institutions like the *maẓālim* tribunal and the public market inspector. Importantly, however, Jackson qualifies that all such expressions of authority and legal institutions were still ultimately derived from and informed by the Quran and the Prophet's precedent. Muslims did not recognize "any ontologically 'higher truth' that can independently or automatically override scripture."[55] *Siyāsa*, the *maẓālim*, and the market inspector were thus still "Islamic" and religious in Jackson's view. Though not secular in the dominant, macro-secular, Western conception of the word, for Jackson everything outside of *fiqh* constituted an 'Islamic secular' space in that it was not directly determined by *fiqh*'s revealed sources and hermeneutic processes.

Here, however, Jackson seems to be arguing strenuously for a distinction without much meaning – for him the *maẓālim* tribunal is still "Islamic law," and its judge is still constrained by and committed to ruling by the Shariah. But for Jackson the *maẓālim* is not Shariah. Why insist on this? Jackson's attachment to this distinction is more comprehensible when we consider his motivating anxieties. First, he is haunted by the insistence of Islamist-driven discourse in the twentieth century that *fiqh* be Muslims' lodestar, a course that led to an abysmal failure to produce not only cogency in areas from economics to science but also any alluring culture. Second, for Jackson, excluding the political realm from the Shariah is essential to protect the Shariah from the embarrassing or immoral policies of today's Muslim rulers. As understandable as these concerns are, however, Jackson's thesis breaks from the dominant scholarly trend that sees the Shariah as a more encompassing aegis in theory and practice.[56]

For my part, I share the conclusions of Hallaq, Quraishi, and others that Muslim jurists, judges, and rulers conceived of the Shariah as having an expansive reach that included *siyāsa* institutions like the *maẓālim* tribunal. That is certainly the position advanced by al-Māwardī, Davānī, and Cevdet Paşa. Fortunately, this book has more to offer than merely adding another piece of evidence to the '*maẓālim*-was-always-part-of-the-Shariah-and-not-secular' pan of the scale of debate. As misguided Muslim rulers and radical reformists alike have found, making the claim that some action or policy is 'Islamic' is easy enough provided one need offer no evidence. What I am interested in, however, is precisely the details of the Islamic scriptural and legal arguments made for *why* certain things were allowed in the *maẓālim* tribunal but not in ordinary courts. I am interested not in mere claims but in how these arguments were proffered and how their evidence was interpreted on a discursive level. Davānī asserts with certitude that the *maẓālim* is part of God's Law. I want to know how he proves it in detail, with Quranic verse and Hadith citation. Finally, in this book I am interested in tracking how arguments made for the Shariah-legitimacy of the *maẓālim* tribunal change as *épistémès* shift. When, if ever, do invocations of the *maẓālim* tribunal as a Shariah-legitimate solution to crises of the mismatch of law and justice cease working as organic and sincere expression and start to come across as contrived against a changed epistemological background? This last question will be taken up in this book's Conclusion.

1

A History of *Maẓālim* Tribunals

In the historical, literary, and legal heritage of Islamic civilization, one finds the notion of *maẓālim* as both a concept of political philosophy and an actual institution (i.e., the grievance tribunal). As a concept it can be invoked at the most abstract levels of legal and political discourse to denote injustice and unjust acts. The great eighteenth-century Indian scholar Shāh Walī Allāh (d. 1176/1762) remarks that one of God's main aims in sending prophets is "removing injustices (*maẓālim*) from among mankind."[1] Muslim political treatises frequently mention the ruler's duty to 'remove injustices' (*rafʿ al-maẓālim*) from his subjects, and chronicles often lavish encomium on rulers for doing so. But these are musings or meditations on ideal rule and cannot be read as references to particular institutions, let alone to a legal forum.[2]

Indeed, even when looking only for concrete mentions of *maẓālim* as an institution, one still finds an elusive construct, shifting across and along Islamic civilization's broad temporal and spatial axes.[3] Unlike the surprisingly consistent institution of the judge's court, the form and function of the *maẓālim* tribunal in Abbasid Baghdad differ markedly from those of Mamluk Cairo or Mughal Agra. Yet there are consistent themes bound up together in the imaginary of the *maẓālim* tribunal. They are sometimes laid out in treatises and more often mentioned off hand in the innumerable texts and chronicles circulated in Islam's millennium republic of letters. These themes are referenced in its mundane forums of adjudication or manifest dramatically in the theatres of justice staged by those rulers whose idiom of sovereignty garbed them in that republic's mantle.

So perennial is the imaginary of the *maẓālim* that scholarship on the administration of justice in Islamicate societies has often assumed the existence of a *maẓālim* tribunal and tended to see them wherever a familiar trace or reference to this construct appears. Thus, audiences during which petitions were submitted to the sultan have been interpreted as manifestations of the *maẓālim* tribunal even when historical sources did not refer to that setting in such terms.[4] Furthermore, scholarship has sometimes associated the *maẓālim* tribunal with a conception of 'secular' law and justice, either outside or even against the Shariah. As a result, there has been the temptation to use the label *maẓālim* for anything that seems to be other than what is self-evidently the Shariah or the judge's court.[5]

Yet in many, if not most, Islamic societies, a legal venue has existed that brings together three salient themes in particular: those of the ruler's executive power, his obligation to see that justice was done for his subjects, and the assumption that this duty existed, at least in part, outside the normal purview of the judge. It is in the comingling of these three themes in some setting that the construct of the *maẓālim* tribunal merits treatment as a historical continuity – if not always as a consistent reality, then as a rubric under which the threads of rule, legitimacy, and law were woven and mended.

Such venues were a manifestation of 'royal justice,' provided by the ruler and guaranteed for his subjects. What follows is an attempt at a history and phenomenology of this rubric. I carry it out with full acknowledgment of the diversity of shapes and forms of the grievance tribunal, and even of the subject matter that passes underneath it, confident in the justification afforded by Wittgenstein's notion of a 'family resemblance.' In what he might call their 'overall similarities,' sometimes 'overlapping and crisscrossing,' one recognizes the constellation of practices, theories, and institutions orbiting the construct of the *maẓālim* tribunal when one sees them.[6] This rubric is rendered all the more elusive by the notable brevity on the part of Muslim jurists and political theorists regarding the details or proper functioning of the *maẓālim* institution they so often reference. This near-silence merits explanation in itself.

THE QUEST FOR *MAẒĀLIM* TRIBUNALS

As we have noted, there has been a tendency in Western scholarship on Islamic legal history to conflate any instance of petitioning royal justice or any application of 'secular' justice with a *maẓālim* tribunal. This gloss occurs because that scholarship long viewed *siyāsa* as secular, and one of the institutions in which *siyāsa* expressed itself was the *maẓālim*. We have already glimpsed the debate over the supposed secularity of *siyāsa* and the *maẓālim* tribunal. Irrespective of that point, however, *siyāsa* and *maẓālim* did conceptually overlap. But they were not coterminous either in concept or in application.[7]

One institution of *siyāsa* that strongly resembled the *maẓālim* tribunal, sometimes intersected with it, and seems to have emerged at around the same time was the crimes tribunal (*wilāyat al-jarā'im*), which evidently overlapped with the activities of the police (*shurṭa*) in cities like Abbasid Baghdad and later in Mughal India.[8] The earliest surviving work theorizing the *maẓālim* tribunal, namely that of al-Māwardī, also includes the earliest surviving theorization of the crimes tribunal, which al-Māwardī mandates that the ruler hold for the prospective hearing of violent or severe crimes that the ulama/judges considered beyond their capacity to investigate properly or punish. Like his discussion of the *maẓālim*, al-Māwardī seems to draw on the existing practices of ruler-emanating organs of justice like the police force. As he conceived of them, the crimes and grievance tribunals shared a great deal in common, primarily in the form of the extraordinary power available to the magistrate but not to normal judges. In both venues, the magistrate can use intimidating interrogation and even the infliction of pain on the accused if enough evidence has already been provided and this seems the route to ascertaining the truth. Both can hear the testimony of witnesses who would not be admissible in most judges' courts, particularly if they had specific expertise or were large in number.

Despite these similarities, and despite al-Māwardī conceiving of the *maẓālim* as an extra-ordinary catchall for legal problems that might well include the criminal, clear differences appear. The grievance and crimes tribunals stand out from one another in al-Māwardī's conception in that the *maẓālim* centers on disputes between known parties and the wrongs done between them. In the case of the crimes tribunal, by contrast, offenders may be unknown or difficult to identify using normal evidentiary procedure. Unlike the *maẓālim*, the crimes tribunal has at its heart an anxiety about public order and safety. Its magistrate, for example, is described uniquely as empowered to sentence repeat offenders to lengthy prison stays to safeguard the community from them.[9]

We do not find frequent mention of a crimes tribunal prior to the eleventh century. The Samanid dynasty held one regularly in ninth-century Khurasan, and a tenth-century government scribe in Baghdad discusses what seems to be the cooperation of jurists and the police force in a criminal tribunal.[10] Prior to this period, it seems that the criminal-court function was vested more in the institution of the *shurṭa* (police). In the early Islamic period the *shurṭa* (and its head, the *ṣāḥib al-shurṭa*) often appear as an enforcement mechanism for the judge's rulings, as when the scholar/judge al-Ḥasan al-Baṣrī (d. 110/728) instructs the "agent of the *shurṭa*" to carry out a punishment in Basra. But the *shurṭa* could also take on the appearance of a legal forum. In Kufa in the mid-700s CE, the *shurṭa* is referred to as a separate crimes tribunal manned by the same corps of ulama who served as judges.[11] In Fatimid Egypt, the police carried out Hudud and criminal law punishments, often without the involvement of judges, though Lev notes they still operated within the general framework of Shariah.[12]

As a result of this ambiguity in both concept and institution, the *maẓālim* tribunal was often only one of the forums in which *siyāsa* expressed itself. In the Mamluk period, for example, cases of Hudud punishment and serious crimes were handled by Mamluk royal justice rather than by judges alone. But these cases were heard before a military crimes tribunal (*wilāyat al-ḥarb*), while a separate, formal venue called the *maẓālim* was devoted mainly to hearing complaints against government officials. In southwestern Persia in the same era, however, the *maẓālim* swallowed up the function of the crimes tribunal.[13] The Ottoman judicial system famously dispensed with the *maẓālim* tribunal outright. But, according to a prominent seventeenth-century

Ottoman judicial manual, judges should send cases of public security (*nizâm-i memleket*) and crimes with capital or severe corporal punishments to the provincial governors or their representatives.[14] In the Ottoman city of Kayseri in that same period, representatives of the governor would attend criminal cases that were held in the judge's court.[15] There appears to be some regional variety, however. In seventeenth-century Ottoman Bursa, judges handled criminal cases, including capital cases and those of bandits considered to be "spreading corruption in the land." In eighteenth-century Ottoman Aleppo, by contrast, judges sent such cases to the governor's council.[16]

Other functions normally associated with the *maẓālim* construct could be absorbed by other government bodies. The Ottoman state expressed consistent concern for remedying wrongs (*ẓulm* or *maẓâlim*), but it did so through standing imperial and provincial councils (*dîvân*), shuttering the longstanding Mamluk *maẓālim* tribunals in Egypt and Syria after the Ottoman conquest of those regions.[17] The sixteenth-century Sultanate of Melaka, thriving off the Asian spice trade, assigned tending to "all those who have suffered injustice" to the powerful harbormaster (*syahbandar*).[18]

In its *maẓālim*-linked function of providing oversight of legal institutions, royal justice could also express itself without taking any institutional form. In 1881, for example, the sultan of Morocco sent a senior judge to Marrakesh with the task of certifying the qualifications and performance of official witnesses and those charged with managing pious endowments and the estates of orphans.[19] Conversely, royal justice need not be involved at all. Some functions associated with the *maẓālim* as a guarantee of justice could be achieved through institutional or informal means with no direct link to the ruler's executive power. David Powers has shown how respected senior scholars, consulted in their capacity as muftis, could function as appeals authorities for litigants who felt they had been wronged by the rulings of judges in late fourteenth-century Granada.[20] In Morocco in the same time period, Powers shows that the judge's court in the capital city functioned, in effect, as a forum for appeals.[21] Leo Africanus (d. *circa* 970/1560) recalls that Fez of the late fifteenth century had one superior court tasked with hearing appeals against unjust or flawed rulings in the city's lower courts.[22] In Ottoman Sofia judges in the provincial capital at times functioned as appellate authorities, reversing the rulings of local judges.[23]

THE INSTITUTIONALIZATION OF ROYAL JUSTICE: THE ABBASID THROUGH THE MAMLUK PERIODS (8TH–15TH CENTURIES CE)

According to both surviving textual evidence and later Muslim historians, the institution of the *maẓālim* appeared in the mid eighth century CE. Certainly, it had ancient antecedents. The rulers of the Persian and Roman empires had held themselves out as the ultimate guarantors of justice in their realms, available for petition, and even Hammurabi had declared that in matters of law it was the king's duty to hear particularly serious cases as well as appeals.[24] Modern scholars follow classical ones like al-Yaʿqūbī (d. *circa* 292/905) in tracing the Islamicate institutionalization of petitioning royal justice to the Sassanid tradition of the ruler as the guarantor of God's justice on earth.[25] Yet there is also no reason to think that an informal or semi-formal process of bringing grievances to the chieftain was foreign to the Arabian tradition of rule.

By the late 700s CE 'rectifying injustices' (*radd al-maẓālim*) was being presented as a key feature of a just Muslim ruler, as is the case with an early hagiography of the Umayyad caliph ʿUmar b. ʿAbd al-ʿAzīz (r. 99/717–101/720).[26] There are reports of some recognizable *maẓālim* tribunals in the late Umayyad period. The Basran Sufi and engaging early Muslim intellectual historian Abū Ṭālib al-Makkī (d. 386/996) offers an oddly detailed description of how Umayyad rulers or governors would hold *maẓālim* tribunals with jurists (*muftī*) to their right and left to provide the ruling when they themselves lacked sufficient knowledge.[27] Al-Kindī's (d. 350/961) landmark history of judges describes several Umayyad-era officials in Egypt taking up people's 'complaints' (*qiṣaṣ*). The litterateur al-Iṣfahānī (d. 356/967) quotes the Kufan scholar and Umayyad confidante al-Shaʿbī (d. *circa*

103/721) describing himself as overseeing the *maẓālim* of Kufa *circa* 690 CE. And Ibn al-Jawzī (d. 597/1200) describes one scholar from Egypt, Zabbān b. Fā'id (d. 155/771–2), as the last person that the Umayyads appointed to oversee the *maẓālim* tribunal in that province. But these sources greatly postdate the events they describe, and they may well be anachronistic in their terminology.[28]

Contemporaneous evidence from the early Islamic period suggests that the institution of the *maẓālim* per se began with the Abbasids after their assumption of power in 132/750. The caliph who quickly took the reins of the new dynasty and built its capital Baghdad, Abū Ja'far al-Manṣūr (r. 136/754–158/775), appointed a respected jurist to handle *maẓālim* cases.[29] A surviving work of Abū Yūsuf (d. 182/798), Abū Ḥanīfa's acolyte and himself chief judge of Abbasid Baghdad, includes mention of the *maẓālim* that assumes the institution was already known by his time. Abū Yūsuf advises the caliph Hārūn al-Rashīd (r. 170/786–193/809) to hold a *maẓālim* session once every month or two. The caliph should do so "to hear the complaints of the oppressed and to denounce the wrongdoers," settling cases in an egalitarian, first-come-first-served manner. This would show his concern for his subjects, explains Abū Yūsuf, and would help prevent abuse by officials.[30] As Maaike van Berkel has shown, there were clearly procedures for petitioning senior government officials in both the provinces and the capital by the ninth century, though how regularly these were handled by an institution known as the *dīwān al-maẓālim* or merely done by direct petition to some powerful official is unclear.[31] An institutional setting seems clearer in the writings of the scribe and scholar Qudāma b. Ja'far (d. 337/948), who worked in the Abbasid administration in Baghdad and wrote a short instruction on how the magistrate of the *maẓālim* (*ṣāḥib dīwān al-maẓālim*) should collect, process, and return petitions turned into the office.[32]

The *maẓālim* institution in early Abbasid Baghdad seems to have been first and foremost a forum for seeking royal justice for redress against wrongs by government officials. Historical and literary sources provide a number of accounts of caliphs such as al-Manṣūr, al-Ma'mūn (r. 189/813–218/833), and al-Muhtadī (r. 255/869–256/870) returning property usurped by royal officials – sometimes even by the caliphs themselves – or cancelling crushing tax burdens on the people of southwestern Iran (Fars) or southern Iraq.[33] One case involves a Christian monk in Upper Egypt complaining about a local official seizing the people's property despite all taxes having been paid. There were also cases of civil dispute, however, for example between shopkeepers or between local farmers and traders over the proper size of a bridge.[34] Disputants from Anbar, a day's travel from Baghdad, dissatisfied with their local judge's handling of an inheritance case, brought it to the capital *maẓālim*.[35]

The early Abbasid caliphs either oversaw the *maẓālim* tribunal themselves or placed their viziers in charge, though judges might also be appointed. For example, the caliph al-Mahdī (r. 158/775–169/785) appointed the jurist and known Hadith transmitter Ibn Thawbān (d. 165/781–2) to oversee the Baghdad *maẓālim*.[36] The theme of the ruler personally guaranteeing justice through the *maẓālim* was powerful in the early Abbasid period, and the caliph al-Mahdī still examined the petitions and rulings passed by his *maẓālim* magistrate after every session.[37] By the time of his successor al-Hādī (r. 169/785–170/786), the royal *maẓālim* seems to have been held in a special facility known as the House of Grievances (*dār al-maẓālim*), and a century later al-Muhtadī built a special domed pavilion (with four doors) called the Dome of Grievances (*qubbat al-maẓālim*).[38]

By the early tenth century, *maẓālim* tribunals had multiplied within Baghdad. The large district west of Baghdad, Bādūrayā, whose inhabitants one Abbasid bureaucrat referred to as exceptionally stubborn (*jalad*), had three separate *maẓālim* tribunals: one for issues involving pious endowments, one for taxes and fees (*rusūm*), and one for official documents (*qirṭās*).[39] In the ninth century the Abbasids also held a *maẓālim* tribunal specifically for the army (*maẓālim al-ʿaskar*).[40]

Early Abbasid-era *maẓālim* tribunals could also serve as a judicial organ that expressed the caliph's legal authority over and against the judges of Baghdad and Iraq. During the infamous inquisition (*miḥna*) initiated by the caliph al-Ma'mūn, in which the Abbasid government sought to enforce rationalist theology on the Sunni scholars of the realm, the chief judge and main agent of the inquisition, Aḥmad Ibn Abī Du'ād (d. 240/854), was placed in charge of the royal *maẓālim*. Mathieu Tillier has shown that the Abbasids also established provincial *maẓālim* tribunals. Sources report individuals, usually ulama/judges, assigned to preside over *maẓālim* tribunals in the Caspian region of Jurjān in the late 700s CE; in Egypt (Fusṭāṭ); in the Jibāl region of western Iran; in the northern Iranian entrepôt of Rayy, the Khurasani center of Marv and as far east as Bukhara, all in the mid-800s CE (with mention of appointment to a grievance tribunal in Nasā in Khurasan in the mid-900s).[41] One scholar, Muḥammad b. Ḥassān al-Ḍabbī, was appointed to the *maẓālim* tribunals of northern Iraq, Qinnasrīn, the Byzantine border (*al-'awāṣim wa'l-thughūr*), Mosul, Armenia, and Raqqa, all in the 830s CE.[42]

Local *maẓālim* tribunals seem not always to have been permanent. At times they were ad hoc courts set up by decree from the caliph to deal with local crises (particularly in the garrison cities of southern Iraq) or to act as an assertion of caliphal authority against local judges who did not comply with central policy. Ibn Abī Du'ād had the judges of Isfahan removed and placed all courts under the magistrates of the local *maẓālim*.[43] Local judges might even be brought before the *maẓālim* for their insubordination. Conversely, when Ibn Ṭulūn (r. 254/868–270/884) wanted to create a local judiciary in Egypt loyal to him and not his Abbasid suzerain, he appointed local scholars to the *maẓālim* in Fusṭāṭ.[44]

Provincial *maẓālim* tribunals continued during the local dynasties that arose under or against the Abbasid caliphs starting in the late ninth century. The Samanid dynasty held a *maẓālim* tribunal presided over by the ruler (Ismā'īl b. Aḥmad, r. 279/892–295/907, is named as one example) in Samarqand.[45] Both the Saffarid rebel state in Sistan and later the Ghaznavids in Khurasan continued the *maẓālim* institution.[46] Some sources note that Ibn Ṭūlūn was the first ruler to "hear grievances" in Egypt, in sessions held twice weekly. But under his successors the practice lapsed and was not revived until six decades later with the Ikhshīdid takeover of Egypt in 323/935.[47] The *maẓālim* tribunal in Egypt under the local Ikhshīdid dynasty is noted prominently by Muslim historians of the judiciary there. The Ikhshīdid ruler Kāfūr (r. 355/966–357/968) presided over the *maẓālim* tribunal every Saturday, with ulama/judges and non-judge ulama in attendance, and was so active and attentive in his supervision of the judge's court that a long-serving judge felt the sultan was a serious constraint on his rulings.[48] It is interesting to note that in Egypt in this period serving on the *maẓālim* tribunal as well as overseeing endowments were duties that could be given to a judge in addition to his duty overseeing his ordinary court. Or they could specifically be withheld from him.[49]

It is thus clear that, by the mid-800s CE, ulama were regular participants in the *maẓālim* forum. It had become common for ulama/judges to be appointed to oversee Abbasid *maẓālim* tribunals or for them to be present to advise the magistrate, who was often a grand vizier.[50] Muḥammad b. ʿAbdallāh al-Anṣārī (fl. 190/800) was appointed by the caliph al-Amīn (r. 193/809–189/813) as both the chief judge and magistrate of the *maẓālim* of Baghdad in 193/809.[51] Such appointments seem to have been possible even for early Sunnis, despite their being anathema to the Ḥanafī/rationalist-theologian elite of the empire's judiciary in the early Abbasid period. Ṣakhr b. Muḥammad al-Minqarī (d. *circa* 230/845) studied with leading scholars like Mālik in Medina. Though he was criticized for his lackluster Hadith transmission, he clearly fell into the network of early Sunnis. Yet he served as a *maẓālim* judge in Jurjān.[52] Aḥmad b. ʿUmar al-Wakīʿī (d. 235/849–50), seen by other early Sunnis as exemplary of their group, was appointed to oversee the *maẓālim* in Marv for twelve years (presumably during the *miḥna*) and boasted that "no ruling (*ḥukm*) was presented to me but I knew a Hadith for it, so I did not need to resort to judicial reason (*ra'y*) or its partisans."[53] Another early pivot of Sunni Hadith transmission, Ismāʿīl b. ʿUlayya (d. 193/809), also held the position of magistrate for the Baghdad *maẓālim*, though he was criticized by his fellow Sunnis for such close relations to the state and subsequently repented for his role.[54]

By the 900s CE, such anxieties over government service had relaxed among Sunnis in the Central Islamic lands. Al-Ḥākim al-Naysābūrī (d. 405/1014), one of the leading Sunni Hadith scholars of his era, was appointed to the *maẓālim* tribunal of Nasā in Khurasan, continued his Hadith studies and teaching apace and, indeed, would come to be known by his title as *maẓālim* magistrate (*ḥākim*).[55]

Maẓālim tribunals might also be overseen by members of the caliph's household, as was the famous case in 306/918 when the caliph al-Muqtadir's (r. intermittent 296/908–320/932 CE) mother appointed her female courtesan Thumal to oversee the caliphal *maẓālim* in Ruṣāfa. She heard people's petitions every Friday, with the judge Abū al-Ḥusayn al-Ashnānī present along with other ulama. Observers noted that Thumal issued sound rulings, though the caliph himself also read cases brought to his attention.[56]

As the Abbasid caliphs lost real power, their protectors would assume control of the *maẓālim* institution. After the Shiite Buyids established themselves in Baghdad in 945 CE, the *maẓālim* arrangement seems to have continued but was placed under the direction of the Shiite nobility such as al-Sharīf al-Raḍī (d. 406/1016) and his brother al-Sharīf al-Murtaḍā (d. 436/1044).[57] One approving chronicler recounts how the powerful Buyid ruler 'Aḍud al-Dawla (r. 367/978–372/983) had an official, designated as *amīr dādh* (Commander of Justice), assigned to hold the *maẓālim* tribunal. Beside him would be a scholar/judge so the official could take his opinion and "implement what the Shariah commands for the subjects and the army."[58] One feature of the Buyid-era *maẓālim* may have been an emphasis on distinguishing its functions from the ordinary courts, including concerns over its use for appeals. A *maẓālim* magistrate in Baghdad in the 930s CE is noted for handling cases involving the government and taxation while directing matters that judges (*ḥukkām*) should handle to them. A letter of appointment in 380/990 included clear instructions that, though the *maẓālim* magistrate's mandate was to look into difficult and recondite cases, he should not reverse judges' rulings.[59]

The first Seljuq Turkic sultan in Baghdad, Toghril Beg (r. 431/1040–455/1063), who replaced the Persian Buyids as 'protector of the caliph,' held *maẓālim* sessions every Sunday and Wednesday. In fact, the Seljuq sultan at times assigned the caliph to the post of *maẓālim* magistrate.[60] With the Seljuq takeover, however, generally the vizier or senior Sunni judges returned to overseeing the tribunal, officially appointed by the caliph. Powerful Abbasid caliphs like al-Nāṣir (r. 575/1180–622/1225) appointed Ḥanbalī judges as the *maẓālim* magistrate. One late Abbasid caliph, al-Mustanjid (r. 555/1160–566/1170), even presided over sessions himself.[61]

Another development in the later Buyid and then the Seljuq periods seems to have been an increasing overlap between the *maẓālim* tribunal and the crimes tribunal (*aḥkām al-jarā'im, wilāyat al-jarā'im*).[62] In the ninth century, the Samanids in Khurasan held a crimes tribunal on Sundays and Wednesdays.[63] The historian al-Ṭabarī (d. 310/923) recounts how, in 277/890, the magistrate of the imperial *maẓālim* in Baghdad instructed the chief of police (*ṣāḥib al-shurṭa*) not to release anyone from prison without him first reviewing the prisoner's petition, so in this case at least the head of the *maẓālim* tribunal seems to have assumed some oversight in criminal law enforcement.[64] A literary reference alludes to the possible rivalry between the two venues due to an overlap in the cases they might handle. Al-Ḥarīrī's (d. 516/1122) famous *Maqāmāt* prose drama includes an episode in which the protagonist, faced with a possible encounter with authorities, remarks on the severity of the judge (*qāḍī*) overseeing the *maẓālim* tribunal in Tus in comparison with the governor/supervising official (*wālī*) overseeing the crimes (*jarā'im*) tribunal.[65]

Written in the twilight of Buyid rule, when there was real hope for a reinvigorated Sunni caliphate, even al-Māwardī's theorizations of the *maẓālim* and crimes tribunals overlap substantially. Both are rooted in imperium and political power as opposed to the legal authority of the judges. Both are ideally presided over by the ruler or his representative (*nāẓir*). And both enjoy tools and tactics not available to judges in order to ascertain the guilt or innocence of accused parties: they can both consider circumstantial evidence, they can both imprison the accused while they carry out an investigation as long as the authority considers it necessary (the judge can only do this for someone who has been convicted), and they can both administer beatings within the range of accepted discretionary punishment (*ta'zīr*) to test the truth of an accused person's statement.[66]

In Egypt and Syria, the Fatimid period (mid-tenth through mid-twelfth centuries CE) would prove foundational for the institution of the *maẓālim* tribunal. References to appeals to a formal *maẓālim* are relatively frequent in the Fatimid period.[67] Although the Shiite Fatimids appointed a judge ruling by Shiite law to preside over the *maẓālim* in the late 900s CE after they had conquered Egypt, the new dynasty initially continued the *maẓālim* procedures that had become so active under the Ikhshīdid state.[68] When the Fatimids assumed control of Egypt, the caliph al-Muʿizz (r. 341/953–365/975) assigned one of his coteries to oversee the *maẓālim* tribunal. When this appointee began exceeding his mandate, which seems to have been limited specifically to disputes amongst the Fatimid army that had come from North Africa, and started signing his rulings as 'The judge of Cairo (*miṣr*) and Alexandria,' members of the local Sunni judicial corps confronted him for trying to supplant the authority of the long-serving Sunni judge in Fusṭāṭ, Abū Ṭāhir al-Dhuhlī (d. 368/979). The Fatimid ruler took the side of the serving Sunni judge and ordered his *maẓālim* appointee to rein in his claims.[69]

Especially in the first half of the twelfth century CE, however, the *maẓālim* tribunal under the Fatimids took on a new shape marked by increased bureaucratic ornateness. All petitions would ultimately have to be presented to the tribunal in carefully formatted written form. Petitioners would bring complaints to the gate of the palace and present them, either orally or in writing, to an official, who would record and then deliver the written petition and documents to the *maẓālim* tribunal. Marina Rustow has argued that the Fatimid dynasty's novel elaboration of a specifically formatted petition document served as part of the dynasty's claim that it stood ready to address the injustices suffered by any of their subjects. This was, of course, not new in Islamicate political culture or the Near East more generally. But Rustow argues that the theme was particularly prominent in the texts which Fatimid ideologues drew on from the heritage of the Family of the Prophet.[70] This written format would become a regular feature of the *maẓālim* institution and associated forums of complaint from this time on.[71] As in the high Abbasid state, in theory, these petitions would ultimately be reviewed and signed by the Fatimid caliph himself. By the mid-1100s CE, the grand vizier was assigned to hear *maẓālim* cases, with the chief judge, two notaries, and several other senior bureaucrats and scribes in attendance. Unlike the Ikhshīdids, this new Fatimid *maẓālim* tribunal sat two days instead of one day a week.[72]

The types of cases brought before the Fatimid *maẓālim* in the twelfth century are as varied as those we have already seen in the Abbasid period, though there seem to be more communal petitions from non-Muslim groups, such as Rabbinic and Karaite Jews who were in dispute over leadership of an academy in Palestine (non-Muslims likely constituted a larger portion of Egyptian society than they did in Iraq and Iran at the time). Other examples include a baker petitioning to have his creditor allow him to pay his debt in installments and the family of a slave who had been imprisoned pleading that they now had no breadwinner.[73] Many cases were about property seizure by government officials.[74]

The linked Zangid and then Ayyubid dynasties of Syria and Egypt, which first challenged and then replaced the Fatimids, built in stone what their predecessors had rendered in paper. They established a lasting, formal institution of royal justice: the House of Justice (*dār al-ʿadl*). This was built in part on the highly formalized Fatimid system of *maẓālim*, with an elaborate process for government officials receiving and processing petitions.[75] The Zangids/Ayyubids erected several such buildings, first *circa* 560/1163 at the behest of Nūr al-Dīn Zangī (r. 541/1147–569/1174) in the capital of Damascus. Also known as the Hall of Uncovering Wrongs (*dār kashf al-maẓālim*), it was located close to the Damascus citadel, and the tribunal was presided over by Nūr al-Dīn twice a week. During Saladin's (r. 564/1169–589/1193) time, normal, regular *maẓālim* sessions continued, often attended by the sultan. Another House of Justice was built in Aleppo in 1189 CE by Saladin's son al-Ẓāhir Ghāzī (r. 582/1186–613/1216), and finally one was built in the citadel of Cairo *circa* 1207 CE as well. Nasser Rabbat has argued that convening the *maẓālim* tribunal in the House of Justice, with the array of ulama/judges and scribes, "visually represented" the dynasties' claim to just and legitimate Islamic rule.[76]

The Zangid/Ayyubid tradition of the *maẓālim* in situ was continued by their Mamluk successors. When in Damascus, the early Mamluk sultans would be sure to preside over *maẓālim* sessions in the House of Justice, and their representative would take their place when the sultans were absent.[77] During the period of the Baḥrī Mamluks (*circa* 1250–1390 CE), the *maẓālim* tribunals were presided over either by the sultan, a delegated representative (*nā'ib dār al-ʿadl*), or a regional governor. Although ulama/judges could be assigned to handle specific cases, the primary *maẓālim* officials were all drawn from the military class that made up the Mamluk elite.[78] However, as has been mentioned, members of the ulama were an essential presence. According to an early fifteenth-century appointment deed, a specially appointed expert jurist (*muftī*) of the House of Justice was supposed to ensure that the rulings of the council were in accordance with the Shariah.[79]

The history and character of the *maẓālim* and other forums of royal justice in the Mamluk period have been well studied, thanks to the plentiful information provided by the period's primary sources. The Baḥrī Mamluks held the *maẓālim* tribunals in Cairo's House of Justice in the citadel or in the citadel's newly constructed Great Portico (*īwān*).[80] During the lengthy third reign of al-Nāṣir Muḥammad (r. 708/1309–741/1341), the sultan presided over two sessions weekly (Monday and Thursday), except during Ramadan. Seated with the city's four chief judges (one from each Sunni school of law) next to him and the senior administrative and military officials of the regime arrayed around him, this grand setting brought every component of the ruler's mechanism of authority together in a visual synecdoche of power.[81] In the mid-1300s CE a position was created uniquely for the *maẓālim* tribunal: the aforementioned mufti of the Dār al-ʿAdl, whom the secretary al-Qalqashandī (d. 821/1418) describes as sitting in the tribunal along with the four judges, representing each school of Sunni law.[82] A shift came with the Burjī Mamluk takeover, when, in 1387, the *maẓālim* was moved to the royal stables and set on Tuesdays and Saturdays.[83] Though this might seem unusual, stables, in this case located in the lower part of Cairo's citadel, had long been known as a place for seeking refuge in Turkic tradition.[84]

As seen in earlier writings like those of al-Māwardī, Mamluk-era chroniclers like al-Maqrīzī (d. 845/1442) describe how the *maẓālim* tribunal was referred to as *siyāsa* justice.[85] Though we have discussed how the two concepts do to a considerable extent overlap, the notion of *siyāsa* (executive authority, royal justice, administrative law) was broader in scope than the *maẓālim*. Modern scholars all agree that in the Mamluk period the relationship between *siyāsa* and *maẓālim* became increasingly complex. As we will see, to a great extent this is because the relationship between *siyāsa* and the Shariah was becoming more complicated in the wake of the Turko-Mongol takeover of the Islamic Near East.

Precisely the nature of how royal justice in general and the *maẓālim* in particular were understood and how they manifested have been greatly contested in modern scholarship on the Mamluk period and its legal institutions. Some scholars have concluded that royal justice in its various forms had by that time occupied the space originally taken by the Shariah, which these scholars claim had been increasingly vitiated by the Mamluk age. Nielsen argues that the preceding centuries had seen Muslim jurists allowing more and more flexibility in the substantive rulings of the Shariah and granting more discretion to royal authority. By the Mamluk period, Nielsen contends, the Shariah only applied in limited areas such as personal status laws. The ulama had become content to have the Shariah maintained in a position of "symbolic supremacy," providing legitimacy even if its substance was unimportant.[86] Other scholars have argued that royal justice was invoked as a poor legitimation of the Mamluks' criminal syndicate state.[87] Another narrative, articulated by Wael Hallaq, holds that the *maẓālim* was the institution that the state used to hold itself accountable to the Shariah, responsible for trying the abuses of government officials, while the judge's court and the Shariah overall were independent of the state.[88] The tension, perceived or unperceived, between the Shariah and the 'secular' justice of the *maẓālim* will be taken up in full in Chapter Five. In any case, it is clear that jurists and, apparently, sultans as well throughout the Mamluk period still adhered to the idea that the *maẓālim* was, or at least should be, approved by the jurists and fell within the Shariah.[89]

Rapoport has offered a remarkably comprehensive description of the characteristics and historical development of the different *siyāsa* (he translates it as royal justice) tribunals in the Mamluk period, when they emerged as a forum parallel to judges' courts with some overlap in subject matter jurisdiction. Rapoport shows that *siyāsa* tribunals formed part of the legal infrastructure of Mamluk state and society, albeit one contested to varied degrees. He makes the key observation that, for both rulers and ulama/judges, it was clear that the exercise of *siyāsa* was "a requirement of the Shariah, not an external intrusion." "The *siyāsah* of the sultans and the amirs was necessary for the continuous application of Shariah norms," he explains, so "the expansion of the *siyāsah* jurisdiction set out to bolster the Shariah rather than defeat it."[90] Famous and respected ulama/judges did push back against the activities of *siyāsa* courts, sometimes with barbed critiques. But they were not rejecting or condemning the exercise of executive justice or institutions like the *maẓālim* tribunal. They were merely (and rightfully) condemning the manner in which royal justice sometimes exceeded what they considered the Shariah's outer limits and ensuring that it did not threaten the Shariah's ideological underpinnings.

Rapoport identifies three periods of historical development in the Mamluk-era *maẓālim* and royal justice:

1) 1265–*circa* 1350 CE: During this period the structure of the Mamluk legal system was established, with its well-known four chief-judge positions, and royal justice took the shape of the military court (*wilāyat al-ḥarb*) that would adjudicate criminal cases. These included crimes such as theft, public intoxication, and banditry, which were punished corporally or capitally. These military courts proved particularly useful when a lack of witnesses or documentary evidence meant that the judges' courts proved unable to guarantee or achieve justice. In this regard, the military court resembled the criminal tribunal described by al-Māwardī. It was described approvingly by Ibn Taymiyya (d. 728/1328), who noted that this appropriate manifestation of *siyāsa* had become the established custom (*'urf*) in the Mamluk realm.[91]

This military court was distinct from the *maẓālim* tribunal, which in this part of the Mamluk period seems to have been more for usurpation of property or abuse by officials (ironically, Ibn Taymiyya himself was brought before it for his controversial fatwa against triple divorces). The royal *maẓālim* court was held in the Ayyubid-era House of Justice, presenting a formal manifestation of the sultan's judicial role. As Nielsen observed, the *maẓālim* tribunal in this period was generally seen as respecting the Shariah and not arbitrary.[92] Ibn Baṭṭūṭa (d. *circa* 770/1370) observed the sultan al-Nāṣir sitting to hear grievances and assigning each case to one of the chief judges seated beside him.[93] Nielsen even found mention of an instance in 713/1313 when a cadre of judges disapproved so much of how one *maẓālim* magistrate was ruling on cases involving pious endowments (*awqāf*) that they were able to pressure the sultan to prohibit him from ruling on such matters.[94] At times, the *maẓālim* tribunal might also handle criminal cases or cases concerning the Hudud, such as a 1288 CE case in which a Christian man was caught cohabiting with a Muslim woman (he was executed, she was lashed one hundred times).[95]

2) *Circa* 1350–1468 CE: In this period, Rapoport explains, the jurisdiction of royal justice sometimes expanded into areas previously reserved for the judge, namely matrimonial cases and issues of debt. This occurred with the expansion of the power of the chamberlain (*ḥājib*), the Mamluk court official charged with dealing with disputes amongst court officials and government folk. From there, the chamberlain began hearing cases of debt and marriage disputes from outside the Mamluk ranks. The description offered by al-Qalqashandī of the chamberlain's adjudicative duties closely resemble those usually associated with the *maẓālim*. Like the *maẓālim* tribunal elsewhere, the chamberlain's court became a forum for bringing complaints about unsatisfactory judge rulings as well.[96] Many cases brought to the *maẓālim* tribunal in this period concerned disputes over pious endowments (*waqf*) or land grants. One was brought against an

official who had turned a church into a mosque, and several involved European merchants requesting goods they were owed be turned over to them.[97]

In the fifteenth century, the Mamluk *maẓālim* tribunals thus often ran concurrent to the judges' courts in their subject matter. There were still, to be sure, cases of people complaining about abuse or injustices suffered at the hands of officials, such as in a 821/1418 case in which the Mamluk sultan had the governor of Cairo whipped after he had fined a man whose son had died but did not have enough money to bury him.[98] But there were numerous cases that would previously have been resolved by the judge's court or, more likely, informal mediation. In one case brought to the Cairo *maẓālim* tribunal, a soldier who had married a young girl with the understanding that the marriage would not be consummated until she was physically mature raped her before then. The magistrate ordered him whipped and had him pay his wife compensation. There were several cases of husbands brought to the tribunal for failing to provide for their wives or for not consummating their marriages to begin with. These often resulted in the magistrate legally ending the marriage. Several husbands brought their wives to the *maẓālim* tribunal to demand they be disciplined or fined for infidelity.[99]

3) 1468–1517 CE: Finally, the two late Mamluk sultans, Qāyitbay (r. 872/1468–901/1496) and Qanṣawh al-Ghūrī (r. 906/1501–923/1517), took on a much more active role in administering royal justice, assuming the role of the representatives of the Shariah even against the fervent objections of ulama/judges. These two sultans involved themselves in numerous cases of theft and fornication, sometimes ignoring well-established procedural norms for avoiding Hudud punishments and carrying out excessive punishments.[100] There were less dramatic cases as well, such as a 913/1507 case in which a Mamluk amīr stabbed a boatman he claimed would not repay a debt, and the man's sons brought this (unsuccessfully) to the *maẓālim* tribunal.[101]

AL-ANDALUS AND THE ISLAMIC WEST

To the west of Egypt, the institution of the *maẓālim* seems to have been well known, especially by the institutional title of 'Rulings on Grievances' (*aḥkām al-maẓālim*). Evidence suggests that in the Islamic West it was also ulama/judges who were appointed to oversee *maẓālim* tribunals, which were located in major centers such as Cordoba, Valencia, and Játiva (Shāṭiba).[102] 'Ubaydallāh b. Muḥammad b. Adham (d. 486/1093) was a very respected scholar and judge who was, prior to being a judge, appointed to head the *maẓālim* in Cordoba. Aḥmad b. Yazīd al-Umawī (d. 652/1254) of Cordoba was a judge appointed to the *maẓālim* in Marrakesh.[103]

In his expansive study of the judiciary in classical Islamic civilization, the Lebanese scholar Emile Tyan contends that the phenomenon of the *maẓālim* in the West differed substantially from that in the East. He sees the *maẓālim* in the West as a strictly legal office not enjoying the aegis of royal justice or authority (Tyan ascribes this to the lack of a Persian heritage in the West). Furthermore, reports suggest that the office of judge enjoyed more authority than the magistrate of a *maẓālim* tribunal.[104]

Müller's more focused study on the *maẓālim* tribunals of Cordoba during the first five centuries of Muslim rule, however, suggests much more similarity with the institution in the Abbasid east. As in the Abbasid realm, the *maẓālim qua* ruler-addressing-grievances began as an appeal to royal justice in person, either to the ruler or a designated senior member of his court, who sat for such a purpose once or twice a week. This person was usually an official in the royal court or even a member of the royal household. Here, the case of the eunuch Masarra being appointed to the tribunal parallels the courtesan Thumal's appointment in Baghdad.[105] As in the east, in the 900s CE there was a shift away from the *maẓālim* being overseen by a member of the royal entourage, whose proximity to the ruler counted more than legal expertise, and towards an institution with a purpose-built venue and overseen by an appointed scholar/judge. The Umayyad ruler (*amīr*) 'Abdallāh (d. 275/888–300/912) built a special Gate of Justice (*bāb al-ʿadl*) by the royal passageway in Cordoba into the communal mosque to hear grievances. Then, in 325/937, ʿAbd al-Raḥmān III (d. 300/912–350/961), now carrying the title of caliph, established an independent office of *ṣāḥib al-maẓālim*. This magistrate was drawn from the ranks of ulama/judges. The rubric of royal justice, however, was still clear. Müller observes that, when he was moved from magistrate of the *maẓālim* to a senior judgeship in 394/1004, Ibn Fuṭays switched his garments from those of a vizier to those of a jurist (*faqīh*).[106]

As in the east, in the Islamic West the functions of *maẓālim* tribunals as well as those of *siyāsa* more broadly found homes in various fora. Leo Africanus recalls that Fez had four courts: one in which judges heard cases of "canon law" (perhaps civil cases and those involving pious endowments, *awqāf*), another dealing with issues of marriage and divorce, a third which seems to have been the crimes tribunal (responsible for capital and severe corporal punishment), and finally one court for appeals against unjust or flawed rulings by other judges.[107] This differs slightly from the description of Cordoba's legal venues made earlier by an eleventh-century judge. He describes the judge's court, the offices of the police force (*shurṭa*), the market police (*ḥisba*), the *maẓālim* tribunal, and what he called the *ṣāḥib radd*, "to which the judges (*ḥukkām*) appealed if they had doubts or misgivings" (this seems similar to interlocutory appeal in the US legal system).[108]

There is limited information about the functioning of *maẓālim* tribunals elsewhere in the Islamic West. In his ethnology/geography, al-Idrīsī (d. *circa* 560/1165) reports that the ruler of Ghana paid allegiance to the Abbasid caliphs and held mobile *maẓālim* sessions, walking around his capital with his entourage.[109] The Egyptian encyclopedist al-ʿUmarī (d. 749/1349) notes that the king of Mali in the 1300s CE held regular *maẓālim* sessions.[110] Much later, a senior scholar and member of the ruling family of the Sokoto Caliphate, ʿAbdallāh dan Fodio (d. 1245/1829), included a description of the *maẓālim* tribunal, drawn from al-Māwardī and later Mālikī scholars, in his practical guide to rulers.[111] Much more work needs to be done on how Mālikī law and state institutions functioned in Sudanic Africa, however, and it is impossible at this point to know if al-ʿUmarī was describing an actual *maẓālim* institution in Mali or just a ruler offering royal justice to his subjects.

ROYAL JUSTICE IN THE POST-MONGOL ERA

One of the most important recent observations in the study of Islamic legal history is the evident increase in the role of Muslim rulers/states from the eastern Mediterranean to India in the application, selection, management, and even constitution of the Shariah from the 1200s CE to the early modern period (in the Conclusion we will see how modernization reforms like the codification of the Shariah in the nineteenth century could be seen as a continuity of this trend). This can be seen most clearly in the fifteenth-century Ottoman and Timurid creation of state mufti (*shaykh al-Islām*) positions, in Ottoman and Mughal assumption of the ruling dynasty's right to adopt a state school of law and select particular opinions from that school to apply, and in the widespread phenomenon of dynastic law (such as the Ottoman *kânûn*).[112] As scholars like Samy Ayoub, Guy Burak, and Anne Broadridge have observed, the role of the ruler/state in defining and applying the Shariah was not new. In his study of the Ḥanafī *madhhab*, for example, Ayoub points out that the ruler had always been granted discretion in areas of law. But as Burak notes, what was new was the enhanced extent of that role and, equally important, its legitimization.[113]

This novel element turns on a hotly debated question: why did this intensified state involvement in the Shariah happen at this time? The most convincing argument, elaborated by John Woods, Broadbridge, Burak, and others, is that the gradual domination of the Nile-to-Ganges region by Turkic states and the dramatic impact of the Mongol invasions introduced a new conception of sovereignty and legitimacy in this region.[114] From the beginning of Islam until the Mongol period, Muslim states had ruled as custodians of God's revealed law and the shepherds of Muhammad's *umma*. The Turko-Mongol heritage of the newly regnant states was totally distinct and novel. This was particularly true for what Marshall Hodgson called

"Mongol prestige," or a heavenly ordained right to universal empire claimed by the Golden Family of Chinggis Khan.[115]

After the Mongol takeover of the Middle East and India and the knock-on effects of their invasions on Turkic polities even outside their range, such as the nascent Ottoman state, new ideas and ideals were introduced to the adjudication of justice. For the first time in Islamic history, rulers applied law legitimized by a perception of sovereignty independent of God's revelation. Turko-Mongol states had varied but definite attachments to traditions of laws such as those referred to enigmatically as the Yasa of Chinggis Khan and, more importantly, to the ruler's and dynasty's right to make law. After converting to Islam in the early 1300s CE, the Ilkhanid Mongol dynasty in Iran, as well as later Muslim Mongol states, made significant efforts to reconcile their regimes with the Islamic ideals of sovereignty and government that had reigned before the Mongol invasions.[116] Yet so dramatic was the shift brought by the Mongol conquests that the Ilkhanids and their successors introduced major changes in the perceptions and practices of Islamic sovereignty and law.[117] Burak proposes that the unprecedented role of states like the Ottoman and Mughal Empires in the Shariah was the result of trying to reconcile the Shariah, which existed before and outside the state, with what they understood as their right to dynastic law.[118]

The core distinction between *siyāsa* as understood in the pre-Mongol realms and in later realms like the Ottoman Empire, Burak explains, is that post-Mongol states like the Ottomans rooted their right to shape law and institutions in their dynastic identity and its claims to legitimacy. Pre-Mongol states, by contrast, engaged in *siyāsa* not because their dynasty conveyed such authority but because they were Sunni Muslim heads of state. Burak elaborates:

> [Ottoman *kânûn*] traces its origins to the eponymous founders of the dynasty, whereas the Mamluk discourse of *siyāsa* does not have, and in fact rejects, this dynastic dimension: the right of the Mamluk sultan to issue *siyāsa* laws and regulations rested on the recognition of his legitimacy as an Islamic (Sunni) sovereign, a

> legitimacy that had little to do with his lineage, in cases in which he could trace it.[119]

The new notions of sovereignty and the new claims made by post-Mongol rulers considerably altered the relationship between institutions of royal justice and jurists' discourse on *siyāsa*.[120] In the early years of Ilkhanid Mongol rule in Iraq and Iran, Ann Lambton notes that the new rulers divided the administration of justice into two forums, that of the khan and that of the Shariah judge (*qāḍī*). In the khan's court, Mongol tradition was applied by Mongol officials, while the judges' courts suffered neglect and decayed into simony. Lambton observes that this changed with Ghazan Khan (r. 694/1295–703/1304) and the Ilkhanid conversion to Islam. Under Ghazan, judges were newly re-empowered. They were once again assigned to oversee or advise the *maẓālim* tribunals. The khan ordered a biweekly *dīwān al-maẓālim*, which was tasked with handling disputes between Mongols or between Mongols and Muslims. In particular, this *maẓālim* tribunal was to handle particularly challenging cases. It was attended by a cadre of administrative and military officers as well as ulama/judges, who ensured that cases were decided in accordance with the Shariah.[121]

While the notion of royal justice was central to the political cosmologies of the Mongol and post-Mongol rulers, the institution of the *maẓālim* tribunal was not often mentioned in their historical records. This stands in stark contrast with the contemporaneous Mamluk lands, where the *maẓālim* was well known and well documented. In the post-Mongol period, therefore, the transregional labeling of certain legal venues as *maẓālim* becomes fairly complicated.

Clearly, there was a division of labor in judicial venues, both between the judge's court and a crimes tribunal and between the judge's court and dynastic matters. The great traveler (and scholar/judge) Ibn Baṭṭūṭa describes a marked subject-matter distinction between what he considered Shariah and dynastic custom during his visit to Khwarazm. He observed that a local ruler there would sit to hear legal complaints with the judge and his ulama advisors seated to one side and a group of Turkic elders seated on the other. Cases that the ruler deemed to fall under the Shariah would be directed to the judge, all others to the elders and amirs.[122] That Ibn Baṭṭūṭa observes a similar division of cases performed by the vizier of the sultan of Mogadishu, outside the reach of Mongol prestige, which suggests that this division of labor was less a product of Mongol imperial ideology than a matter of rulers distinguishing between public and private law, or perhaps between matters of policy/administration and those less oriented towards the ruler and his government. But the fact that in Mogadishu the issues falling outside of the ulama's purview were merely handled by "amirs and viziers" as opposed to venerable experts in a culturally steeped dynastic tradition – or perhaps the culture of the political elite – highlights the singular aspect of the Mongol legacy, namely its legitimate and articulated tradition of dynasty and ruling culture as a source of law.[123]

'Mongol prestige' received a powerful booster with the supremely successful conquests of Timur (r. *circa* 771/1370–807/1405), whose tremendous personal power and appeal to Chinggisid legitimacy convinced countless followers of his mandate-of-heaven right to universal empire.[124] The legal code that governed the application of royal justice under Timur and many of his successors was "the *törä* of the Lord of the auspicious conjunction," which Subtelny describes as representing "Turko-Mongol custom as practiced by Timur, his descendants, and their Chaghatay followers," sometimes complementing, sometimes taking the place of, and sometimes synonymous with the Chinggisid Yasa.[125] Timurid royal justice was manifested formally in the dynasty's *yarghu* courts, the military tribunals where the *törä* was applied by specialized officials. They were arbitrary and non-formal in comparison with Shariah judges' courts, with no formal process for accrediting witnesses, the casual use of torture, hasty execution, and the expropriation of property.[126] Mongol/Timurid royal justice was transmuted into Islamic form when the inheritor of the core of Timur's realm, his son Shāh Rukh (r. 807/1405–850/1447), assumed the mantle of *pādishāh-i Islām* (Emperor of Islam) and caliph. In 1411, he claimed to abolish the *yarghu* courts in favor of Shariah courts.[127]

The Persianate/Mongol traditions of royal justice continued in the Timurid successor states. In Iraq and western Iran the Aqquyunlu dynasty established a supreme administrative council (*dīvān-e aʿlā*), which, in addition to other administrative issues, dealt with legal cases that were submitted to it.[128] The late-sixteenth-century Safavid historian Būdāq Munshī Qazvīnī (fl. 985/1577) recalls the legal activity in the *dīvān* of the renowned Aqquyunlu sultan Ūzūn Ḥasan (r. 851/1457–883/1478), a figure whom the sixteenth-century Ottomans also saw as a paragon of effective and just rule:

> When Ūzūn Ḥasan had finished the morning prayer, the 'drum of justice' would be sounded to indicate the convening of the court of appeals. There he would appear in person clothed in dervish attire consisting of a camel's wool waistband and a plain, leather-trimmed lamb's wool jacket. He would seat himself on a golden dais while the princes and generals took their places on the right and on the left. Needy, indigent plaintiffs were then summoned to present their suits through a public official who acted as their advocate and intermediary. Cases would be settled immediately and the secretaries in attendance would draft and issue the orders. The plaintiffs would leave the court with firm decisions not subject to change or alteration.[129]

Davānī's treatise on the *maẓālim* tribunal, which is at the center of this book, suggests that, while in Mamluk Egypt the use of royal justice to investigate and prosecute difficult criminal cases seems to have moved mostly under the jurisdiction of the military court, in post-Timurid Persia it was the *maẓālim* tribunal that subsumed all royal justice. While al-Māwardī's writing on the *maẓālim* tribunal focused on resolving grievances, Davānī's treatise shifts attention markedly to violent crimes whose perpetrators are unknown or difficult to convict. That in sixteenth-century Persia the *maẓālim* tribunal may have swallowed the crimes tribunal function is also suggested by one of Davānī's students, Faḍlallāh b. Rūzbahān Khunjī (d. 927/1521). In a political advice work, Khunjī provides an almost verbatim Persian translation of al-Māwardī's chapter on the *maẓālim*. But then, within the same *maẓālim* chapter, Khunjī addends the near-verbatim contents of al-Māwardī's crimes tribunal chapter as well.[130]

THE OTTOMAN EMPIRE

Much like their Near-Eastern predecessors and contemporaries, the Ottoman dynasty drew considerable legitimacy from an imperial discourse about justice and its dispensation.[131] Along with the Near-Eastern/Mongol notion of the ruler as the apex and guarantor of peace and justice in a multi-ethnic, multi-religious empire, the Ottoman political tradition also absorbed the Mamluk-era scholarly contribution of *siyāsa sharʿiyya* (legitimate governance), which stressed the ruler's obligation to uphold God's law, pursue its ends, and protect the Muslim *umma*.[132] Ottoman sources reflect an expectation that the ruling dynasty prevent and remove oppression in the realm.

These sources do not, however, mention an institution within the Ottoman legal system that was labeled *dīwān al-maẓālim*. In fact, the Ottomans actually abolished the *maẓālim* tribunal in the Mamluk realms when they conquered Egypt, Syria, and the Hejaz.[133] Scholars like Haim Gerber and Wael Hallaq have interpreted this abolition as an attempt by the Ottomans to increase the authority of judges over other judicial offices and institutions.[134] Yet recent studies of the Ottoman legal system, most recently by James Baldwin, have seriously qualified both the claim that the Ottomans centered all legal activity in the office of the judge and, more importantly, that the *functions* of the *maẓālim* institution disappeared.[135] Rather, those functions were absorbed into another royal justice body, namely the provincial councils (*dîvân*) of governors and the Imperial Council in Istanbul (*dîvân-i hümâyûn*).

Michael Ursinus has provided an excellent study of the *Record of Complaints* registers from Monastır, the administrative capital of the Balkan Rumelia province, for the years 1781–83 CE. These volumes contain a trove of petition cases presented to the governor's council, the provincial counterpart to the Imperial Council in Istanbul, for redress of injustices and to which the sultan and his representatives devoted surprisingly consistent bureaucratic attention as part of their self-conscious duty as the ultimate guarantors of justice in their realm.[136] Based on an analysis of hundreds of these complaints cases from innumerable Muslim, non-Muslim, male, female, slave, and free subjects, involving civil disputes, criminal matters, concerns about financial abuse by officials, and more, Ursinus concludes that this provincial *dîvân* functioned "as a kind of *mazalim* or equity court" as well as a court of appeals.[137] In the case of some provincial centers such as Aleppo, the provincial *dîvân* handled cases of severe, violent crimes and threats to law and order like banditry.[138] This public/criminal law aspect overlapped with crimes tribunals and *maẓālim* tribunals in other eras and regions. A famous Ottoman legal guide, the seventeenth-century *Kânûnnâme* of Nişâncı ʿAbdürrahman Paşa (d. 1103/1692), instructs judges (*qāḍī*) to send cases of public security (*nizâm-i memleket*), capital, and severe corporal crimes to the sultan's representatives, i.e., the *dîvân*s.[139]

But what made individuals submit their complaints (*şikâyet*) to the provincial *dîvân* instead of taking them to the regular law courts? In the case of Monastır, the answer seems to lie in the *dîvân*'s appellate function and in its procedural flexibility, both originally core characteristics of the *maẓālim* tribunal. As in Davānī's treatise, in the criminal cases that Ursinus examines the offenders were very often unknown. This would be a challenge for judges' courts, where both parties were required to be present. In many of the civil cases, petitions were often appeals from subjects displeased with the rulings they had received from the law courts and who were hoping for a different result upon appeal. In fact, the *dîvân*s accepted repeat petitions more than once.[140] In the case of the governor's *dîvân* in Ottoman Cairo, Baldwin argues that there is not much to distinguish the petitions sent there from ordinary law court traffic in terms of subject matter. What does distinguish cases heard by the Cairo *dîvân*, however, is that the plaintiffs were disproportionally drawn from Egypt's elite. The governor's council in Cairo, then, was a forum of justice sought out by elites who thought it could advantage them.[141]

The cases that Ursinus finds in the Monastır records resemble those we have seen in other *maẓālim* tribunals. In addition to administrative complaints about things like excessive taxation, there are a large number of criminal cases, such as a (Jewish) petitioner's relative disappearing on a country road along with all their goods; a local headman accused of killing his own wife and dumping her body in a lake; a Christian accusing another Christian of impregnating his two daughters and raping his wife; and a Christian shepherd boy killed and his sheep stolen. There are also civil complaints aplenty, such as loans not repaid and disputes over inheritance.[142] In the case of Baldwin's research into the cases heard by the High Council (*al-dīwān al-ʿālī*) in Cairo, the majority were private disputes. There were also criminal matters, like two drunken Christians accidentally shooting a passer-by in the street. Its procedures did not differ dramatically from the law court.[143]

It is thus certainly false that the function of the *maẓālim* tribunal was abolished by the Ottomans in favor of the judge's law court. But the error of that claim is nonetheless illustrative for understanding how non-law-court institutions fell within the purview of the Shariah under Ottoman rule. In his reading of the Ottoman complaint registers, Haim Gerber noted the prominent role of judges (*qāḍī*) in the procedures as evidence of judges' near monopoly over judicial function in the Ottoman Empire. But, as Ursinus points out, this was not because there were no forums that mattered other than the law courts. It was because the *dîvân*s were a Shariah institution and the Ottomans were very conscientious about having ulama/judges present and often presiding.[144] In both the imperial and provincial *dîvân*s, judges (*qāḍī*) were almost always present, and imperial legal manuals instructed governors to adjudicate alongside them.[145] Ottoman legal directives (*kânûn*) in Egypt stated that a government official (*wālī*) should not punish anyone absent a judge's decision (though, as Baldwin observes, police often punished offenders on the spot). The governor's high legal tribunal (*al-dīwān al-ʿālī*) in Cairo was overseen by the governor, the chief Ḥanafī judge, many notaries, and then the leading judges of the other Sunni schools of law as well. A lower *dīwān* legal council, which met every day, was presided over only by a judge, an office known as the *qāḍī al-dīwān*.[146] Baldwin's study of the High Council in Cairo shows that judges there performed the same kind of work they did in the ordinary courts, drawing on the same body of Islamic law (*fiqh*) as those courts in evaluating evidence and rendering rulings.[147]

As Baldwin has shown, Egyptian subjects also sent petitions to the Imperial Council in Istanbul, sometimes involving serious matters of administrative abuse but also often involving private issues like arguments over inheritance or even neighborhood squabbles. In 1697 CE one woman sent a petition, along with her legal documentation, that shop properties she owned in Cairo's Khān al-Khalīlī be turned over to her. When it was feasible, the Imperial Council issued a ruling. If the matter required local investigation, it referred it to a local judge to investigate "according to the Shariah."[148]

One question remains, however. As we will see, the chief advantage the *maẓālim* tribunal had over the judge's court, at least in many times and places, is that it could draw flexibly from across the Sunni schools of law. Was this a feature of the Ottoman *dīvān*s as well, contributing to their ability to offer justice beyond what a normal court could provide? We know that the provincial *dīvān* in Cairo was staffed with judges from the four Sunni *madhhab*s. But Egypt was a land of legal diversity, with a strong presence of the Shāfiʿī, Mālikī, Ḥanafī, and even Ḥanbalī schools. The rest of the Ottoman Arab provinces and even eastern Anatolia also had pronounced legal diversity. Their *dīvān*s may only have been reflecting their constituencies. From what I have been able to ascertain, however, it is not at all clear that Ottoman provincial *dīvān*s were *intentionally* staffed with ulama/judges from diverse schools of law for the purpose of offering legal flexibility. In areas like the Balkans, where the Ḥanafī school prevailed, it is not clear that the *dīvān* would have been able to offer flexibility beyond an openness to the non-standard opinions offered within the Ḥanafī tradition, particularly since such *dīvān*s were required to rule by Ḥanafī law when they were hearing cases of first instance. The *dīvān* did offer a chance to appeal what litigants believed was a misapplication of Ḥanafī law, as shown in two cases on contract dispute presented to the Imperial Council in Istanbul during the seventeeh century. Many more cases, however, such as complaints about rulings not enforced and debts not paid, reveal the real advantage afforded by the *dīvān*'s royal justice: namely the imperium and intimidation that the ruler's name offered over and above what was often the more limited practical authority of a mere judge.[149]

THE SAFAVID EMPIRE

To the east, much like their Ottoman counterparts, Safavid Persian dynasts also held to the ideal of the dispensation of royal justice. Shah Ismāʿīl I (r. 907/1501–930/1524), the founder of the Safavid polity, established a *yarghu* tribunal to judge wayward governors. Ismāʿīl's successors also used this forum for trying state officials. Since the Safavid court was then an itinerant one, provincial subjects could submit their petitions and complaints when the shah visited their province. When Shah ʿAbbās I (r. 995/1588–1038/1629) visited Isfahan in 1590, for example, he invited the local population to submit their complaints about oppressive governors and officials. Moreover, according to Safavid prescriptive manuals, the grand vizier was expected to come to the Guard House or the *Dawlat* Gate of the royal palace to collect subjects' petitions.

In addition to petitions, the Safavids established a council of justice (*dīvān-e ʿadālat*), which coexisted alongside the judges' courts, both at the imperial center and in the provinces. Occasionally, but apparently not always, the shah himself attended the *dīvān*. Generally, the *dīvān-e ʿadālat* was under the responsibility of the *dīvān-begi*, an office that the Safavid dynasty adopted from their Timurid and Aqquyunlu predecessors.

The *dīvān-e ʿadālat* assumed different forms. During the reign of Shah Ismāʿīl and his son Ṭahmāsp I (r. 930/1524–984/1576), the tribunal (*dīvān-khāneh)* was held in a tent. Under Ismāʿīl II (r. 984/1576–984/1577), the *dīvān* was held at the court hall that the shah had built at the gate of the Chehel Sotūn (Forty Pillars) palace in Qazvin. Shah ʿAbbās I used to adjudicate standing at the gate of his palace. In seventeenth-century Isfahan, the *dīvān-begi* was expected to sit with the *ṣadr*, who supervised the endowments and other scholarly institutions, including the judges' courts, in session four days a week, usually at the main gate of the royal palace, and two additional days in his residence.

Fairly little is known about the Safavid royal justice *dīvān* in terms of procedures, and it is therefore difficult to establish how they differed from those of the law courts. Contemporary observers, however, pointed out that torturers were occasionally employed in the *dīvān,* a fact that may suggest that certain forms of evidence not used in the courts were admissible there.[150]

Royal justice tribunals and the discourse about the responsibility of the ruler for dispensing justice continued well into the twentieth century. In Qajar Iran, as Irene Schneider has argued, the dynasty maintained a system of courts and petitioning channels in addition to the judges' courts. Beyond that, a system of imperial courts, often referred to as the *'orfī* (customary or *siyāsat*) jurisdiction, existed throughout the Qajar realm. The Shah himself presided over the *dīvān-e shāh,* the highest royal court of justice. Muḥammad Shāh (r. 1250/1834–1264/1848) established a *dīvān-e 'adālat,* which was later reorganized by Nāṣir al-Dīn Shāh's (r. 1264/1848–1313/1896) chief minister, Mīrzā Taqī Khān (known as Amīr-e Kabīr) during his three-year tenure from 1848–51 CE. In 1858 the *dīvān* was transformed, unsuccessfully, into a department of justice, known as the *dīvān-khāneh-ye 'adliyye.*[151] As was the case in the Ottoman Empire, a certain degree of legal pluralism from the litigants' perspective existed in Qajar Iran, as litigants seem to have addressed their cases to both the judges' courts and the *dīvān-e 'adliyye.*[152]

INDIA AND THE MUGHAL EMPIRE

Further east but still within the Persianate and Turko-Mongol/ Timurid pale, legal institutions in Islamicate India seem to have followed in the tradition of Persianate Mirrors for Princes and Mongol royal prestige. This is reflected in both how royal tribunals functioned and how the forum was conceived. Under the Delhi Sultanate in the mid-1300s CE, the famous sultan Muḥammad b. Tughluq (r. 725/1325–752/1351) presided over a *maẓālim* tribunal every Tuesday and Thursday, along with his chamberlains and senior commanders (*amīr*). Interestingly, Ibn Baṭṭūṭa makes no mention of scholars or judges present. Had they been present, he likely would have mentioned them, as he spent many years in the sultan's entourage as a judge and scholar. But other sources note that some grievances presented at the *maẓālim* sessions would be taken up by a judge assigned to these cases.[153] In the later Delhi Sultanate, Sikandar Lōdī (r. 894/1489–923/1517) heard *maẓālim* cases in a pavilion called the House of Justice (*dār al-ʿadl*), with jurists and judges present.[154]

Ruling from the mid sixteenth-century until 1857 CE, the Mughal (i.e., the Indian Timurid) emperors crafted elaborate personas as the ultimate guarantors of God's justice on earth. As with other Muslim states we have seen, the Mughal emperors and their court chroniclers enveloped the judge's court and its *fiqh*, along with *siyāsat*, dynastic decrees, and local custom all within the larger fold of royal justice while stressing Islam's primacy and terming the whole system 'Shariah.'[155] Akbar (r. 963/1556–1014/1605) held sessions for royal justice that his famous court chronicler Abū al-Faḍl (d. 1011/1602) envisioned along the same lines as al-Māwardī's and Davānī's works. The emperor assigned senior scholars to hear cases in the House of Justice. There are also elements similar to the Aqquyunlu royal tribunal, such as the custom of announcing these sessions with the beating of a large drum. There were also always ulama/judges in attendance. Jahāngīr (r. 1014/1605–1037/1627) ordered (or at least wanted it known that he had ordered) the installation of the 'Chain of Justice,' a golden chain with bells attached that could be pulled by petitioners to whose grievances court officials had failed to attend (see cover illustration).[156]

A Mughal court historian noted the regular system of appeals in operation under Jahāngīr's son Shāh Jahān (r. 1038/1628–1068/1658). Litigants unsatisfied with local judgments could appeal first to the regional judge and then, if still unsatisfied, they could appeal by a petition to the emperor, who would usually be represented by either the chief judge or the head of the royal court (*dīvān*). Shāh Jahān devoted all Wednesday to hearing petitions, with ulama/judges in attendance for him to consult.[157] A Venetian resident in the court tells stories of the emperor hearing petitions and reversing *qāḍī* judgments on appeal with Solomonic flare. In one case, the emperor deduces that a slave girl was the slave of a scribe and not a soldier from watching her ably pour water into an inkstand. In another he compensates Dutch merchants whose warehouse had been looted because Mughal officials had not caught the culprits.[158]

In his rulings on petitions, Shāh Jahān was said to dispense justice according to the principles of the Shariah, a theme further developed by his overtly orthodox Sunni successor Awrangzīb (r. 1068/1658–1118/1707). According to a long-term European observer at the royal court, Awrangzīb would devote one day a week to open petitions at the Pavilion of Justice (*'adālat-khāna*), with the two chief judges in attendance. In addition, on another day of the week he would hear the petitions of ten individuals from the lower orders of society. This would take place even when the emperor was traveling. Part of that emperor's well-known tack toward the formally Islamic, Awrangzīb showed great anxiety that justice be dispensed according to the Shariah. One chronicler describes him taking the legal rulings from the ulama in attendance before pronouncing them. In 1702 CE he even renamed the sessions held in the Pavilion of Justice the *dīvān-e maẓālim*, which suggests that the scholarly strain so verbosely inaugurated by al-Māwardī and endorsed by Davānī granted a distinct orthodox imprimatur.[159]

The Mughal system of addressing grievances and royal justice was thematically quite similar to the Ottoman system, but it was much less institutionally defined and bureaucratically robust. It should probably best be understood as part of their Timurid heritage, with Awrangzīb's formally naming it a *maẓālim* tribunal echoing his Timurid predecessor Shāh Rukh's more orthodox turn. As with other states we have seen, a number of petitions sent to the emperor involved criminal cases in which the culprit was unknown or evidence unavailable. Several from the mid 1600s CE dealt with criminal matters, such as a man murdering his wife and an oppressive employer detaining and then potentially killing (fate unknown) their employee.[160]

SUMMARY: THE BIOGRAPHY OF THE *MAẒĀLIM* TRIBUNAL IN A SAUDI EPITOME

In one sense, we have already seen the transformation of the *maẓālim* tribunal in the modern period and the era of the nation state. *Siyāsa*, as a legitimate authority and jurisdiction within the Shariah, gradually expanded to consume or nearly eclipse what had previously been the most expansive forum of the Shariah: the judge's court (more on this in the Conclusion). It was allowed to do so because this was a conscious process of state centralization and expansion pursued by the holders of *siyāsa* and validated by ulama/judges who had, for several centuries, been increasingly subsumed into a state structure. The *maẓālim* may have only been a small component in this great kinematic recombobulation that Rachel Scott has termed the "recasting" of Islamic law.[161] In fact, in the Ottoman realm the *maẓālim*'s function had long been absorbed into provincial and imperial councils. But the *maẓālim* tribunal was arguably the most conspicuously Shariah-legitimate *siyāsa* forum. It is no coincidence that the Mughal emperor most interested in overt adherence to the Shariah, Awrangzīb, labelled the age-old, Near-Eastern, Perso-Indian, Turko-Mongol theatre of royal justice the *maẓālim*. And it was for the *maẓālim*, as articulated and legitimated by al-Māwardī and Davānī, that Cevdet Paşa reached in his effort to shore up the Islamic credentials of modern Ottoman legal centralization and state domination of law.

Yet there is at least one remaining *maẓālim* tribunal consciously phrased in a relatively un-'recast' idiom: the Board of Grievances (*dīwān al-maẓālim*) of Saudi Arabia (it even has its own X handle, @saudibogrv). Interestingly, the historical development of this forum since the time of the Kingdom's founder, King Abdulaziz Ibn Saud (d. 1373/1953), in many ways epitomizes the history of the *maẓālim* in Islamic history more broadly.

In 1926 King Abdulaziz, having recently added the cosmopolitan and thus very suspicious province of the Hejaz to his austere Bedouin kingdom of Nejd, announced that his subjects could deposit any grievance they had in an official 'Complaint Box' (*ṣandūq al-shakāwā*).

Only the king had the key. No administrative process was laid out for these complaints, though they had to be signed, and false complaints would be punished. But the king's gesture was as clear a continuity of age-old royal justice as one could imagine in the twentieth century. Administrative reforms in 1954 aimed at remaking the Kingdom's overall governance structure for a more complex and increasingly wealthy state transformed the Complaint Box into institutional form: the Board of Grievances. This ministerial department was charged with receiving grievances on any matter, investigating them, and then forwarding suggested rulings to the king for his final decision. In 1982 the Board of Grievances' structure and functions were focused and further explicated: its mandate was narrowed almost exclusively to grievances against some aspect of government administration, overreach or malfeasance by state officials, or cases in which the government was a party.

Interestingly, beyond the theme of formally institutionalizing the process of appeal to royal justice, the functioning of the Board of Grievances recalls other trends and moments passed through in this chapter. For example, the primacy of the Shariah and ulama/judges was clear. Regulations (and Saudi ulama/judges' objection) made it clear that the Board of Grievances had to respect the authority of ordinary *qāḍī* courts. And the Board's magistrates were themselves products of the Kingdom's Ḥanbalī Shariah judge training (though they often also added higher legal degrees as well). And yet the Board has applied laws issued by the Saudi government that the Kingdom's Ḥanbalī judges regard as Islamically illegitimate. Like *maẓālim* tribunals of the past, the Board of Grievances has had a more expansive view of the Shariah's outer bounds.[162]

Further reforms in 1982 allowed the Board of Grievances to extend its jurisdiction "temporarily" into criminal and commercial law matters. It also received sole competency to enforce foreign judgments and foreign arbitration agreements.[163] This ambiguous expansion is reminiscent of the *maẓālim*'s overlap with the crimes tribunal in Davānī's treatise and its occasional historical conflation with *siyāsa* areas writ large, such as foreign legal dealings. Finally, in 2007 the Board's mandate was reined in, and it was folded into the government's administrative court system. It now serves as the government's venue for complaints regarding administrative wrongs, bribes, graft, objections to administrative law verdicts, etc., as well as complaints between government departments. And yet we see the same adaptive potential in the *maẓālim* that we will soon see in Davānī's and Cevdet's invocation of the institution. In Saudi Arabia, the Board of Grievances remains a liminal forum for *siyāsa* and legal change. Like Cevdet and Davānī, many Saudi administrative law experts have viewed the Board of Grievances as a crucial instrument for dealing with novel domestic and international issues. It is even referred to by functionaries in the judiciary as "the shadow court" (*qaḍā' al-ẓill*).[164] The Board still seems to be the venue authorized to enforce foreign judgments. And it is also responsible for ruling on crimes resulting from violating the Kingdom's prohibition on commercial dealings with Israel.[165]

As this chapter has demonstrated, despite significant differences and variations, institutions of royal justice existed in many, if not most, Islamicate societies. While not all these institutions were *maẓālim* tribunals and, even when they had *maẓālim* functions, they were not always so named, family resemblances abound. Among them were the notion of the ruler as the ultimate guarantor of justice, an element of public law in which the ruler exhibited interest in public order and criminal law, and a venue for extraordinary adjudication for instances when normal justice seemed to have failed.

In the early and middle Abbasid periods the *maẓālim* tribunal was mainly a forum for petitioning against government wrongs or appealing judgments. Under the more imposing military patronage state (to use Hodgson's term) of the Mamluks, the *maẓālim* was matched by equally powerful forums for royal justice but also extended its reach under the influential supervision of the chamberlain. In the parts of Islamicate civilization swallowed by the Mongol conquests, the *maẓālim* tribunal became a more inchoate setting for an expansive demonstration of royal justice, at times engulfing the crimes tribunal function. Where the Turko-Mongol legacy was effectively bureaucratized, like the Ottoman Empire, the functions of the *maẓālim* were largely absorbed into the provincial and imperial *dīvāns*. In the

Mughal Empire, the *maẓālim* retained its important symbolic function as a theatre for royal justice. But, unlike other Timurid successor states, the crimes tribunal (*ʿadālat*) emerged as the dominant venue for justice alongside the *qāḍī* court.

Moreover, as this historical overview shows and as will be further discussed in the following chapters, the historical sources attest to the essential presence and involvement of ulama/judges in royal justice tribunals: as judges, consultants, and legitimating observers. The role of the jurists in these jurisdictions challenges the narrative that situates the *maẓālim* tribunal in opposition to the *qāḍī*'s court, let alone in tension with the Shariah. Yet their presence also raises important questions with regard to the reluctance of jurists over the centuries to write prescriptively about these tribunals. Some influential jurists, however, did write treatises about the *dīwān al-maẓālim*. It is to these treatises that we now turn.

2

From Baghdad to Istanbul: The Genealogy of a *Maẓālim* Treatise

In investigating how the *maẓālim* tribunal came to serve as an institutional answer to instances of incongruity between law and the expectations of justice, this book takes as its focus the treatise by Jalāl al-Dīn Davānī. Every text has a context, but Davānī's treatise has an unusually prominent and impactful prior and afterlife. It came to the attention of scholars only because it was pulled from the recesses of history by an influential Ottoman jurist and administrator in nineteenth-century Istanbul to justify his court reforms. Meanwhile, Davānī's treatise itself was shaped by a context far removed from the modernizing Ottoman metropolis. More than most of Davānī's *oeuvre*, his *maẓālim* treatise emerged from his immediate experiences as part of the elite in southwestern Persia during a time of chaos and reflects the features of post-Mongol Islamic thought. Davānī, in turn, was remolding and adding to a work from a still earlier and more distant world. He drew on a book that had been penned over four centuries earlier by two of the most prominent judges of Abbasid Baghdad. He chose that text as a model because it was, at the time, not only the most voluminous but also the only real effort we know of to theorize the *maẓālim* tribunal and describe its features in detail.

THE ORDINANCES OF GOVERNMENT (*AL-AḤKĀM AL-SULṬĀNIYYA*) AND THEORIZING THE *MAẒĀLIM* IN ELEVENTH-CENTURY BAGHDAD

The source on which Davānī relied was the chapter on the *maẓālim* tribunal in the famous *Ordinances of Government* (*al-Aḥkām al-sulṭāniyya*), a book or, more properly, two books, that present a rare challenge in intellectual history. Two texts entitled *The Ordinances of Government* were penned by two leading judges of Baghdad, both with close connections to the governing elite, and likely in the same decade (between 430–440/1038–1048). The two books have identical structures, themes and, in fact, *nearly* identical texts. One was either written as a slightly adjusted copy of the other or they were both closely modeled after a third, previously existing book. These two *Ordinances* versions came from the capable and accomplished minds of the renowned Shāfiʿī jurist and polymath of Buyid Baghdad, Abū al-Ḥasan al-Māwardī (d. 450/1058), and his contemporary, the city's leading Ḥanbalī jurist and theologian, Abū Yaʿlā Ibn al-Farrāʾ (d. 458/1066).

AL-MĀWARDĪ: ESTEEMED SHĀFIʿĪ JUDGE AND POLITICAL ADVISOR

Al-Māwardī was born in Basra in 364/974 to a merchant family (his last name means 'Seller of Rosewater'). As a youth he studied law in Basra under the Shāfiʿī master and judge ʿAbd al-Wāḥid al-Ṣaymarī (d. 386/996).[1] The young man formed a close relationship to the city's chief judge, who would later become the chief judge of Baghdad. It was not long before al-Māwardī began a career as a teacher himself, first in Basra and later in Baghdad.[2] We do not know exactly when al-Māwardī moved to Baghdad. It seems likely that, at first, he and his brother traveled between the two cities in the course of his studies and early teaching career.[3] He must have spent some prolonged time in the capital before the age of forty-two (in 406/1016), since he studied Shāfiʿī law extensively with the leading light of Shāfiʿī *fiqh* in

Baghdad at the time, Abū Ḥāmid al-Isfarāyīnī, who died that year. As he gained his own reputation as a scholar and author, al-Māwardī seems to have toured southern Iraq's major cities, such as Wāsiṭ, to teach in their mosques.[4]

For much of his career, al-Māwardī served as a judge, first in several towns in the environs of Basra and Baghdad and eventually in Baghdad itself.[5] Although he was often referred to by the honorific 'supreme judge' (*aqḍā al-quḍāt*) (a title bestowed on him by the Abbasid caliph al-Qā'im, r. 422/1031–467/1075), this was not an official post. Contrary to popular opinion, al-Māwardī never actually served as the chief judge of the Abbasid capital.[6] There is no doubt, however, that he was an extremely respected member of the scholarly community centered there, in particular amongst Shāfi'ī scholars.[7] When he died in his early eighties, his funeral prayer was led by no less than the city's leading Sunni Hadith scholar and historian, al-Khaṭīb al-Baghdādī (d. 463/1071).[8]

Although it was not unusual for leading scholars in his time to have relationships with rulers and their courts, al-Māwardī's were particularly close and varied. His career was marked by close relationships to the Abbasid caliphs al-Qādir (r. 381/991–422/1031) and his son al-Qā'im. But he was also a trusted advisor of the Shiite Buyid family, who ruled Iraq and Iran and served as the 'protectors' of the caliphs. In particular, he had a close relationship with the powerful Buyid sultan Jalāl al-Dawla (r. *circa* 416/1025–434/1043) and other leading members of the Buyid family.[9] Serious conflict within the Buyid family was common, and al-Māwardī was often used as an emissary or mediator during intra-family and inter-regional tensions.[10]

Al-Māwardī's reputation seems to have been one of integrity. In 429/1038, after Jalāl al-Dawla had solidified his hold on Baghdad, prominent ulama weighed in on the question of whether it was acceptable for the Arabic title 'king of kings' (*malik al-mulūk*) to be added to the sultan's public honorifics. (Buyid grandees jockeyed endlessly over such titles, which were granted them by the caliphs). Leading jurists of the city acceded, explaining that, if there was a chief judge (literally, 'judge of judges'), then why could there not be a 'king of kings'? Indeed, the Buyids had long referred to whichever prince had achieved preeminence by the Persian equivalent, *shāhānshāh*. One historian recorded in detail, however, that al-Māwardī disapproved of the title, since the Prophet had disliked it. Rather than punishing him for denying the request of his longtime patron, this resistance only increased Jalāl al-Dawla's respect for al-Māwardī.[11]

As Buyid power faded, Jalāl al-Dawla neared death, and the forces of the Sunni Seljuq Turks moved steadily across Iran towards Baghdad, the caliph al-Qā'im sent al-Māwardī as an emissary to the Seljuq chieftain, Toghril Beg (r. 431/1040–465/1063). He would act as an emissary between Baghdad and the Seljuqs for several years. But around 437/1046 al-Māwardī mostly withdrew from political life.[12] The Seljuqs finally took over Baghdad in 1055 CE and, though al-Māwardī no longer played a prominent role in court, he remained a respected and prominent personality. Chroniclers note that in 448/1056–7 he was one of the leading attendees at the wedding of the caliph al-Qā'im to the niece of Toghril Beg, the new 'protector of the caliph.'[13]

Al-Māwardī was first and foremost a jurist and judge. His writings on jurisprudence were copious and influential. Upon the request of the caliph for each of the four dominant Sunni schools of law to provide an epitome summarizing their views, al-Māwardī was asked to contribute the Shāfiʿī volume.[14] In the field of law, by far al-Māwardī's most famous book was his massive *al-Ḥāwī al-kabīr* (Great Compendium), an extensive commentary on the school's formative text, the *Mukhtaṣar* (Abridgement) of al-Shāfiʿī's acolyte al-Muzanī (d. 264/878). Although it would not become as influential as a comparable work by al-Māwardī's younger Khurasani contemporary, al-Juwaynī (d. 478/1085), its contents were quickly incorporated into the school's body of law and would be cited often.[15] Al-Māwardī contributed to other Islamic sciences as well, compiling a book documenting reports proving Muhammad's prophethood (*Dalā'il al-nubuwwa*) and penning a Quranic exegesis that has been surprisingly influential and had made its way to Al-Andalus within decades of its author's death.[16]

Al-Māwardī was a leading scholar of Shāfiʿī law in the late Buyid/Seljuq era. But, in this regard, he was one of many. Whereas other leading jurists were also accomplished theologians, such as al-Juwaynī and al-Ghazālī (d. 505/1111), al-Māwardī made his distinct mark in the genre of political theory and 'Mirrors for Princes' advice literature. This genre emerged in the late Umayyad period among chief administrators in the caliphal court, but it bloomed in the early Abbasid period as the philosophical and political heritages of the Near East were translated from Greek, Syriac, and Persian. Mirrors for Princes works came to include a telltale blend of realpolitik maxims and tales of exemplary conduct. These were all framed within the concept of the Circle of Justice, in which a ruler maintained all the component parts of his realm and state functioning in their proper roles for the sake of prosperity but even more so for the secure future of his dynasty. Moreover, they elaborated on the proper characteristics of effective rulers and the proper practices for overseeing an administration. Common exempla were Alexander the Great, Persian emperors, and early Islamic rulers.[17] By the mid-eleventh century it was not uncommon for prolific scholars to contribute a treatise to the genre, as both al-Juwaynī and al-Ghazālī did. But no jurist matched Māwardī in either impact or sheer volume of production in the Mirrors for Princes genre.

Al-Māwardī wrote at least five treatises on the theories, practice, laws, and institutions of government. His close relations to a number of powerful rulers and patrons over his career probably meant that he was asked repeatedly to pen such works. Understandably, this may have resulted in a number of not entirely original efforts. *The Ordinances of Government* stands out, however, while his other Mirrors for Princes works overlap a great deal in their contents and with other scholars' contributions to the genre.

Al-Māwardī rarely left clues as to when or for whom he wrote his books, and scholars have come to different conclusions about his motivations. Riḍwān al-Sayyid has mapped the works out as follows. The *Durar al-sulūk fī siyāsat al-mulūk* (The Pearls of Comportment in the Rule of Kings) was probably written around 393/1003 by a young al-Māwardī (then around twenty-nine) for the Buyid ruler

Bahā' al-Dawla.[18] Around 420/1029 he composed the *Adab al-dunyā wa'l-dīn* (The Etiquette of Worldly and Religious Affairs), a fascinating tour of the Near-Eastern/Islamic amalgam that was Mirrors for Princes along with a rational justification of Islam's teachings. In 427/1035, he wrote the *Qawānīn al-wizāra wa siyāsat al-mulūk* (The Vizier's Laws and Kingly Rule), a book of philosophical and practical ethics for viziers written in ornate rhythmed prose (*saj'*) for an unnamed vizier. Finally, the *Tashīl al-naẓar wa ta'jīl al-ẓafar* (Easing Examination and Hastening Victory) is yet another Mirrors for Princes amalgam but perhaps the author's most impressive, written around 432/1040 for the Buyid ruler Jalāl al-Dawla. Some have argued that al-Māwardī wrote another book, the *Naṣīḥat al-mulūk* (Advice for Kings), but its authorship has been seriously challenged.[19]

The Ordinances of Government was not only likely the last book that al-Māwardī wrote on the broad topic of politics, it also differed dramatically from his previous works. If we were not familiar with how the conventions of the Mirrors for Princes and legal genres differed, we might think the books did not issue from the same author.[20] Unlike the polyglot mixture of Greco-Roman, Pre-Islamic-Near-Eastern and Islamic philosophical wisdom that dominates his Mirrors for Princes work, *The Ordinances* is markedly a book of Islamic law. Al-Māwardī states in the introduction that he had been requested by an unnamed superior to compose an accessible guide on the legal rulings necessary for a sovereign who was too busy for more involved references.[21] Although H.A.R. Gibb proposed that *The Ordinances* was written at the behest of one of the two Abbasid caliphs whom al-Māwardī served, Riḍwān al-Sayyid has made a compelling argument that it was written towards the end of al-Māwardī's life, sometime after 435/1043 and likely around 445/1053, for the vizier Abū al-Qāsim 'Alī b. Maslama (d. 450/1059).[22] Melchert's conclusion is similar. Based on a date referenced in the *Ḥāwī*, he surmises that al-Māwardī was composing that legal compendium around 440/1048–9. If, as Melchert also asserts, *The Ordinances* relies on the *Ḥāwī*, then it was written even later than that.[23]

ABŪ YAʿLĀ IBN AL-FARRĀʾ: ḤANBALĪ JUDGE AND THEOLOGIAN

Abū Yaʿlā Ibn al-Farrāʾ was sixteen years al-Māwardī's junior, born in Baghdad in 380/990 to a scholarly family that followed the Ḥanafī school of law. His father was so respected a jurist that he was invited to serve as the chief judge of Baghdad. But he was too pious to accept. When his father died when Abū Yaʿlā was only ten, the boy's education was left to a Ḥanbalī teacher. Abū Yaʿlā was cemented in this new school of law when he graduated to study under the towering figure of Ibn Ḥāmid (d. 403/1012), the leading Ḥanbalī of Iraq.

Abū Yaʿlā succeeded his professor in his teaching position and exceeded him in his written *oeuvre*. He penned over fifty-seven books, excelling in the topics of law, Hadith, and theology. He was one of the first Ḥanbalī scholars to engage polemically and productively in the speculative theology tradition developed by al-Ashʿarī (d. 324/935–6) and embraced by many Shāfiʿīs and Mālikīs. His text on Ḥanbalī legal theory (*uṣūl al-fiqh*) represents an effort to combine that school's Hadith-based tradition with Ashʿarī epistemology and hermeneutics. His most well-known theological works were his abridgment of his own larger theological work, the *Muʿtamad*, and a book refuting the figurative interpretation of reports about God's attributes (*Ibṭāl al-taʾwīlāt li-akhbār al-ṣifāt*). The latter text, written in 432/1040, seemed to endorse anthropomorphism and caused a major theological controversy in Baghdad. But Abū Yaʿlā was so respected for his intense piety and asceticism and was so strongly supported by the caliph that he weathered this storm.

Like al-Māwardī, Abū Yaʿlā was a prominent member of the Abbasid judiciary. He served as a notary witness with Baghdad's chief judge and was eventually invited by the Caliph al-Qāʾim to preside over the court in the palace (*qāḍī al-ḥarīm*). He held this position for the rest of his life, along with concurrent judgeships in a number of other locales. He died in Baghdad at age seventy-eight in 458/1066.[24]

It is not clear when Abū Yaʿlā penned his *Ordinances of Government*. It must have been after 428/1036, since he states in his introduction that he had written an earlier book on governance (*imāma*), which he had either included in or merely mentioned in a now lost work which we know he completed sometime before 428/1036.[25] Abū Ya'lā states that this earlier book actually included much more material on the subject of governance, including the differing positions of the schools of law as well as their evidence. With *The Ordinances*, he explains, he decided to write a more focused guide for rulers about the legal rulings concerning their duties.[26]

WHO WROTE *THE ORDINANCES OF GOVERNMENT* FIRST AND WHY?

Scholars remain divided on who wrote the book first.[27] As they have noted, the two *Ordinances* are so similar, with the same topics in the same order and often the same text verbatim, that they must be related. But the two books differ in a few noticeable ways. While Abū Ya'lā refers almost exclusively to the opinions of Ibn Ḥanbal and his scriptural evidence, al-Māwardī regularly notes the positions of his Shāfi'ī school, along with those of the Ḥanafī and Mālikī ones. His version also contains much more historical and literary material. Melchert has argued that, in light of these differences, it seems more likely that al-Māwardī was adding material to an already existing text.[28] There is another indication that Abū Ya'lā laid the foundation for the book: he states in his *Ordinances* that he had already written an expansive book on governance but that he now wanted to write a monograph on the topic, removing some material and adding chapters. If his *Ordinances* is an outgrowth of his earlier writings, then he is either the originator of the shared text or – more cynically – he had read al-Māwardī's book or some unnamed original and wanted to make a subtle accusation of plagiarism.

As Melchert notes, however, in important ways, the relationship between the two texts and who influenced/'plagiarized' whom does not matter. That the two books are so similar shows how much agreement there was on their contents among Sunnis in Baghdad in the mid-eleventh century.[29] That both authors were intimately aware of the dynamics and institutional workings of the government and legal institutions of their time further bolsters the shared landscape they present in their books. Thankfully, for our purposes, whether al-Māwardī or Abū Ya'lā wrote the book first is not relevant. The section on the *maẓālim* and related material in the two versions are almost identical in their descriptions of the institution and its functions. But because al-Māwardī's text is likely later and constitutes a larger accumulation of legal and literary material, and because *The Ordinances* has mostly been associated with al-Māwardī, we will refer to the book either just by its title or to al-Māwardī as the author.

Such has been the assumption that al-Māwardī was the sole mind behind *The Ordinances* that it has been his motivations alone that have attracted scholarly attention. Gibb and others have argued that *The Ordinances* aimed to show that the caliphate was essential even if it was only ritual and symbolic and that al-Māwardī was offering this argument at a crucial point: when the power of the existing 'protector of the caliphate' was crumbling and a new one (the Seljuqs) might not see the utility of patronizing it any further. As Ovamir Anjum succinctly observes, *The Ordinances* was an effort to provide a realistic and viable theoretical reconciliation of the ideal of a Muslim *umma* and a Shariah presided over by a (symbolically) unifying caliph with a reality in which neither the caliph nor the larger Muslim community had any real political power. It was Islamic law and politics as 'the art of the possible.'[30]

MAẒĀLIM IN *THE ORDINANCES*: IS IT ACCURATE?

For our purposes, the question of what motivation or vision lay behind the writing of *The Ordinances* only matters to the extent that it colors the work's prescriptions and descriptions of the *maẓālim* tribunal. How accurate or realistic was the model *maẓālim* presented in the book?

While Western scholarship has been skeptical about how much *The Ordinances* can be read as a source for the actual nature of the caliphate in Abbasid Baghdad, there is much more confidence about how accurately the latter part of the book reflects the mundane functions of financial and legal organs like the *maẓālim*.[31]

We will explore the details of al-Māwardī's portrayal of the *maẓālim* tribunal and its procedures in the coming chapters. Here it suffices to note the most salient features of the tribunal as he and Abū Ya'lā knew and/or conceived of it. Most prominent is, not surprisingly, the *maẓālim*'s setting and foundation in imperium. Whether presided over by the ruler directly or, more likely, by a judge, vizier, or other official designated as magistrate, the ability to project raw power is crucial for the *maẓālim*'s functioning. Often results are achieved (or imagined to be achieved) by simple *irhāb*, intimidation, and the provocation of fear. It is this intimidation that can compel truth directly, or it is the use of investigation and even evidence not as proof (it would not be admissible in a judge's court anyway, notes *The Ordinances*) but to frighten a party into admitting the truth. So a document would be held up in a defendant's face because its contents were likely to frighten that defendant into admitting their wrong even though the document itself could not be admitted as evidence.[32]

A second salient feature of the *maẓālim* in *The Ordinances* is that, despite the prominence and indispensability of sovereign power and intimidation, the tribunal is very often envisioned as working through mediation between the disputing parties. In fact, such arbitration and mediation are frequently delegated to more junior officials, such as judges or notaries and even to community leaders.

The final theme that pervades al-Māwardī's and Abū Ya'lā's *maẓālim* is that, despite its reliance on the ruler's imperium, it is nested in, facilitated, and ultimately bounded by the Shariah. Judges (*quḍāt, ḥukkām*) and notarial witnesses are the experts turned to constantly for legal answers and the officials relied on to move cases forward. They are the investigators, mediators, and, as a last resort, the administers of oaths and issuers of final rulings. In the text of *The Ordinances*, the *maẓālim* is distinguished from the judge's court never because it can go beyond the Shariah but because it can utilize the Shariah's full range. Its magistrate can resort to what is permitted (*jā'iz*) within the Shariah's outer boundaries as opposed to the judge, who is constrained by what is required (*wājib*) by his school of law.

As al-Māwardī says clearly, "adjudicating according to the *maẓālim* does not render permissible what the Sacred Law has prohibited."[33]

Several of these themes are corroborated by our most prolonged discussion of the *maẓālim* forum prior to al-Māwardī and Abū Ya'lā. It comes from a scribal manual written in Iraq roughly a century before their time, and it both confirms in description much of what *The Ordinances* prescribes for the tribunal and also adds color. The author, one Ibn Wahb (fl. 950–1100 CE), seems to have been a scribe familiar with institutions in Baghdad.[34] He offers a familiar description: the *maẓālim* tribunal's concern is rectifying usurpation, preventing abuse and "restoring to people their rights (*ḥuqūq*)." Ibn Wahb adds the interesting note, however, that this is done on the basis of "prevalent information (*al-khabar al-shā'i'*) and what is well and widely known." This corroborates al-Māwardī's and Abū Ya'lā's reference to how the magistrate of the *maẓālim* can accept testimony, documents, or facts that are corroborated by a large accumulation of reports (*taẓāhur al-akhbār*).[35] Ibn Wahb describes the duties and skills needed for scribes working in the *maẓālim* tribunal as similar to those of officials working in the judge's court, except they do not need to deal with vetting witnesses, taking their testimony or examining certified documents (*lā yaḥkumu bi-shay' yusajjalu bihi*). This accords with *The Ordinances'* repeated references to such procedures as either being irrelevant, since the magistrate of the *maẓālim* tribunal might not be constrained by them, or as being delegated by the magistrate to subordinate judges or expert notaries. Like al-Māwardī's and Abū Ya'lā's texts, if the evidence brought forth in the *maẓālim* tribunal is too conflicting or ambiguous and the *maẓālim* officials cannot find a solution that the disputants agree on, the case can be delegated to judges, who can administer oaths to the disputants to arrive at a final ruling.[36]

At times Ibn Wahb's image differs distinctly from al-Māwardī's and Abū Ya'lā's *Ordinances*. In their instructions for the *maẓālim*, we see a forum that combines in alternation the essential power of intimidation by a representative of the sovereign and efforts to mediate between disputing parties with the aim of achieving resolution. Ibn Wahb's description seems only to touch on the *maẓālim* as a setting for mediation. This difference may lie in Ibn Wahb leaving unstated what is essential and implied: the magistrate of the *maẓālim* can succeed in mediation *because* the disputants are intimidated by his ultimate authority. A more obvious disjunct is that, while *The Ordinances* portrays a forum open to high and low alike, Ibn Wahb recommends the *maẓālim* as a workplace whose personnel only mix with upstanding and respected citizenry. They need not engage with the wide range of people we see seeking royal justice in other sources. In this regard, the *maẓālim* of Ibn Wahb resembles more the High Council in Ottoman Cairo than other *maẓālim* tribunals or fora for royal justice we have seen.[37] This does not necessarily impugn the accuracy of how the *maẓālim* tribunal is portrayed in *The Ordinances*, however, since there could be diversity among contemporaneous institutions even in one state, as the different Ottoman provincial *dīvān*s show.

JALĀL AL-DĪN DAVĀNĪ: THE LAST GREAT SUNNI THEOLOGIAN OF IRAN

Muḥammad b. Asʿad al-Ṣiddīqī al-Davānī, known as Jalāl al-Dīn (d. 908/1502), was born around 1426 in the village of Davān,[38] which sits in the hills just north of Kāzerūn, a town now a two-hour journey west of Shiraz.[39] His father, Saʿd al-Dīn, had received impressive scholarly training with famous Hadith masters, the leading Shāfiʿī jurists of Iran, and even the famous theologian and philosopher Sayyid Sharīf al-Jurjānī (d. 816/1413). Davānī the elder served as the judge of Davān as well as a teacher in the Jāmeʿ al-Morshedī madrasa in Kāzerūn. It was from this accomplished father that the young Davānī acquired most of his initial training in the Islamic sciences, particularly Hadith, Quranic exegesis, logic, and dialectical theology. The young Davānī later sought knowledge in the metropolis of Shiraz, and amongst his teachers were Ḥasan Baqqāl, Humām al-Dīn Gulbārī, Ṣafī al-Dīn Ījī, Maẓhar al-Dīn al-Kāzerūnī, as well as al-Maḥbūbī al-Lārī. Davānī boasts that he received a general permission to transmit Hadith from the famous Cairean Ibn Ḥajar al-ʿAsqalānī

(d. 852/1449) when he wrote an *ijāza* (permission to transmit Hadith and books studied by that scholar) to the whole city of Shiraz.[40] Davānī also sought knowledge elsewhere.[41] He traveled to and spent time in Najaf and Baghdad. He devoured the Islamic sciences ravenously, as illustrated by a reputation for borrowing books for annoyingly long periods of time.[42]

Davānī soon emerged as a master of numerous sciences, particularly the rational sciences of theology, ethics, and philosophy, and he was sought out by students from as far off as Central Asia and Egypt. Davānī was a proud Shāfiʿī in his jurisprudence and a staunch Ashʿarī in theology. Regarding his involvement in Sufism, in an *ijāza* to a student Davānī mentions that he had studied the *Ḥizb al-Baḥr* of the famous Sufi Abū al-Ḥasan al-Shādhilī (d. 656/1258), around whom the Shādhilī Sufi order had formed. But Davānī expresses greater pride in having been initiated into the spiritual chain of teaching back to Abū Isḥāq Ibrāhīm b. Shahriyār al-Kāzirūnī (d. 426/1033), the epicenter of a Sufi brotherhood that flourished in the region of Shiraz and traced its inspiration back to that sage's teacher, Ibn Khafīf (d. 371/982) of Shiraz.[43] Interestingly, Davānī's refutation of using weak Hadiths to declare actions recommended (*mustaḥabb*) is highly reminiscent of Ibn Taymiyya's unique take on that topic.[44]

Davānī also set foot early on in the political realm.[45] As a young man he was appointed as a senior religious official (*ṣadr*) under the Karaquyunlu rulers of Shiraz, though he soon resigned and turned to teaching in the Begum Madrasa (also known as Dār al-Aytām) in Shiraz. Al-Sakhāwī mentions that, as of 1491–2, Davānī had been appointed the chief judge of Shiraz and the Fars province by Yaʿqūb (r. 883/1478–896/1490), the sultan of the Aqquyunlu Turkic nomadic confederation that had bested the Karaquyunlu and conquered all of Iran. Davānī's administrative duties and scholarly interests led to continued travel. As a mature scholar he visited Tabriz (in late 1467, where he completed his *al-Zawrā'* epistle). He later visited Kashan, Gilan, and Herat. But he lost none of his enthusiasm for scholarship, and it seems that he continued to write and teach even when serving as chief judge.[46]

Davānī enjoyed a particularly strong and sustained relationship with the Aqquyunlu rulers of Iran. He received extended patronage from the dynasty's powerful builder, Ūzūn Ḥasan (r. 861/1457–882/1478), whom Davānī praised as the renewer (*mujaddid*) of the ninth Islamic century as well as the rightful caliph of God and His Prophet.[47] Though Davānī at times criticized his successor, Ya'qūb, for excessive or tyrannical control, the scholar cultivated a fruitful relationship with him as well.[48] Davānī also enjoyed the favor of Ya'qūb's successor, Rustam (r. 898/1493–902/1497) and received patronage from Ūzūn Ḥasan's son Khalīl, who was governor of the Fars province. As demonstrated by Lambton and John Woods, in return Davānī drew on the rich Persianate genre of Mirrors for Princes to provide moving literary and administrative elaborations of the dynasty's cosmic role as God's shadow on earth and the guarantor of His justice. The Shariah was the law that would best model God's justice, but it was the crucial person of the ruler who ensured it was applied. Any righteous and powerful ruler was fulfilling the mantle of the caliphate, and so Davānī referred to Aqquyunlu rulers like Ūzūn Ḥasan by this lofty title.[49]

Davānī was also well aware of political vicissitudes far from Shiraz, and he paid tribute to other rulers who sought to honor him or whom he respected. He dedicated (with effusive praise) several works to Sultan Maḥmūd I of Gujarat (r. 862/1458–917/1511), an ambitious patron whose realm was quickly emerging as a magnet for Muslim scholarly talent. Interestingly, some of Davānī's descendants would later flourish in the Mughal court in Agra. And Davānī composed at least one treatise for the Ottoman sultan Bayazit II (r. 886/1481–918/1512), with whom he also exchanged letters and whose father had tried to convince him to move to his realm.[50]

The last years of Davānī's life were traumatic. His political patronage and protection vanished as the Aqquyunlu state fragmented in internecine strife and the shadow of Safavid expansion grew. In 1497 there was an uprising against the local Aqquyunlu ruler of Shiraz, Qāsim Beg Purnāk, and in the fall of 1498 the city was taken over by the Afshar clan in the midst of an Aqquyunlu civil war. These events seem to have led to Davānī's flight or exile from the city.[51] The *maẓālim* treatise presented in this book was penned by Davānī after he had fled his native haunts, and he describes himself poignantly as being far from home and in the region of Lār, close to the Persian Gulf. His reference to the rulers of Lār, to whose sultan he addressed the epistle, suggests he took refuge there. We know from what Kātib al-Chelebī (d. 1067/1657) considers Davānī's last work that towards the end of 1499 Davānī found himself even farther from home, in the locality of Jarūn on the island of Hormuz near modern day Bandar Abbas, where he says he had ended up after having been "exiled from homelands, cast about by regions and toyed with by misfortune (*ḥidthān*)."[52] His *Unmūdhaj al-ʿulūm*, dedicated and sent to the sultan of Gujarat, reads in part like a C.V. sent with a plea for patronage. And Davānī's near apotheosizing praise for the sultan strongly suggests that he wrote this work after having lost hope for a return to stability in the Aqquyunlu state. He seems to have found a way home again, however, after the Aqquyunlu prince Abū al-Fatḥ Bāyandur recovered Shiraz from the Afshar pretenders in late 1499/early 1500. It is reported that the old scholar fell ill on a visit to Abū al-Fatḥ's camp near Kāzerūn and died there in 1502. He was in buried in Davān.[53] The ruler of Sind invited Davānī to his court, but the great scholar had died by the time the invitation arrived.[54]

The great bulk of Davānī's writings concerned the *ʿaqliyyāt*, Islam's rational sciences. In particular, his works engage Islamic theology (*kalām*) and logic (*manṭiq*), ranging from monographs such as his rational proof of God's eternity (*Ithbāt al-wājib al-qadīm*)[55] to small treatises such as *The Levels of Existence* (*Marātib al-wujūd*) and *The True Nature of the Human and the Soul* (*Ḥaqīqat al-insān wa'l-rūḥ*). More famous were Davānī's commentaries and glosses on mainstay texts of theology, philosophy, and ethics, which gained great renown as staples of madrasa curricula in both South Asia and the Ottoman world.[56] Particular favorites were his *Ḥāshiya ʿalā al-Shamsiyya* in logic, his commentary on the *ʿAqā'id al-ʿAḍudiyya* theological compendium of ʿAḍud al-Dīn ʿAbd al-Raḥmān al-Ījī (d. 756/1355), and what became known as the *Ṭabaqāt al-Jalāliyya*, an amalgam of theological and logic commentaries that had resulted from a scholarly rivalry memorialized with epic joy in Ottoman sources. Davānī had written a commentary (*al-ḥāshiya al-qadīma*) on an existing commentary by 'Alā' al-Dīn al-Qushjī (d. 879/1474) on the *Tajrīd al-kalām* of Naṣīr al-Dīn al-Ṭūsī (d. 672/1274). In this Davānī critiqued another commentary written by a rival scholar in Shiraz, Mīr Ṣadr al-Dīn Dashtakī (d. 903/1498). Dashtakī then wrote a *ḥāshiyya* rebutting Davānī, which he sent as a tribute to the Ottoman sultan Bayazit II. Davānī countered with a second *ḥāshiya* (*al-jadīda*), only to have it rebutted by another commentary by Dashtakī. Davānī penned a third *ḥāshiya* as a rebuttal (*al-ajadd*), but by that time Dashtakī had died. His son, Ghiyāth al-Dīn Dashtakī (d. 948/1541), was undeterred and wrote a final rebuttal in his father's stead.[57] Ottoman scholars layered many more supracommentaries on top of the *Ṭabaqāt al-Jalāliyya*, with one Ḥājjī Ḥasanzāde even composing *The Trial of Davānī v. Mīr Ṣadr* (*al-Muḥākama bayn al-Dawānī wa Mīr Ṣadr*).[58]

Other well-known works by Davānī include a theosophical commentary, *Shawākil al-ḥūr,* on the *Hayākil al-nūr* of the Sufi martyr al-Suhrawardī (d. 578/1191); a digest sampling a range of the Islamic sciences (*Unmūdhaj al-ʿulūm*); several exegetical works on the short Quranic chapters of *al-Ikhlāṣ*, *al-Kāfirūn*, *al-Falaq*, and *al-Nās*; as well as what was likely a collection of forty Hadiths on politics and statecraft entitled *al-Arbaʿīn al-sulṭāniyya fī al-aḥkām al-rabbāniyya.*[59]

Doubtless Davānī's reputation was promoted by his many students who settled and found patrons throughout the Persianate world, from the Indian subcontinent to the Ottoman lands. In his biographical dictionary of the Ottoman learned hierarchy in the fifteenth and sixteenth centuries, Taşköprüzade (d. 968/1561) lists several scholars either as Davānī's students or as affiliated with his circle who had migrated to Ottoman lands and entered the service of the dynasty's evolving learned hierarchy. Among the at least half a dozen scholars who either traveled to India after studying with Davānī or returned home there after doing so, two would settle in the wealthy, rising powerhouse of Gujarat and teach the future chief judge of the Mughal Empire.[60] Davānī's commentaries became mainstays of the madrasa curricula in Muslim South Asia.[61] Combined with the widespread fame of his writings, the prominence of his students fixed Davānī firmly in the imperial pantheon of esteem.[62] Moreover, his ethical work, the *Akhlāq-e Jalālī*, was extremely popular throughout the Persianate world, from the Indian subcontinent to the Balkans.[63] Davānī's position in the intellectual-political landscape of the post-Mongol Persianate world of the fifteenth century onward, and particularly in the heartlands of the Ottoman Empire, would have made him particularly attractive to anyone seeking an authority to legitimize a claim, as Cevdet Paşa's later reliance on Davānī shows.

There is dispute over whether or not Davānī converted to Shiism towards the end of his life. Sunni sources make no mention of this. A few distinctively Shiite treatises have also been attributed to Davānī, including the introductory parts of the surviving treatise on legitimate authority (*Nūr al-hidāya fī al-imāma*). Writing several decades after Davānī's death, the Iranian Shiite transplant to Mughal India Shūshtarī (d. 1019/1610) asserts that "there is no hesitation about Davānī's Shiism."[64] The Shiite biographer Khwānsārī (d. 1313/1895) claims that "the spirit of right guidance" struck Davānī as he was penning his third rebuttal of Dashtakī, which would have been after 1498 but before Davānī's death in 1502.[65] Yet Andrew Newman points out that as late as 1499 Davānī was clearly very Sunni, since that year he composed his commentary on the *'Aqā'id al-'Aḍudiyya*, which was openly anti-Shiite (Shūshtarī admits this but suggests that Davānī wrote this book at the behest of a Sunni patron and concealed his Shiism in an act of cautionary dissimulation, *taqiyya*).[66] In the three years or so that remained of his life, Davānī could have converted to Shiism. There is no way to know, since the internal dynamics of such scholarly inquiry render it insoluble: Sunnis deny any claim or attribution of embracing Shiism as Shiite fabrication, and Shiites explain away any overt Sunnism as dissimulation (*taqiyya*). At any rate, Davānī died about two years before the Safavid capture of Shiraz in 1504, when the city's leading Sunni scholars were forced to convert or were executed. Kāzerūn suffered particularly badly, with the Safavid Shah executing the leading scholars of the town along with their families.[67]

DAVĀNĪ'S *MAẒĀLIM*: CRISIS AND RECTIFICATION

As with al-Māwardī's chapter, we will investigate the procedural, substantive, and constitutional issues raised in Davānī's treatise at length in later chapters. Some of its salient features, however, are worth noting here, particularly as pertains to the historical development of the *maẓālim* and Islamicate royal justice. First, though Davānī openly builds his treatise on *The Ordinances' maẓālim* chapter, he borrows only from al-Māwardī's sections on the history of the *maẓālim* in the early Islamic centuries, his layout of the *maẓālim*'s subject matter jurisdictions and, in particular, the ways in which the *maẓālim* magistrate enjoys more authority and less restrictions than the judge. Having done this, Davānī abruptly departs from al-Māwardī's text and moves on to cases he knows of or himself adjudicated in Shiraz.

These are all criminal cases, and Davānī's departure from al-Māwardī's chapter shifts the focus completely from *The Ordinances'* dry discussion of what procedures the magistrate should follow in resolving disputes over expropriated land to the crisis precipitated by judges' inability to provide justice in cases of murder and theft. Where al-Māwardī's text centers on rulers addressing grievances mainly sparked by their own government officials, Davānī's subject is a crisis of law and order that necessitates the *maẓālim* magistrate's enhanced powers and greater procedural latitude. The crisis that Davānī perceives in the provision of justice extended beyond criminal matters. In fact, it would resonate in many countries today: ordinary courts are stalled by lawyerly, obstructive defendants who abuse legal minutiae to exhaust plaintiffs, and judges are too often complicit.

Were Davānī himself not a respected judge and venerated Shāfiʿī scholar, one might almost read his critiques as subversive. One anecdote in his treatise includes a brief remark that subtly undermines a fundamental plank of Shariah court procedure. Davānī tells how, in one instance of theft, suspicion had fallen on a pious man who would spend all of Ramadan reading the Quran. When Davānī responds that such a crime "would not come from him," he was merely following a common assumption in Shariah procedure that how the claims of plaintiffs, defendants, and witnesses were weighed depended in part on their reputations for piety and virtuous conduct. But he then reports that this 'pious' man had, in fact, been guilty!

For Davānī, the judiciary's dire condition has resulted in what he touches on again and again in his treatise as intolerable for ulama/judges and rulers alike: the rights of God's servants (*ḥuqūq al-ʿibād*) were being denied them. The *maẓālim* tribunal was essential to rectify this. As indispensable as this *siyāsa* forum was in Davānī's view, however, the final, salient theme in his treatise is his response to the accusation that the *maẓālim* was an illegitimate decamping from the Shariah, namely Davānī's vociferous insistence that "the judgment of the grievance tribunal is the judgment of the Sacred Law."

INVOKING DAVĀNĪ IN MODERNITY: AHMET CEVDET PAŞA AND OTTOMAN REFORMS

Davānī's remarkable treatise on the *maẓālim* tribunal would likely have languished in some archival eddy had it not been brought forth by the third generation in the history of this text, the peerless Ottoman scholar, administrator, and intellectual Ahmet Cevdet Paşa (d. 1312/1895).

Born in Lovec (in modern-day Bulgaria) in 1238/1823 to a well-established family of administrators and jurists, Ahmet Cevdet was sent to the Ottoman capital for his education. Soon he was studying with some of the leading jurists and scholars of the day. The young Cevdet's talents quicky stood out, and he came under the wing of some of the capital's most notable scholars, such as the reformist grand vizier Mustafa Reşid Paşa (d. 1274/1858) and the chief imperial mufti, *şeyhülislam* Ârif Hikmet Beyefendi (d. 1275/1859). In 1844, Cevdet was appointed to his first position in the Ottoman imperial learned hierarchy and served as the judge of the Albanian district of Permedi (Përmet). In the following years, Cevdet served in different judgeships and teaching positions. In 1855, he became the official imperial chronicler of the empire (*vakʿanüvis*) before he was appointed the chief judge of several important jurisdictions, such as Galata, Mecca, and Istanbul. He served on the Committee on Education (*Maarif Meclisi*) and the Supreme Committee of the Empire's massive and comprehensive reform project (*Meclis-i 'Âli-i Tanzimat*) from 1857 to 1861.

Cevdet's star continued to rise, and in 1863 he was appointed the chief justice of the Anatolian and Arab provinces of the empire (*Anadolu kadiasker*). In an unprecedented turn, in 1866 this position was converted into a cabinet-level administrative position, which meant that Cevdet left the ranks of the Ottoman ulama corps (*ilmiye*) and assumed the senior administrative title (and garb) of Paşa. He soon thereafter was appointed the governor of Aleppo, a position he held for two years and during which he reorganized the province. Throughout this period, Cevdet took part in drafting and issuing regulations and laws, such as the land code of 1858, and other legal elements of the *Tanzimat* reforms.

Most importantly, in 1868 Cevdet was appointed to head the newly created High Court of Justice (*Dîvân-ı Ahkâm-ı 'Adliyye*) and served in the also relatively new position of the Minister of Justice. From the 1860s he led the establishment of the *Nizâmiyye* courts and was involved in drafting some of the laws and regulations that were intended to guide the new jurisdiction's operation. During those years, Cevdet also led the committee that compiled the empire's first major civil law code, better known as the *Mecelle* (or *Mecelle-i Ahkâm-i 'Adliyye*, 1869–76), which he proudly attested was based solely on Ḥanafī jurisprudence.[68]

In addition to his administrative and judicial roles, Cevdet was an accomplished historian and litterateur. His *oeuvre* included works on grammar, Islamic history, logic, and law. His most important historiographical work was his twelve-volume chronicle, *Târîh-i Cevdet* (completed in 1884). He also left his memoirs, which he intended to assist his successors as imperial chronicler.

Cevdet continued to serve in different high-ranking administrative positions under Sultan Abdülhamid II (r. 1293/1876–1327/1909), including a very short tenure as the grand vizier in 1879. Soon thereafter, he was appointed once again as the Minister of Justice (*'Adliyye nâziri*). After 1882, however, Cevdet lost much of his influence and power in the Ottoman administration. In 1895, he died aged seventy-two in Istanbul's waterside neighborhood of Bebek.[69]

CEVDET'S 'DISCOVERY' AND DEPLOYMENT OF DAVĀNĪ'S *MAẒĀLIM* TREATISE

Despite Davānī's place in the Ottoman scholarly firmament, his treatise on the *maẓālim* tribunal was not well known at all. In fact, though it survived in Istanbul's libraries (which hold two evidently nineteenth-century copies), it had never been published or, to my knowledge, cited by scholars before Cevdet. It was not even listed by the compendious Ottoman bibliographer Kātib Chelebī in his *Kashf al-ẓunūn*. What drew Cevdet's attention to Davānī's treatise when he could have consulted a much better known and canonical text, namely al-Māwardī's *Ordinances of Government*? Was Cevdet's interest in Davānī's text merely antiquarian?

Here we must remember that what has become canonical in the modern period, among intellectual historians and lay readers alike, has not always been so. Al-Māwardī's *Ordinances* actually did not enjoy strong name recognition in the Ottoman scholarly heritage. As Hüseyin Yılmaz has observed, during the heyday of Ottoman rule, al-Māwardī's tome "remained untranslated [into Ottoman Turkish] and rarely referred to."[70] Davānī's name, by contrast, enjoyed a stellar and quite canonical reputation among Ottoman scholars. His ethical and philosophical works had been madrasa staples for centuries. Davānī was thus actually a more respected name among the Ottoman elite than al-Māwardī. And it was this fame and renown that Cevdet required even more than the detailed contents of al-Māwardī's extensive *maẓālim* chapter.

Dropping Davānī's name in the process of an argument was a trend in Cevdet's writings. On several occasions he cited the scholar's well-known ethical works for authority. In Cevdet's *History*, it was Davānī's name that he invoked to remind his audience that the sovereign's two principal duties (*vazîfe*) were ensuring the security of his subjects through military means and securing the rights of God's servants (*ihkâk-i hukûk-i ʿibâd*).[71]

Yet for what particular task did Cevdet choose to invoke Davānī's obscure *maẓālim* treatise? He did so, it seems, in two instances. Both concerned the legitimacy and functioning of the Empire's new *Nizâmiyye* (statutory, 'regular,' or state-promulgated) court system, of which Cevdet was a chief architect. This new court system was a core component of the Ottoman Empire's systematic program of legal reform and modernization, which took shape in the two decades after 1864 as part of a comprehensive reorganization, hierarchization, and centralization of the Empire's entire administration. The *Nizâmiyye* courts were created parallel to the existing law courts (*mahkeme-i sherʿiyye*), still presided over by ulama/judges. In every province a tripartite court arrangement was established: a civil court (*mahkeme-i hukûk*), a crimes tribunal (*maclis-i ceza*), and a commercial tribunal, though they were all mostly administered by the same judges. The *Nizâmiyye* courts handled civil, criminal, and commercial issues, while the law courts continued to handle personal status issues like marriage, divorce, inheritance, and the ubiquitous institution of pious foundations (*vakf*). The crimes tribunals were manned by judges produced by the new *Nizâmiyye* Imperial Law School (*Mekteb-i Hukûk-i Şahane*, 1878) and who would eventually come to work under the newly formed Ministry of Justice (*ʿAdliye Nezâreti*), while the civil courts were manned by the same corps of ulama/judges who staffed the existing law courts. Following the French model, the *Nizâmiyye* system had three levels: courts of first instance were spread out at a sub-district level, there was an appeals court (*istinâf*) in each province, and finally a court of cassation (*mahkeme-i tamyîz*) in Istanbul.[72]

At the core of his new system was Cevdet's greatest accomplishment: the *Mecelle*, a codification of Ḥanafī law on civil matters such as contracts, sales, torts, conversion, and debts (but excluding family law) alongside those subjects that essentially made up civil procedure. The *Mecelle* provided the substance and initially part of the procedure for the *Nizâmiyye*'s civil courts and also for the existing law courts (until their own law of procedure was passed in 1917).

When a new Code of Civil Procedure was passed for the *Nizâmiyye* courts in the 1870s, it was an amalgamation of the French code and the procedural parts of *Mecelle* and was produced by the same committee of ulama/judges who had compiled the *Mecelle* under Cevdet's direction. The *Nizâmiyye's* new code of criminal procedure, by contrast, was almost a wholesale translation of the French criminal code.[73] But Islamic criminal law has always been overwhelmingly discretionary and left to judges, with guidance on discretionary punishment (*taʿzīr*) provided in *fiqh* manuals or by *siyāsa*.

The first instance of invoking Davānī's *maẓālim* treatise, Cevdet recounts in his memoirs. Some ulama, whom this late Ottoman titan considered more ignorant samples of that scholarly class, had been opposing the establishment of the Supreme Court of Justice (*Dîvân-i Ahkâm-i ʿAdliyye*) and the *Nizâmiyye* court system that followed it. The empire already had a court system, they objected, and this new one was totally unnecessary (*bunca mahâkim-i şerʿiyye var iken mahâkim ve-mecâlis-i nizâmiyye tertîbine ne hâcet var idi*).[74]

In 1868, as a response to this questioning, Cevdet translated large sections[75] of Davānī's treatise and presented his rendering to his critics in a meeting. In his brief commentary on the text, Cevdet explains how the *Nizâmiyye* courts were nothing more than the latest fulfillment of the age-old principle of protecting the rights of God's servants, which had been embodied in several institutions over the centuries, from the early days of the Ottoman state up to the recent Supreme Court of Justice. He wrote:

> With this, Your Highness became familiar with the essence of Davānī's discourse on the topic. Even at that [earlier] time, it was extremely necessary to establish tribunals (*dîvân*) other than the law courts (*mahâkim-i şerʿiyyeden*). Now, commercial and interpersonal transactions (*muʿâmelât*) have increased in number, and the Well-Protected Domains [i.e., the Ottoman Empire] have expanded significantly. When examining and contemplating these [issues] and comparing [different times and conditions], it is obvious why it is extremely necessary to establish [new] tribunals in the Supreme State.

The first task of political regimes is to defend the rights of the servants [of God] (*ihkâk-i hukûk-i ʿibâd*), and in every time period the fulfillment of this task is managed in one way or another. In some countries, the scribes and servants of the Shariah are called upstanding witnesses (*ʿudûl*), and they have been tasked with serving as witnesses [i.e., procedural notaries] for the cases that transpired in the law courts (*mahâkim-i şerʿiyye*) and to certify the documents of court decisions and testimonies with their signature, all with the purpose of protecting the common good (*mesâlih-i âmme*) from damage. But, even in those earlier times, this practice had degenerated to the point that Jalāl al-Dīn Davānī complained that most of these upstanding witnesses (*ʿudûl*) were not actually upstanding.

In its early period, the Supreme State paid utmost care to its most important task: the protection of the rights of the servants [of God]. It is reported that in the area of the Imperial Palace where the imperial Eid ceremonies currently take place – more particularly, in the area where scholars gather and wait during these ceremonies – there was a chamber, known as the Old Chamber of the Imperial Council (*ʿAtîk Dîvânhâne*), where a tribunal (*dîvân*) was set up twice a week for bringing cases. And the sultan of the time attended the meetings of this tribunal in person. Later, with the expansion of the state, it was moved to Beneath the Dome (*kubbe-altı*, i.e. the Imperial Council chamber built in the 16th century). And it was led by the absolute representative of the sultan (*vekîl-i mutlak*, i.e. the grand vizier), while the sultan of the time observed the session from behind a grill (*kafes*). It continued this way until recently.

Lately, these cases came under the supervision of the Shaykh al-Islam [i.e., the head of the religious establishment and judiciary]. However, for political and administrative issues, the High Council of Judicial Ordinances (*Meclis-i Vâlâ-i Ahkâm-ı ʿAdliye*), which was intended to serve as the grievance tribunal (*dîvân-ı mezâlim*), was established. Nevertheless, due to the extraordinary expansion in the number of [people's] dealings and the resulting increase in legal issues, it is well known that the High Council

> became swamped. Now, His Excellency, the Shadow of God, following the natural requirements of the time, divided these issues into two, thus separating the task of protecting the rights of the servants [of God] from other tasks of the state. For this purpose, he ordered the establishment of the Supreme Court of Justice (*Dîvân-ı Ahkâm-ı ʿAdliye*)....[76]

According to Cevdet's recollection, presenting Davānī's text silenced the critique. He recounts that the ulama and the other members of the Council who attended his presentation agreed that "After someone like Jalāl al-Dīn Davānī saying so, what can one say?"[77]

The second instance of Cevdet invoking the authority of Davānī's *maẓālim* treatise took place in the wake of Ottoman religious and citizenship reforms. Driven by outside pressure from European states and internal worries about dissatisfaction among the Empire's Christian subjects, in the 1850s and 1860s Ottoman reformers committed to ending religious discrimination before the law. Although religious minorities actually prized some legal distinctions (like exemption from military service), the *Nizâmiyye* courts dispensed with almost all of the Shariah's distinctions between Muslims and non-Muslims.[78]

Cevdet was confronted by Ottoman ulama and administrators over the Shariah legitimacy of such reforms. How could Muslims, non-Muslims, Ottoman subjects, and foreign merchants all have their testimony accepted equally in the Empire's courts, since the Shariah had generally not allowed non-Muslims to serve as witnesses against Muslims?[79] According to Turkish historians Ebül'ula Mardin and Niyazi Berkes, Cedvet referred to the *maẓālim* treatise to state that Davānī, for one, did not consider this restriction valid in that tribunal. In the *maẓālim*, witnesses from all religions and backgrounds could be heard. Here we should note that Cevdet was clearly reading this into the text. His interpolation is certainly plausible, but Davānī does not explicitly state this in his treatise.[80] It is to the details of Davānī's fascinating treatise that we now turn our attention.

3

A Post-Mongol Treatise on the Grievance Tribunal: A Translation of Jalāl al-Dīn Davānī's *Resāle dar dīvān-e maẓālem*

THE ATTRIBUTION OF THE *MAẒĀLIM* TREATISE TO DAVĀNĪ

Cevdet's discovery of Davānī's treatise on the *maẓālim* is surprising, since it was not one of Davānī's well-known works. In fact, it seems to have been quite unknown for a long time. The works by some of Davānī's students, most notably Khunjī (d. 927/1521), do show that his circle of students was very interested in the institutional aspects of the *maẓālim*. In his *Sulūk al-mulūk,* the political advice work that Khunjī authored in the service of the Uzbek Khan 'Ubaydallāh (d. 946/1539) in Bukhara after fleeing political chaos in the former Aqquyunlu lands, Khunjī devotes a detailed discussion to the *maẓālim* in a manner reminiscent of his teacher. Much like Davānī, Khunjī patterns his discussion on the *maẓālim* chapter in al-Māwardī's *Ordinances.*[1]

Thankfully, writing less than a century after Davānī's death, Shūshtarī (d. 1019/1610) does list a *Resāle dar dīvān-e maẓālem* among Davānī's writings, deducing that it was written in the environs of Lar for its ruler at the time, Niẓām al-Dīn Malik 'Alā' al-Mulk (fl. 1500 CE).[2]

CONVENTIONS OF TRANSLATION

Underlined text means a direct translation or gloss summary of a passage from al-Māwardī's *Aḥkām al-sulṭāniyya.*

Italicized sections are reproduced in Cevdet Paşa's Ottoman Turkish rendering of the text.

TRANSLATION OF TEXT: EPISTLE ON THE GRIEVANCE TRIBUNAL

In the name of God, the Most Gracious, the Most Merciful, whose complete and perfect aid we seek. To Him all praise is due for His most general blessings. And may prayers be upon His prophet, sent to raise up the signposts of the true faith and to lift away the injustices of the blameworthy people, and also upon his Family and Companions, who follow in his noble footsteps, traveling the straight path.

To proceed, these are some issues concerning the grievance tribunal (*dīvān-e maẓālem*), based on authoritative books such as *The Ordinances of Government*, written by the Supreme Judge[3] Abū al-Ḥasan al-Māwardī, who was the imam of his age and whose book has been consulted and acted on by the perspicacious great scholars, as well as from other books and principles of legal interpretation (*qavāʿed-e estenbāṭ*).

It is my hope that those charged with the law's rulings, those governors of the people of Islam, will consult [this treatise] and act on it, that they might deserve goodly mention in this life and a reward in the hereafter, and that through them the rights of the Muslims might not be squandered and that the regime for the welfare of God's servants not come to ruin.

Firstly, these issues are offered up before his royal presence, he whose inner garments are sovereign power and whose outer garb is ennoblement, that heir of great kings and powerful potentates, that joy of all creatures, that relief from hardship and destruction, that order of rule, of the state and the faith, ʿAlāʾ al-Molk [of Lār],[4] may

God aid him in supporting the faith and guide him to assure the welfare of the Muslims.

Such it is that, in these days this pauper has found himself far from his dear home and familiar places, a bereft foot stretched through a rent robe. May this all be mended, if God most high so wills it, and may [the Sultan] be guided by God to read this treatise and act on it, so that it might earn the Creator's pleasure and become a means for welfare and righteousness. The one who is guided receives aid, and it is God from whom all aid is sought.

Now, hearing and adjudicating grievances should be understood as granting succor to the wronged and the oppressed, and removing the transgressions of the oppressors.

*Now, the magistrate (*ḥākem*) of the grievance tribunal must possess executive authority (*seyāsat*) and gravitas more than that found with judges (*qāḍī*). Nay, but he must have great standing, tremendous prestige, be completely God-fearing, and his orders must be obeyed, like a sultan, an amir, a vizier, or someone suitable for such affairs. This is so that the people would fear his dignity and majesty, so that they would refrain from fraud, theft, and underhanded scheming (*ḥīleh*), and so that truth would prevail and the interest of the Muslims not be hindered and impeded. This must be heard, since the judge might have legal motives that seem legitimate but in truth are fraudulent and deceptive. And for this reason, the rights of the people have become wound up in a knot of delay and denial. But the official charged with the grievance tribunal can, with sound opinion and accurate insight, deem such matters untenable and render judgment such that, from then on, they would be known in detail. And another thing that presents an obstacle to the dignity and authority of the official responsible for the grievance tribunal is that [some folk] hide their legal schemes and denial of rights.*

*With the attention of the just magistrate (*ḥākem*), charged with overseeing the grievance tribunal, right would become manifest without delay or fault. Matters that remain bogged down in courts for years would be settled definitively, and right would triumph once the magistrate of the grievance tribunal becomes heedful. And if the Sultan does not pay heed to running the grievance tribunal nor does he appoint someone to that task, he is not fulfilling his duty in protecting the rights* *of his subjects. The Revered Bearer of the Message, may the best of prayers and greetings be upon him, himself took up the investigation of grievances, and in the same manner as the magistrate of the grievance tribunal he passed judgment between Zubayr b. al-'Awwām*[5] *and one of the Anṣār. The two had fallen into a dispute over irrigating their lands. The garden of al-Zubayr lay above and upstream from the other man's garden, so the Prophet ordered,* "Isqi yā Zubayr," *and then he granted that right to the man from the Anṣār, meaning, "First give water to your own garden, Zubayr, and then give water to the Ansārī man." Then the Anṣārī man replied,* "wa innahu ibn 'ammatika," *meaning, "Because he is your paternal cousin?" Then the Revered Bearer of the Message became angry and ordered, "O Zubayr, let the water flow until it reaches up to your ankles, then release it."*[6]

And even before this, it had been reported that the Prophet Solomon[7] *heard the dispute of two women concerning their claim to a child, with each saying that the child was hers. Solomon sought the truth in the case by announcing, "I will cut the child in two and will give a half to each mother." The one who was not related to the child [in reality] exhibited no consternation, while the one who was the mother in reality showed a great deal, saying, "Let her have [the child]!"*

And there is the story of Joseph, whom Zulaykha accused of pursuing her when the case was quite the opposite. The case was settled in the following manner: Joseph's shirt was examined to see if it had been torn from the front or from the back. When it was seen that it was torn from the back, it was known that Zulaykha's words were false and that Joseph was speaking the truth. And such is it mentioned in the glorious Quran.[8] *In this sort [of matter] judgment is passed on the basis of circumstantial evidence (*qarīneh*).*

None of the Four Caliphs paid heed to looking into and adjudicating grievances, since in their time unfairness of this sort did not carry the day, and disagreement was brought before judges. After that, when fraud, falsity, and overweening transgression appeared amongst the people, [the Umayyad caliph] 'Abd al-Malik b. Marwān[9] *assigned one day [a week] for examining the cases of those suffering wrongs. And when he found difficulty on a question, he sought an explanation from the judge Abū Idrīs al-Azdī,*[10] *who was the mufti of that time. And because of the greater concern required due to an increase in the oppression by the rulers and imperious folk as well as the falsity of the people, 'Umar b. 'Abd al-'Azīz*[11] *himself attended to the grievance [tribunal], occupying himself to the extent that he rectified the wrongs [committed even by members] of the Umayyad family. He was exacting with them on this matter, to the point that they said to him, "In the end, I fear that this path will end in the fracture [of our dynasty]." He replied, "Each day that I fear this will be less than the Day of Judgment."*

Then, from among the Abbasid caliphs al-Mahdī,[12] *then al-Hādī,*[13] *then al-Rashīd,*[14] *then al-Ma'mūn,*[15] *each concerned themselves with the grievance tribunal. And it is reported that al-Ma'mūn would sit for the grievance tribunal on Sundays. Fakhr al-Dīn al-Rāzī*[16] *states in his* Manāqib al-Shāfi'ī (Virtues of al-Shāfi'ī) *that Hārūn al-Rashīd had, in the end, made Muḥammad b. Ḥasan al-Shaybānī*[17] *the magistrate of the grievance tribunal and Abū Yūsuf,*[18] *who was also the student of Abū Ḥanīfa, the [chief] judge.*[19] *Towards the end of the Abbasid caliphate, al-Muhtadī*[20] *also occupied himself with overseeing the grievance tribunal.*

*And before all of this, the kings of Persia had recognized this notion as one of the foundational pillars of justice and rule. And, in this respect, they gave it full attention. In the time of Jahiliyya [i.e., Pre-Islamic Arabia], the Quraysh also proceeded in this manner, such that 'Abbās, Abū Sufyān, and the other heads of the Quraysh commemorated an oath and sealed a pact that they would concern themselves with rectifying wrongs and not permit anyone to bring injustice upon another. And the Revered Bearer of the Message, may the best of prayers be upon him, was twenty-five years old at that time [when the oath was taken] in the house of 'Abdallāh b. Jud'ān. After his prophethood, he declared, "*Mā yazīd al-Islām illā shidda,*" meaning "This Islam does not increase this matter but in harshness and strength," meaning that the religion of Islam does not abrogate that [pact]. Rather, it makes it stronger.*[21]

And the Sultan must specify one day [each week] for tending to the grievance tribunal. And if the Sultan refers the governance of the grievance tribunal to another person, that official must also [designate] one day for acting on this matter. The Emperor and Shield of Justice and Goodness, aided with plentiful succor by God, the Sultan, son of the

Sultan and grandson of the Sultan, Abū al-Naṣr [Ūzūn] Ḥasan Beg Bahādor Khān,[22] *may God illuminate his manifest proof, had total concern and care in this matter.*[23] *And the pillars of his princely territory (*īyālat*), which was known as the Royal State (*davlat-e mamālek*), followed this same path, calling that day the Day of the Grievance Tribunal of the Poor. And two days each week they would sit for this matter. In truth, through the days of His Majesty and those of His Noble Successors, especially the Great Emperor Anjum Sepāh Yaʿqūb Beg Khān,*[24] *may God grant him eternal paradise, it was a golden age (*zamāneh nūrānī*), and the totality of God's servants and lands were in the cradle of safety and security, and both field and family were greatly blessed.*[25] *It is hoped that, by the blessing of those Masters of the Heart (*aṣḥāb al-qolūb*),*[26] *welfare triumphs amongst the Muslims, and that they find salvation from this injustice, affliction, constriction (*ḍīq*), and inflation (*ghalā*), God most high willing.*

And in this same sense, it was the continuous custom of the noble sultans of Lar of yesteryear, from time immemorial, that they gathered two days in each week at the court to avail themselves for this, with the notables, ministers, and chamberlains making themselves present as well. Such that, previously, it is reported that the caliph Ma'mūn had assigned Sunday, which was the first of the week's councils, for that [purpose], and that he would spend the whole day settling the cases of the grievance tribunal.

Now, it must be the case that, during that session, the rulings of the Sultan be acted upon, and that he himself must plumb the full depths of the dealings and concerns, that he not lend himself over to impetuosity without God so leading him, since God most high will interrogate him about this [on the Day of Judgment]. And should he assign this to another, this responsibility must not fall from their neck. And, if some ruin should occur in some matter, they should be addressed with the following, "Yā rāʿī al-sū' sharibta al-laban wa akalta al-laḥm wa lam tajbur al-kasīr *(O unfaithful shepherd, you have drunken from the milk and eaten of the meat but you have not set the broken bone).*"[27] *And he must be 'light of access' (*sahl al-ḥejāb*), meaning that those who have suffered wrongs must have access to him. And in his council, there must be present guards, aids, judges, magistrates (*ḥokkām*), jurists (*foqahā'*),* *scribes, witnesses, and a number of people possessed of wisdom and experience.*

Overseeing the grievance tribunal includes ten parts:[28]

First, investigating the transgressions of local governors (*ḥākemān*)[29] upon the subjects. He must examine the conditions of the governors so that, if they are weak, he provides them with force. And if they are unjust, he must restrain or replace them. ʿUmar b. ʿAbd al-ʿAzīz gave a sermon at the beginning of his caliphate in which he said, "I counsel you to have fear of God most high, nothing other than this has any benefit, and God only has mercy on those who cultivate it. And I swear to God, if not for some right practice that had died and then I revived it, or some wrong practice that had been revived but then I dispensed with it, I would not want to live for one instant more. Rectify your Hereafter so that your earthly life might be righteous."[30]

Second, investigating the injustice of tax officials in the collection of money, such that, if they have taken too much, they render it back. And if they have surrendered it to the treasury already, it be given back from there.

Third, investigating the financial records of the members of the chancellery [of finances] (*dīvān*),[31] so that their justness in buying and selling be ascertained.[32]

And in these three parts, it is not necessary for someone to present a request to the magistrate of the grievance tribunal. Rather, he himself must plumb the full extent of these matters without the urging of others.

Fourth, investigating the wrongs suffered by those holding posts and salaries, such that, if the comptrollers (*ʿommāl*) have visited some wrong upon them and given them less than their due, if [the sum] is still in the hands of the administrators, it be taken back from them and given to those who deserve it, and if it had been returned to the treasury, it be given to them from there. One of the comptrollers of the caliph Ma'mūn wrote to him that the soldiers of the army were committing wrongs and raiding. Ma'mūn wrote in reply that, "If you had been just, they would not have been able to commit wrongs, and if you had been strong, they would not have been able to raid," and he dismissed the man from his post.

Fifth, investigating theft and usurpation. If this takes place in the activities of the council [of finances] and the magistrate knows of it, he should return the property to its rightful owners, even if they make no request. And if the magistrate is not aware, whenever the owners make the request, the records of the council should be looked into. If there is proof that so-and-so has taken the property of so-and-so, merely by dint of this [evidence] he returns the property to its owner, with no need for any witness or direct evidence (*bayyeneh*). And if [theft or usurpation] takes place in the dealings of others, he can take back the property by one of four means: either the admission of the person involved, by the magistrate's own certainty (*'elm*) that it has come into the person's possession unjustly, by direct evidence (*bayyeneh*) presented by the plaintiff, or because it is widely and well known, since, if witnessing by widespread [reports] is permitted, it is even more fitting that it be permitted for the magistrate to rule by this.[33]

Sixth, investigating the pious endowments (*avqāf*). If the endowment is public (*'āmm*), the magistrate sees that the stipulations of the endower are abided by and acts accordingly. And in this situation, the books of the endowment's administrators (*'āmelān*) or of the state administrators or written documents whose authenticity seems reliable to the magistrate, such as the edicts of the sultan or local governors, are sufficient, even if there are no [notarial] witnesses. On this matter, there is no need for a petition from anyone in order to proceed. If the endowment is private (*khāṣṣ*) and its beneficiaries are a specific group, then this rests on their petition and wrongs they suffer. Without their petition it is not required for the magistrate to look into [their case] unless something becomes known that they do not know.[34]

Seventh, implementing a ruling that the judge is unable to implement, either due to weakness or due to the power or high standing of the defendant (*ṣāḥeb-e yad*).

Eighth, the implementation of a ruling by the market inspector (*moḥtaseb*) that he is unable to implement.

Ninth, overseeing public acts of worship and the rites of the religion, such as Friday prayer, the two Eid holidays and mourning.[35]

Tenth, inquiring into [disagreements] between opposing parties or disputants in order to pass judgment between them in accord with the Sacred Law (*sharʿ*) on some matter that is not permitted for the judge (*qāḍī*).[36]

And the difference between the adjudication by the magistrate of the grievance tribunal and that done by the judges consists of ten aspects:[37]

First, in that the magistrate must have power and dignity greater than the judge so that he effect actions that the judge is either unable or not permitted by the Sacred Law to do.[38]

Second, in that the scope of adjudication by the magistrate is broader than that of judges, such that, in terms of the Sacred Law, things are permitted for him to do that are not permitted for the judge. For example, in a situation in which he has suspicions, he can inquire from the defendant as to how [some property] came into his possession in order to ascertain the right and wrong of that [case].[39]

Third, in that he can intimidate and greatly frighten the disputants, and he can uncover secrets and causes (*asbāb*) and instructive indications (*amārāt*) so that the truth becomes clear.

Fourth, in that, when it becomes evident that someone has committed a wrong, he can correct and severely chastise him.[40]

Fifth, in that, if he has some doubt despite direct evidence (*bayyeneh*) having been provided [by one party],[41] he can stay the ruling until such time that he has performed a proper investigation (*taḥqīq*) on the basis of circumstantial evidence (*qarāʾen*), instructive indicia (*amārāt*) and consulting those with appropriate expertise. It is not for the judge (*qāḍī*), meanwhile, to delay a ruling in such situations unless both disputing parties consent. If he were to do so without their consent, they would be able to refuse [his ruling], and the judge would be acting wrongfully (*āthem*).

Sixth, in that he can hand over the disputants to intermediaries so that [the dispute] could be resolved by mediation. And it is not for the judge to do so except on the occasion that the disputants are content to do so. If he were to do so without their consent, it could transpire that the disputants not accept [the ruling], and thus the judge would be acting wrongfully (*āthem*).

Seventh, in that he is able to ask the witnesses to swear an oath if he has suspicions.[42]

Eighth, in that he can place the disputants [in detention?] (*sepārad*) and order the attachment [of property?]/have them pursued and followed (*molāzamat*) until such time as the truth of the case becomes evident.[43]

Ninth, in that he can demand that witnesses appear before him and hear their testimony (*shahādat*), though the claim is not well pleaded (*moḥarrar*) according to the custom in courts. Rather, it is sufficient to lay the case out before the magistrate so that he ascertains what is intended.

And none of these matters is permitted for the judge. And when the pleading is brought before the magistrate (*ḥākem*) of the grievance tribunal, if circumstances show that the plaintiff is truthful, such as his having a deed (*qabāleh*) notarized (*mosajjal*) before upstanding witnesses, it is for the best interest (*maṣlaḥat*) either to bring the witnesses before him and request their testimony or to request the denial by the defendant and intimidate (*takhvīf*) him [into telling the truth]. And if the witnesses are absent, he should first try to frighten the defendant and threaten him so that his authority and force of dignity bring the defendant to confess and retract his denial. If this does not transpire, he should order the witnesses to present themselves, if it does not pose too much hardship for them, that the defendant be placed with an appointed receiver (*movakkal*), that some security [i.e., bail] be taken from him. And, if he sees it as in the best interest (*maṣlaḥat*), he should deposit the [contested] property [in receivership], until the truth be ascertained.

And, if no illumination comes from the witnesses, it might be that, as in the case of the Mālikī school of law, he interrogates the defendant as to how this property came into his possession, and he might intimidate and greatly threaten him according to what is in the best interest, though in the schools of Shāfiʿī and Abū Ḥanīfa this is not permitted. This is because the magistrate of the grievance tribunal can act according to best interests (*maṣlaḥat*) within the realm of what is permitted, and it is not required for him to restrict himself to what is required. This is in contrast to the judge, who is not permitted to act [freely] within the [realm of the] permissible but whose adjudication is specified within the required.[44] And if he [i.e., the judge] were to act according to a school of law other than that of his own school's founder (*emām*), the most correct position (*aṣaḥḥ*) is that this is not permissible, in contrast to the magistrate of the grievance tribunal, for whom this is permitted.[45]

And if the witnesses are present but evaluating their upstandingness has not occurred, he must investigate their character and behavior (*aḥvāl*). And if they are [present] but their character and behavior is unknown, he must intimidate the defendant and inquire as to the means by which he came into possession [of the property]. And he should investigate this [by asking the defendant's] close associates and relatives as well as those possessed of expertise and experience. And if the written [documents] of the defendant correspond to the claim of the plaintiff, and the defendant admits that it is his writing, some magistrates consider it obligatory to enforce it, as it is in the Mālikī school of law. And some do not consider this permissible, citing [the legal principle that] "*al-khaṭṭ lā yanṭuqu* (The written word does not speak)." And the correct position (*taḥqīq*) on this is that, if the magistrate of the grievance tribunal acts according to this and orders it enforced, this ruling is to be implemented. And if [the defendant] says, "This is my signature, but the money/property (*māl*) was never paid to me," [the case] should be handed over to mediators (*motavasseṭān*) and appropriate intimidation [used].[46] And if he says, "This is not my writing," and they test [his writing] and it, in fact, resembles his writing some give a ruling rejecting [his defense] (*hukm beh radd*). And some do not hold this to be permissible. Rather, it sets the stage for intimidation and severe threats.[47] And if the record books of the plaintiff's [transaction] with the defendant are in agreement with the claim, intimidation and strong presumption must obtain. And if [the claim] concerns the records of the defendant, and he admits that it is his writing, he has the same ruling as before. In fact, this is even more reliable and credible, even if it is the writing of another.[48]

*The fact of the matter is that, by not having a grievance tribunal, many of the rights of the Muslims are squandered, and the fraudulent and dishonest gain sway over the rights and properties of the people. And when they petition the judge, first, those 'upstanding' individuals, most of whom are not actually upstanding, begin complicating the evaluation of the pleading (*taḥrīr-e daʿvā*). And sometimes it is delayed by an extended period because of their claim that it is not well pleaded and because of the many legal schemes (*ḥīleh*) and deceptions that they employ. And after [the case] has passed this phase and the witnesses are produced, they begin scrutinizing the phrasing or formulation (*ṣīgheh*) of the testimony and bringing up trivial details (*daqīqhā*) and legal dodges and objecting that this formulation is incomplete and[, in doing so,] causing extended delays. And if some end to this predicament comes, they begin scrutinizing the process of establishing the credibility of the witnesses (*tazkeyeh*) and occupy themselves for an extended period with that. And so in the expressions of the witness evaluation legal schemes and deceptions are at work as well. And if they also dispense with this, they put their hand to impugning the witnesses and go back to impeaching the establishment of the witnesses' credibility and to impeaching the impeaching, and so on endlessly. This can be such that sometimes nothing more than raising the claim [before the court] occurs and no decision is made, to the extent that the disputants become weary and fed up. And, if the case itself is a claim of some criminal offense (*jenāyatī*), the purpose is entirely missed.*[49]

*And these harms are all due to the lack of concern from the magistrate of the grievance tribunal, since, if a just and disinterested magistrate were to adjudicate by means of the grievance tribunal, in most of these cases, the dispute could be resolved and right would triumph. And this humble author (*faqīr*) has witnessed much from this ilk where a claim (*morāfaʿeh*) was tied up and delayed in courts and in one instant, when one of the honorable governors tended to it, it came to a decisive conclusion and right prevailed. This is because this is an era of corruption and most people have no fear of God most high. But they do fear the ruler who holds authority (*seyāsat*), and when they know that he is attentive to properly investigating a situation they engage in less deception and legal schemes (*ḥeyal*), and right triumphs.*[50]

It is written in one of the books of the Ḥanafīs that ʿAṣām b. Yūsuf,[51] one of the Ḥanafī masters, was present at the court of one ruler (*ḥākem*), and a person was brought in and accused of theft. He denied it, and the aforementioned master [i.e., ʿAṣām] ruled that the plaintiff should bring a witness or, if he had no witness, that the defendant swear an oath that he had not committed this theft. The ruler did not accept this, and he told his chamberlain and aid to summon the whippers and punishers. When they arrived and dealt the man ten lashes,[52] he made a confession, departed and brought the very things that had been stolen and returned them to the owner. The aforementioned ʿAṣām was shocked and expressed his surprise.[53]

And the wisdom (*serr*) of this is that when God most glorified and high places the reins of the common good (*maṣāleḥ*) of some of His servants in the capable hands of others, and He makes them their rulers, there is His perfect providence (*ʿenāyat*). Thus there is the saying, ʻ*arbāb al-duwal mulhamūn*,ʼ[54] [meaning that God] grants the rulers special inspiration, so that securing the welfare of that realm takes place by their action and words. And with them one beholds wondrous situations, which do not appear with others. Shāfiʿī declared that the words of sultans not be treated casually (*sahl nadānīd*), since their words issue from the tongue of the state (*dawlat*).

And amongst those things that this humble author (*faqīr*) himself has witnessed is that, in part of the province of Shiraz, may it be encompassed in strength, a murder had occurred. And a report of this situation (*ṣūrat*) was written by a person and delivered to the governor of Shiraz, who was one of the great amirs. When the attention of the governor fell on this person and he had heard some of what he had to say, it occurred to the governor that this person who was explaining the situation and who had brought this issue before him was himself the killer and that the origin of the situation lay with him. This was then investigated, and it was just as the governor had guessed through intuition.

And in the same way, there was a lady (*ʿawratī*) in the neighborhood of this humble author (*faqīr*) who had given a loan to people, and a woman (*zanī*) had something valuable with her [as collateral?] and said to her that someone wants to propose marriage to you. And, as is the custom of women, the lady wore whatever jewelry and clothing she had and at night went to the house of that woman, who had arranged for a man to kill her, for she and a daughter of hers had conspired and brought about that lady's death. And no one was aware of this until it became known that, in the neighborhood where that woman resided, a body had been dumped in a well. When examined, they denied [committing the crime]. Then we placed both the mother and daughter in jail and then summoned them separately and interrogated each one until it was ascertained that they had partnered with a man. After being summoned, that man denied this vehemently. But after he was threatened with the infliction of pain (*taʿdhīb*) he gave a detailed confession without the torture even taking place, such that he omitted none of the requirements (*qayd*) [of a legal confession], and they were able to implement retaliatory punishment (*qeṣāṣ*).

Another person from the governorate of Kazerun had gone to part of the Shiraz province and, as is known in that region, through begging (*beh daryūzeh*) and other means he acquired some things. And in the end, one day he hired two people to mount him on 'Jesus' donkey' (*bar ʿīsawiye*)[55] and take him to Shiraz. But then several days passed, and this person was nowhere to be found. So these schemers were questioned and replied, "We brought him to the camp of the amir and delivered him there since there were people living there, and it was night at the time. He remained there. And we do not know where he went." When they were brought to the magistrate's tribunal (*majles-e ḥākem*) they insisted in this same manner. When it was ruled that they would be tortured (*taʿdhīb*) until they told the truth, one of them, who was older, revealed the truth of the situation and made a formal confession (*eqrār mashrūʿ*) that, "We both in agreement did this thing." And the one who was young was [still] denying it. After they turned their attention to torturing him, and after a small amount of torture, he also made a detailed confession, such that all the requirements were observed, and retaliatory punishment (*qeṣāṣ*) was implemented.

And thus there are many thieves who at first denied [their crimes]. But, in the end, with a little [application of] authority (*seyāsatī*) ordered by the magistrate (*ḥākem*), the truth became clear and they returned the money. In one such case, in Jaryūn[56] something had been stolen from someone, and amongst the people who were accused was a person who occupied himself the whole month of Ramadan with reading the Quran. It occurred to this humble author (*faqīr*) that this sort of phenomenon would not come from him. In this vein, I wrote a letter to the constabulary that they not apply torture to him until a letter arrived [with that order]. [But] it was revealed that he had done this deed and most of what was stolen was brought back and surrendered.

*The aim of laying out these introductions is [to show] that the judgment (*ḥokm*) of the grievance tribunal is the judgment of the Sacred Law (*shar'*) and that it is obligatory upon the ruler (*solṭān*) to himself step forward on this matter, as some of the caliphs have done, or to order it referred to a just and disinterested amir who is possessed of great authority (*seyāsat*). And if [the ruler] were negligent in this matter, it would be sinful. And anyone who says "This type of legal authority is not legitimate," has said something illegitimate (*nāmashrū'*), has assigned error to the senior imams and is deserving of serious punishment (*ta'zīr*). Nay, he may be exposed to the danger of unbelief (*kofr*), since, as has been mentioned previously, it has been reported that this type of judgment (*ḥokm*) was exercised by the Revered Bearer of the Message, may God's peace and blessing be upon him, as well as by the caliphs and imams, may God be pleased with them. And these [reports] have been established [as authentic]. So impugning this [type of legal authority] would entail unbelief, and we seek refuge with God from unbelief and disobedience (*ṭoghyān*). So it is most fitting that His Revered Sultanic Emblem (*sho'ārī*) himself justly and properly undertake adjudicating through the grievance tribunal*; that he give no admittance to hastiness; that he not suffice with delegating this to another, since on the Day of Resurrection it will be His Revered Self that will be asked about this, and delegation to others will be no excuse; and that he bring about this adjudication (*aḥkām*), which is purely the Sacred Law; and that he not be blind to this [duty]. And some of the imams of profound and esoteric knowledge (*kashf*) have said that it will be upon this [forum of adjudication] that the promised Mahdi will establish his legal rulings (*aḥkām*).

O God, guide him and all the other sovereigns of Islam to the implementation of this legal authority, to ordering the welfare of the people for the sake of Muhammad, may peace and blessings be upon him, the other prophets and all their kin. So ends this epistle, attributed to the master and senior scholar (*moḥaqqeq*) Jalāl al-Melleh va'l-Dīn al-Davānī, may his soul be sanctified.

4

Maẓālim and Questions of Procedure and Substantive Law

IN SEARCH OF *MAẒĀLIM* THEORY

In 1741 CE, a junior judge from a town near Sanaa wrote to Yemen's most famous scholar of the day with a series of questions. How should judges treat the rules of evidence laid out in the Quran and the Sunna of the Prophet given the tremendous changes in culture and values since these rules were elaborated? Should judges relax them to meet the impious culture of the day, or should they adhere fideistically to them? If judges insisted on upholding the strict procedural rules of the Shariah, what would happen if courts could not protect the rights of litigants and their access to justice? How should judges weigh written documents and oral testimony? What did it mean to be 'just' in that day and age anyway?[1]

Al-Māwardī, Davānī, and Cevdet Paşa each took up the topic of the *maẓālim* tribunal for their own reasons. What joins them together is precisely what the young Yemeni judge felt: a sense of institutional crisis, whether a crisis of politics and law, the institutions of law, the law as an institution, or all three. They also shared the quality of rarity. They were among the very few scholars who provided any substantial prescriptive discussion of the *maẓālim* tribunal. As we have already pointed out, despite the prevalence of these institutions, ulama *qua* jurists wrote remarkably little over the centuries about the *maẓālim* tribunal's procedures and theoretical underpinnings.

Why were jurists so reluctant to discuss institutions of royal justice in general and the *maẓālim* tribunal in particular?[2] While it is difficult to offer a hardy answer to this question, it is possible that

Muslim jurists were invested in the procedural and institutional vagueness of royal justice. It may be that most did not want to articulate the procedures of the *maẓālim* out of fear that such an articulation would encroach on their position as legislators. As Hurvitz suggests, rulers too had an interest in the relative dearth of writings on *maẓālim* and crimes tribunals in juridical books: rulers and their representatives remained unencumbered by jurists' writing on their involvement in public and criminal law.[3] Nevertheless, these rare treatises in which jurists did discuss the *maẓālim* share several themes in common. In this chapter we will take up some of the most salient questions.

Two key issues dominate the historiography of the *maẓālim* institution (and forums of royal justice more broadly) and its treatment in the writings of Muslim jurists. First, what is the relationship between the judges' courts and the *maẓālim* tribunal? In the genealogy we explore in this book, from al-Māwardī to Cevdet, several major issues in this comparison merit particular attention. Is the magistrate presiding over the *maẓālim* tribunal bound by any *madhhab* constraint? To what extent is he free from the procedural restrictions that bind the judge? Finally, what are the different types of evidence available to him as opposed to the judge? This last topic in particular raises the question of the acceptability and the consequences of relying on two forms of evidence, both controversial in theory if not equally provocative in nature: what are the proper roles of written evidence and judicial torture respectively in the judge's court and the *maẓālim* tribunal?

Across the centuries in Islamicate thought, we can perceive two general strands in thinking about the contrasting roles and interaction between the judge (*qāḍī*) and *siyāsa* magistrates, such as those assigned to crimes tribunals and the *maẓālim*. The first is the Māwardian/Davānian strain, which sees the judge as a relatively constrained office and places more expansive powers of investigation and compulsion in the hands of offices like the crimes tribunal and the *maẓālim*. The second strain conceives of the judge as a more unitary office holding many of the same powers as *siyāsa* magistrates. It is inspired by the Egyptian Mālikī jurist al-Qarāfī (d. 684/1285) and Ibn

Qayyim al-Jawziyya's purposivist view of the judge's power. This strain found influential expression in twin impactful judge's manuals. The first was the *Tabṣirat al-ḥukkām fī uṣūl al-aqḍiya wa manāhij al-aḥkām* (Instruction for Judges on the Bases of Cases and Methods of Ruling) of the Mālikī Ibn Farḥūn of Medina (d. 799/1397). The second was the *Muʿīn al-ḥukkām fīmā yataraddadu bayn al-khaṣmayn min al-aḥkām* (The Judges' Aid regarding those Rulings that often Appear between Disputants) of the Levantine Ḥanafī judge al-Ṭarābulusī (d. 844/1441), which often copied-and-pasted directly from Ibn Farḥūn's work. It was via al-Ṭarābulusī's book that this strain became influential in the Ottoman and greater Persianate context.[4]

For the purposivist strain, the Prophet's overall judicial authority and divinely imposed duty to do justice might be devolved onto different offices. But those offices remained fundamentally the products of human convention, and their shared inheritance of that revealed role easily superseded the boundaries between them. They are all, Ibn Taymiyya explains, judges (*qāḍī*). All officials who deal with disputes and claims of wrong, whether governors, the magistrates of the *maẓālim*, or other positions named by convention (*al-asmāʾ al-ʿurfiyya al-iṣṭilāḥiyya*), says Ibn Taymiyya, they all rule by God's command (*ḥukm*). It is incumbent on all who "take up the affairs of the people and rule between any two people to rule by justice and thus to rule by the book of God and the Sunna of His messenger. This is the law revealed (*al-sharʿ al-munazzal*) by God most high."[5]

The second major issue in the historiography of the *maẓālim* tribunal is the looming question of the relationship between the law decreed by an executive authority and the Sacred Law (*sharʿ*, *sharīʿa*) of God. Several questions follow. When and to what extent is royal justice acceptable to the defenders of the Shariah? Does the *maẓālim* tribunal stand within the pale of God's law or outside it? What is the verdict or at least the leading dissenting opinion on the legitimacy of the *maẓālim* tribunal and the exercise of royal justice from a Shariah perspective? Ultimately, the intervention of executive authorities to dispense justice bears on a foundational theological question: if the Shariah needs the intervention of these authorities, then, in Christine Hayes' words, what's divine about divine law?[6]

These two issues and the questions they generate are closely connected. In fact, the first set can be seen as a concrete procedural manifestation of the second, more theoretical one. As such, studying the institution of the *maẓālim* enables us to examine the multiple registers of Islamic law and legal thought. While the first set of issues is predominantly procedural and may fall under the rubric of law applied in court, the second set of questions may be considered, for the lack of a better term, constitutional.

ISLAMIC CRIMINAL AND PUBLIC LAW: THE LINE BETWEEN PUBLIC AND PRIVATE WRONGS

One of the questions posed by Davānī's treatise on the *maẓālim* tribunal, which seems to have swallowed the function of the crimes tribunal in the Aqquyunlu context, is why royal justice should be sought out in a case of murder or theft. Are these not conceived of as private wrongs (torts) in the Shariah tradition?[7] We have already seen how the criminal court emerged and morphed over the centuries, from the Umayyad caliph connecting the functions of *qāḍī* court and the governor's *dīwān* in cases of tortious injury, to the Abbasid-era *wilāyat al-jarā'im*, to the military court of the Mamluk sultanate and the varied involvement of the Ottoman provincial governor councils and Mughal police authorities in criminal law. But this brief sketch does not address an underlying tension: if we understand 'crimes' to be offenses against a community, a state or some sense of public order or morality, is there an Islamic 'criminal law'?[8] What are its boundaries? Put differently, why does the tradition of public law in Islamic civilization (encompassing the details of governance, taxation, border controls and security, etc.) seem to creep into what the Quran and Sunna appear to cast as a distinctly private law of torts, such as killing, injury, and battery?

The Quran's ruling of "a life for a life, an eye for an eye" as well as its rule that "injuries are dealt with through retaliatory punishment (*qiṣāṣ*)" (Quran 5:45, 2:178–9) suggest that even severe injuries are private matters, dealt with by individuals and families, without formal mediation by any public body. Hence the confusion of one questioner, who asked a leading scholar of thirteenth-century Cairo why he could not simply take Quranic law on such matters into his own hands.[9]

The ambiguity over whether killing and tortious injury were private wrongs or public ones becomes clearer when viewed through the lens of the tradition from which we draw these categories, that of Roman law. This is not because the Roman law categories of public and private law were always logically or practically distinct (even to the Romans) or because they were adopted directly by Muslim jurists.[10] Rather, this comparison is instructive because it suggests that the blurring or overlapping of public and private wrongs seems almost a natural byproduct of certain pre-modern legal regimes.[11] Both Rome and the early caliphate were rooted in tribal societies, but they were elevated by ambitions of imperium and the emergence of a burgeoning state. They were limited by technological and logistical constraints, but they consciously aspired to a just rule of law that transcended such limitations (Virgil's call to "crown peace with law," for example).[12] Such states considered injuries to be primarily wrongs between private parties but also sought to insert the state's hand into adjudicating offenses like murder because they represented both a threat to public order and an encroachment on the ruler's presumed monopoly on violence.

Even in its earliest formulations, Roman law set apart as public law offenses against the state and by state officials, as well as those seen as particularly harmful to mores, religion, and (in the later period) social order. But homicide seems to have been dealt with primarily as a private matter. By the middle republic period (*circa* 300 BCE), crimes against the state, fundamental mores, or public order expanded to include fraud and false witness, and by the late republic period the public element of homicide had become more pronounced. Under Augustus (r. 31 BCE–14 CE), the first Roman emperor, such crimes were assigned to an affirmed set of standing courts (*ordo iudiciorum publicorum*). Battery, however, remained mostly a *delict*, or private injury. During the imperial period battery was also absorbed under public criminal law, as were some forms of property crimes like aggravated theft or rustling. But the ambiguity between these public crimes and their original conception as private wrongs remained. There was no public prosecutor, though magistrates might play this role. Criminal cases were still mainly brought by private persons.[13] Even in Justinian's (r. 527–565 CE) Code, in addition to a public criminal prosecution for theft and the victim recovering the value of the stolen item, the victim could still bring a private (delictal) claim for punitive damages.[14]

The Islamic legal tradition progressed through these stages much more rapidly. As the thirteenth-century Cairene scholar above recognized, his questioner was correct: "The original formulation (*al-aṣl*) entailed that individuals were permitted to carry out [Hudud punishments or retaliatory punishment], but the Sacred Law delegated this to the rulers (*imām*)" so that this did not become a source of strife, injustice, and oppression.[15] Despite this publicization of criminal procedure, as in the case of Roman law, the original private nature of many crimes remained in the Shariah's genetic code.

The Quran and Hadiths do not set aside a category of public law or criminal law, but they did ordain a set of procedures, such as strict evidentiary bars, for offenses such as adultery, theft, and public intoxication. And the Hadith corpus further articulated the critical procedural role of the ruler/judge (*ḥākim*) in those crimes as well as other disputes and legal arrangements. For example, a Hadith in which the Prophet discusses the need for women to receive their male guardian's permission to marry leads into the Prophet stating "The authority (*sulṭān*) is the guardian (*walī*) of those who have no guardian."[16]

This concept of *walī*, which denoted someone in close propinquity to another, extended far beyond the role of guardian in marriage. It encompassed those who stand to inherit from the deceased, those relatives deemed wronged when a person is killed as well as those responsible for bringing cases of homicide to trial. So the Prophet's statement that "I am the *walī* of those with no *walī*"[17] in the context of someone with no inheritors in one narration of a Hadith morphs into his taking the role of liability for injuries they cause in another.[18]

Since the Prophet was both the political authority and the judge in Medina, references attributed to him concerning the role of the legal authority became ambiguous when those functions were split.[19] They were later channeled into sometimes competing conceptions of the purview of the judge and the ruler. As Ibn Ḥanbal (d. 241/855) explained after narrating the Hadith of the sultan as guardian, "The *sulṭān* [here] is the judge, because matters of legal rulings and marriage (*furūj*) fall to him."[20] But, as discussed below, there was disagreement as to who inherited the authority to punish serious threats to public safety.

Among early Muslim jurists, the rubric of public/criminal law developed around what were understood as the Hudud crimes (intoxication, certain severe acts of theft, sexual slander, adultery/fornication, violent robbery/banditry and, in some schools of law, apostasy).[21] By the eighth century, Hadiths had been collected requiring the legal authorities to adjudicate accusations of crimes like adultery and theft. They could not be left as private wrongs.[22]

The vague Quranic diptych of banditry (*ḥirāba*) *cum* "causing corruption in the land" (*ifsād fī al-arḍ*, sometimes referred to as *si'āya*) (Quran 5:33) linked the Hudud crimes to a more abstract notion of punishing violations of public order and security.[23] As Johansen and others have noted, this led to the weaving of a legal fabric in which the judge's purview of justice was only a part. With the exception of the Mālikī school, the Sunni schools of law all reserved punishing banditry/causing corruption to the ruler's, not the judge's, discretion.[24]

This duty to protect public welfare undergirded the authority of the crimes tribunal (*wilāyat al-jarā'im*). As described by al-Māwardī, unlike the judge, the official overseeing the crimes tribunal could imprison repeat, unreformed offenders for extended periods to protect the public from them. Unlike his restrictions on judges, al-Māwardī allowed the crimes tribunal to consider circumstantial evidence, such as the reputation of an alleged thief or the fact that he had been found with stolen property on him, when determining guilt.[25] The Ḥanafī master of Central Asia al-Sarakhsī (d. *circa* 490/1096) concurred. *Siyāsa* meant that it was the duty of the ruler to protect the public from substantial criminal harm. Al-Sarakhsī gives the example of a person who had been accused of murder and had a reputation as a dangerous criminal. Even if there were only circumstantial evidence that he committed the crime, it was the duty of the ruler (*imām*) according to *siyāsa* to execute him.[26]

The same delegation of conceptually private wrongs to public authorities applied to *qiṣāṣ* (talion or retaliatory punishment and compensation). This delegation had certainly become a legal reality by the late eighth century CE. Al-Shāfiʿī (d. 204/820) stated that whoever exacts retribution for injuries or killing without the sultan's permission must be punished (*ʿuzzira*).[27] By the twelfth century CE it had become a matter of consensus that the legal authority was an indispensable element of the individual's right to retaliation, and no execution or Hudud punishment could take place without the ruler's permission (though there were some exceptions, such as some cases of owners punishing their slaves).[28]

The involvement of the state in 'private' injuries may be the result of some structural drive for the state to direct all employment of violence. But the early Islamic government also seems to have been involved by dint of its roles in the enterprise of the early Islamic conquests and the distribution of the spoils they generated. This gave the early state leverage in garnishing incomes to make sure compensation was paid. Al-Kindī (d. 350/961) describes how the caliph Muʿāwiya (r. 40/660–60/680) created a new policy for judges in Egypt, which directed them to hear and rule on cases of tortious injuries (*jirāḥ*). But the caliph also instructed the judges to refer those cases to the governor (*ṣāḥib al-dīwān*) so that he could garnish the annual spoil stipends (*ʿaṭāʾ*) of the liable parties.[29]

Yet these glimpses of a public criminal law are obscured in the writings of Muslim jurists, who often seemed loath to acknowledge their need for the ruler's muscle. For example, the Iraqi Ḥanafī al-Khaṣṣāf's (d. 261/874) manual for judges paints an image of the scholar/judge in complete control of the life of the law and its application. But the author occasionally admits the role of the ruler, such as when the judge must call upon the governor (*wālī*) as muscle to compel a defendant to come to court.[30]

Yet the public law element of the Shariah surfaces precisely in those instances in which the mechanisms of addressing a private wrong break down even in theory. In general, as specified in the Quran and the Hadiths, it is up to the heirs of the deceased to bring the accusation of wrongful death. But as al-Shāfiʿī notes, "If a man intentionally kills someone with no heirs/guardians (*walī*), it falls to the ruler (*sulṭān*) to have his killer executed. Or he can choose to take the compensation payment (*diya*) and pay it to the Muslim community overall."[31] Seeking a scriptural anchor for this approach, the Ḥanafī al-Sarakhsī ties it to the Prophet's Hadith regarding marriage: "The ruler is the guardian of those with no guardian."[32] The breakdown of society's normal means of redressing private wrongs – when the guilty party cannot be identified – was also taken up to a certain extent by the state, as in cases when someone dies in the crowd at Friday prayer.[33] These rules are based in what is perhaps the Hadith corpus' most salient case of public/criminal law involvement: the Prophet's decision to use public funds to pay the compensation for a person who had been found murdered but whose killer could not be proven according to the requirements of evidence.[34]

Muslim scholars also acknowledged that there were other areas of law and governance that fell exclusively within the purview of executive authority. The problem of soldiers dying on the battlefield without witnesses to hear their last wills and testaments was resolved directly by the Mamluk sultan Baybars (r. 658/1260–676/1277) because it was an issue of military law.[35] As stated by the sultan's contemporary, the Shāfiʿī master al-Nawawī (d. 676/1277), it was the mainstream position of scholars that the judge's remit covered all areas of law except "what is particular to securing the realm (*ḍabṭ al-bayḍa*) and the monies collected in land taxes."[36] Later scholars like Ibn Taymiyya, Ibn Qayyim al-Jawziyya, and the Ḥanafī judge of Jerusalem al-Ṭarābulusī stated that the exact boundary between the judge's purview and *siyāsa* was dictated by the custom (*ʿurf*) of every place and time.[37] In the Mamluk period, for example, matters of diplomacy were at the discretion of the ruler, and Muslim scholars often gladly deferred to the ruler on contractual disputes with foreigners from outside the Abode of Islam or crimes involving religious minorities within it.[38] Al-Qalqashandī preserves a *maẓālim* complaint made by Frankish merchants asking the sultan to ensure that their rights were preserved in conducting business.[39] In 687/1288, the Mamluk *maẓālim* tribunal ordered a Christian man executed for living with a Muslim woman, who was lashed.[40] Taxation could be a matter of sensitivity to the ulama, who often spoke out against oppressively heavy taxation or taxes lacking any Shariah legitimacy. But in this area the rule was deference to executive authority.[41]

MADHHAB IN THE JUDGE'S COURT AND THE *MAẒĀLIM*

One of the main themes reiterated as a distinction between the judge's (*qāḍī*) court and *maẓālim* tribunal is that the magistrate of the *maẓālim* is free from many of the procedural limitations constraining the judge. As described by al-Māwardī, the magistrate can proceed according to the full range of what the Shariah allows (*jā'iz*) in terms of procedure and evidence, while the judge is restricted to what is required (*wājib*). What al-Māwardī means when he coined this unusual phrase, which he uses several times in his chapter on the *maẓālim*, becomes clear in its context: in most cases, al-Māwardī invokes "what the Shariah allows" to describe the magistrate crossing *madhhab* lines and acting according to what one *madhhab* allows but others do not.[42]

According to al-Māwardī and Davānī, the magistrate enjoys procedural freedom greater than that of the judge so that he can achieve equitable resolutions and see justice done. In a case in which there is not even probable evidence supporting one side in a dispute over the other, al-Māwardī reminds us that the magistrate has more procedural and evidentiary means at his disposal because the *maẓālim* tribunal aims at attaining the best and most judicious ruling (*al-aṣlaḥ*). This is in contrast to the judge, whom al-Māwardī imagines as being at least prudentially constrained by his own school's requirements.[43] Al-Māwardī gives as an example the case of a scribe who is upright and swears to the authenticity of a document he drafted. In this case, the magistrate can treat the scribe himself as a witness in a case in which the document appears as evidence. If the claimant in the case also swears an oath, then the magistrate can rule based on one witness (the scribe) and the plaintiff's oath (*shāhid wa'l-yamīn*), which the Ḥanafī school does not allow but which the other schools do to varying degrees. Al-Māwardī explains that the magistrate would do so "either according to [his] *madhhab* or according to executive authority (*siyāsa*) entailed by the circumstances of the case (*taqtaḍīhā shawāhid al-ḥāl*)."[44]

It seems odd that al-Māwardī would phrase as 'requirement' what seems to us to be a restriction on the judge. But this may, in fact, fit very well the conception that judges in al-Māwardī's era had of their own position. They may have felt constrained more by a sense of internal obligation to a legal methodology than by top-down restrictions from a government authority. Along similar lines, one puzzling feature of al-Māwardī's treatment of the *maẓālim* is that he argues fervently in both the chapter on judges (*quḍāt*) in *The Ordinances* and in his thick judge's manual, the *Adab al-qāḍī*, (itself replicating the chapter on judging from his enormous *Ḥāwī fiqh* compendium) that judges are actually *mujtahids*, i.e., independent jurists qualified to derive rulings directly from the scriptural sources of the Shariah. This means that they must rule in a case according to their own understanding of the sources of law (*ijtihād*) and cannot be restricted to one *madhhab*. Rather, they can rule by whatever *madhhab* they see fit on a legal question, since the ultimate governor of their choice is the result reached by their own *ijtihād*.[45]

Why, then, is the magistrate any freer in his actions than the judge in matters of crossing *madhhab* lines? The explanation may lie in al-Māwardī's tacit acknowledgment that his judges-as-*mujtahids* position was both unrealistic and not widely applied. He even admits that some within his own Shāfiʿī school require a judge to rule by his own *madhhab* alone, since, if he were to shift from school to school depending on the situation, this would lead to suspicion and accusations of tailored justice. This had already been remarked on over two centuries earlier in an anti-Sunni satire on juristic flexibility.[46] And well over a century before al-Māwardī was writing, such independence had begun to attract understandable suspicion. Contemporaries of Ibn Ḥarbawayh (d. 319/931) observed that, though this chief judge of Egypt followed the *madhhab* of Abū Thawr (soon to become extinct), he would "exercise choice in his rulings in such a way that would not have been accepted from others." It was only his prodigious knowledge and, more importantly, his reputation for fairness and probity that shielded him from criticism.[47] Al-Māwardī recognizes that, in his own time, ruling consistently by one school is what sound political judgment (*siyāsa*) requires in the wake of the gelling of the *madhhab*s (*istiqrār al-madhāhib*) and people settling into different schools of thought.[48]

Did judges in al-Māwardī's time, in fact, act as independent *mujtahid*s? For the Abbasid period, a lack of evidence to the contrary suggests that it was assumed that judges would rule by their own school. But there seems to be no evidence that this was forced upon them by their administrative superiors.[49] It is the exceptions that are noted. Biographers remarked that, while he was the judge of Qayrawan, the famous Mālikī teacher Saḥnūn (d. 240/854) appointed the city's leading Ḥanafī jurist to a judge position. Yet he required him to rule by the Mālikī school.[50] This impression is further supported by the surprise expressed by some Muslim jurists of the time that the Shiite Fatimids, when they conquered Egypt in the mid tenth century, required the Sunni judges that they appointed to rule by Shiite law, not their own *madhhab*s.[51] When a leading Shāfiʿī jurist of Nishapur, Abū Muḥammad al-Juwaynī (d. 438/1046–7) (the father of the famous Imām al-Ḥaramayn), wrote that he would not be bound by any *madhhab* but rather would write a book of law based directly on his interpretation of the Quran and the Sunna, this sparked serious rebuke from fellow Shāfiʿī scholars.[52] Evidence suggests that, in the tenth century, even veering from the principal position of one's school in favor of minority opinions within it could raise eyebrows, as in the case of a respected Mālikī judge who served in Basra, Baghdad, and then finally in Egypt.[53] Though not a judge, ʿAbd al-ʿAzīz al-Dārikī (d. 375/986), a very senior and respected Shāfiʿī mufti in Nishapur and later Baghdad, caused some controversy on occasions when he answered fatwa requests by ignoring his school and ruling directly from Hadiths he considered pertinent.[54] Later sources from the thirteenth century show us that the expectation that a judge would rule by their own school of law was standard.[55]

Davānī seems much less concerned by the question of *madhhab* restriction. His treatise omits much of al-Māwardī's text on the topic and bypasses the question by concluding simply, "if [the judge] were to act according to a school of law other than that of his own imam, the most correct position (*aṣaḥḥ*) is that this is not permissible, in contrast to the magistrate of the grievance tribunal, for whom this is permitted."

This would seem a reasonable summary of what was the main position in the Shāfiʿī school in the fifteenth and sixteenth centuries: a judge who had attained the level of a *mujtahid* (a nearly unattainable standard according to the Egyptian jurist al-Shaʿrānī, d. 973/1565) could rule according to any of the four *madhhab*s (and even outside those schools in his personal life). A judge who did not meet the requirements of being a *mujtahid* must follow the ruling of his school and not depart from it.[56] Mālikī judges in Egypt and North Africa seem to have been stricter in expecting and enforcing uniformity, although some judges claiming the seniority of a *mujtahid* dissented.[57] In 786/1384 the Mālikī chief judge in Cairo was removed from his position after fellow Mālikī scholars heavily criticized him for ruling on a case contrary to their *madhhab*, a fate barely escaped the previous year by another Mālikī judge.[58] In the Ḥanafī school of the time, if all three founding figures in the *madhhab* (Abū Ḥanīfa, Abū Yūsuf, and al-Shaybānī) agreed on a point, the judge had to rule by that. If Abū Ḥanīfa took one stance and his two pupils another, then a judge capable of *ijtihād* could choose between them, but any lesser judge had to follow the instructions of senior judges. There was no ruling from outside the Ḥanafī school.[59]

Although it is often stated that only the Ḥanafī school allowed rulers to require judges to rule by one school of law, this seems to have been more widely accepted. One Mālikī judge in Egypt in the early 900s CE was appointed as a stand-in (*istanāb*) for a more senior Ḥanafī judge and ruled by the Ḥanafī school on at least one point of controversy on which the two schools differed. In another instance, it seems that it was Egypt's ruler who actually insisted on this.[60] The Shāfiʿī judge Taqī al-Dīn al-Subkī (d. 756/1355) holds that judges have to obey rulers if they specify a school of law by which to rule (and they must rule by the main position of that school on any question, unless they are a *mujtahid* in that school).[61] Much later, the Shāfiʿī authority Ibn Ḥajar Haytamī (d. 974/1565) clarifies that it had long been the position of his school that rulers could instruct judges what school of law they should rule by. He affirms the opinion of his Egyptian predecessor al-Bulqīnī (d. 805/1403) that not only is it permitted for the sultan to require judges to rule according to one particular ruling from any of the four *madhhab*s, but also that such a command from the ruler makes it prohibited for the judges to then rule by any other ruling.[62]

SUBJECT MATTER JURISDICTION BETWEEN THE LAW COURT AND THE *MAẒĀLIM*

As we saw in the historical function of various *maẓālim* tribunals as well as related royal-justice forums like the Ottoman *dîvân*s, there was no neat separation of subject matter jurisdiction between the judge's court and the *maẓālim* tribunal. There was an inherent overlap between the purview of the judge and that of the *maẓālim* magistrate, not least because one of the tasks of the magistrate was to enforce the judge's rulings when he was unable to do so himself.

Al-Māwardī is conscientious that, when the magistrate is acting within the judge's purview in terms of the subject matter of the case, he should respect the restrictions and rules of that office. When resolving disputes between parties in such circumstances, he "is not permitted to pass judgment between them except in the same manner as the judges do." This is essential, al-Māwardī continues, because "it may be that the magistrate becomes confused (*ishtabaha*) regarding judgment in the *maẓālim*, so that they are oppressive in their rulings and thus pass the limit of what is acceptable."[63]

Davānī seems much less concerned with the magistrate respecting the judge's procedures when acting in his role. As we shall see, this is because he was much laxer on what the Shariah considered 'unacceptable' on the part of judges. He does, however, note in two *maẓālim* cases that the magistrate ultimately ensured that the accused party's guilt was established by formal and legal confessions (*eqrār-e mashrūʿ*) for which all the procedural conditions had been met (see below on the Use of Judicial Torture to Elicit Confession).

Many petitions brought to *maẓālim* tribunals over the centuries involved complaints about some wrong or excess committed by government officials, especially concerning taxation or the expropriation of property. This was the case for the Abbasid *maẓālim* of the ninth and tenth centuries CE, as shown by Van Berkel, as well as during the Baḥrī Mamluk state of the thirteenth and fourteenth centuries.[64]

There is evidence of a wide range of other subjects as well, however, and this range suggests that al-Māwardī's categories of issues that the *maẓālim* tribunal could hear corresponded to reality. Van Berkel shows evidence of a dispute between farmers and traders over the size of a bridge and a dispute between shopkeepers in the Abbasid era.[65] In one instance in Baghdad in the early 900s CE, a case was submitted by someone who saw a vision of the Abbasid dynasty's ancestor, the Prophet's uncle ʿAbbās, complaining how every time he tried to construct a building, the vizier at the time would undermine him (this was ultimately a ruse to oust the vizier).[66] The *maẓālim* also frequently functioned as a court of appeals for rulings made by judges, especially regarding inheritance. In the early 900s CE a woman in Nishapur went to the *maẓālim* tribunal with a complaint about how a special magistrate assigned to inheritance issues (*ṣāḥib al-tarakāt*) had ruled regarding her rights.[67] Around the same time in Cordoba a case was brought to the city's *maẓālim* judge, one ʿAbd al-Ra'ūf (d. unknown), seemingly because it was extremely perplexing. A slave woman had claimed that she had been wrongly enslaved during a civil conflict and was originally a free Muslim. But then several days later she had retracted this claim. The *maẓālim* magistrate sought out opinions from other respected scholars, some of whom said she should be freed because her initial claim should be believed, in which case her subsequent statement could not be accepted because it was impermissible for a Muslim to enslave themselves. Others said her recanting should be heeded.[68] In Mamluk Egypt the sultan ordered a widower who had seized all of his deceased wife's wealth to redistribute it according to the Shariah rules of inheritance (though Nielsen's study of *maẓālim* cases under the Baḥrī Mamluks suggests personal status issues seem to have been exceptional, such as cases involving members of the Mamluk elite).[69] Davānī's treatise provides examples of the *maẓālim* tribunal taking up cases of theft and homicide that, as he describes them, could not have appeared before the judge due to a dearth of evidence. Thieves and alleged murderers were also brought before the *maẓālim* audiences of the Mughal emperor Awrangzīb.[70] Here, the *maẓālim* institution blends with the crimes tribunal of the Abbasid era. Similarly, as we have seen previously, the Ottoman Imperial Council and the provincial councils of the governors dealt with a similar range of cases, from excessive taxation to unjust acts by provincial officials and judges to petty civil disputes and criminal cases (as with Davānī's treatise, often with unidentified perpetrators).

Other times, the *maẓālim* took up public law issues. One Mamluk case dealt with an issue specific to the military: there were no witnesses to hear the last wills of dying soldiers, so their children were being deprived of potential inheritance. In consultation with the chief judge, the sultan Baybars issued an order that unit leaders select certain people to act as witnesses in such cases.[71] Several Mamluk-era cases were brought because the ordinary judge did not have the power to settle it or enforce the ruling.[72]

Because the *maẓālim* tribunal was seen as a forum for the legitimate exercise of sultanic authority, there may have been a risk that rulers might exploit the tribunal for political purposes. This raises the question of whether political cases, such as trying those accused of sedition or some 'dangerous' heresy, also fell under the jurisdiction of the *maẓālim*. Nielsen identified several trials for blasphemy or heresy in the *maẓālim* tribunal during the Mamluk period. In 712/1312, for example, Ibn Zahra al-Maghribī was called to the *maẓālim* to respond to accusations that he had deprecated the Quran, and was subsequently imprisoned. A few decades earlier someone had been convicted in the Dār al-ʿAdl for claiming to be a prophet.[73]

Of course, rulers needed no forum to carry out their will on the accused. 'Royal justice' could amount to no more than a ruler ridding himself of someone with no trial, as the caliph al-Mutawakkil did with his vizier Ibn al-Zayyāt in 233/847–8, torturing him to death in an iron maiden device the vizier himself had invented.[74] The mystic al-Ḥallāj (d. 309/922) does seem to have been tried in a *maẓālim* setting, presided over by the grand viziers with ulama and judges in attendance and after seeking out fatwas from leading scholars as to the proper fate of the accused.[75] The same may also have been the case for the maverick Quran reciter of Baghdad, Ibn Shanabūdh (d. 328/939). He was tried in the house of the grand vizier, with jurists and judges in attendance, for reciting anomalous (*shawādhdh*) readings of the holy book.[76]

SEPARATE BODIES OF LAW?

The parallels between the *maẓālim* tribunal and the courts of equity in the common law tradition are remarkable. Both were housed under royal authority and drew on royal justice, and both responded to cases in which ordinary courts could not meet the demands of justice. There is at least one possible limit to this comparison, however. In the case of the common law tradition, equity developed its own, admittedly terse, body of jurisprudence, known as the maxims of equity. The institutional tradition of the *maẓālim* tribunal, by contrast, never built up its own storehouse of law and precedent or even its own legal literature. Both Tyan and Nielsen conclude that the *maẓālim* tribunal was not defined by some separate body of substantive or procedural law. In practice, Nielsen states, it was "an institution defined by its bureaucratic processes."[77] This sense is buttressed by the famous Mālikī jurist and exegete al-Qurṭubī (d. 671/1272), whose discussion of which law should be applied by judges hearing cases between non-Muslims locates the *maẓālim* tribunal in the generic space of some 'common sense' *ius gentium.*

While a judge can use either the Shariah or the law of the denominational minority, al-Qurṭubī says that, on issues of *maẓālim*, the judge should simply "take from their strong and give to their weak" in defense of wronged parties.[78] The *maẓālim* tribunal is not about the law applied but rather about providing an equitable resolution to a matter where whatever law had been applied had fallen short.[79]

Furthermore, the *maẓālim* tribunal did not need its own body of law because, as described by al-Māwardī, Davānī, and others, a vast sea of law already existed, namely the *madhhab*s of the Shariah. They provided an assorted grab-bag of rulings. The *maẓālim* magistrate's ability to provide equitable rulings resulted in part from the flexibility he enjoyed in picking and choosing from the diverse bodies of law within the different *madhhab*s.

This may actually present more of a similarity than a difference between *maẓālim* tribunals and courts of equity. Scholars of common law are divided as to whether the maxims of equity (originally, in the sixteenth century, 'the rules of equity and good conscience') and the common law were two distinct bodies of law or whether they shared a common origin and retained some intrinsic and significant relationship.[80] But there is no doubt that a separate body of jurisprudence came into being and was referred to in the English courts of equity. More recently, however, Henry Smith has argued that the tradition of equity should be conceived less as a stream parallel to the law and more as "meta-law," a second-order system that operates above the law in order to help the law achieve justice in the type of complex, multi-polar, or clash-of-rights cases that law's generality finds challenging. Equity is not *contra* law or independent of it, Smith argues. Equity aids the law or, as one maxim of equity puts it, "equity follows the law."[81] Similarly, the *maẓālim* tribunal can be viewed as a meta-law forum in that it is meta-*madhhab*.

The dependency of the *maẓālim* institution on *fiqh* is further illustrated in Tillier's observation that, though the ulama of Islamic civilization produced numerous biographical dictionaries of judges, there is none known to have been devoted to magistrates of *maẓālim* tribunals.[82] While Tillier suggests that this might reflect the *maẓālim*'s illegitimate standing in the eyes of the ulama, it seems more likely that they simply did not consider overseeing the *maẓālim* to be a legal office distinct enough to merit separate treatment, as the biographies of ulama/judges, senior administrators and governors were recorded in the biographical dictionaries penned by the ulama and administrative class. The magistrate of the *maẓālim* was ultimately a bureaucratic position, one to which judges were often appointed.

THE USE OF JUDICIAL TORTURE TO ELICIT CONFESSIONS

Our texts on the *maẓālim* repeatedly assert that one crucial distinction between the coercive tools available to its magistrate and not the judge is that the magistrate of the *maẓālim* is allowed to use the physical infliction of pain (*taʿdhīb*, i.e., beating, lashing)[83] to extract confessions or testimony, while the judge is not. Interestingly, both al-Māwardī and Davānī may have belonged to a more conservative school of thought on this issue, as it was much more complicated than their *maẓālim* treatises suggest. This was particularly true in Davānī's time, when the use of force to elicit confessions was widespread and controversial amongst scholars of his Shāfiʿī school. This complexity is alluded to in Davānī's cryptic remarks that, in the instances he witnessed or heard of confessions being made after some sort of pain infliction, all the requirements for a "legitimate confession" were nonetheless met.[84]

In his discussion on interrogation by beating (*imtiḥān bi'l-ḍarb*), Ibn Taymiyya notes three positions on its use by the judge or the political authority (*wālī*). First, both offices are allowed to use beating in order to extract a confession from the accused, a position he attributes to some Mālikīs on the basis of al-Ashhab's (d. 204/819) early stance. Second, neither is allowed to use beatings, but both can detain the suspect in jail (*ḥabs*) pending an investigation or to compel him to confess. Ibn Taymiyya associates this stance with the Mālikī al-Aṣbagh (d. 225/840), some Shāfiʿīs, and many Ḥanafīs. Third, only the political authority can resort to beating the accused. He attributes this position to none other than al-Māwardī and Abū Yaʿlā Ibn al-Farrāʾ.[85] Yet Ibn Taymiyya's taxonomy only scratches the surface of a much more complicated and diverse debate, which involved questions of a judge's right to employ discretionary punishment (*taʿzīr*), burden of proof, liability for injury, and the overall effectiveness of a court system.

In general, Muslim jurists agreed that pain infliction or physical compulsion had its place at the final stage of a judicial process. A defendant whom a judge had found to be withholding someone else's property or denying them their rights could be physically compelled to comply with the verdict, if need be by the bailiffs or police force (*shurṭa*).[86] Conversely, the application of pain was hotly debated if applied *during* the investigative phase of a trial. Muslim jurists generally did not approve of confessions made under naked duress (*ikrāh*), since the Quran made it clear that duress invalidated even something as serious as a confession of unbelief (Quran 16:106).[87] As Mohammed Allehbi has shown, coercive forms of interrogation, though well established in the Late Antique Near East, entered into Muslim law enforcement very slowly. Early ulama/judges like the Abbasid chief justice Abū Yūsuf (d. 182/798) did not approve at all of police forces using beating to extract confessions or solve cases.[88] Waters were muddied, however, by Hadiths appearing in the mainstay Sunni Hadith collections of the ninth century that described the Prophet imprisoning *suspected* thieves in order to elicit confessions[89] and even Hadith evidence (much more ambiguous) that he had permitted beating or lashing for this purpose.[90]

For those who accepted that the Prophet had inflicted pain on suspects as part of an investigation, one solution to resolve the tension with the Quran's invalidation of coerced statements was to assume that the infliction of pain was, in effect, legitimated retroactively if it produced external evidence of guilt, such as an alleged thief revealing the location of stolen goods after a beating. The main Prophetic Hadith that affirmed beating a suspect suggested that no wrong had occurred if the beating led to retrieving the stolen goods. Some Mālikī, Shāfiʿī, and Ḥanafī jurists specified that, in such cases, it was not the confession made under physical duress but rather the discovery of external evidence that cemented guilt. This justification was adopted by Ottoman criminal law in the sixteenth century. This did not convince some Muslim jurists, however, since external evidence such as locating lost goods was circumstantial and fell far below the bar of direct evidence normally required by the judge, namely confession or upstanding witness testimony.[91]

Another method of reconciling the Prophet's use of prison or beating was to assume that not all infliction of pain constituted duress, as in al-Nawawī's and the Ottoman Mullā Hüsrev's (d. 885/1480) definition of duress as stemming not from beating but from "severe beating" (*ḍarb shadīd*) or the Mālikī opinion that it was "beating that causes pain."[92] But drawing a bright line between the acceptable infliction of pain and duress was difficult.[93] The early Ḥanafī master al-Shaybānī (d. 189/805), for example, is quoted by later proponents of judicial beating as allowing beating a suspected thief as long as it does not "expose bone."[94] An influential fifteenth-century Ḥanafī judge's manual, however, cites al-Shaybānī as leaving it up to the judge's discretion to determine what is acceptable and what is coercion in any particular place and time.[95] The use of limited imprisonment while an investigation into allegations was carried out was not controversial amongst jurists.[96]

In practice, prior to the Mamluk period, the use of torture for investigative purposes seems to have been restricted to matters of state security, such as uncovering spies, and for compelling recalcitrant taxpayers to pay.[97] For al-Māwardī, infliction of pain as an investigative tool was only available to the *maẓālim* and the crimes tribunals, whose presider he states could use limited beating to test the truthfulness of the accused and could imprison him pending the completion of an investigation. But, according to his perspective in the Shāfiʿī school, a judge could not do so.[98]

Pace both al-Māwardī's theorization and Ibn Taymiyya's taxonomy, by the 1300s CE it seems to have become widely accepted that a judge could order someone suspected of theft to be beaten until he admitted it or surrendered the stolen item, and this was all the more acceptable if the suspect had a reputation for crime.[99] This became enshrined in the Ottoman criminal law in the sixteenth century, though it was the minority position in the Ḥanafī school.[100] Citing Hadiths, Ibn Taymiyya's student Ibn Qayyim al-Jawziyya insists that the Prophet "imprisoned on the basis of accusation and punished (*ʿāqaba*) on the basis of accusation" when he found circumstantial evidence that suggested the guilt of the alleged.[101] Another of Ibn Taymiyya's admirers, the Ḥanafī scholar Ibn Abī al-ʿIzz (d. 792/1390), repeats a digest of Ibn Taymiyya's taxonomy on the various positions on the use of force with suspects, but he ends by saying that the position of the "great majority of jurists" was that it was permitted to beat a suspected thief if he was "known for his bad conduct (*fujūr*)." He cites the same Hadiths referred to as evidence by Ibn al-Qayyim.[102]

There is a strong sense amongst proponents of permitting the beating of a suspect that it was necessary for the proper functioning of the judiciary at the time. Ibn Abī al-ʿIzz concludes that the practice "is what is available to people and is acted on (*huwa alladhī yasaʿu al-nās wa ʿalayhi al-ʿamal*),"[103] which dovetails with Ibn al-Qayyim's concern that a judge "who lets free every accused person, making them swear an oath and then letting them go, despite knowing that they are well known for causing corruption in the land and for frequent theft, saying 'I will not take him except by two upstanding witnesses'" is contradicting proper governance.[104]

Some jurists, however, particularly from the fourteenth to sixteenth centuries, found inflicting pain on a suspect entirely problematic. Abū Dāwūd (d. 275/889), a disciple of Ibn Ḥanbal and compiler of a famous Hadith collection, had early on noted that the proper understanding of Prophetic Hadiths on the subject was that there was to be no infliction of pain until *after* the confession.[105] Al-Nawawī had already pointed out the contradiction inherent in permitting the beating of a suspect while prohibiting confessions under duress, an objection confirmed by a later prominent commentator on his works, al-Khaṭīb al-Shirbīnī (d 977/1570). Shihāb al-Dīn al-Adhraʿī (d. 783/1381), a Shāfiʿī judge in Aleppo under the Mamluks and a famous mufti, complained that beating defendants accused of theft, injury, or other wrongs had become common practice for the military judges and governors of his time, and that all such practices constituted invalidating duress.[106]

Ḥanafī scholars evinced the most consistent concern and often prohibited inflicting pain on suspects.[107] The ninth-century scholar al-Khaṣṣāf allowed accused parties to be imprisoned pending an investigation, but they could not be placed in any prison where there was risk of injury from other inmates. There was simply no legal basis for allowing harm to befall the defendant.[108] This was even the view of some jurists in sixteenth-century Central Asia. The renowned Ḥanafī mufti of Bukhara, Shams al-Dīn al-Quhistānī[109] (d. *circa* 953/1546), cites the story, mentioned by Davānī, of the amir of Bukhara ordering a suspected thief lashed ten times (well below the Ḥanafī limit on *taʿzīr*) to the horror of the early Ḥanafī scholar ʿAṣām, who remarked, "I have not seen oppression (*jawr*) more closely resemble justice than this." For al-Quhistānī, this suggests that beating a thief to force him to confess "contravened the Sacred Law (*khilāf al-sharʿ*)," which was also the position taken in the influential early fifteenth-century Ḥanafī legal manual the *Fatāwā al-Bazzāziyya*.[110] So foreign was the permissibility of investigative torture to the Ḥanafī methodology that, as Johansen noticed, its acceptance in the fifteenth century came through cutting and pasting sections on the topic from more permissive Mālikī legal manuals.[111]

In the Ottoman lands, however, by the late fifteenth century, leading jurists, such as Mullā Hüsrev, had become much more accepting. And the early-nineteenth-century Ibn ʿĀbidīn (d. 1252/1836) was a forceful advocate of the permissibility of a judge using discretionary punishment (*taʿzīr*) during an investigation. He allowed this for someone who was merely suspected of a crime such as theft, based only on the report of an upright person (*ʿadl*) or on the judge's knowledge, for example, if he knows that the accused had a reputation for criminal conduct (*fasād*). Ibn ʿĀbidīn considered this to be the *siyāsa* of the judge and states he wrote a whole treatise (*risāla*) on the issue of inflicting chastisement on the accused suspect (*taʿzīr al-muttaham*).[112]

Beating an alleged criminal raises the interesting question of liability if the accused turns out to be innocent. In one of the principal Hadiths on the topic, the Prophet tells those who had accused a man of theft that, if he were to have the man beaten, but he turned out to be innocent, that the Prophet would "take from your backs like what I took from his."[113] In the Ḥanafī, Mālikī, and Ḥanbalī schools, the state or judicial authority held no liability for the injuries or deaths caused either in the case of applying Hudud punishments or discretionary punishments.[114] If an innocent defendant suffered bodily injury or death, however, the Ḥanafī school did hold the accuser liable for compensation payment (*diya*).[115] In the case of someone who died as the result of Hudud punishment, by the time of Davānī it was agreed upon amongst Shāfiʿī scholars (and many others, according to Ibn Ḥajar) that the ruler or judicial authority had no liability. One exception amongst Shāfiʿī scholars was if a person died as the result of the Hudud punishment for intoxication if the lashes were dealt with a whip instead of the Sunna practice of using cloth or shoes and if it were done over the Sunna number of forty lashes. In this case, the public authority had to pay the compensation amount (*diya*) to the decedent's family. This was also true if someone died as the result of discretionary punishment, but the sixteenth-century Egyptian jurist al-Shaʿrānī admits he had never heard of a sultan paying any *diya* for any such injury.[116] Yet there is evidence that al-Shaʿrānī's anecdotal observation did not reflect the entirety of the Ottoman judicial scene in his time. The influential Ottoman Shaykh al-Islām Ebü Süʿūd Efendi (d. 982/1574) issued a fatwa that, when a man accused of theft died after the governor had him tortured, the governor was liable for compensation for the death (*diya*) and the person who had accused him should be punished (*taʿzīr*).[117]

THE USE OF DOCUMENTARY EVIDENCE

Even more important than the infliction of pain in evidentiary procedure, though not as provocative, is the use of written evidence. Overall, scholarship on the acceptability of documentary and other written evidence in the judge's court has suffered from generalizations that elide remarkable internal diversity in the Shariah tradition. Hallaq and Schacht agree summarily that documents only served as "aids to memory" in Shariah procedure, with their contents admitted as evidence only when attested to by witnesses to the transaction or by notaries.[118]

This conclusion is not surprising given the overall skeptical attitude of Muslim jurists towards documentary evidence. Since the early Muslim community, it had become almost uniformly understood amongst judges that a document such as a will or deed could not be accepted on its own as dispositive evidence for a claim in court. It had to be accompanied by the testimony (*shahāda*) of an upright witness vouching that the document's contents represented the intended message of its author. As reported from the Mālikī judge Muḥammad b. al-Ḥārith (d. 361/971), accepting the contents of a written document as a reflection of some past will or transaction was hearsay (*shahāda ʿalā shahāda*). The document was like an unaccredited, unknown, anonymous person claiming someone wanted their estate or property disposed of in some way.[119]

Arguing that Muslims' theoretical skepticism towards written evidence (and the conclusions of scholars like Schacht made on its basis) was not borne out in practice, Tyan demonstrated how the 'writing as hearsay' risk could be and was easily avoided by having documents notarized by a judge or by his vetted official witnesses.[120] In such cases, a judge presented with a notarized document was not weighing evidence anew. He was considering a document already authorized by a court, and no testimony was required. Provided judges followed accepted conventions of sealing and sending documents, Tyan argued, it was generally permitted for judges to enforce written instructions or notarized documents from other courts.[121]

In weighing the 'Shariah only accepts oral testimony' school of thought against the 'notarization gives documents the force of oral testimony' school, there is little recourse other than to scattered studies of court records from across the breadth and depth of Islamicate civilization. Several studies support the claim that documentary evidence had little power.[122] The court records of a late-fourteenth-century Shāfiʿī judge in Jerusalem studied by Müller suggest that, without the oral corroboration of witnesses, signed contracts could not withstand the challenge of a party who denied the claims made by a plaintiff. But Müller also located several cases of notarization being used to prevent future disputes, though he argues that it was ultimately the testimony of the notaries and not the documents themselves that would be needed in court. These cases include a document attesting to a deceased master emancipating his slave and copies of claims made in an inheritance case and distributed to the heirs.[123] Ergene's study of court records from provincial Anatolia in the seventeenth and eighteenth centuries suggests that documents were not commonly used in provincial Ottoman Shariah courts.[124] On the other hand, Jessica Marglin has shown that, in Moroccan Shariah courts in the nineteenth century, notarization was a major portion of the court's activity. This allowed documentary evidence to be submitted regularly in disputes.[125] But the development of a distinctive class of notary-witnesses indicates that the predominant Mālikī view, which in general accepted documents as uncorroborated evidence, required the development of institutional mechanisms to authenticate specific documents.

In light of the most recent studies, generalization about the acceptability or prevalence of documentary evidence is dangerous. Theory, practice, and the relationship between the two varied by time and place, as it often did with distinctions in social class, subject matter, or industry. Schools of law could differ. Even within one school of law, in one state, regional variations could be dramatic. Within Ottoman Ḥanafism, local court custom in Syria was much more accepting of documentary evidence than the law courts of Istanbul.[126] The type of document, by whom and how it was issued, mattered a great deal. The Ḥanafī school was generally unwelcoming of documents and required oral testimony, for example. But certain forms of written documents enjoyed privileged standing in court practice, particularly those involving state bureaucracy and powerful commercial interests. As Baber Johansen has shown in one of the most comprehensive studies of the use of documents in the Ḥanafī legal tradition, as early as the eleventh century jurists such as al-Sarakhsī and Qāḍī Khān (d. 592/1196) argued that documents and records that did not have witnesses but were produced by the commercial and political elites should be accepted as reliable evidence.[127] Writing in defence of relying on Ottoman state documents, and specifically the imperial registers (*defter*), in court, the

Mufti of Damascus ʿAlāʾ al-Dīn al-Ḥaṣkafī (d. 1088/1677)[128] noted that, since the time of al-Sarakhsī and particularly since the fifteenth century, scholars had widely agreed that it was permissible to rely on the document issued by the mufti (*khaṭṭ al-muftī*), the letters of safe conduct carried by foreigners in the Abode of Islam (*kitāb ahl al-ḥarb bi-ṭalab al-amān*), as well as the records of merchants, moneychangers, and brokers (*daftar al-bayyāʿ wa'l-ṣarrāf wa'l-simsār*).[129] It seems, however, that, in comparison to his eleventh-century colleagues, al-Ḥaṣkafī sought to justify the Ottoman imperial use of documents across long distances and much longer timeframes.

Finally, there might be contemporary internal disputes within one school of law in one locality. Al-Ḥaṣkafī's view was challenged by other jurists who operated across the Ottoman lands, such as his teacher, Khayr al-Dīn al-Ramlī (d. 1081/1671). Al-Ramlī adhered to the view within the Ḥanafī school that registers should not be admitted as evidence without the supporting testimony of witnesses. Later, in early- and mid-nineteenth-century Istanbul, Ottoman state recognition of commercial documents presented by European merchants prompted a call by Ottoman merchants for similar treatment, so Cevdet's *Mecelle* civil code admitted any documentary evidence free from suspicion of fraud and categorically authorized documents notarized and kept in a court's records.[130] But even after the fall of the Ottoman Empire, influential Ottoman/Republican Turkish jurists still insisted that, aside from official documents, written evidence without oral testimony corroborating it should not be accepted in law.[131]

Our texts on the *maẓālim* tribunal agree on the greater flexibility allowed for admitting written evidence in this forum. But for al-Māwardī, that flexibility is marginal at best. In his *Ordinances*, Māwardī prescribes the proper use of documentary evidence in the *maẓālim* procedure:

> The fifth situation regarding the strength of a claim occurs when the plaintiff produces [a document] that concerns the contested issue in the defendant's handwriting. Here, the grievance tribunal

> requires the defendant be questioned regarding the handwriting. If he is asked, "Is this your writing?" and he acknowledges it, he needs to be asked about the authenticity of the content. If he acknowledges the authenticity of its content, then he confirms [the accusation], and he is obliged to accept the resolution [based on his] admission. If he does not admit the authenticity of the content, some magistrates of the grievance tribunal would rule against him based on his writing if he had admitted it was his, even if he did not admit the accuracy of the contents, seeing this as a type of circumstantial evidence according to prevailing conventions (*wa-ja'ala dhālika min shawāhid al-ḥuqūq i'tibāran bi'l-'urf*). Scrupulous scholars and all the jurists among them,[132] however, argue that the magistrate is not allowed to rule on the basis of the writing alone (*mujarrad al-khaṭṭ*), unless [the accused] also acknowledges the document's contents, because adjudicating in the grievance tribunal does not allow (*lā yubīḥu*) what the Sacred Law (*shar'*) forbids.[133]

Even when using documentary evidence that would not be permitted in the judge's court, the *maẓālim* magistrate can only deploy it to intimidate a litigant, not as evidence formally admitted.[134] Moreover, if the case cannot be resolved due to the lack of evidence corroborating the authenticity of the document, and if the parties refuse mediation, al-Māwardī states the case has to be resolved by having both parties swear oaths. In other words, even in the forum of the *maẓālim* tribunal, al-Māwardī exhibits the mainstream Islamic juridical suspicion of the use of documentary evidence and prefers oral testimony, admission, and oath.[135]

Davānī is much more flexible. Although he acknowledges that the use of uncorroborated written documents was debated, he argues for greater reliance. For Davānī, al-Māwardī's most permissive approach is the norm:

> And if the signature of the defendant corresponds to the claim of the plaintiff, and the defendant admits that it is his signature, some magistrates consider it obligatory to enforce it, as it is in

> the Mālikī school of law. And some do not consider this permissible, citing [the principle], "writing does not speak" (*al-khaṭṭ lā yanṭuqu*). The correct position (*taḥqīq*) on this is that, if the magistrate of the grievance tribunal acts according to this and orders it enforced, then this ruling is to be implemented.[136]

As in using torture to extract evidence, we find that the flexibility allowed for the *maẓālim* by Davānī was not too far removed from contemporaneous practices in some judges' courts. A similar attitude towards the use of written evidence can be found in the *Mu'īn al-ḥukkām*, a famous Ḥanafī judge's manual written in Jerusalem slightly before Davānī's time. The manual notes that custom and necessity had led to judges accepting written documents as evidence in situations in which this had previously been prohibited, such as concluding that a document had been written by a defendant based on a hand-writing comparison.[137] Even in Davānī's own Shāfi'ī school of law, a flexibility regarding documentary evidence seems to have emerged, ironically through means very similar to the choices offered by the *maẓālim*. The Cairene Shāfi'ī Taqī al-Dīn al-Subkī writes in a fatwa that Shāfi'ī judges can send cases in which written evidence features prominently to a Mālikī court, whose judges have more relaxed rules on accepting documents.[138] Similarly, in Ottoman Cairo two centuries later, Ḥanafī judges sometimes ordered cases referred to other judges, such as Ḥanbalīs, for particular transactions to be notarized.[139]

Following Davānī, Cevdet agrees that occasionally the resolution of a case can be based on evidence that may be uncorroborated and doubtful. This followed a trend in the official ranks of the Ottoman ulama/judge corps. As has been argued above, some jurists, such as the officially appointed Damascus mufti al-Ḥaṣkafī, tried to demonstrate that the greater reliance on uncorroborated written evidence is based on principles found in the (Ḥanafī, in his case) judge's manual literature. Al-Ḥaṣkafī argued that the authenticity of the Ottoman archival documents was guaranteed by Ottoman archival practices, which rendered the corroborating support of the witnesses' testimony redundant.[140] By drawing on al-Māwardī's *Ordinances* and

Davānī's treatise, Cevdet followed a different path. He based support for the use of written evidence uncorroborated by testimony on the principle underlying the *maẓālim* discourse: the need to prevent injustice, promote the wellbeing of the Muslim community, and protect the rights of the servants of God.

5

Can God's Law Be Unjust? Equity and the Rights of God's Servants

In 1352–3 CE a group of Persians on business in Cairo found that the local Egyptian merchants who owed them money were refusing to pay. They had even, unconvincingly, pleaded bankruptcy. The standard recourse available to the foreigners would have been to take their claim to the law court of the Ḥanafī school. All schools allowed a debtor to claim relief by declaring bankruptcy, but in Mamluk Cairo it was the Ḥanafī school that was seen as having the strictest standards for testing this. It allowed the debtor to claim bankruptcy only after spending a period in prison – a cost many would-be shirkers were unwilling to bear.[1]

The contested sum in this case must have been substantial, because the Egyptian merchants were apparently happy to choose a short stint in jail over paying the money they owed. With even the strictest *madhhab*'s court option failing to pry the Persians' due from local hands, an obvious injustice was being done. So the foreigners appealed to the *maẓālim* tribunal. The chamberlain (the presiding Mamluk official in that era) swiftly ordered the local merchants to be punished corporally until they paid, which they soon did.[2] As in the cases of theft and murder that Davānī described in the region of Shiraz, the rule of law provided by the judge's court in this case had failed to meet the reasonable expectations for justice and compensation on the part of those who had been wronged.

THE SAFEGUARD OF PROCEDURAL FORMALISM

The ordinary legal procedures and restricted punishments that failed the Persian merchants and the victims mentioned by Davānī were not senseless or the results of a feeble legal system. They often originated directly in the revealed texts of the Quran and Prophetic Hadiths, which established them to protect the wrongfully accused and minimize the abuse of power by judges. Already by the ninth century Muslim scholars were insisting on procedural limitations on the judge arriving at rulings based on his own conclusions about a case or on knowledge of the facts gleaned from something other than testimony or evidence proffered in court. He had to have at least some formal reliance on witness or notary testimony. This would prevent judges from pursuing their own agendas against litigants or the accused falling victim to biases. Or, at the very least, it would prevent what the early Kufan scholar al-Qāsim b. ʿAbd al-Raḥmān (d. 116/734–5) called "suspicious doubts" spreading amongst the population about the integrity of their judiciary.[3] Agreement soon formed that judges could not rule on capital or even serious corporal crimes on the basis of their own knowledge of the truth of an accusation. Most schools of law did not allow a judge to rule by his knowledge in other types of cases either, but the Shāfiʿī school eventually allowed this.[4]

Early Muslim jurists consciously articulated a notion of rule of law based on a presumption of innocence and the inviolability of life and property. As Abū Yūsuf insisted in his work on governance and taxation, "It is not for the ruler to extract anything from anyone's hands without an established and known right (*ḥaqq thābit maʿrūf*)."[5] As stated in a Prophetic Hadith, any claim made that attempted to alter the status quo by imposing a duty, liability, or challenging de facto ownership had to be supported by evidence (*bayyina*).[6] If a plaintiff lacked such evidence, the defendant against whom the claim was made had only to swear an oath in order to clear themselves. As the Central Asian Shāfiʿī jurist al-Khaṭṭābī (d. 388/998) wrote, it is beyond question to all Muslims, scholars, and laymen that "neither property nor life is forfeited (*yustaḥaqqu*) except by some direct evidence (*bayyina*)."[7]

As Baber Johansen has observed, this legal philosophy ushered in a strong strain of formalism in Shariah legal procedure and evidentiary law (the common understanding of formalism being that rules and processes should be followed without excessive consideration for the matter passing through them).[8] This formalism was rooted in the belief that God and the Prophet had laid down certain concrete rules for the welfare of mankind, and these had to be trusted. Al-Māwardī was a committed exponent of such formalism. He explains, for example, that the number or quality of witnesses brought by a disputant to support a claim makes no difference once the formal requirement for direct evidence – usually two upstanding male witnesses – had been met. Al-Māwardī freely acknowledges that more and better witnesses sway hearts towards the truth of a claim, but this is irrelevant. "God most high has specified the numbers for testimony," he explains, "So these specific texts preclude interpretive effort (*ijtihād*) on a greater or lesser number."[9]

Though anchored in revelation, al-Māwardī's position also expressed a profound commitment to the presumption of innocence and freedom from liability. All things being equal, the defendant triumphed because it was the plaintiff who had the burden of justifying a change to the status quo. Even if the plaintiff could provide a hundred witnesses, al-Māwardī explains, if the defendant brought the minimum two witnesses, his response would stand.

This conservative formalism did not dominate juristic discourse completely. As Johansen and others have shown, this formalism was greatly reduced after the late thirteenth century.[10] But even before then some strains of legal thought and practice allowed more flexibility in procedure and more space for circumstantial evidence. In the late Umayyad period, there was a tradition of Basran judges paying attention to circumstantial evidence, though this was later superseded by oaths.[11] A judge in late-eighth-century Egypt weighed possession of a disputed item along with one witness's testimony as better proof than multiple witnesses produced by the plaintiff.[12] The Shāfiʿī jurist al-Iṣṭakhrī (d. 328/940), who served as a judge in southwestern Iran as well as Qom, would not even consider the claim made by a plaintiff if the circumstances of the claim and the parties involved (*qarāʾin al-ḥāl*) strongly suggested it was false.[13] In the Ḥanbalī and Mālikī schools, a person who claimed a lost object found by someone else only had to describe it accurately to have the finder turn it over. They did not have to provide witness testimony (*bayyina*) to their ownership.[14] Based on an analogy to this situation, Ibn Ḥanbal ruled that, if the owner of a dwelling and his tenant each claimed to be the owner of property found buried there, the one who could accurately describe the buried property was awarded ownership.[15] Also based on an analogy to this, an eleventh-century Andalusian judge deemed that, if highwaymen or thieves had property with them when they were captured, plaintiffs who alleged they had been robbed of that property could reclaim it if they could accurately describe it even though they lacked direct evidence (*bayyina*) of their ownership. The word *bayyina*, this judge advanced in a functional argument based on the root meaning of the word, is what brings 'clarity' to a matter. So any evidence that does so is, in effect, *bayyina* even if it does not meet *bayyina*'s common formal requirements.[16]

Culture and custom also strongly influenced evidentiary burdens, since they helped shape presumptions of where that burden lay. Long prior to the thirteenth/fourteenth-century CE turn away from formalism, in the Ḥanafī school, if a husband and wife disputed ownership of household items, the default ruling would be that the man would receive items usually associated with men and the wife those associated with women.[17] Al-Māwardī himself notes how his Mālikī colleagues tried to convince him of their position on competing claims made by a husband and a wife on whether their marriage had been consummated, which greatly affected the portion of the dower that the husband received back in the case of divorce (the husband was given back half the dower if the marriage was not consummated, Quran 2:237). Given the unfeasibility of finding evidence beyond the couple's claims, Mālikīs argued, the fact of the couple having secluded themselves, along with the wife's testimony, was a convincing circumstantial indication that sexual intercourse had occurred. Al-Māwardī did not agree. Prior to the dispute, the status quo for the bride and groom had been an absence of consummation. Only by evidence that met the formal requirements of the law could a new duty or liability be imposed.[18]

Even in al-Māwardī's Shāfiʿī school of law there was a range of opinion on accepting circumstantial evidence and custom as a factor in placing the burden of proof. Al-Shāfiʿī himself had not always held the above-mentioned, formalistic position on weighing witness testimony. Al-Māwardī's younger contemporary al-Juwaynī explains that the initial stance (*qadīm*) of their school's founder later changed to the position that the judge should evaluate the aggregate probity and convincingness of the witnesses by their individual reputations and number.[19] Sometimes the question of accepting circumstantial evidence itself hinged on circumstance. Al-Juwaynī and his famous student al-Ghazālī (d. 505/1111) rejected the circumstantial evidence claim of other Shāfiʿī scholars that, in an inheritance dispute, the person in possession of an asset should be the presumed rightful recipient (in general, all things being equal, the person in possession of an item had a stronger claim to ownership).[20] But this was not because al-Juwaynī and his student felt this broke with the formal rules of evidence as set forth in the revealed sources. Rather, it was because they looked at circumstances beyond mere possession. The asset had come into the heir's possession via the process of inheritance, which was precisely what was in dispute.[21]

PROCEDURAL JUSTICE AND SUBSTANTIVE WRONG? THE TALE OF NŪR AL-DĪN ZANGĪ

Beyond stymying the efforts of merchants to recover debts, the procedural formalism so prominent in Shariah discourse could be seen as hobbling the very capacity of the Shariah to provide justice and order. In a book the late Cornell Fleischer called the "classic statement of Ottoman social and political morality," the Ottoman judge and intellectual Kınalızade ʿAlī Çelebī (d. 979/1572) invokes the tale of how the notables of Mosul had pleaded with their famously pious sultan, Nūr al-Dīn Zangī (d. 569/1174), to exercise "a little bit of *siyāsa* (*bir mikdār siyāset*)" and send soldiers to the city because the "mere rules of the Sacred Law did not suffice" to manage those seeking to do harm in the city. Zangī replied that the Shariah was the most perfect of all laws, promoting man's welfare and proscribing harms. If God had wanted to add something to His perfect law, Zangī stated, He would have.[22]

Before delving into how the provocative story of Nūr al-Dīn Zangī and Mosul has been understood, we must appreciate a profound irony. Kınalızade's rendition adds flourishes found nowhere in the original account. In fact, it alters it altogether. Originally found in the chronicle of the Syrian scholar Abū Shāma al-Maqdisī (d. 665/1268), the notables of Mosul write to Zangī asking him to restore law and order in their city after a rash of thefts there had become so serious that the situation, as they describe it, "required some sort of *siyāsa*." This crisis resulted from Zangī earlier instructing the city's officials not to do anything not ordered by the judges, with the consequence that the head of the police (*shiḥna*) had ceased his enforcement (*siyāsa*). But the thieves and bandits plaguing the city were not deterred by the more constrained punishments that judges could employ. The letter insists that only harsher responses like executions and crucifixions would stop them. Zangī's reply is just as Kınalızade describes. He refuses to offer anything more than what the Shariah prescribed (read, what the judges could do), since the wellbeing (*maṣlaḥa*) of the people was to be found in God's law, and if God had wanted to add something to His perfect law He would have.[23]

Crucially, however, in the original version of the report, the appeal by the notables of Mosul for the sultan's aid includes no hint of any shortcoming in the Shariah. In fact, problems had only arisen when Zangī's orders resulted in one of the main organs of Shariah law enforcement – the *siyāsa* of the police force – being shut down. As we have seen in our treatises on *maẓālim*, the ulama recognized the need for the ruler's imperium, that brute executive authority needed to actually implement law and order. For the community to enjoy the protection of the Shariah, it needed royal authority (*siyāsa*) to underpin it.

This was particularly true in the areas of criminal law, where the Quranic crime of armed robbery or banditry (*ḥirāba*) and "spreading corruption in the land" (*ifsād fī al-arḍ*) fell clearly within the ruler's legal purview, not that of the judge. The Mosul appeal was an obvious call for the sultan to punish the thieves tormenting the city for this Quranic crime, even referencing the punishments that the Quran ordains for it, namely crucifixion and execution (Quran 5:33). This fell squarely within the bounds of the Shariah as set forth in the Quran. But it was the ruler's, not the judges', responsibility to carry it out.[24] So Zangī's pious rebuke was misplaced. Ironically, it was the sultan's erroneous conflation of the Shariah with the judges' courts alone and his flawed formalism that left Mosul in a predicament. Protecting public welfare was the duty of the sultan.

This has not been, however, how the sultan's reply to the ulama of Mosul has been understood. The story has been told and retold over the centuries as a foil for challenging or affirming the relationship between the Shariah and justice. Sometimes enhanced with dramatic alterations, the vignette of Zangī and Mosul would surface again and again in debates over whether the legal regime of the Shariah was sufficient to guarantee justice and order in changing times. This is how Kınalızade used it: as a lesson for those notables in his own time who claimed that the noble Sacred Law was "insufficient" to rectify the problems of an age in which "the people of corruption, thieves, and bandits had so multiplied." Like Zangī, argued Kınalızade, righteous Muslim rulers should not heed such arguments. The Shariah was sufficient.[25]

This story highlights the perennial tension between the rule of law and equity, in the sense of some notion of justice or fairness outside the formal rules of law, a tension recognized at least as far back as Aristotle.[26] It is a tension that can arise when discordance appears between a community's expectations of justice and the regime of law to which that community is committed, whether that commitment inheres through some measure of conviction or merely by tradition. This tension is wound all the more tightly when it is God's law, not some customary law, that seems to be falling short. As al-Sarakhsī neatly summed up, "The Sacred Law does not command injustice."[27]

The case of the Shariah adds another layer of complication: the divine law had staked its claim to authority in part on rescuing mankind from mankind's own flawed perceptions of justice.[28] As Ḥanafī jurists (and, at the opening of this book, al-Saqqāf) often wrote in their disparagement of conventional notions of right and wrong as opposed to revealed norms, revealed texts (*nuṣūṣ*) cannot be based on falsehood, while human convention can.[29] So a life-and-limb 'lapse' of the Shariah regime was compounded by the fact that pious Muslims experiencing it should, in theory, deny that their own perception of that shortfall had any merit. In these fraught circumstances, Muslims have been faced with a more intensified version of the same dilemma faced by other communities. What does one do when the rule of law and equity seem to contradict one another?

JUSTICE OUTSIDE OF SCRIPTURE? EQUITY AND THE RIGHTS OF GOD'S SERVANTS

There is a foundational tension in Islamic legal hermeneutics, as there is in Islamic scriptural hermeneutics in general. The text of scripture empowers itself as the source of norms and reference for truth and justice; "It is the truth of certainty" (Quran 69:51), and "Whoever rules by other than what God has revealed, those are the unbelievers" (5:44). But it also empowers aspects of the world outside of scripture with normative weight; bequests should be given and spouses treated according to "what is right by custom (*ma'rūf*)" (2:180, 2:229). This tension has created pronounced threads of ambiguity in Islamic rule-making throughout the centuries, such as dispensations (*rukhṣa*) to rules permitted due to necessity (*ḍarūra*) or some pressing need (*ḥāja*). The Quran prohibits pork and carrion, but it allows them to those driven by necessity (*uḍṭurra*, Quran 2:173, 6:145, cf. 6:119). The Prophet prohibited silk clothing for Muslim men but allowed the smooth fabric for those with rashes.[30] Revelation provides rules but also communicates that there are goods that sometimes trump them. These goods are often absent from the immediate scriptural contexts of those rules but are either endorsed elsewhere in scripture (like the value of life) or inducted by Muslim scholars from a wholistic survey of the teachings of God and the Prophet (like a presumption of innocence).

Yet what should the proper relationship between these licenses and the ordinary rules of the Shariah be? When do needs and necessity justify deviating from the normal rulings of the Shariah? And, concretely, what principles trump the normal rulings?[31] A tension between justice on the one hand and the rule of law as set forth in scripture on the other assumes at least a tacit recognition of some notion of justice and equity outside of that scripture. Or, at the very least, that scripture must convey an overarching and abstract sense of justice distinct from the scripture's more detailed rulings. Sunni legal scholars would come to identify this notion of justice via two means that would converge on a common conclusion. Legal theorists utilized a limited form of natural law reasoning to identify, apart from revealed sources, certain objective goods sought by human beings. And early Muslim jurists abstracted certain concrete rights from a holistic appreciation of the law they were deriving.

Whether or not human reason could grasp a notion of justice or 'good' without recourse to revelation was fiercely debated by Muslim theologians from the eighth to the eleventh centuries CE. Most Sunni theologians denied the capacity of human reason to chart an abstract path of natural law reasoning, such as that found in the thought of Stoics and Roman jurists such as Gaius (fl. mid 100s CE), which assumed that human reason could arrive at high-level truths about justice and morality such as the equality of human beings or the immorality of lying. Sunni theologians did recognize that reason could identify certain 'goods' outside of scripture, but these were more biological necessities required by humans as a species, such as the desire to procreate and protect one's kin.[32] This was more along the lines of the basic natural law reasoning of the Roman jurist Ulpian (d. *circa* 228 CE).[33]

By the late 900s CE, this more limited and baseline good was theorized as *maṣlaḥa* (welfare, common good) in the nascent Ashʿarī school of Sunni theology, which defined *maṣlaḥa* as what leads to benefit (*al-nafʿ wa'l-anfaʿ wa'l-manfaʿa*) and pleasure (*ladhdha*).[34] This common good of *maṣlaḥa* would become more elaborately understood, particularly after the thirteenth century, as attaining the aims (*maqāṣid*) of the Shariah. In the eleventh century, these would converge on the natural rights and duties that Muslim jurists understood as emanating from the concept of justice embedded both in the explicit texts of the Quran and the Sunna as well as in the potential that jurists would derive from them.

The notion of justice permeating Quranic discourse is that of *ʿadl* and *qisṭ*. The two words are often used interchangeably in the scripture to mean 'equitable action,' 'justice,' or 'fairness,' though in their semantic fields *ʿadl* is more justice in decision or passing judgment, while *qisṭ* is more justice as fair apportioning.[35] God instructs the Prophet to rule on disputes brought before him by *qisṭ* (Quran 5:42), which may be borrowed from the Greek *κόστος*, as Muslim scholars like al-Suyūṭī (d. 911/1505) suggested, as might the Quran's metaphor of the scales (*qisṭās*) of justice.[36] *ʿAdl* comes from the Arabian image of the *ʿidlān* (also *ʿadalān*), or the two sides of the pack animal's load that must balance each other.[37] Using that root, the Quran thus tells Muslim men that they will not be able to treat multiple wives justly or equally (*lan... taʿdilū*, 4:129). *ʿAdl* thus seems to be almost an "original position" in the Rawlsian sense, a notion of justice as 'equality-is-equity' prior to any appearance of distinction between equality and equity. To abuse a metaphor, there may be some camels whose body shape or gait requires one side of their load to be heavier than the other, but the presumption is that both sides of the load must be equal. Similarly, the presumption is that all people are equal and deserve equal portion and consistent treatment.[38]

Another important concept making up the Quranic discourse on justice is that of *ḥaqq*, meaning 'truth' or 'right,' which overlaps with *qisṭ* in its semantic capacity as one's due share.[39] God and His revelation are "the truth (*ḥaqq*), absolute," but a person's due is also their *ḥaqq*, and the portion of wealth due in charity is its "known right (*ḥaqq*)" (Quran 70:24). *Ḥaqq* is also associated with a correct ordering, in which each component of a system is in its proper place. Thus God "did not create the heavens and the earth except in *ḥaqq*" (Quran 16:3). The notion of *ḥaqq* as justice therefore overlaps with Aristotle's understanding of justice as deserts and justice as defined in Justinian's *Code* as "the constant and perpetual will to render to each his due." This is exemplified in the Prophet's Hadith that God ordered that "everyone with a *ḥaqq* be given his *ḥaqq*."[40] It also overlaps with Plato's notion of justice as proper ordering within a system, with each actor playing their proper role.[41]

The assumed synonymity of justice (*'adl*) with equity or fairness would continue as a prominent theme in Islamic legal thought.[42] But as Muslim scholars further theorized justice in the wake of their conquest of the Near East and its philosophical and political heritage, the concept of justice as virtue/the golden mean and proper order became more developed.[43] A standard definition of justice/*'adl* was 'placing each thing in its proper place,' with injustice resulting from something being out of its proper place.[44] In his *Etiquette of Worldly and Religious Affairs* (*Adab al-dunyā wa'l-dīn*), al-Māwardī explains that excess and extremes are the enemy of justice, while moderation/evenness is its key, since *'adl* is derived from proportionality or moderation (*i'tidāl*).[45]

Since the Islamic genre of political advice literature grew out of and drew effusively on the Near Eastern genre of Mirrors for Princes, its discussion of justice transcended Islam and its scriptures even as it was applied within an assumed Shariah framework.[46] The main objective was assuring the continued stability and prosperity of the dynasty, so justice was not an end in and of itself.[47] It was the essential program to achieve the desired result. According to al-Māwardī, worldly good (*maṣāliḥ al-dunyā*) can only be achieved if six factors are present: a religion followed by the subjects, a powerful ruler, comprehensive justice, general security, economic prosperity and hope among the populace.[48] *Dīn* (often glossed as religion) was thus but a useful tool in this enterprise, though it brought the important benefit of assuring felicity in the Afterlife as well.[49] But it was justice that was truly essential. As al-Māwardī and many Muslim scholars writing in this genre after him stressed, "Dominion can survive disbelief (*kufr*), but it cannot long survive injustice (*ẓulm*)" (this was even, erroneously, cited as a Prophetic Hadith in some Mirrors for Princes works).[50] Of course, a Muslim jurist like al-Māwardī would never marginalize God's law. But, in the context of political philosophy and good governance, the Shariah's value was functional. If a king exceeds God's law (*shar'*) in collecting taxes, for example, the repercussion that al-Māwardī highlights in one of his Mirrors for Princes works is not that the act is sinful before God or morally wrong. It is that the king's subjects will begin to resent and resist him.[51]

In the conceptions of justice predominant in both political theory and juristic writings, justice-as-balance and justice-as-rights were closely linked. In what became a famous epistle in the Mirrors for Princes genre, the Abbasid governor Ṭāhir b. Ḥusayn (d. 207/822) writes that judgeship is a crucial pillar of state because "it is God's scale by which conditions on earth are moderated (*ta'tadilu*)" and by which "people attain their rights (*ḥuqūqahum*)."[52] The Abbasid chief judge Abū Yūsuf writes that one of the ruler's chief jobs is "returning rights to those owed them."[53]

The conception of *ḥaqq* as right or claim developed in Islamic jurisprudence dovetailed with this discourse on political philosophy, though Muslim jurists focused on defining more concrete claims. From the eighth through the tenth centuries CE, Muslim jurists (particularly in the Shāfiʿī and Ḥanafī schools) elaborated a framework of basic rights of property, contract, and security. And they distinguished those rights or claims that people owed each other through contracts or basic duties regardless of faith (*ḥaqq ādamī*)[54] from those rights that Muslims owed God (*ḥaqq Allāh*).[55] While, as noted in the Hadith corpus, the ultimate "right of God" is to be worshipped without partner, as Johansen observes, the rights of God also included the claims of the state and community on individuals.[56] Public order was thus a right of God. And God held as one of His rights the freedom of non-Muslims legally enslaved by Muslims.[57]

As inducted by jurists in the ninth century from their scriptural proof texts, these basic human rights (literally, *ḥaqq ādamī*, the 'right of a human;' or more often *ḥuqūq al-ʿibād*, literally, 'the rights of the slaves of God,' i.e., human beings) included notions of a right to physical integrity (*ʿiṣma, nafs*), to property and the right to own (*māl*), and some sort of due process (*al-barāʾa al-aṣliyya*, i.e., the basic presumption of innocence or non-liability). These concepts were not theorized clearly by early jurists and found expression only later, particularly in the tenth century CE, as explanations for concrete rulings derived from proof texts in jurisprudence.

In the eleventh century, this rights discourse converged with the limited natural law reasoning that was occurring among legal theorists and theologians. The Ashʿarī legal theorist al-Juwaynī proposed that the prohibitions of the Shariah function to preserve bodily integrity (*dam*), chastity (*furūj*), and property (*amwāl*), a concept that his student al-Ghazālī developed into the famous Five Universals (*uṣūl*) that constitute the aims of the Shariah (*maqāṣid al-sharʿ*): protecting the integrity of life (*nafs*), reason (*ʿaql*), religion (*dīn*), lineage/paternity (*nasl*), and property (*māl*).[58] Their Ḥanafī contemporary, al-Sarakhsī, similarly concluded that the rules of the Shariah "are policies set down for the common good of human beings (*siyāsāt mashrūʿa li-maṣāliḥ taʿūdu ilā al-ʿibād*)." These were primarily the protections of rights that the Shariah acknowledged for *all* its subjects, whether Muslim or not: those of physical integrity, property, religion, reason, family, and honor (*ʿirḍ*) (though, theoretically, non-Muslims had less right to honor or dignity than Muslims).[59]

The requirement that these rights be protected emerged as a prominent theme in Islamic legal discourse.[60] Even if an act of theft could almost never meet the evidentiary bar to be punished as a Hudud crime, the thief was still subject to discretionary punishment and liable for compensating the victim because the latter's property right had been violated.[61] Eleventh-century CE jurists arguing for an increased acceptance of written evidence in court argued that, if the judge could not examine them, then many rights (*ḥuqūq*) of the Muslims would be lost.[62] A fourteenth-century Andalusian judge wrote that, if courts upheld too stringent requirements for witnesses and did not accept the testimony of local notables even when they fell short, "then the rights (*ḥuqūq*) of the weak and strong alike would be lost."[63] A similar conclusion was reached by judges in the same period in Tlemcen regarding affidavits.[64] A 1672 CE decree by the Mughal emperor Awrangzīb set guidelines for the empire's crimes tribunals (*ʿadālat*), instructing the heads of local administrations and judges to work together to safeguard subjects' rights. This meant ensuring that no one was detained longer than necessary during an investigation but also assigning appropriately harsh punishments in cases where a crime did not meet the evidentiary bar for Hudud crimes.[65]

WHAT IF JUSTICE AS RIGHTS AND *FIQH* CONFLICT? THE PLACE OF THE *MAẒĀLIM* TRIBUNAL

What should Muslims do if this overarching conception of justice, rights, and the regime of law as set forth by certain interpretations of Islam's scriptural sources conflicted? One response offered was that of a fideistic formalism, which turns away concerns about worldly wrongs by an appeal to total divine justice. This response resonates strongly with the position of the dominant Ashʿarī school of Sunni theology, which holds that good and bad are dictated solely by divine fiat, and can be seen in statements such as that of the prolific nineteenth-century Yemeni scholar al-Shawkānī (d. 1250/1834): "Justice (*ʿadl*) is what accords with what God has decreed (*sharaʿa*), and injustice is what contravenes it."[66] This was present in al-Māwardī's discussion of burdens of proof, and it appears again clearly in his rules of evidence. Against what had become accepted convention in his time, al-Māwardī decried judges relying on their own store of documents even though they did not remember signing them or when they were witnessed.[67] He simply rejects the argument that judges not accepting such documents as evidence would result in many Muslims losing their rights (*ḥuqūq*). To second guess the laws derived from revelation based on speculations about what harm this might do is to violate the Quranic order not to follow "that of which you have no knowledge" (17:36).[68]

Fideistic formalism long predated al-Māwardī, and it has appeared often since. The Umayyad caliph ʿUmar b. ʿAbd al-ʿAzīz, famed for his piety, refused to endorse the criminal procedure of *qasāma* (compurgative oath), which sought to offer some form of compensation and justice when a person was murdered, but the murderer was either unknown or the evidence of his guilt did not meet the formal requirements of *bayyina*. To punish anyone without such evidence would be unjust, the caliph explained, since one could not impose liability without the evidence required by God's law. God would grant justice to the victim and punish the killer in the Hereafter.[69] A similar example is the ruling for manslaughter. As laid out in the Quran and Prophetic Hadiths, the killer's agnatic kin group (*'āqila*) should pay the compensation payment.[70] As non-Arab jurists quickly realized, however, communities in Persia, Central Asia, and elsewhere did not have these kinship structures. While most jurists sought functional equivalents to pay the compensation, such as neighborhoods, guilds, or, ultimately, the public treasury, even in the early modern period some Mālikī jurists in North Africa argued formalistically that, with the process set out by God and His Prophet gone, no compensation payment was owed. There was no justification for second-guessing the formalities of revealed law.[71]

A second response to the clash of equity and the regime of law is to push back against formalism by embracing a purposivist vision, or the interpretation of rules with the assumption that they had some original aim that must be fulfilled. It was to insist that the rule of law *must* yield justice since that is law's main purpose. Beyond broad Quranic assertions that "God does not wrong any of His servants" (Quran 3:182, 8:51, 22:10), advocates of this response could point to the provision of dispensations (*rukhaṣ*) in the Quran and even more so in the Hadith corpus. In one Hadith, the Prophet allows the poor to buy food in return for a future portion of their crop not yet ready for harvest despite the Prophet's command "not to sell what you do not have."[72] On the basis of a contested Prophetic Hadith, many schools of law allowed the judge to set aside the limitations on women's testimony in court and to accept the testimony of a single midwife as persuasive on issues pertaining to a child's birth, since only women were present.[73]

But since this purposivist approach defines itself, in effect, against the specific rulings or formal precedents of the Quran and Sunna in favor of the implied imperative for justice in those sources, its main evidence comes from the later legal reasoning of Muslim jurists. So, though the Prophet had refused to fix food prices in Medina during a time of inflation, his explanation that he did not want to exert control that might wrong (*maẓlima*) anyone was understood by many later scholars as proof *for* the permissibility of fixing prices in situations in which *not* doing so would cause injustice.[74] This legal reasoning took its clearest shape in the notions of *istiḥsān* (equitable reasoning) in the Ḥanafī and Mālikī schools or need (*ḥāja*) as demonstrated in the Shāfiʿī and Ḥanbalī ones.[75] The Shāfiʿī school, for example, did not permit a man to look at the face of an unrelated woman without some pressing need, but leading scholars allowed it for male teachers teaching female students the Quran.[76]

In matters of procedural law, this push back against formalism was most vociferously argued by Ibn Qayyim al-Jawziyya. Amid debates over the legitimacy of *siyāsa* and questions over the Islamic pedigree of Mamluk and Muslim Mongol rule, Ibn Qayyim wrote that just law is God's law, and God's law must provide justice. Labels we apply are mere convention, for, "if the signs of justice (*ʿadl*) are manifest and its face revealed then, by whatever path it came, there is the law of God." Those judges, like al-Māwardī, who cling parochially to formal rules of evidence are failing in their duty to provide just and proper governance. According to Ibn Qayyim, they "would have the Shariah fall short (*qāṣira*), not tending to the interests of God's servants."[77] In contrast, Ibn Qayyim launched the most comprehensive defense of circumstantial evidence and the position that direct evidence (*bayyina*) was not limited by formal requirements but was whatever gave the judge confidence to rule.[78]

Finally, a last response is to concede to at least some of the demands of equity by reining in the inherent formalism of the rule of law while still affirming its validity. This could be achieved through a conscious (if controversial) regime of legal stratagems and fictions, such as the legal devices (*ḥiyal*) used in the Ḥanafī school (and, with less willing admission, in others).[79] According to Abū Ḥanīfa, a judge could not rule on the basis of what he himself knew to be true. Yet if he had personally witnessed a man divorce his wife, for example, but that man now denied this in court and his opponent had no evidence, how could the judge not grant the wife the separation she desired and that she claimed had occurred? The solution, Ḥanafī scholars wrote, was for him not to terminate the marriage but rather merely to separate the man and woman on the basis of 'ordaining right.'[80]

A concession to equitable needs while still affirming the validity of the Shariah's formal requirements could also be accomplished by temporarily suspending accepted rules within the judge's court. A glaring example of this is the insistence, which continues in Saudi Arabia to this day, that judges are and must be qualified *mujtahid*s (i.e., qualified to derive rules directly from scriptural sources) in the face of the undeniable fact that few, if any, are.[81] Acknowledging this dissonance goes back at least as far as al-Jāḥiẓ (d. 255/869), who mocked it in the ninth century, to al-Iṣṭakhrī a century later, when he urged accepting the rulings of non-*mujtahid* judges if they accorded with "the truth" (a very flexible criterion), and to the scholar-vizier Ibn Hubayra (d. 560/1165), who plainly admitted judges all fell short of this bar.[82] A typical explanation for this decision comes from the Damascene Shāfiʿī jurist Ibn Firkāḥ (d. 690/1291), who remarked that the rulings of such a judge were to be implemented regardless of his lack of stature due to "the corruption of the age" (*fasād al-zamān*).[83]

Unlike the purposivist resistance to legal formalism exemplified by the likes of Ibn Qayyim, who cast an attachment to formalism as a misunderstanding of God's intention in the Sacred Law, this last approach more narrowly justified exceptions to formal rules. It did so by drawing on formal concepts of need and necessity, in this case the necessity of protecting the rights of the community, and the license necessity created. This was well established in the Quran and the precedent of the Prophet. For example, the Quran allowed Muslims to have non-Muslims bear witness to their wills if no Muslims were available while they were traveling (Quran 5:106). This license was affirmed by several schools of law, though it broke with the otherwise consistent rule that non-Muslims could not act as notarial witnesses for Muslims.[84] Looking across the four Sunni schools of law, the Egyptian al-Shaʿrānī (d. 973/1565) offers the explanation that some schools had embraced lower requirements for who could serve as a witness in the law court in order to protect the rights of the Muslims.[85] This was certainly the argument offered by the Mālikī judge al-Nubāhī in late fourteenth-century Granada, where he felt a refusal to reconcile requirements for witnesses with the realities of social life would lead to an inability to safeguard the rights of the strong and weak alike. This was seconded by the Mālikī jurist al-Ḥaṭṭāb al-Ruʿaynī (d. 954/1547) two centuries later, who cited the widespread corruption of the age as justification.[86]

Finally, conceding to the demands of justice and equity could also be done by creating a separate legal forum in which the more restrictive procedures and burdens of the rule of law are excluded. This was what was done in Britain with the formalization of the court of equity presided over by 'the conscience of the king,' the royal chancellor. Still nested in and reliant on the common law of the land, the English equity courts allowed innovations in procedure and remedies that enabled them to administer justice in cases that "escaped the meshes of the ordinary courts."[87]

And this was what was done with the *maẓālim* tribunal and similar forums of royal justice, such as the crimes tribunal. As Tyan noted, the *maẓālim* tribunal, like the English courts of equity, had a subsidiary (*subsidiaire*) character. They functioned to catch what had fallen through the cracks of the judge's court or when the institution of that court or the person of the judge proved impotent in the face of some greater force.[88] Like the English equity court, the *maẓālim* tribunal did not claim superiority over the ordinary law of the land. But the magistrate presiding over the *maẓālim* wielded the temporal muscle of royal authority, and this gave him an *ad hoc* power to respond directly to petitions, to intervene in disputes, or overturn the rulings of ordinary judges.[89] As Tyan observed, the separate venue of the *maẓālim* tribunal proved so valuable to Muslim jurists and rulers alike because it allowed ulama/judges and their rulers a rubric under which to legitimately place the legal exercise of royal authority.[90]

Davānī stresses the importance of the *maẓālim* tribunal as a crucial bulwark for protecting the rights (*ḥuqūq*) of the ruler's subjects. In the opening of his *maẓālim* treatise, Davānī states that he wrote it so that "the rights of the Muslims might not be squandered and that the regime for the welfare of God's servants might not come to ruin." Commenting on Davānī's treatise, Cevdet Paşa explains that "the first task of regimes is to defend the rights of the servants [of God]."[91] While Johansen stresses that, in Ḥanafī jurisprudence at least, the state's role in guaranteeing the 'rights of God' was a minimalist one, leaving most legal ground to the jurists' law,[92] al-Māwardī, Davānī, and Cevdet Paşa remind us that it was also the ruler's/state's responsibility to act as the ultimate guarantor of its subjects' rights, "the claims of the servants of God." Davānī had written that assuring that all subjects received their rights and did not infringe on the rights of others was "the greatest governance" (*seyāsat-e 'oẓmā*).[93] This actually requires the increased intervention of the state or the ruler in the otherwise non-state legal affairs of the judges' courts.[94]

One might object that the discourse drawn on by Davānī and others around "protecting the rights of God's servants" was a foreign entrant into Islamic law via Islamic political thought and its absorption of the Near Eastern, Greco-Persian heritage. In short, it was a use of 'un-Islamic' *siyāsa* ideology to subvert 'Islamic' Shariah. But we must remember that the whole concept of *ḥuqūq al-'ibād* was actually developed from the legal ground up by early Sunni jurists poring through the Quran, Hadiths, and nascent Muslim law and uninterested in the Near-Eastern, Greco-Persian heritage.

From this perspective, *siyāsa* intervention is by no means a Schmittian 'state of exception,' in the sense that it is not a suspension of the Shariah. The ruler's intervention is described as the implementation of one of the foundational principles in Islamic legal thought, the protection of the rights of God's servants. In al-Māwardī's and Davānī's expositions, it was the *maẓālim* tribunal that embodied this royal justice duty. In Cevdet's case, it was the new *Nizâmiyye* courts.

Of course, advocates of the purposivist approach exemplified by Ibn Qayyim considered this concession-by-institution approach to be a grave misunderstanding of the application of justice in the Shariah. Relying heavily on Ibn Qayyim's vast anti-formalistic writings, al-Ṭarābulusī's judges' manual specifically criticizes al-Māwardī and his writings on the *maẓālim* and crimes tribunals for advancing the flawed position that only the officials of those bodies and not the judge can rely on *siyāsa* to achieve justice. After summarizing al-Māwardī's list of procedures and evidence available to the magistrate of the *maẓālim* or the crimes tribunal but not the judge, al-Ṭarābulusī retorts that his Ḥanafī school allows the judge to avail himself of the *majority* of these tools as well.[95]

Delineating these three options for addressing the failure of *fiqh* rules to protect rights should not delude us into thinking they were necessarily mutually exclusive. One jurist could advocate all three in different matters. Such is the case with Ibn al-Amīr al-Ṣanʿānī (d. 1182/1769), the senior Yemeni scholar whose opinions were sought at the beginning of the previous chapter. Asked whether judges should adhere to the rules of evidence regarding how many witnesses were required for specific kinds of cases or if judges could drop these standards and simply rule by what they considered most probable, al-Ṣanʿānī's scripturalist formalism was undaunted. Turning away from the rules on witnessing stated clearly in the Quran and the Sunna was out of the question. Presaging al-Saqqāf, he wrote that the Lawgiver had "taken into consideration the realm of mankind's wellbeing," and "He knew that the conditions of His servants would change" when He revealed those rules. But as for doctrines not defined explicitly in Islam's scriptures but rather elaborated by later jurists, such as what exactly constituted an upstanding witness, al-Ṣanʿānī turns purposivist. Dispensing with centuries of juristic definitions, he ingeniously cites a Hadith to assert that individuals considered upstanding by their peers are upstanding for purposes of witnessing, and those who are not are not. Peer approval is the only criterion that matters. When it comes to whether a judge should give more weight to written documents or to witness testimony, al-Ṣanʿānī defers to the deteriorated condition of culture and legal institutions at the time. If written documents are seen as repositories of reliable claims, they should be honored. If people see that judges and notaries are corrupt and that the infrastructure of documents is unreliable, only oral testimony should be accepted.[96]

IS THE *MAẒĀLIM* PART OF THE SHARIAH; OR HOW CAN GOD'S LAW FAIL?

If the purviews of the *maẓālim* tribunal and the judge's court never overlapped, then the question of the *maẓālim*'s place within the Shariah would be simple. We could conclude that it provided complementary subject matter jurisdiction to the judge's court, handling issues outside it by agreement of all involved. But, as we have seen, there was overlap, and it cannot be explained away as mere appellate oversight.[97] If the *maẓālim* tribunal seems to infringe upon the territory of the clearest protagonist of God's law, the judge, then is the *maẓālim* ultimately part of the Shariah or a tool of justice outside it?

For numerous leading Western scholars, beginning with Joseph Schacht, the answer unambiguously is that the *maẓālim* was outside the Shariah.[98] In his study of *maẓālim* tribunals in the Baḥrī Mamluk period, Nielsen observes about the institution that, "in strict Shariah, it had no place."[99] Khadduri concludes that the ulama/judges did not consider the *maẓālim* tribunal to be a real court at all, since "it applied essentially a set of political (almost secular) laws and not necessarily the Shariah." The late Bernard Weiss wrote that the *maẓālim* magistrate "was not bound by the rules of Islamic law."[100] Knut Vikør places the *maẓālim* under the rubric of "*non-sharʿī* courts."[101] Hurvitz treats the *maẓālim* tribunal as a category separate from "Shariah courts."[102] Ronald Jennings called it "a non-Islamic secular court operated by the government...."[103] In his history of criminal law in medieval Egypt, Yaacov Lev includes a chapter on the *maẓālim* tribunal within a section entitled "Judicial Institutions outside the Pale of Islamic Law." So, when Davānī declared vociferously that the *maẓālim* was an integral part of the Shariah, was he wrong?

Davānī did not spring to the defense of the *maẓālim* for no reason. In the three centuries before him, cries of outrage from prominent Muslim jurists inveighing against the imposition of the ruler's profane notions of justice on the sacred body of the Shariah certainly suggest that many ulama considered the *maẓālim* to be a threat to the Shariah's monopoly on legal legitimacy. It was during the Mamluk period that these anxieties reached an unprecedented peak. Even within the Mamluk period, however, the attitudes of the ulama/judges towards the application of royal justice differed as it changed over time.

In the first century of the Mamluk period (Rapoport's first period in his periodization of Mamluk *siyāsa*), we observe the approval of senior ulama/judges like al-Qarāfī and Ibn Taymiyya, as well as Ibn Taymiyya's arch-critic Tāj al-Dīn al-Subkī (d. 771/1370). They consider it appropriate for the ruler or local governor (*wālī*) to investigate and punish public crimes like theft and the public consumption of intoxicants.[104] Al-Subkī offers firm correction as well, however. He calls on these officials to constrain themselves to the public sphere, respecting the Quranic commands to honor the private space of the home and private conduct (*satr*), not seeking out wrongdoing there (*tajassus*) (Quran 49:12). He severely criticizes those officials who force people out of their homes in the process of their investigations or who apply excessively violent lashings that exceed Shariah norms. All of this violates "the boundaries (*ḥudūd*) of God," states al-Subkī.[105]

As royal justice in the form of the chamberlain (*ḥājib*) and the *maẓālim* expanded into a forum parallel to the judges' courts (during Rapoport's second period), ulama like the historian al-Maqrīzī (d. 845/1442) stepped up their objections. He describes the chamberlain as settling cases sometimes by Shariah and sometimes by "what they call *siyāsa*," a "Satanic term" that al-Maqrīzī inaccurately claims was derived from the Mongol word *Yasa*.[106] These ulama critics complained that the chamberlains inappropriately removed cases from the jurisdiction of the judge. In the Mamluk realm ulama/judges pushed back against the expanding jurisdiction of the chamberlain, sometimes trying to have debtor cases moved back to the judge's court. These efforts were met with the sultanic rebuke that *siyāsa* "runs the same course as the Shariah."[107] The intensity of ulama anxiety over royal justice diverging from the Sacred Law, however, is clear in a passage written by Tāj al-Dīn al-Subkī (translated by Rapoport):

> We say: the chamberlain should refer all affairs to the Shariah, and should not think that the *siyāsa* brings any benefit. Rather, the *siyāsa* brings harm to the land and to the subjects and leads to chaos. The best interests of men are served by the laws handed down by their Creator, who knows best what brings them benefit and what brings them harm. The Shariah of our Prophet

> Muhammad (pbuh) guarantees all the benefits to humanity in this world and the next, and only harm comes when it is set aside. But whoever follows it finds that his days are good and calm... If you like, look at the annals of the just and unjust kings and amirs, and see which of the two is more secure and which is longer lasting. I have observed these, and found that anyone who thought that he could better the world with his intellect, and rule the land through exercise of personal opinion and *siyāsa (bi-ra'yihi wa siyāsatihi),* and go beyond the limits and warnings of God, had suffered ill fate, and his days were dark and troubled... And as for someone who thinks that his affairs will not succeed if he does not shed blood with no just reason and if he does not beat innocent Muslims, let him know that he is a rebel, an ignoramus, a stupid ass, whose dominion will soon perish and whose fall is imminent... If one of those asses says: "How should I know that? I am a Turkish simpleton *('āmmī)* who knows not the Book and the Sunna." Tell him that this would not help him with God. Ask someone who knows. Otherwise, you will come to the Day of Judgment with your adversaries, those you have beaten and punished, dragging you over the mountains face-down. Then no excuse will help you. If it is impossible for you to understand, then what business do you have in taking on this job? Leave it.[108]

Yet we must remember that this did not entail a total rejection of royal justice or *siyāsa*. Ambiguity around the term *siyāsa* confuses scholars to this day and was played on by figures like al-Maqrīzī in their criticisms of government overreach. As a result, even highly competent modern historians have misread authors like Ibn al-Jawzī (d. 597/1200) as condemning *siyāsa* as fundamentally outside of and in competition with revealed law. This famous Baghdad historian, jurist, and preacher certainly seems to be doing so when he writes that a ruler excusing his actions by "making the claim of *siyāsa* is making the claim that there is a flaw in the Shariah." But this is to misread Ibn al-Jawzī. Elsewhere in the same book Ibn al-Jawzī uses the term *siyāsa* simply to mean the management of political affairs. What he is actually condemning is made clear in a parallel passage.

Ibn al-Jawzī is calling out those who excuse or encourage conduct that contravenes God's law by claiming it actually fulfills it, a criticism he launches jointly at unjust, transgressive rulers and antinomian Sufis alike. Rulers indulge in oppression and kill the innocent when "their own opinion is made to seem goodly to them... and they are deluded into thinking that this is *siyāsa*." Like Sufis who violate the Shariah with the claim that this will actually lead to true piety, such rulers kill people unjustly "and call that *siyāsa*." So it is not a ruler's authority or discretion in making law or policy that Ibn al-Jawzī dislikes. It is when the ruler uses that right to excuse violating God's law.[109] As he writes in another work, rulers err when they engage in *siyāsa* without heeding what the Sacred Law (*shar*ʿ) has commanded, since "it is the Law that is *siyāsa*, not the ruler acting on his own opinion or whims."[110]

From Ibn al-Jawzī to Ibn Taymiyya, Tāj al-Dīn al-Subkī to al-Maqrīzī, all embraced the use of *siyāsa* as long as it was in conformity with the Shariah. They just urged rulers to heed this limit.[111] In fact, such *siyāsa* was required. The influential Mālikī judge Ibn Farḥūn (d. 799/1397) divides *siyāsa* into just *siyāsa* (*siyāsa ʿādila*) and unjust *siyāsa* (*siyāsa ẓālima*). The former is necessary for preserving people's God-given rights, the latter infringes upon them. This is misunderstood by some jurists and rulers alike, Ibn Farḥūn observes, with some jurists denying a role for just *siyāsa* because they mistakenly view it as departing from the principles of God's law (*al-qawāʿid al-sharʿiyya*) and some rulers indulging in unjust *siyāsa* because they incorrectly conclude that God's law requires what they see as necessary excess.[112] Ibn Farḥūn's distinction became influential and was popularized in the Mamluk context by al-Maqrīzī.[113]

Al-Subkī penned an even fierier condemnation of those rulers or officials who think that any welfare or dynastic power lie in the application of *siyāsa* that exceeds the Shariah's bounds, since all welfare in this world and the next lies within God's law. His biography of the great Seljuq vizier Niẓām al-Mulk (d. 485/1092) idealizes him as the consummate just minister, and al-Subkī offers the remark that, "when he sat for the *maẓalim* tribunal, he applied the Quran and the Sunna."[114] Al-Subkī's criticism of the chamberlain's justice and *siyāsa* not in conformity with the Shariah seem primarily rooted in concern over excessive use of violence against the population. Here he echoes Abū Shāma al-Maqdisī's (d. 665/1268) praise of Nūr al-Dīn Zangī for not meting out the excessive punishments resorted to by latter-day rulers. Zangī required witnesses and direct evidence (*bayyina*) before applying "the lawful punishment" prescribed by the Shariah.[115]

But if acceptable *siyāsa* is part of the Shariah, what does it mean for it to be, as scholars often described it, 'in conformity with the Shariah'? If it is part of the Shariah, isn't it already in conformity with it? Reflecting on a debate with a Shāfiʿī scholar who had (correctly) argued that "There is no *siyāsa* except what accords with the Law (*sharʿ*)," the Baghdad Ḥanbalī Ibn ʿAqīl (d. 513/1119) explained that there was no disagreement there. *Siyāsa* was what promoted wellbeing (*ṣalāḥ*) among the people and warded off harm, even if neither God nor the Prophet commanded it. If that Shāfiʿī scholar had meant that *siyāsa* cannot "contradict what the Law has articulated," this was correct. But if he meant that it could only be "what the Law has articulated (*naṭaqa*)," then that was wrong, since *siyāsa* was by definition a realm of policy and regulation authorized by revelation but left unarticulated. This had been clear since the time of the Companions, explained Ibn ʿAqīl, who had themselves made their own totally legitimate *siyāsa* decisions.[116] As the Ottoman Syrian jurist Ibn ʿĀbidīn (d. 1252/1836) would later explain, *siyāsa* "is included within the bases of the Law (*qawāʿid al-sharʿ*) even if the Law does not specify it in particular textual indicants (*nuṣūṣ*)."[117] So *siyāsa* is part of the Shariah in that it is an area of law authorized by the Shariah, though its details are left to the political authority to define. *Siyāsa* conforms to the Shariah as long as those details do not transgress the boundaries of that area.

In general, Muslim jurists' attitudes towards *siyāsa* were thus mostly consistent over time. Tāj al-Dīn al-Subkī, al-Maqrīzī, and other Mamluk-era ulama disturbed by the misuse of *siyāsa* but grateful for its use within the limits of the Shariah were no different from al-Māwardī centuries earlier. His guidelines for the magistrate of the *maẓālim* assumed that the Shariah encompassed the activity of adjudication and permeated its lacunae. In the context of doing something that Mālik allows but Abū Ḥanīfa and al-Shāfiʿī do not, al-Māwardī states that the magistrate may choose whichever body of law ends the dispute between the litigants. "Otherwise," he adds, presumably referring to cases in which no established law can be found, "he should settle between them by what the Sacred Law (*sharʿ*) entails."[118]

Perhaps more importantly, the Sacred Law sets firm limits. In a clear statement about the boundaries of the *maẓālim* forum, al-Māwardī affirms that "adjudicating according to the *maẓālim* does not render permissible what the Sacred Law has prohibited."[119] The inclusion of *maẓālim* justice within the Shariah is affirmed in al-Māwardī's discussion of how the magistrate should phrase his instructions to an official to whom he delegates a ruling. The official should issue a ruling "by nothing but the truth and legal right (*ḥaqq*) that the ruling of the Sacred Law (*sharʿ*) requires."[120] There is thus no noteworthy tension between royal justice and the Sacred Law in al-Māwardī's work. Absent from his discussion is the anxiety over 'bad' *siyāsa* found in later centuries. Unlike Muslim jurists writing after the Mongol conquests, when the powerful legacy of Mongol law and legitimacy stood as a specter over the ulama, al-Māwardī understood *siyāsa* as no more than routine political decision-making and executive leadership. The *siyāsa* of the ruler is the same as the *siyāsa* of a general leading his army (*yasūsu al-jaysh*). It is essential and non-threatening to Shariah legitimacy.[121]

Relatively consistent attitudes towards *siyāsa* should not be mistaken for a static relationship between the ruler and the jurists in matters of law. Prior to the Mongol period, by and large, the rights of the ruler to shape the application of the law and 'provide justice' were delimited by the jurists. *Siyāsa* took place in the spaces that the jurists left mostly blank. Rulers could disagree with jurists about their duties or the scope of the *siyāsa* sphere, as Nūr al-Dīn Zangī did, but the jurists had the right to determine what would be considered a legitimate legal act. Put differently, conceptually, *siyāsa* was a discursive construct of the jurists within which rulers could and did negotiate their duties. It is also worth pointing out that in the pre-Mongol period in the eastern Islamic lands the ruler's legislation was perceived as *ad hoc* intervention, not compelling precedent. This may have been the reason for the jurists' reluctance to systematically articulate the 'ruler's law,' and adhere, instead, to fairly vague principles.

In the post-Mongol period, the dynamics between the rulers and the jurists were markedly different. Not only did some post-Mongol sultans and rulers claim to have their own sultanic/dynastic laws, the legitimacy of which came from the divine imperium of the ruling dynasty (be it Chinggisid or otherwise, as in the case of the Ottomans), some issued detailed legislation and regulations describing procedures and administrative/legal practices. This was exemplified by the Ottoman sultans and, to a lesser extent, the Mughal emperors. The Ottoman state, with its bureaucracy – or learned hierarchy – of jurists, argued that these procedures and practices were compatible with the Shariah, as they issued from "those in authority amongst you," whom the Quran ordered Muslims to obey (Quran 4:59).[122] They also drew on arguments and ideals of rule that predated the Ottomans, such as the notion that the sultan was responsible for dispensing justice in his domains. However, it was evident that Ottoman sultanic/dynastic legislation was an independent legal corpus that positively described the role of the sultan as legislator and adjudicator. It is therefore no coincidence that jurists who opposed the legal claims made by the Ottomans did not consider them a manifestation of legitimate *siyāsa* but, rather, yet another instantiation of the Mongol Yasa.[123]

Of course, it is in the modern period that anxiety about turning completely away from God's law has reached a crescendo. In the mid twentieth century, the anecdote about Zangī's pious (but poorly informed) refusal to legislate was reread with new pathos by Muhammet Zâhit Kevsarî (d. 1371/1952), a capacious mind and the last academic Shaykh al-Islam (*shaykh dars*) of the Ottoman Empire, who lived out his post-Ottoman career in exile in Cairo. Retreading Kınalızade's footsteps, Kevsarî casts Zangī as an exemplary contrast to the Kemalists and secular Arab reformers who had either replaced the Shariah entirely with European civil law codes or relegated it to family law. But what seems to the reader like a direct quotation of the story from al-Maqdisī's thirteenth-century chronicle is in reality a paraphrase even more embellished than Kınalızade's had been. Instead of merely petitioning the ruler to come and fulfill his Shariah duty of punishing the crime of brigandage, the deluded ulama and notables of Mosul are portrayed as complaining – explicitly – that God's law is weak and insufficient. Interpolating material totally absent from the original report, Kevsarî has them beg the sultan to punish accused criminals without even waiting to prove them guilty. When Zangī refuses, his response is thus an affirmation of the primacy and efficacy of God's law in the face of those who wrongly dismiss it as obsolete and overly constraining in its procedural safeguards. It is also a defense of due process against authoritarians.[124] Zangī is portrayed as the ideal but absent modern Muslim ruler who refuses the deluded and blasphemous pleas of secular lawmakers and statesmen, whose vision of law is both godless and oppressive.

Yet were the Mosul notables of Kevsarî's grossly embellished telling right in their alleged complaint that God's law is weak and inadequate? The question of how we should conceptualize the justice capacity of law when we see that sometimes law does not do justice is an ancient one. For Plato, written laws compiled by the skillful and wise men of a state are the most one can expect in terms of the provision of justice. Only the philosopher king, who can access truth and justice directly, could supersede them.[125] Only a living lawgiver can achieve perfect justice because written laws cannot listen or speak.

Aristotle went further than his teacher in grappling with this question. He wrote that the essential nature of equity as opposed to law is that equity "is a rectification of law where law is defective because of its generality." Equity is a manifestation of justice that must be applied alongside the rule of law because it must rectify the rule of law when it falls short. And the law *must* fall short, Aristotle explains, because it is necessarily a "general statement." It is its generality – its formal consistency – that convinces a people that they are being dealt with fairly. As with all generalizations, though the law provides just solutions to the majority of cases, it must inevitably miss the mark on some. And of this the law itself is aware. Aristotle provides this crucial insight: the inherent failing in a regime of law "does not make it a wrong law; for the error is not in the law nor in the lawgiver, but in the nature of the case: the material of conduct is essentially irregular."[126] The law creates rules for categories and deals in generalities. Equity evaluates the exceptional case of an individual.[127]

The question of how to understand the mismatch between law and equity is hardly unique to the Islamic tradition, but in the Islamic tradition it is at its most fraught. Though his observations still apply, Aristotle did not have to worry about a body of law that was divinely inspired. In the modern period, the query 'Is the *maẓālim* within or outside the Shariah?' carries along with it a more threatening corollary for Muslims. Put plainly, if God is the infallible source of the law applied in the judge's court, why does that law need some outside corrective? If the judge's rules of substance and procedure, derived and elaborated by the ulama, truly extend from God's perfect, ideal law, how could one call for a whole legal forum that is in great part justified by its exemption from these rules? Khadduri phrased it well when he observed that it seems "strange indeed to speak of equity as a higher form of justice... in a system of law claiming to be the embodiment of Divine Justice."[128]

Two points help resolve this tension. First, Muslim jurists always admitted that their enterprise to manifest God's Shariah in the earthly realm was probabilistic (*ẓannī*).[129] With the exception of clear rulings agreed on by all schools of law, the rulings of *fiqh* were characterized by tremendous diversity. This was by the fact of scholars' disagreement over the reliability of some sources, such as specific Hadiths, and also by the nature of their interpretive process. Because ulama/judges accepted that their school of law was a best-guess approximation of God's will, they generally granted full faith and credit to courts applying other schools of law, at least on matters of import.[130]

Second, the Islamic legal tradition offered a clear admission to the question 'Can the law be unjust?' Yes, it can, because the texts of the Sunna make it clear that the judge is a highly constrained figure who is limited in the bases on which he can rule. The Sunna of the Prophet characterizes judgeship as a locus of temptation and potential abuse, with the judge more likely than not to fall into perdition due to the enormity of his responsibility. A famous Hadith warns that, for every judge in Heaven, two will be in Hell, one for intentionally and another for accidentally "squandering people's rights (*ḥuqūq*)."[131] The evidentiary restrictions placed on the judge are meant to minimize the misuse of judicial discretion, intended or unintended, and to protect the innocent from wrongful rulings.

The claim to truth in the judge's law came from its origins in revelation. But those very revealed texts portrayed the judge as a fallible officer unable to pierce the veil of the unseen and a hostage to procedures designed to restrict abuse. Modeling the ideal judge, even the Prophet admits he can only rule based on the evidence presented and cannot know the unseen truth of the case. In a famous and procedurally consequential Hadith, the Prophet tells two disputants who had come before him, "I am but a man. Disputants might come before me, and it might be that one of them is more eloquent in presenting their proof than the other." If one deceives the judge and, as a result, the judge rules in his favor, the Prophet warns that he has only earned a slice of Hellfire.[132] As Johansen explains, bringing a case before the judge does not necessarily lead to justice or expose the truth of a situation: "the place to find religious truth is not the judge's audience hall." (My translation.)[133]

Of course, the Shariah prizes and considers itself a reliable means to substantive justice, namely the idea that justice comes when a court yields a just result. But, like many legal traditions and in great part due to Hadiths like those on judges above, the Shariah also places great emphasis on procedural justice – the formalist notion that justice overall relies on the impartial application of a consistent set of processes aimed at protecting rights and fairness.

Few would deny that impartiality and consistency, the chance to have one's day in court and be treated without bias, are essential for people to feel that justice is being done. But the intuitive importance of procedural justice leaves us with a paradox. The impartial and formally consistent application of the law can yield results that are substantively unjust. As Lawrence Solum asks, "What solace can procedural justice be to someone who has suffered a substantive wrong?"[134] What happens if, as in the cases of murder described by Davānī, a great injustice has been done, but it is the letter of the law that seems to be protecting the culprit from punishment? What happens when, as asked by those pleading for Nūr al-Dīn Zangī's aid, there is no witness to the robbery perpetrated on the lonesome highway? Such cases can occur at any time, but they proliferate rapidly when social or economic change outstrips the pace at which legal institutions can be reformed. In such cases, the Shariah's emphasis on procedural justice leads to a denial of substantive justice. In such situations it is the *maẓālim* tribunal, with its more flexible rules of evidentiary and judicial procedure and with the expanded discretion of opening up the entirety of the Shariah tradition and not just one school of law, that steps in to provide substantive justice.

The *maẓālim* tribunal lies fully within the borders of the Shariah because, like Aristotle's description of the ruler stepping in with equitable resolution when the rule of law seems to fail, the regime of law in the judge's court *must* inevitably fall short of substantive justice on some occasions. The *maẓālim* resolves exceptional circumstances in which normal procedures fall short. And that falling short is a certainty guaranteed by the commitment to procedural justice and the regime of procedural law promulgated for judges. This understanding became a common theme among scholars in the Mamluk era and thereafter, such as the Cairene Mālikī al-Qarāfī. The expanded flexibility in choosing rulings (*tawsiʿa*) found in the *maẓālim* tribunal "is not contrary to the Sacred Law (*sharʿ*)," he states. Rather, al-Qarāfī explains, the legitimacy of this flexibility is testified to by important legal maxims (*qawāʿid*), such as judges choosing different rulings based on changes in time and culture as well as *maṣlaḥa mursala*, or the overall goal of pursuing the common good provided it does not contradict specific ordinances of the Shariah.[135] This is reminiscent of al-Māwardī's statement that the *maẓālim* tribunal aims at attaining the best and most judicious ruling (*al-aṣlaḥ*).[136] Davānī is the bluntest in asserting the Shariah legitimacy of the *maẓālim* tribunal. The magistrate's rulings are "purely the Sacred Law." "Anyone who says 'This type of legal authority is not legitimate' has said something illegitimate (*nāmashrūʿ*)" and may even have committed unbelief (*kofr*).

Confusion over the status of the *maẓālim* stems from two mistaken assumptions: first, that the *maẓālim* and royal justice were coterminous or synonymous; second, that the judge's court was coterminous with the Shariah's application. Concerning the first error, the *maẓālim* tribunal was only part of a larger field of royal justice. In the Mamluk era, when we see significant concern expressed by ulama over the Shariah legitimacy of royal justice, the *maẓālim* tribunal is not the object of this ire. It seems clear that the *maẓālim* tribunal was viewed as falling within the acceptable and uncontroversial part of the *siyāsa* spectrum. This misreading is understandable, since scholars like al-Maqrīzī slung mud at the term *siyāsa* with remarkably little sympathy for their own efforts elsewhere to parse it into good and bad.

The second error is also quite understandable. For the ulama, the judge's court represented only one part of the procedures and personnel that adjudicated God's law. But the *fiqh* manuals that the ulama produced lacked any chapter devoted to the *maẓālim*. Observing this, Nielsen concluded that the *maẓālim* tribunal must have been one of secular justice, falling outside of the Shariah. But *fiqh* manuals only covered those areas of substance and procedure that ulama/judges understood to be within their remit. And, while the *maẓālim* tribunal seems to have fallen squarely within the realm of the Shariah, it certainly lay outside the judge's court.[137] The mistaken conclusion that what lies outside of *fiqh* also lies outside of the Shariah may result from the misleading truism that *fiqh* is 'comprehensive.' As observed by M.K. Masud, *fiqh* is indeed comprehensive from a Western perspective on law, in that it includes areas that the modern Western tradition views as distinctly 'private,' such as worship, ritual purity, and personal piety. Indeed, it considers these the very foundations of the law. This is certainly much more comprehensive than what the average American thinks of as law. But *fiqh* is *not comprehensive* in that jurists left crucial areas of law to the ruler's discretion.[138] As long as the ruler and his officials did not violate the outer limits of the Shariah, by indulging in excessive punishment or levying oppressive taxes, for example, their conduct was part of the Shariah. In fact, as Davānī, the nobles of Mosul, and countless other ulama/judges observed, it was an essential part.

Conclusion

Does the *Maẓālim* Tribunal Make Legal Reforms 'Islamic'?

When Cevdet Paşa produced Davānī's treatise to silence ulama questioning the new *Nizâmiyye* courts, he was claiming that the *maẓālim* tribunal was a truly Islamic precedent that justified his legal reforms. Was he correct? Davānī's warning against doubting the legitimate place of the *maẓālim* tribunal and *siyāsa* more broadly in the Shariah system was aimed at his peers. It could also be read as a challenge to modern Muslims concerned with the legitimacy of legal reform and to the Western scholars who have studied their production. Both are groups that have been haunted or fascinated by the question of what makes law or a legal system truly 'Islamic.'

One of the most prominent manifestations of this question has been a longstanding debate among Muslim scholars and Western academics alike over whether the past century and a half of Islamic legal history – essentially the modern period – represents a rupture in an otherwise organic development of Islamic law or a continuity of thought and institutions whose gradual development was only accelerated. This question is not merely academic. Rightly or wrongly, perceived behind it is a grievous implication. A continued, organic development of the Shariah tradition is arguably a legitimate and authentic expression of an Islamic *épistémè*. In this view, it is possible for law today to be truly and organically 'Islamic.' A rupture brought about by contact with the modern West and colonialism, by contrast, is arguably an inexorable sign of foreign contamination and epistemic loss.

Addressing these questions means taking one of two paths. Either we adopt an external perspective, developing and applying our own standard of what is or is not 'Islamic law.' Or we defer to voices inside the Islamic tradition and their standards for the authenticity of their endeavors. Unfortunately, neither path is satisfying. As we shall see, external standards differ, and it is not clear why one should overrule another. Nor is it clear that such external criteria would hold any weight for Muslim practitioners of the law themselves. Interior perspectives also differ, often between ulama/judges of comparable and unimpeachable credentials.

Still more challenging is gauging the sincerity or intentions of the Muslim actors and speakers involved, since in an interpretive tradition devoted to authenticity the new is most persuasively phrased in the garb of the old. How do we tell when an *épistémè* has been extended organically as opposed to being stretched unnaturally to cover over an epistemic rupture? Cevdet Paşa seems to have sincerely believed he was reshaping Islamic legal institutions in a manner loyal to the Shariah tradition. How do we tell the difference between a Cevdet Paşa and Abdullah Cevdet (no relation, d. 1351/1932), an Ottoman intellectual who admitted later in life that he had been disguising his advocacy for Western customs and 'scientific' ideas by "stitching them onto an Islamic jacket."[1]

But if finding a conclusive answer to the continuity vs. rupture in tradition and *épistémè* debate eludes us, then at least charting the detailed arguments made can be illuminating. As with the questions of whether *siyāsa* and the *maẓālim* tribunal are part of the Shariah or apart from it and whether the *maẓālim* is 'secular' or 'Islamic,' the answers often follow from the terms one sets. More fruitful than trying to answer definitively the question 'Do the *maẓālim* tribunal and *siyāsa* more broadly legitimize Islamic legal reform' is seeing the detailed evidence that each side musters and assessing the consequences of their arguments.

AN INSIDER VIEW

A plausible reading of Islamic legal history is one of *siyāsa* institutions gradually encroaching onto the judicial terrain of ulama/judges and their elaboration and application of God's law, ending with the modern state engulfing those roles completely. Early Muslim rulers' basic role of appointing judges and the relatively unambitious functions of the Abbasid-to-Seljuq-era crimes and *maẓālim* tribunals gave way to the more expansive Mamluk-era military courts and ulama acceptance that rulers could designate which *madhhab* and even which opinion within a school judges should apply.

Then the Turko-Mongol wave crashed over the Abode of Islam. It reshaped this landscape into one of rulers whose dynastic prestige allowed them to promulgate detailed laws in those areas that the ulama had always left to *siyāsa* discretion but which had never been filled with anything as ample or confident as Ottoman criminal and land law. In the 1550s CE the Ottoman sultan and his state mufti introduced a fifteen-year statute of limitations on lawsuits, restricting what the Empire's Ḥanafī school had never restricted before. And they enforced the school's minority opinion, which required a bride to have her male guardian's permission to marry, over its dominant opinion, which did not.[2] The sultan's Mughal contemporary declared himself above the *madhhab*s altogether and qualified to select which opinion should be applied where they disagreed.[3] Whereas prior to the Mamluk period the *siyāsa* office of market inspector (*ḥisba*) had limited what materials could be used and regulated trades like baking, late-Mamluk- and Ottoman-era jurists discussed much more directly the ruler's right to legislate by restricting the permissible (*taqyīd al-mubāḥ*) on questions like banning smoking.[4]

In the nineteenth century, a wave of new European administrative technologies, capacities, and ambitions, such as the telegraph and state centralization, drew the attention of Muslim states from Istanbul to the Malay sultanate of Johor. On other Muslim states they were imposed through colonial rule. Joining in this modernizing trend, state ulama like Cevdet Paşa were charged with formatting *fiqh* into the novel, clear, and specific shape of a code. What had once been the production of ulama/judges was now appropriated and promulgated in the voice of the state. Whereas the Ottomans' Ḥanafī school once had several potential rulings on a question, which judges might draw on in varied contexts, codes only had one for universal application.

And whereas judges in the Mamluk, Ottoman, or Mughal realms had on occasional issues encouraged litigants to head to another *madhhab*'s court for a more equitable ruling, new national codes like the Ottoman Family Law of 1917 or the Moroccan family code of 2004 borrowed rulings liberally from different schools.[5]

These new Shariah law codes were applied in an even greater expansion of *siyāsa*'s role: new court systems that ran parallel to and quickly encroached on the old judges' courts. Whereas crimes tribunals and the *maẓālim* had once supplemented the ordinary courts of the ulama/judges, the *Nizâmiyye* system and its modern counterparts from Egypt to Indonesia absorbed all areas of law other than family issues like marriage, divorce, and inheritance.[6]

If by the nineteenth century *siyāsa* meant the state could pick which rule to apply from the rich grab-bag of the Shariah's heritage and create laws where discretion allowed, the *siyāsa* of the twentieth century entailed states creating law from whole cloth. While even codes like Cevdet's *Mecelle* had drawn their contents solely from *fiqh* books, a century later the law codes of Muslim countries from Egypt to Pakistan and Malaysia are either totally original in their contents or modifications of British or Dutch colonial-era law. The law codes of several Arab states were drafted by a French-trained Egyptian jurist with Islamic inclinations, ʿAbd al-Razzāq al-Sanhūrī (d. 1391/1971), who, as Clark Lombardi puts it, "reimagined the Shariah as a series of principles that could be uncovered through an inductive study of the *fiqh* literature." These could then be manifested in legal codes that addressed modern needs, shared much in common with other legal systems (particularly European), and yet were truly 'Islamic.'[7] Whether the 'Sanhūrī codes' of Egypt and Iraq or Malaysia's hybrid of British and Shāfiʿī law, what makes all these law codes 'Islamic' is that they aspire to embody what jurists have determined to be the principles of the Shariah or that national courts have declared that they do not transgress the Shariah's wide outer boundaries.[8] In the twentieth century, what had previously been a marginal question of the ruler delimiting the permissible on issues like smoking became a robust exercise of the state's authority to shape the Shariah. From abolishing slavery in Tunisia, Saudi Arabia, and elsewhere to restricting child marriage in Egypt and Syria, 'restricting the permissible' had become an indispensable pillar of Muslim states' 'Islamic' legislative power.[9]

Viewing Islamic legal history along this trajectory of *siyāsa* expansion, the *maẓālim* encapsulates the dramatic transformation of the Shariah in the modern period. Cevdet Paşa drew on the *maẓālim* institution to justify the *Nizâmiyye* courts because its *siyāsa* mandate to safeguard 'the rights of God's servants' embodied the institutional flexibility and adaptability needed by a burgeoning modern state in a time of rapid change. The parallel between the *maẓālim* tribunal and the Anglo-Saxon equity court is again felicitous. As the victory of one procedural model and forum over another, *siyāsa*'s – here represented by the *maẓālim* – domination of the judge's court resembles the victory of equity over common law in America as the two were merged in the 1930s. In important ways, the resulting hybrid Federal Rules of Civil Procedure resembled equity more than law, with their acceptance of written evidence (in contrast to common law's preference for testimony in court), parties themselves being able to testify (at common law they had been deemed too biased), with the possibility of injunctive relief (law offered the recovery of damages), and equity's conscious emphasis on the consideration of justice.[10]

Moreover, Henry Smith's argument that equity should be viewed less as parallel or a competitor to law and more as 'meta-law,' a forum or approach that draws on law's rich offerings to provide justice in situations difficult for normal courts, seems an apt take on the *siyāsa* domination in modern Islamic law.[11] *Maẓālim* courts again epitomize modern Islamic legal reform, a pillar of which has been the *maẓālim* magistrate's ability to pick selectively from different schools of law. Since the late nineteenth century, drawing selectively (*takhayyur*) first from among the four Sunni *madhhab*s and then even from non-Sunni schools or ulama who predated the formation of such divisions has proven a crucial tactic.[12] Though the permissibility and frequency of taking from different *madhhab*s had long differed regionally and historically, by the early 1800s in the Ottoman Empire adherence to the official Ḥanafī school had become much stricter.[13] This changed with the two most influential movements of Islamic legal reform, both the Islamic modernist notion of re-forming Islamic law by bypassing the accretion of *madhhab* tradition and returning to the Quran, well-verified Hadiths, and the spirit of *maṣlaḥa* (advocated by influential figures like Rashīd Riḍā, d. 1354/1935); and the blending of European law codes with the principles seen as imbuing the totality of *fiqh*, an approach termed Islamic legal revivalism by Leonard Wood and best exemplified by al-Sanhūrī and the Syrian Muṣṭafā al-Zarqā (d. 1420/1999).[14] Examples of *takhayyur* in the law codes of modern Muslim states are many, but a common one is the guarantee of inheritance to a grandchild whose parent had died. This position was offered by the Ḥanbalī school, while the other schools of law considered this grandchild to be cut off from inheritance by their parent's death.[15]

Reasonable minds can disagree on the details or the linearity of this long trajectory of *siyāsa* domination. But the trend seems clear. Along the spectrum of the Shariah, *siyāsa* has expanded to minimize or even overwhelm the independent purview of the ulama. 'Islamic law' has moved from an uncodified law developed by jurists outside the state as the sole law of the land, enforced by *siyāsa* and acknowledging its role, to codified law elaborated and applied by state-authorized jurists in national courts in the ultimate expression of *siyāsa cum* national sovereignty. As Omar Gebril ably notes, *maṣlaḥa* (common good), an essential justification for the exercise of *siyāsa*, is no longer determined by the peerless authority of ulama/judges. It is determined by the state, which had slowly but surely drawn in ulama/judges and coopted them. The interests of that state now define what the common good is.[16] But is this a rupture or merely an evolution, an outcome very different from its origin but with each stage building contiguously on the one that came before? After all, if the past centuries have seen more and more of the ulama/judge class absorbed into the state or aligned with it, how much would their assessment of *maṣlaḥa* differ from the state's?[17]

Sometimes the evidence for a rupture seems overwhelming. Such is the case of Egypt, the center of intellectual gravity in Islamic thought for the past century.[18] Egypt gained increasing autonomy from its Ottoman suzerain in the nineteenth century before suffering direct British takeover in 1882. Even before that, Egypt's default to European creditors had opened the doors to British and French administrators, who began reshaping Egyptian law in the 1870s. When the British abruptly occupied the country in 1882 they razed existing Shariah institutions and imposed European law codes. Recent Ottoman reforms, such as the introduction of the *Nizâmiyye* courts and limiting the judges' courts to family law, were superseded by a new tripartite system of family law courts (*maḥākim sharʿiyya*); 'Native Courts' (*maḥākim ahliyya*), which handled civil, criminal, and commercial disputes among Egyptians; and 'Mixed Courts' (*maḥākim mukhtalaṭa*), which handled all disputes between Egyptians and the Europeans who now swarmed into the country, along with many real estate issues. The family law courts were staffed by ulama/judges and applied uncodified *madhhab* law, though the draft family code compiled by the senior Egyptian administrator Qadrī Paşa (d. 1306/1888) on the basis of the Ḥanafī school was often used. The Native Courts were staffed at first by the corps of *Nizâmiyye* judges and later by graduates of Egypt's new French-inspired law school, the Mixed Courts by European and American judges. Both the Native and Mixed courts applied new codes of criminal and civil law and procedure directly based on the French Napoleonic Codes. This system continued until it was folded into Egypt's National Court system in 1949.[19]

Many luminaries of Islamic law in Egypt have deemed the changes wrought by British occupation to be a clear rupture in the country's Shariah tradition. This was noted by figures like the influential activist scholar Rashīd Riḍā, who in 1898 decried the imposition of foreign, non-Islamic laws on Egypt. He later wrote that one British policy aim in the country was "the death of the Law (*sharʿ*) and destroying Muslims' trust in it."[20] His scathing criticism was echoed by more conservative ulama/judges like Aḥmad Shākir (d. 1377/1958) and even by clerics appointed to the pinnacle of Egypt's state religious institutions, such as the Shaykh al-Azhar ʿAbd al-Ḥalīm Maḥmūd (d. 1398/1978) and Shaykh al-Azhar Muḥammad Sayyid Ṭanṭāwī (d. 1431/2010). They made it clear that Egypt's civil and criminal laws were not 'Islamic' and pointed out the unambiguous imposition of laws totally foreign to Egypt and the Islamic tradition (though Ṭanṭāwī insisted that only 2% of Egypt's statutes contradicted the Shariah).[21]

Yet not everyone noticed this rupture or assessed it as such. Aside from prescient thinkers like Riḍā, who was almost obsessively attuned to the colonial politics in and around Islam, prior to the 1920s there was little public opposition to the imposition of French law or worry about a crisis of the Shariah. How could this have been missed for four decades? In part, the rupture was not as obvious as we might think. Many Egyptians familiar with the judiciary saw the new Native Courts as continuities of the *Nizâmiyye* court system, whose officials often staffed the new courts. The Mixed Courts, with their special treatment of Europeans as well as their local Christian proteges, were seen as the latest version of Ottoman capitulations. These agreements had been negotiated by European states after 1838 and obliged the Ottoman state to offer favorable trading rights and preferential legal protection to Europeans in its realm. For many educated Muslims in Egypt, however, the rupture was not missed. It was just too daunting to resist. Many Egyptians felt they could do little to oppose British military and administrative might. The British empowered minority Christian groups in Egypt to oversee these reforms. These Armenians, Copts, and Greeks generally had little interest in the Shariah. Moreover, many in Egypt felt that the situation would return to normal after the British left.[22]

Armando Salvatore offers another insight, one which harkens back to the notion of the Shariah as both an ideal much loftier than whatever laws were applied and a system much broader than mere courts. Unlike the *fiqh*-centered Islamism of the mid-to-late twentieth century, between the 1880s and the 1920s many in Egypt did not see courts and a specific body of law as coterminous with the Shariah. In fact, for many in the new professional, white-collar class of educated Egyptians produced by Ottoman reforms and then European influence, the ulama and their courts seemed benighted betrayals of Islam's promise of justice and progress. For this new class, many of whom were committed Muslims like al-Sanhūrī, the Shariah was not the *ancien régime* of law. It was an ideal that guided reform from an authentic past into an equally authentic and ideal future.[23]

Certainly, major figures, from mercurial reformists like Riḍā to senior state clerics like Maḥmūd, have taken the side of 'rupture.' But equally qualified and authoritative Muslim voices have considered the laws of modern Egypt to be totally 'Islamic.' In a 1979 response to the question of whether Egypt was ruled by the Shariah, the state Fatwa Ministry (*dār al-iftā'*) and its head, Shaykh Jād al-Ḥaqq 'Alī Jād al-Ḥaqq (d. 1416/1996), wrote that "the Shariah, as a law (*qānūn*), is truly applied to all Egyptians." It is, he explained, the main source behind the country's laws.[24] Writing in 2005, not just as Egypt's state Mufti but also one of the most respected ulama globally, Shaykh Ali Gomaa ('Alī Jum'a) wrote that Egypt's Islamic legal reforms had never abandoned or betrayed the substance of the Shariah. They only reformed it for Muslims' needs in the modern world. Egypt is "an Islamic state," he wrote, and Egyptians "have never considered removing the Shariah."[25]

Yet how could anyone familiar with the imposition of blatantly French law in Egypt make such confident assertions of continuity? In part they rest on an argument from the early 1900s, ironically formulated to help justify the adoption of French law, that French law and the Mālikī and Ḥanafī *madhhab*s overlapped substantially or even that French law was originally based on the Mālikī school.[26] In part assertions of Islamic continuity depend on the state's post-'Abduh minimalist understanding of the Shariah, which limited the Sacred Law's fixed features only to rules explicit in the Quran and undisputed Hadiths, with God leaving everything else up to the pursuit of justice and public benefit.[27] In part they rest on Egypt's post-1971 constitutional commitment to the Shariah as a source (after 1980, "the principal source") of the country's laws, understood as meaning that the country's Supreme Constitutional Court would reject laws it determined transgressed the Shariah. Finally, claims of continuity rest in part on the claims of the drafters of Egypt's laws themselves, in particular al-Sanhūrī, that their codes represented the Shariah's substance and values.

The question of continuity vs. rupture (and hence, the implication of organic, Islamic authenticity vs. foreign, non-Islamic imposition) is much murkier in cases in which direct colonial imposition is absent and in which legal reform occurred indigenously and gradually. Such is the case of the Ottoman imperial center in the nineteenth century, specifically in Istanbul of Cevdet Paşa's time. Scholarship on the question of indigeneity/continuity vs. foreignness/rupture in Ottoman legal reform has been divided, with much disagreement stemming from scholars' civilizational outlooks and political leanings. A narrative of Ottoman/Turkish secularization was developed and embraced by Turkish scholars working in the Republican Turkish tradition and by Western scholars for whom secularization and Westernization made obvious sense as part of history's inevitable movement towards the modern. This secularization narrative held that the nineteenth-century Ottoman legal reforms overseen by figures like Cevdet were part of a greater secularization process and an imitation of Western models like France. According to this narrative, this gradual distancing from the Islamic heritage culminated in the founding of the committedly secular and avowedly Westernizing Turkish Republic of Mustafa Kemal Atatürk in 1923.[28]

As in the more dramatic case of Egypt, there were noteworthy figures at the time who did sense in these Ottoman reforms a dangerous shift in *épistémè*. They perceived a turn away from Islam's scripture and Shariah tradition towards normative sources outside them. Even at the very dawn of Ottoman reform efforts, Muḥammad Saʿd al-Tilimsānī (d. 1264/1848) left his position as the chief judge of the Ottoman Algerian city of Tlemcen when he saw that "law was moving from the rulings of the Shariah to secular, positive law (*qānūn ʿaqlī*)."[29] We see how complicated it could be for ulama/judges to navigate these situations in another semi-autonomous Ottoman province that was engaged in its own reform process, one that was driven by internal desires to modernize but also with an eye towards currying European favor. In Tunis, the drafting committee for what would be the state's 1861 constitution included a number of prominent ulama/judges. The head of the state clerical establishment, Muḥammad Bayram (d. 1278/1861), suggested that he and his fellow scholars remain silent if a decision by their political colleagues contradicted the Shariah. But the chief minister preferred the ulama find some

Shariah justification, drawing on the full range of opinions from various *madhhabs* if need be. Ultimately, however, the ulama withdrew from the drafting committee with the excuse that it was not appropriate for them to deal with political matters (*al-umūr al-siyāsiyya*).[30]

Later, some Ottoman thinkers saw the *Nizâmiyye* reforms as driven by or imitating the West and thus as posing the risk of religious treason and surrender to Western encroachment. Ziyâ Paşa (d. 1297/1880), an Ottoman administrator turned reformist exile, supported legal reforms but warned "there can be no greater mistake than to fail to benefit from 'the sea-without-shore that is the Shariah (*Şerîat*)' and instead sink into some intellectually corrupt (*fikr-i fâsidi*) legal system." Establishing the *Nizâmiyye* system and marginalizing the existing legal courts had no other purpose "than to do away with the Shariah and appear shrewd before Europe." Another influential regime critic and reformist intellectual, Nâmık Kemal (d. 1306/1888), echoed the objections that had prompted Cevdet to cite Davānī's treatise. He argued that creating a dual-track legal system made no sense and that "there is no need to take on the laws of foreigners when there exists the 'sea of Truth' that is the body of *fiqh* gathered by the study of scholars for a thousand years."[31]

This sentiment, however, surfaced primarily among politically active intellectuals and especially the Young Ottoman reformers, whose calls for diffusing and limiting royal power Ziyâ Paşa and Nâmık Kamal had led. It was found far less among ulama/judges, who tended to be more ensconced in the Empire's scholarly and judicial edifice. There was a political valence to these critiques of Ottoman reforms. The real target was often the centralizing authority of the sultans, in particular Sultan Abdülhamîd, whose authoritarian rule undergirded the legal reforms. This is most evident in the writings of 'Abd al-Raḥmān al-Kawākibī (d. 1320/1902), the sharpest and most effective critic of the late Ottoman state's efforts to centralize institutional control. This Syrian administrator, scholar, and journalist painted the *Nizâmiyye* court system as an expression of Abdülhamîd's despotism. The new courts, he argued, removed procedural safeguards and punished the accused based on mere supposition (*ẓann*) and the testimony of witnesses who fell short of upright character (*'adāla*).[32] An exception that in some ways proves the activist-political character of this strain of critique is Mustafa Sabri (d. 1373/1954), a tremendously gifted member of the Ottoman scholarly establishment who would later serve as its penultimate head (*şeyhülislâm*) after World War I. But from the late 1890s Sabri had devoted himself to journalism and reformist politics, writing an 1898 condemnation of the Empire's "Europeanization" (*Avrupalılaşmak*).[33]

Against this narrative of inevitable rupture and Western-inspired secularization, the last two decades have seen scholars like Butrus Abu-Manneh, Alp Eren Topal, and Iris Agmon show how major nineteenth-century Ottoman legal reforms were rooted and phrased in indigenous Islamic paradigms (such as the Prophetic notion of renewal, *tajdīd*) and sometimes originated not in the West but in the practical experiences of the Ottoman provinces.[34] Many of the most active Ottoman reformists among groups like the Young Ottomans and the more radical Committee for Union and Progress (CUP), including many ulama, were motivated by Islam and their desire to defend it against foreign defeat. Whether they were all sincere or not, they repeatedly described the 1876 Ottoman constitution and the Empire's need for it as entirely in line with the Shariah and indeed required by it.[35] Even during the last years of Ottoman reform, from 1909–20, Islam was actually *increasingly* invoked as essential for the health and security of the state and society.[36]

Most crucially for our purposes, Avi Rubin's comprehensive studies of Ottoman legal codification and the *Nizâmiyye* reforms have shown that influence from the West was selective and resulted in creative amalgamations of French and Islamic law.[37] Rubin has demonstrated that, far from knowingly engaging in a secularization project, leading nineteenth-century Ottoman legal reformers "consciously preserved" the Islamic character of their systems and did not at all think of themselves as secularizers.[38] Rubin and Ruth Miller have also shown that, in reforms like the codification of laws and the comprehensive standardization of legal institutions, Ottoman officials were not laggards aping a more advanced West. They were participants in a *global* nineteenth-century project of centralization and routinization. In fact, the Ottomans preceded some Western states in this. In seeing the Napoleonic legal system as an ideal model, the Ottomans were just another European state trying to replicate a successful strategy.[39] Jun Akiba has noted how ulama/judges of the existing legal courts and serving the Empire's religious establishment played a crucial role in manning the *Nizâmiyye* courts in great part because of their experience in adjudication.[40] Despite the creation of a new *Nizâmiyye* law school to train judges and eventually an examination system that ensured that only graduates of that school could man *Nizâmiyye* courts, until the final years of the Empire "the preference for *ilmiyye* [i.e., ulama] members as civil court judges was a consistent policy for the judiciary."[41]

A fascinating example of how rupture and the secularization narrative have been read into Ottoman legal reforms, one that directly implicates the boundaries of the Shariah, what is 'Islamic' and what is 'secular,' is the tendency of historians to conflate the terms Shariah (*sharīʿa*), namely the Sacred Law, and *sharʿiyya*, an adjective that simply means law or legal. Though it was not uncommon for premodern Muslim scholars or even some modern ones to use both Shariah (*sharīʿa*) and law (*sharʿ*) to refer to the Sacred Law, habitually treating the two as synonyms can lead to disastrous conflation when studying the period of late Ottoman reform.[42] The new *Nizâmiyye* courts that Cevdet established were added to the centuries-old, existing Ottoman judges' courts, which had always simply been called 'law courts' (*mahkeme-i sherʿiyye*, pl. *mahâkim-i sherʿiyye*). But, if one translates *sharʿiyya* not as law/legal but as Shariah, and particularly if one understands late Ottoman reforms as an ineluctable step away from religious backwardness towards a secular Turkish destiny, then the *Nizâmiyye* courts seem clearly to be alternatives to Islamic law courts. And these legal reforms are then inevitably perceived as creating a secular alternative to the Ottoman Empire's Islamic system.[43] No less an accomplished scholar than Şükrü Hanioğlu can thus mistransliterate – and hence misconstrue – Ottoman legal reforms. If *sharʿiyya* courts are not law courts but "*sharīʿa* courts," i.e., 'Islamic' courts, then the new *Nizâmiyye* court system displacing them must be secular. It must be a case of a state replacing an Islamic legal system with a secular one.[44] In light of this huge misunderstanding, it makes sense why many Ottoman studies scholars have translated *Nizâmiyye* courts as 'secular' courts, when a more apt rendering would be state-order (*nizâm*) or statutory courts.[45]

At a certain point, members of the Ottoman clerical and administrative establishment did sense a move towards secularization and what many viewed as a Westernizing betrayal of Islam. But this did not come until after the final 1909 deposition of Sultan Abdülhamîd and the capture of control over the government by the now blatantly Westernizing Committee for Union and Progress. It was thus only in 1909, some forty years after Cevdet had used Davānī's treatise to argue for the legitimacy of the *Nizâmiyye* courts, that the traditionalist Ottoman Ulama Association launched a campaign entitled "We Want the Shariah."[46]

This highlights one of the challenges of discerning 'rupture' from 'continuity,' as one cannot deny the importance of the sincerity of the actors involved and their subjective sense of their own actions. One could hypothesize that an endeavor is 'Islamic' as long as some ulama endorse it. But, empirically speaking, there have always been ulama willing to endorse anything. What one does notice, however, in the course of the Ottoman reforms of the 1910s and their by-then fairly open secularization, is that even ulama/judges who had previously felt they could sincerely support them began to walk away. Mustafa Hayri Efendi (d. 1339/1921) was a staunch CUP supporter, a two-time Minister of Pious Endowments (*avkâf*), and accepted the position of heading the CUP government's clerical establishment (*şeyhülislâm*) in early 1914. More radical reformists, however, soon advocated for limiting the *şeyhülislâm* to overseeing purely "religious" (*diyaniye*) matters and moving even the family-law courts and seminaries (*medrese*) into the Ministries of Justice and Education. When this was adopted by the Parliament in 1916, it proved too much for Hayri. He resigned and was replaced by the even more pliant Mûsâ Kâzim Efendi (d. 1338/1920). Even a person as attuned to the Islam/West political dynamic as Mustafa Sabri acknowledged in retrospect that many of the pro-CUP ulama of 1909 to 1923 had been pious and devout, like the imam of the main Aya Sofya Mosque, Monastırlı İsmail Hakkı (d. 1330/1912). Those who would stay on after the Turkish Republic's abolishment of the caliphate, categorical adoption of European law codes, and abandonment of the Arabic script, however, he dismissed as "phony ulama" serving a "godless" religious establishment.[47]

THE VIEW FROM THE OUTSIDE

Among Western scholars of Islamic legal history, the case for modernity rupturing the Shariah tradition has been most fervently argued by Wael Hallaq, whose monograph *The Impossible State* is devoted to the topic. Loath as I am to rely on block quotations and quick as readers' eyes are to pass over them, James Baldwin's summary of Hallaq's influential view is too clear not to employ:

> The nineteenth-century legal reforms in the Ottoman Empire and Egypt, undertaken by Ottoman Muslim statesmen, represent the intrusion of alien, European concepts and ideals into the Islamic legal sphere just as much as the reforms of colonial governments in Algeria, India, and Indonesia. The subjection of the law to state authority, codification, the founding of modern law schools, the introduction of new tribunals staffed by bureaucrats in the Ottoman Empire and by British judges in India: these changes constitute a single phenomenon across the Muslim world and are the fundamental rupture in Hallaq's narrative. The intrusion of the modern state is so alien to Hallaq's concept of Islamic law that he regards the reformed legal systems of the modern Muslim world as inauthentic by definition, regardless of the claims they make about compliance with Islamic law.[48]

For Hallaq, in premodern Islamic civilization the Shariah existed outside and beyond the claim of Muslim states and dynasties. These, like almost all premodern states, were limited in their powers and reach. The Shariah was the civil-society production of the ulama/judges and provided the dominant ethical and legal worldview, orienting its subjects towards God. Modern states, by contrast, demand supreme sovereignty, permeate all areas of life through their bureaucracies and are culturally hegemonic. Sharing Talal Asad's view of secularism as a pervasive orientation of modernity that was spawned by and serves the modern state, Hallaq sees modern Islamic legal reform as the state's usurpation of the Shariah and subordinating it to the only object of devotion that the modern state deems worthy: the state itself.[49] The same harsh assessment has been arrived at by others. The liberal Muslim reformist Abdullahi An-Na'im writes that efforts by Muslims to forge modern states that are 'Islamic' never actually bridge modernity's rupture from the Islamic past. Rather, they are stuck in the modern trying to recreate what never was. What they have created in Iran or Pakistan is "in fact, a postcolonial innovation based on a European model of the state and a totalitarian view of law and public policy as instruments of social engineering by the ruling elite."[50]

Other scholars have been much more cautious about declaring a clear rupture. They stress the continuities of Islamic legal history and are more likely to see modernization as a series of step-changes.[51] The nineteenth- and early-twentieth-century reforms of Muslim states like the Ottomans appear less as a departure in kind and more as adaptation and the adoption of novel forms and technologies. Hallaq and those who share his view see codification of the Shariah as a betrayal of that law's internal flexibility and the all-powerful modern state stripping it from the civil-society hands of ulama/judges.[52] Samy Ayoub, however, argues that the most famous code, the *Mecelle,* was a continuity of Ḥanafī legal tradition.[53] This is certainly how Cevdet and the vast majority of ulama viewed it. Similarly, Brian Wright, Tobias Heinzelmann, and the late Rudolph Peters have argued that the codification of criminal law in nineteenth-century Istanbul and Cairo were continuities of the earlier Ottoman-Islamic legal tradition, sometimes very consciously so.[54] The Hudud, so symbolically important, had by intention almost never been implemented. The bulk of criminal law the *madhhab*s had left up to judges as discretionary punishment (*ta'zīr*), sometimes with school guidelines, or to *siyāsa* to set. When the Ottoman state adopted French criminal law in its 1858 Criminal Code, it was merely using its *siyāsa* authority to replace one set of *ta'zīr* guidelines with another. The Code's preamble reaffirmed the rights and commitments of the Sacred Law (*Şer'*).[55]

In a recent book, Rachel Scott summarizes the continuity vs. rupture debate and suggests reframing it as Islamic law being 'recast' in the modern period. According to this view, there is continuity in the substance, the matter, of the Shariah. But this has been reshaped and repurposed by the modern nation state to express its identity and cement its domination over the role of religion in society. Scott's framing acknowledges the continuities of Islamic legal history, but she agrees with Hallaq that the Shariah is no longer paramount. The Shariah has been consumed by the modern state and "recast in its service."[56]

Another push not just against the 'rupture' argument but, more uncommonly, against the argument that the modern state is a unique creature that must dominate religion and life comes from Sherman Jackson. In one sense, Jackson's assertion that the Shariah was always a much smaller part of a greater Islamic whole than al-Māwardī, Davānī, Cevdet, or Hallaq would admit serves him well: even if the Shariah were dominated by the modern state, that is not the same as the state dominating Islam.[57] A more broadly applicable objection comes when Jackson warns us that Hallaq's paradigmatic modern-state Leviathan is often an abstraction. In reality, states are not metaphysical new gods. They are "not driverless" but are shaped and controlled by people. And undeniably modern states like the U.S. and post-WWII Germany have imposed real and meaningful limitations on their powers over law, life, and their citizens' beliefs.[58]

SIYĀSA AS A PROBLEM OR SOLUTION? THE AZHAR TO IGGY AZALEA SPECTRUM

Another of Jackson's concerns blends his insider/outsider perspectives, reflecting his ambition to provide an academically convincing definition for the Shariah and the secular as well as his sensibilities as a Muslim. One reason that Jackson feels compelled to limit the Shariah to *fiqh* and exclude *siyāsa* from its canopy is that to do otherwise would "confer an ominous degree of *sharʿī* insulation and legitimacy upon [the state's] discretionary acts."[59] To put it more plainly, if political decisions are part of the Shariah, then the Shariah has to answer for the panoply of dubious or undeniably awful policies and actions of contemporary Muslim rulers. If one denies a rupture has occurred and affirms that *siyāsa* carries 'Islamic' legitimacy, do the political or legal deviations of Muslim states mar the Shariah?

No doubt the most egregious misuse of *siyāsa* would be for a Muslim ruler or state to pass a law requiring Muslims to do something prohibited (*ḥarām*) by the Shariah, like drinking alcohol, or prohibiting something required (*wājib*), like performing daily prayers. Not only would the Shariah prohibit Muslims from obeying such laws (unless under tremendous duress) on the basis of the Prophet having unambiguously condemned this, it would also arguably require them either to overthrow that regime or emigrate.[60] It was, in fact, a notional guarantee *not* to impinge on Muslims' basic religious freedom that allowed them to accept living under European colonial rule.[61]

Muslim governments issuing laws totally irreconcilable with the Shariah has been rare even in the modern period. In cases cast as such, government bodies have almost always located loopholes in the *madhhab*s' diverse interpretive heritage. In 1996, for example, Egypt's Supreme Constitutional Court excused a ban on face veils in public schools in part because not all *madhhab*s required wearing it. The face veil was thus not an unambiguous Shariah obligation.[62] Instances of total deviation from the Shariah usually occurred during the twentieth-century wave of Arab, Turkish, and Iranian nationalism, as well as socialism and communism. In such cases, governments made no pretense that what they were doing accorded with the Shariah.[63] A rare occasion of a government proffering a Shariah argument for the validity of such a law was the Tunisian president Habib Bourguiba's infamous 1960 on-air declaration that Tunisians should not fast during Ramadan and that the country's senior Ḥanafī and Mālikī scholars, Muḥammad Juʿayṭ (d. 1389/1970) and the venerable Muḥammad al-Ṭāhir Ibn ʿĀshūr (d. 1393/1973), would affirm this decree. They very publicly did not and were both dismissed.

Much more common is for Muslim scholars to remain silent in the face of governments or rulers engaging in official actions or making policy that violates the Shariah, either out of prudence or out of quietist principle. In 2023 the pop-singer Iggy Azalea appeared in concert in Riyadh. Controversy was sparked when she performed one song with the idolatrous chorus "Bow down to the goddess," another about how "It's a woman's world" and finally when her dress split open entirely on stage. Whether or not hosting Azalea's performance accorded with Shariah sensibilities, Saudi authorities did actually halt her concert after her dress mishap (she claimed the show was stopped due to her feminist message).[64] And I have not found any evidence of Saudi ulama actually *defending* such events.

Clearly, since the accession to *de facto* power of the crown prince Mohammed bin Salman in 2017, Saudi Arabia's previously formidable religious establishment has been utterly cowed. In the face of 'cultural activities' like the Azalea concert and hosting some of the world's biggest raves, Saudi ulama have either remained silent or simply say that it is not appropriate to openly criticize 'the holder of political authority' (*walī al-amr*), the most common (if contested) political stance of Sunni ulama dating back to the ninth century CE.[65] Silence in the face of a ruler or administration engaged in policies or actions that blatantly violate the Shariah may not be the ideal for Muslim scholars. But it surely has never been exceptional. Chronicles, generally written by the ulama, tend to lionize the former and pass over the latter as unremarkable.[66] Taqī al-Dīn al-Subkī offers us a glimpse of this mundanity when he complains about Mamluk sultans being too obsessed with worldly power to fully carry out their Islamic duty as rulers and about his fellow ulama being too absorbed in their scholarship and worship to confront them.[67]

Since ulama have long acknowledged that the ruler can restrict the prohibited or make the recommended required, there is also the risk of the misguided employment of *siyāsa* corrupting the actual shape of the Shariah itself. The ruler's right to 'restrict the permissible,' however, hinges on this pursuing some general good (*maṣlaḥa*). Furthermore, it is a separate question if the ruler's edict actually changes the ethical valence of an act, rendering it obligatory or sinful in God's eyes even if done or omitted in private. The main position in the Shāfiʿī school, where the most robust discussion of this issue unfolded, is that Muslims are required to obey such rules in public and private provided they were actually promulgated in pursuit of some common good. So the state's prohibition on slavery is a religious obligation, not merely an administrative rule. If the law is not issued for some general good, it is only required to obey the law publicly. The prohibited act does not become a sin in God's eyes if done privately.[68]

Of course, the impact of misguided *siyāsa* on Islam as perceived and practiced is more a social question than a theoretical one. Part of the *siyāsa* domination of the Shariah spectrum in the last century has been the state's monopolization or at least control over as many areas of religious life as possible, whether that state be a 'secular' state like Turkey or an 'Islamic' one like Saudia Arabia.[69] In this light, whatever the state's choice is in drawing the line between national law and the Shariah is certainly likely to shape public belief by the sheer force of state power and media control. In recent decades, however, the trend in Muslim public discourse on the proper relationship between state law and the *ḥalāl* and *ḥarām* of the Shariah points less to positively defining the Shariah through state law than to negatively defining it by stressing that religiosity is up to individuals, provided those individuals do not form organizations outside state control. It is most common to read Muslim opinion stressing that national laws should *not* reflect Shariah sensibilities on questions like appropriate dress, financial interest, or alcohol, but that individual Muslims should make their own choices on such matters. Ironically, this discourse often seeks to exonerate Muslim states and their laws from their *failure* to apply Shariah law. Of course, as scholars like Fahd Ṣāliḥ ʿAjlān have written, such negative shaping of the Shariah is still highly consequential. It demonstrates that Muslim states lack a commitment to encouraging Islamic values.[70] But this sort of influence of *siyāsa* on Islamic norms in society is certainly more a function of the global trends of secularization and liberalization than the result of empowering *siyāsa* as part of the Shariah.

Much global Muslim outrage at modern Muslim rulers for egregious transgressions of Islamic norms has centered not on domestic law but on foreign policy. Here not only questionable policy but also bizarre whim receives Islamic imprimatur. When Mohammed bin Salman announced a comprehensive and aggressive boycott of Qatar (2017–21), the Saudi state mufti justified it as promoting the common good (*maṣlaḥa*) of Muslims.[71] Abdallah bin Bayyah, the head of the Fatwa Council of the United Arab Emirates (UAE), Saudi Arabia's close partner in the boycott, immediately issued a statement supporting it.[72] When the UAE announced the normalization of diplomatic and trade relations with Israel, Bin Bayyah again proclaimed his support, saying the decision was wise and for the best interests of the UAE and Palestinians. He explained to his many detractors that this was a *maṣlaḥa* decision and fell into the *siyāsa* purview of the ruler.[73]

As aggravating as some of these policies are, Bin Bayyah correctly voices the dominant trend in Islamic law, which granted the ruler broad discretion in foreign policy. Nor is securing Shariah legitimation for dubious foreign policy a product of modernity. The Ottomans had received religious approval to make war on Muslim enemies like the Karamanids, the Aqquyunlu, and the Mamluks with the justification that, in resisting the Ottomans, these states were aiding the enemies of the faith. It was thus the Ottomans' Shariah 'duty' to remove them.[74] And, with or without ulama approval, awful ethical decisions in war and treaty are nothing new for Muslim rulers. The ruler of Damascus, Muʿīn al-Dīn Önör (d. 544/1149), resisted a siege by Zangī by allying with the Crusader king of Jerusalem. And the Nasrid ruler of Granada aided Fernando III (d. 1252) of Castille in his conquest of Muslim Seville.[75]

Without a doubt one of the most distasteful abuses of political authority involves neither law nor foreign relations. It is the obsequiousness modern Muslim rulers evoke by incentive, intimidation, or even inexplicable sincerity from the learned representatives of Islam. Examples of such unmerited and open fawning on the part of ulama are numerous. But the 2014 public comparison made by Saʿd al-Dīn al-Hilālī, a professor of Islamic law at Al-Azhar, between Egypt's dictator, ʿAbd al-Fattāḥ al-Sīsī, and Moses is among the most egregious. It proved too much even for the Shaykh al-Azhar, who condemned it.[76]

Again, however, such toadyish encomium is nothing new for ulama/judges in Islamic history. Davānī's flowery and extended praise for the Aqquyunlu ruler Ūzūn Ḥasan makes al-Hilālī's praise seem modest. Al-Bayḍāwī (d. 691/1292) came from an accomplished family of ulama, served as the Shāfiʿī chief judge of Shiraz, and remains renowned worldwide for his commentary on the Quran, which has served as a mainstay in madrasa curricula from Istanbul to Java. Al-Bayḍāwī enjoyed the patronage of the Ilkhan Mongol rulers and penned hyperbolic praise for Hülegü (r. 654/1256–663/1265), the same Hülegü whose armies had only a few years earlier sacked Baghdad, killed and raped hundreds of thousands of Muslims over a period of weeks, and slaughtered the Abbasid caliph. He lauded Hülegü and his son, who had similarly bloody inclinations, as rulers who had "inclined towards justice and compassion and who favored the Muslims entirely."[77]

Jackson's effective rejection of Davānī's and Cevdet's argument that the *maẓālim* tribunal extended the Shariah umbrella over *siyāsa* certainly pushes against the notion that *siyāsa* has gradually come to dominate the Shariah spectrum. Removing the Shariah legitimacy from *siyāsa* powers and institutions, however, presents a much thornier problem for Muslims and their most widely accepted understanding of what 'Islamic law' means today. Some scholars may judge *siyāsa* to be too risky for Shariah endorsement or as having grossly overstepped its bounds via the modern state. But if, as Gebril observes, it is now the state that determines the common good that the Shariah should pursue, the state seems often to get it right. *Siyāsa* has offered the most compelling solutions for serious challenges to Islamic morality, law, and hermeneutics in the modern period. Every Shariah argument for permitting the abolition of slavery and, indeed, obligating it, hinges on the *siyāsa* authority of Muslim rulers, specifically their power to restrict the permissible.[78] Many Muslims around the world feel intense discomfort at the Quranic verse (4:34) allowing husbands to strike their wives as a last resort in correcting their behavior. Ibn ʿĀshūr's interpretation that the verse places this authority in the hands of the judge, hence the state, seems to many to be the most compelling and well-grounded in the Shariah tradition. It turns on *siyāsa* legitimacy.[79] For well over a century, Muslim women have pointed to the abuse of one type of Islamic divorce, *ṭalāq*, which is only available to the husband and can be uttered unilaterally and irrevocably in any setting, even, according to some *madhhab*s, while drunk.[80] *Siyāsa* has offered a practical and seemingly successful solution. In Morocco, Indonesia, and Malaysia the husband must pronounce *ṭalāq* in court. In fact, in Malaysia to do so outside the court is a crime.[81] Such laws and institutions have arguably contributed to the material betterment of Muslims' lives. They have also markedly eased the burden on faith created when the dictates of scripture seem to clash with the demands of justice. As part of the Shariah, they have ensured the protection of 'the rights of the slaves of God.'

Appendix I

Maẓālim – An Annotated Bibliography

For the most comprehensive or instructive studies of *maẓālim*, see H. F. Amedroz, "The Mazalim Jurisdiction in the Ahkam Sultaniyya of Mawardi," *Journal of the Royal Asiatic Society of Great Britain and Ireland* July (1911): 635–674. This must be read along with Mathieu Tillier's historiographical review; Mathieu Tillier, "Mazalim in historiography," in *The Oxford Handbook of Islamic Law*, ed. Rumee Ahmed and Anver Emon (Oxford: Oxford University Press, 2018), 357–380 as well as idem, "Maẓālim courts," in *Encyclopaedia of Islam Three* (Brill). Much scholarship on the *maẓālim* either still relies on or references the ever-essential Emile Tyan, *Histoire de l'organisation judiciaire en pays d'islam*, 2nd ed. (Leiden: Brill, 1960), 476–481. Another excellent overall study is Nimrod Hurvitz, "The Contribution of Early Islamic Rulers to Adjudication and Legislation: The Case of the *Mazalim* Tribunals," in *Law and Empire: Ideas, Practices, Actors*, ed. Jeroen Duindam et al. (Leiden: Brill, 2013), 135–156.

For *maẓālim* in the Abbasid period and Umayyad Iberia, see Tillier, "*Qāḍīs* and the political use of the *maẓālim* under the 'Abbāsids," in *Public Violence in Islamic Societies*, ed. Christian Lange and Maribel Fierro (Edinburgh: Edinburgh University Press, 2009), 42–66; Maaike van Berkel, "Abbasid *Maẓālim* between Theory and Practice," in *Le Pluralisme Judiciaire dan l'Islam Premoderne*, ed. Mathieu Tillier, special issue, *Bulletin d'Études Orientales* 63 (2014): 229–242; Christian Müller, "Redressing Injustice: *Maẓālim* jurisdictions at the Umayyad court of Córdoba (eighth-eleventh centuries CE)," in *Court Cultures in the Muslim World*, ed. Albrecht Fuess and Jan-Peter Hartung (New York: Routledge, 2011), 93–104.

As with almost all areas of cultural production and history, the Mamluk period remains the most amply sourced period for the study of the *maẓālim*. See Jørgen Nielsen, *Secular Justice in an Islamic State: Maẓālim under the Baḥrī Mamlūks, 662/1264–789/1387* (Leiden: Nederlands Historisch-Archeologisch Instituut te İstanbul, 1985); Albrecht Fuess, "*Ẓulm* by *Maẓālim*? The Political Implications of the Use of *Maẓālim* Jurisdiction by the Mamluk Sultans," *Mamlūk Studies Review* 13, n. 1 (2009): 121–147; Yossef Rapoport, "Royal Justice and Religious Law: Siyāsah and Shari'ah under the Mamluks," *Mamlūk Studies Review* 16 (2012): 71–102.

Appendix II

A Translation of al-Māwardī's Chapter on the *Maẓālim* Tribunal from *The Ordinances of Government (al-Aḥkām al-sulṭāniyya)*

CONVENTIONS OF TRANSLATION AND SOURCES

Italicized text in the translation that follows is text that appears in Davānī's *Maẓālim* treatise either in direct translation into Persian or in summary gloss (Arabic words in parentheses to note original wording are also italicized).

Underlined sections represent text absent from Abū Ya'lā Ibn al-Farrā's *Aḥkām al-sulṭāniyya* recension. Occasional alternative wordings or the rare item present in Abū Ya'lā's text but absent in al-Māwardī's are noted in the footnotes, with **M** indicating al-Māwardī and **Y** Abū Ya'lā.

§ breaks are my interpolation, while 'Section' in the text comes from the original.

Text in **bold** is of particular significance to this book or referenced more than once.

This translation of al-Māwardī's *Aḥkām* is based on:

1) Baghdādī's 1989 edition (*al-Aḥkām al-sulṭāniyya wa'l-wilāyāt al-dīniyya*, ed. Aḥmad Mubārak al-Baghdādī [Kuwait: Dār Ibn Qutayba, 1409/1989]), which relied on the earlier printed edition by Maṭba'at al-Bābī al-Ḥalabī, an eleventh-century manuscript from the Chester Beatty Library (some folios evidently written by the author himself), another

fifteenth-century manuscript from the same library and, finally, an admittedly error-laden nineteenth-century manuscript.

2) Enger's 1853 edition (*Maverdii: Constitutiones Politicae*, ed. Maximilian Enger, [Bonn: Adolphum Marcum, 1853]), which, despite its age, often appears more accurate than al-Baghdādī's edition. It relied on a twelfth-century manuscript from the Bodleian Library, a fifteenth-century manuscript from the Bavarian State Library, an additional Arabic copy and, finally, a Persian rendering.
3) Comparison with the Fiqī edition of Abū Ya'lā's *Aḥkām al-sulṭāniyya* (*al-Aḥkām al-sulṭāniyya*, ed. Muḥammad Ḥāmid al-Fiqī [Beirut: Dār al-Kutub al-'Ilmiyya, 1421/2000, reprint]).

There have already been at least two translations al-Māwardī's *Aḥkām al-sulṭāniyya* in its entirety into English, one by Asadullah Yate (*Ordinances of Government* [London: Ta-Ha, 1996]) and another by Wafaa H. Wahba (*The Ordinances of Government* [Reading: Garnet, 1996]). My choice to provide this chapter translated here is not a judgment on either of their efforts, which I consulted in the process of my translation.

CONCERNING THE TRIBUNAL OF GRIEVANCES

Adjudicating grievances (*maẓālim*) means leading disputing parties toward equitable agreement using one's high standing and steering them away from denying one another's [claims] using intimidation and rebuke. Thus, among the conditions required of the magistrate overseeing the resolution of grievances is that of high standing, such that his orders be obeyed, that he enjoy great prestige and display evident probity, such that he not be avaricious but scrupulous in piety. For in his oversight this magistrate must combine the authority of an armed guard with the firmness[1] of a judge. He must combine

1 M: *thabt* / Y: *tathabbut*.

the characteristics[2] of both these offices, being of lofty standing and one whose orders are obeyed in both respects, like a caliph or those to whom the caliphs have delegated oversight of public matters.[3] If he is among those authorized to look into public matters, like ministers or commanders (*umarā'*),[4] his tending to matters [such as the grievance tribunal] does not require any specific appointment (*taqlīd*), since that is subsumed under his existing general appointment. But if he is not among those delegated to tend to public matters, then he requires a specific appointment. He can take it up if he meets all the aforementioned conditions.

If the official is to adjudicate grievances generally [meeting such conditions] is likely only in the case of those who could be chosen as a successor to rule, as an authorized minister, or as the governor of a region. But if overseeing the grievance tribunal is limited to executing what judges cannot or implementing what they lack the means to implement, then it is permissible for this official to be of lesser standing or power, provided that he fear no reproach in upholding truth and that avarice not leave him vulnerable[5] to bribery.

*And the Messenger of God, may God's peace and blessings be upon him, adjudicated grievances (*maẓālim*) in the matter of irrigation in which al-Zubayr b. al-ʿAwwām,[6] may God be pleased with him, and a man among the Anṣār disputed. He himself took this up, saying to al-Zubayr, "Irrigate using the water, O al-Zubayr, then the Anṣārī man can." The Anṣārī man said, "Because he is your paternal cousin, O Messenger of God?" So [the Prophet] was angered by his words and said, "O Zubayr, let the water flow in its course until it reaches up to your ankles."*[7] And he only said "Let it flow in its course" to discipline [the man] for his presumptuousness with him. And the reason why

2 M: *ṣifāt* / Y: *ṣifatay*.

3 The clause about caliphs or their delegates is missing from Enger's edition of M, appearing in only one ms. in the Baghdādī edition.

4 Y here overlaps with some mss. of M, explaining M mss. disparity. Y has: So if he is among those authorized to look into public matters, like caliphs or those to whom the caliphs have delegated public matters, like ministers or commanders....

5 M: *yastashiffuhu* / Y: *yastakhiffuhu*.

6 The famous Companion (d. 36/656), his mother was the Prophet's paternal aunt.

7 *Ṣaḥīḥ al-Bukhārī*: *kitāb al-musāqā, bāb shurb al-aʿlā qabl al-asfal.*

he told [al-Zubayr] to let the water flow until it reached ankle-height has been disagreed on. Was this the proper right he was clarifying for the two of them as a ruling, or was this something permissible that he ordered as a rebuke to the two responses?[8]

And none of the first four caliphs paid heed to grievances because they lived in the early period, when faith was manifest among those whom fairness would lead to the truth and whom admonition would dissuade from wrongdoing. Disputes would but arise among them in ambiguous matters that the ruling of a judge[9] *would clarify*. If any of their uncouth Bedouins acted unjustly, admonition would persuade them to withdraw, or violence would lead them to desist.[10] So the caliphs of the early generations limited themselves to resolving disputes by their ruling and legal judgment, placing every right in its place and relying on people's willingness to heed it. And 'Alī, may God be pleased with him,[11] when his time in leadership was delayed and people fell into dispute regarding it, required more sharpness in governance (*siyāsa*) and increased vigilance in arriving at rulings on obscure matters. He was the first to take this path and did so on his own. He did not set up [an office] for looking into grievances, however, due to his sufficiency in this. He said, regarding the *Minbariyya* question, "Her eighth becomes a ninth."[12] And he ruled, regarding the girl who bit, the one who fell and the one whose neck was broken, that the compensation

8 This incident raises the question of whether the Prophet issued this ruling out of anger, which contradicts his command that judges not rule when angry. The general response of Muslim commentators is that this would be impossible for the Prophet due to his infallibility (*'iṣma*). In his *Sunan* (*al-Mujtabā*), al-Nasā'ī places this Hadith under the chapter title of 'License for the Trustworthy Judge to Rule when Angry.' Another argument, mentioned by al-Khaṭṭābī, was that the Anṣārī man had committed apostasy by speaking to the Prophet as he did and had therefore invalidated his property right. The Prophet thus was treating him gently; Ibn Ḥajar, *Fatḥ al-bārī*, 5:49; al-Khaṭṭābī, *Ma'ālim al-sunan*, 4:182.

9 M: *ḥukm al-qaḍā'* / Y: *ḥukm al-quḍāt*.

10 M has *yuḥsina* (to do good), but one ms. has *yaḥbisa* (to constrain, desist) / Y has *yakhshuna* (to be rough, crude), which makes little sense. All are orthographically similar.

11 Enger's edition of M has *'alayhi al-salām* instead of *raḍiya Allāh 'anhu*.

12 This is a famous and complex question of inheritance law that 'Alī was asked about while on the pulpit (*minbar*) of the mosque in Kufa.

payment be in thirds.[13] And he ruled, regarding the boy over whom two women were disputing, with a judgment that settled the matter [i.e., the Solomonic judgment].

Then, after him, matters began to spread, to the point that people began openly wronging and transgressing one another. Rebuke and admonition no longer restrained them from mutual quarrel and deprivation. So they needed an office looking into grievances (*maẓālim*) to deter usurpation and provide fair settlement for those who were wronged, an office that blended the power of political rule and the justice of judgeship. The first to devote a specific day to such wrongs and to sorting through the complaints presented by wronged parties, without addressing them directly, was *ʿAbd al-Malik b. Marwān.*[14] *When he came across something particularly difficult or needed a ruling to be implemented, he directed it to his judge Abū Idrīs al-Awdī,*[15] who would implement his ruling, thanks to the opposing parties' fear of ʿAbd al-Malik b. Marwān and his awareness of the dispute and his having identified the cause. So Abū Idrīs dealt directly with the matter, while ʿAbd al-Malik provided the authority behind him.

Then the injustice of governors and the wrongdoing of the arrogant increased such that only the strongest of hands and most binding of commands could restrain them. *So [the Umayyad caliph] ʿUmar b. ʿAbd al-ʿAzīz,*[16] *may God be pleased with him, was the first to assign himself to examining grievances and removing them, observing just precedents (*sunan*). And he removed the injustices (*maẓālim*) done by*

13 In this case, ʿAlī was asked about three girls who were playing. They climbed onto each other's shoulders, then the girl on the bottom bit the girl in the middle, who then fell, leading the girl on the top to fall and break her neck. He ruled that the compensation payment was due from the families of the bottom two girls, but he reduced it by a third because the topmost girl was partially responsible for her own death.

14 The Umayyad caliph, r. 65/685–86/705.

15 This is likely actually ʿĀbid Allāh (or ʿĀʾidh Allāh) b. ʿAbdallāh al-Khawlānī (d. 80/699), who served as a judge from 684–699 CE and whom al-Māwardī and Abū Yaʿlā may have confused with ʿAbdallāh b. Idrīs al-Awdī of Kufa (d. 192/808), a famous Hadith transmitter about whose death date many erred; Wakīʿ, *Akhbār al-quḍāt*, 618; Ibn Saʿd, *al-Ṭabaqāt al-kubrā*, ed. ʿAlī Muḥammad ʿUmar (Cairo: Maktabat al-Khānjī, 1421/2001), 9:451; Judd, *Religious Scholars and the Umayyads*, 106; al-Dhahabī, *Siyar*, 9:42–44.

16 R. 99/717–101/720.

[his own] Banu Umayya clan, such that he was told, after being strict and severe with them, "We fear that you will face consequences for removing them." He responded, "May I not be spared any day that I fear or am wary of other than the Day of Resurrection."

After that, a number of the Abbasid caliphs sat to [address grievances]. The first to do so was al-Mahdī,[17] then al-Hādī,[18] then al-Rashīd,[19] then al-Ma'mūn.[20] And the last to do so was al-Muhtadī, such that properties were returned to their rightful owners. And the kings of Persia had considered this to be one of the bases of rule and the canons of justice, without which righteousness cannot prevail and equity cannot obtain.

And during the age of ignorance before Islam, the Quraysh tribe, when its chieftains had grown in number, its primacy had spread and they had begun seeing usurpation and contention that could only be restrained by a powerful authority, they concluded a pact to remove wrongs done (*maẓālim*) and to do justice for those wronged. The cause of this was recounted by al-Zubayr b. Bakkār[21] [as follows]:

A man from Yemen, from the Banu Zabīd clan, had come to Mecca on pilgrimage, bringing with him goods for sale. A man from the Banu Sahm clan, said by some to be al-ʿĀṣ b. Wā'il, bought them from him. But the man cheated him of his due, so [the Yemeni man] asked him for his goods back, and he refused. So the [Yemeni] man stood up on a rise and recited at the top of his lungs:

> O family of Quṣayy [i.e., the Quraysh], for one wronged of his goods,
> in the valley of Mecca, far from home and kin,
> Hair matted, still in the pilgrim's state,
> Between the station [of Abraham], the enclosure [of the Kaaba] and the [Black] stone.
> Will any among the Banu Sahm rise for their responsibility,
> Or will the property of this pilgrim vanish in error?

17 R. 158/775–169/785.
18 R. 169/785–170/786.
19 R. 170/786–193/809.
20 R. 189/813–218/833.
21 Noted genealogist, historian, and judge from Medina, d. 256/870.

And Qays b. Shayba al-Sulamī sold some goods to Ubayy b. Khalaf. But [Ubayy] cheated him out of his due, so he sought aid from a man from the Banu Humuj.[22] But he offered him none. So Qays recited, in the *rajaz* meter:

> O Quṣayy, how can it happen in the Sacred Precinct,
> With the sanctuary of the House and its noble, allied protectors,
> That I am wronged and not shielded from the one who wronged me?

So al-ʿAbbās b. Mirdās al-Sulamī responded:

> If your protector has done nothing to help you,
> And you've drunken great draughts from the cup of humiliation,
> Then go to the houses and stand before their families,
> You'll find in their redress neither obscenity nor wrong.
> And whoever seeks refuge by the House, will find Ibn Ḥarb [i.e., Abū Sufyān] and ʿAbbās.
> My people, Quraysh, perfect in character, in glory and strength as long as they live and toil,
> Tend to the pilgrims, while this one spreads division, for glory is handed down generation after generation.

So Abū Sufyān and al-ʿAbbās b. ʿAbd al-Muṭṭalib rose and had [Qays'] property returned to him. And the various clans of Quraysh gathered and swore a mutual oath in the house of ʿAbdallāh b. Judʿān to address injustices (maẓālim) *done in Mecca, to let no one commit injustice there and to render unto those wronged their rights. And the Messenger of God, may God's peace and blessings be upon him, was present with them on that day, before his prophethood, when he was just twenty-five years old. They swore this Alliance of Virtue* (ḥilf al-fuḍūl) *in the home of Ibn Judʿān. And the Messenger of God said once, recalling that moment, "I was present in the home of ʿAbdallāh b. Judʿān for the swearing of the alliance of virtue. And if I had been called to swear to it, I would have. It would have been*

22 Enger has *Jumaʿ* instead of *Humuj*.

more precious to me than red camels [i.e., a rare and valuable type]." He recounted the story and added, "Islam only increases this in strength."[23] And someone from Quraysh said, regarding this alliance:

> [The clans of] Taym bin Murra, if you asked, of Hāshim,
> And Zuhra, the best, all in the house of Ibn Jud'ān,
> Swearing the oath of allegiance to magnanimity as long as
> Leaves tremble on any branch or twig.

And though this was an act done in the age prior to Islam and called for by the needs of governance, the presence of the Messenger of God, may God's peace and blessings be upon him, and his affirmation of it renders it a legitimate rule of the Sacred Law (*ḥukm shar'ī*) and a prophetic act.

§

Thus, if a person is appointed to preside over the grievance tribunal, he should announce an assigned day for this, so that aggrieved parties can seek it out and disputants can bring their claims before him. In this way, the other days are free for his other leadership and management duties, unless he be an official appointed solely to respond to grievances on all days of the week. And he should be easy to access and keep only reputable company.

§

Sessions devoted to the task [of adjudicating grievances] absolutely require the presence of five types of officials:

First, guards and assistants to manage the strong and discipline the unruly.

*Second, judges (*al-quḍāt wa'l-ḥukkām*) to make known those rights that are established in their view and for their knowledge of procedure between disputants.*

*Third, jurists (*fuqahā'*) to consult on difficult or unclear points.*

23 For this Hadith, see *Musnad Aḥmad Ibn Ḥanbal*: 1:190 (Maymaniyya print).

Fourth, secretaries to record what transpires between disputants and what rights and rulings are decided for and against them.

*Fifth, witnesses and notaries (*shuhūd*) to testify to what rights are required and to certify rulings.*

If a grievance tribunal includes these five, aforementioned groups, the official can begin addressing them.

§

*There are ten types of subject matter that are dealt with in addressing grievances (*maẓālim*):*

The first type is looking into governors' transgressions and arbitrary treatment of their subjects. This is an essential duty of the grievance tribunal, regardless of whether anyone complains of wrongs done. The official [in charge] should regularly examine the conduct and circumstances of governors in order to bolster them if they are just, restrain them if they are arbitrary and even replace them if they are unjust. It is said that ʿUmar b. ʿAbd al-ʿAzīz addressed the people during the early days of his caliphate. Indeed, this was among his first speeches. He said to them:

> *I counsel you all to have fear of God, for He accepts nothing else and welcomes only those possessed of it. Some of those in authority have barred people from their rights until they are bought off and have spread falsehood until they are paid. By God, if not for a truthful tradition (*sunna*) that I'd revived after it had gone extinct or a false tradition that I stamped out as it thrived, I would not wish to live a single day more. Ensure the prosperity of what awaits you all in the Hereafter, and this life will be prosperous for you.* There is none since the time of Adam but death has taken them, they are soaked through by death.

The second type are wrongs done by officials in the collection of taxes. In this case, recourse should be to the just regulations found in the books of leading scholars and enforcing these among the people. Officials should be held to these rules, and it should be assessed whether they collected an excessive amount. If that amount had been sent already to the treasury, it should be returned. And if those officials took it for themselves, it should be returned to its rightful owner.

It has been reported that [the Abbasid caliph] al-Muhtadī,[24] may God be pleased with him, once held a session to hear grievances, and some complaints were presented to him regarding [payments made] in fractions of coins (*kusūr*). [The vizier] Sulaymān b. Wahb[25] said:

> ʿUmar b. al-Khaṭṭāb, may God be pleased with him, collected the land tax from the people of southern Iraq and areas conquered in the east and west in the form of coins and also in kind. And silver and gold coins were minted in that time according to the weights and measures of the Persian and Byzantine emperors. The populace would pay the proper amount in whatever denomination they had available and did not pay heed to how one kind of weight varied from another. Then corruption spread among the people, and those paying the land tax would pay in Tiberias-minted coins, which are each four *dāniqs*, keeping the *Wāfī* coins, which each weighed a *mithqāl* [i.e., 9 *dāniqs*]. When [the Umayyad governor] Ziyād took charge of Iraq, he demanded that payment be made in *Wāfī* coins, obliging them to pay in coin fragments. So the tax officials of the Banu Umayya acted corruptly, until ʿAbd al-Malik b. Marwān acceded to the throne. He examined the two weights and set the weight of a silver coin at seven tenths of a *mithqāl*, leaving the *mithqāl* as it was. Then, later, [the Umayyad governor] al-Ḥajjāj once again required fractions of coins be used, until ʿUmar b. ʿAbd al-ʿAzīz reversed the policy once again. Then it was reversed after him until the time of [the Abbasid caliph] al-Manṣūr,[26] to the point that southern Iraq fell into ruin. So al-Manṣūr removed all coin taxes on wheat and barley, instead applying crop sharing, and these were the two main sources of revenue for southern Iraq. Some few seeds, date palms and other trees were still subject to taxation, as people today are forced to pay in coin fractions and other stock.

24 R. 255/869–256/870.
25 A prominent Abbasid scribe and vizier, d. 272/885.
26 R. 136/754–158/775.

Al-Muhtadī replied, "God forbid that I subject people to injustice, whether it has been done before or not. Remove this [tax] from the people." And al-Ḥasan b. Makhlad[27] said, "If the Commander of the Faithful removes this tax, the ruler's revenue per year will decrease by twelve million dirhams." Al-Muhtadī replied, "I must affirm a right and remove a wrong even if I leave the treasury in ruins."

The third type are [wrongs done by] the administrative scribes, because they are the secretaries trusted by the Muslims with the integrity of their wealth, what they pay and what they are due. So the magistrate [overseeing the grievance tribunal] should monitor them as long as they are charged with those duties. If they veer away from what is right, in increase or decrease, with regards to revenue or expenditure, the magistrate should make them comply with the regulations and provide compensation for their transgressions.

It is said that it reached [the caliph] al-Manṣūr, may God be pleased with him, that a number of his administrative scribes had been inflating and falsifying records. He ordered them brought to him for disciplining. One of them, a young man, recited as he was being lashed:

> May God prolong your life in righteousness
> and glory, O Commander of the Faithful!
> We seek your pardon, and, if you grant us it,
> Then surely you are the protector of all the worlds!
> And we, the scribes, who have done wrong,
> leave us to the scribes most noble [i.e., the angels recording people's deeds]!

So the caliph ordered their release and showed favor to the young man, since he had demonstrated intelligence and honesty.

And in these three above types, the magistrate tending to grievances does not need to wait for a complaint to come from someone claiming to have been wronged.

The fourth type is wrongs suffered by those holding salaries or pensions that are either inadequate or tardy or that have not been

27 Another Abbasid scribe and vizier, d. 269/882.

administered properly. This should be referred back to the ministry charged with granting just stipends and rectified, examined for what had fallen short or been withheld up to that point. If it was taken by the responsible officials, it should be recovered from them. And if they had not taken it, its restitution should come from the treasury.

When a military commander wrote to [the Abbasid caliph] al-Ma'mūn that the soldiers were running wild and looting, he replied, "If you had been just with them, they would not have run wild. And if you had given them their due, they would not have looted." And he dismissed him and lavished their wages upon them.

*The fifth type is the restoration of expropriated property, which is of two sorts. The first is government property (*sulṭāniyya*) seized by unjust officials, such as properties seized from their owners either out of some desire for them or to transgress upon the owners. If this is discovered by the magistrate of the grievance tribunal in the process of looking through administrative matters, he should order it returned before any complaint of wrongdoing is made to him. If he does not so discover it, then it depends on the owners bringing the complaint to him. It is permitted for the magistrate, when such a complaint of wrongdoing is brought, to refer to governmental records. If mention is found in them of that property having been seized from its owner, this should be acted on. And the magistrate should order it returned. He needs no direct evidence (*bayyina*) testifying to this,[28] as what he finds in the records suffices.*

So it has been reported regarding 'Umar b. 'Abd al-'Azīz, may God have mercy on him, that he went out one day to pray. A man happened upon him who had come from Yemen to complain of a wrong done. He said:

> You call to your door those wronged and in confusion,
> And now one wronged has come to you from a distant abode.

He replied, "What is your grievance?" The man answered, "[The earlier caliph] al-Walīd b. 'Abd al-Malik[29] seized some of my property

28 Y has the problematic phrasing: and he does require direct evidence.
29 R. 86/705–96/715.

unlawfully." [The Caliph] called out, "O Muzāḥim [i.e., one of his assistants], bring me the records of the lands held by the Persian nobility (*al-ṣawāfī*)!" He found there that God's servant al-Walīd b. ʿAbd al-Malik had appropriated the property of so-and-so. So he said, "Remove this from the record and let it be recorded that this property is being returned to him, with double its revenue given to him."

The second type of expropriated items are what the powerful have taken control of and used out of sheer force, as if they were the owners. These cases depend on the wronged parties bringing the cases and cannot be recovered from their possession except via four means: either by the admission of the expropriator and their confession, by the magistrate of the grievance tribunal learning of it, in which case he can rule on it based on that knowledge,[30] *by the required number of notarial witnesses (*bayyina*) testifying either to the expropriator's act or that the usurped property belonged to its owner, or finally by the accumulation (*taẓāhur*) of reports to such an extent that conspiring to produce them would have been impossible. And doubt should not shake this since, being that notarial witnesses base their testimony regarding properties on the predominance of reports [regarding who legally owns them], the ruling of those overseeing the grievance tribunal [on the basis of so many reports] is even more reliable.*

*The sixth type [of wrongs done] is found in the supervision of pious endowments, which consist of two types: public (*ʿāmma*) and private (*khāṣṣa*). As for public endowments, [the magistrate] begins by looking through them even if no complainant has come forward with a grievance, so that he can facilitate their proper function and have them operate according to the conditions set by the endower. These he can discover through one of three ways: either from the records of those judges delegated to assure legal rulings [regarding the endowments] are followed, from the state administration's records of transactions that mention the endowments in question, or, finally, from what was written down in [the endowment's records] at some earlier period and which seems to be authentic, though no notarial witnesses can testify to it, since there is no one disputing them. And the [magistrate's] remit is even broader in private endowments.*

30 Y includes the qualification: though it be disagreed on (*ʿalā ikhtilāf fīhi*).

*As for private endowments, his examination of these depends on a person associated with the endowment claiming to have been wronged in a dispute. In such cases of dispute, he acts according to what establishes rights in the eyes of a judge (*ḥākim*). He is not permitted to refer back to government records or what is found in prior, older written records [from the endowment] if there are no vetted notarial witnesses to testify to them.*

*The seventh type [of wrongs done involves] enforcing rulings that had been issued by judges (*quḍāt*) [but were then unenforced] due to the judges being too weak to enforce them and due to their inability to implement them on the losing party because of his strength or standing.* But the magistrate of the grievance tribunal is stronger and has more authority, so he can enforce the ruling for those whose property has been expropriated or who need to pay what they are responsible for.

*The eighth type involves looking into matters regarding public interest that those officials responsible for market inspection (*ḥisba*) are unable to tend to*, such as someone doing unacceptable things openly that they cannot prevent, transgressing [upon others] in the public streets in such a way that they cannot stop it, or impinging on others' rights such that they cannot rectify it. In all such cases, [the magistrate] holds them accountable to the rights of God most high and orders them compelled to perform what is required.

*The ninth type is overseeing public worship such as Friday prayers, Eid, Hajj, and legitimate warfare (*jihād*)* and assuring that there is no negligence in these and that all their conditions are fulfilled. For the rights of God and obligations due Him are the most deserving of fulfillment and performance.

The tenth type involves looking into disputes between parties and ruling between them, during the course of which he should not depart from what the truth and right requires and entails. ***It is not permitted for him to rule beyond the rulings made by judges*** **(al-ḥukkām wa'l-quḍāt).** And it may be that the [manner of] ruling in the grievance tribunal eludes those responsible and that they are then unjust in their rulings and exceed the bounds of what is allowed for in that setting.

§

There are ten aspects in which adjudications by the grievance tribunal are distinguished from those done by judges:

First, the authority and gravitas enjoyed by the official overseeing the grievance tribunal but not by judges allow better for preventing disputants from mutual recrimination and stopping wrongdoers from overweening conduct and quarreling.

Second, the grievance tribunal can go beyond the narrow realm of the required to the wider realm of permissibility, so the magistrate has a wider purview.

Third, he enjoys increased ability to intimidate and investigate types of indicia and **circumstantial evidence** *(*shawāhid al-aḥwāl*)* in a manner not available to judges (*ḥukkām*), allowing him to ensure rights and discover what or who is denying them.

Fourth, he can match those whose wrongdoing is evident with remonstration and those whose enmity is manifest with rectification and discipline.

*Fifth, he can take more time than judges (*ḥukkām*) in repeated questioning of the disputants when their affairs are unclear and their rights recondite, to look in depth into causes and their conditions. This is not available to a judge, who, when one of the disputants asks him to rule on the matter, is not permitted to delay. But this is permitted to the magistrate of the grievance tribunal.*

*Sixth, he can refer recalcitrant disputants to the mediation of trustworthy parties to sort out the dispute between them and to reach a mutually acceptable agreement. The judge (*qāḍī*) cannot do this without the agreement of both disputants.*

*Seventh, he has latitude in ordering the two disputants detained and investigated (*mulāzama*) if indications have made it clear that blatant lying has occurred and to require bail be offered as far as is permitted to him, to encourage the disputants to deal fairly and to discourage them from lying and blatant denial.*

Eighth, he can hear the testimony of witnesses of unsure standing, in a manner beyond the custom of judges (*quḍāt*) hearing [only] the testimony of upstanding witnesses.

Ninth, he can force the witnesses to swear an oath if he has doubts regarding them if they have changed their testimony, and he can bring a larger number of them in order to remove any doubt and suspicion he has. The judge (*ḥākim*) cannot do this.

Tenth, he is permitted to begin by calling the witnesses and asking them what they know regarding the issue disputed by the two parties. The normal practice of judges (*quḍāt*),[31] meanwhile, is initially to place the burden of bringing direct evidence on the plaintiff, and they only hear this evidence after the plaintiff has been questioned.

These are ten aspects in which the conduct of the grievance tribunal and that of judges differ regarding disagreements and disputes. And those two offices are equal in other regards. Now we will clarify in detail these ways in which the two offices differ, God willing.

§

Section:

In light of the aforementioned, a claim brought before the grievance tribunal must fall into one of these three situations: either the claim is accompanied by something that bolsters it, by something that weakens it, or by neither of these two. If it is accompanied by something that strengthens it, then it would be one of six potential situations, which differ in degree regarding the strength of the claim:

The first of such situations is as follows: that the claim is accompanied by documentary evidence (*kitāb*) containing available vetted witnesses [i.e., to testify to the document's contents]. What then concerns the magistrate overseeing the grievance tribunal regarding such a claim are two elements: first, that the magistrate begins by calling the witnesses to give their testimony; second, that he rejects the [defendant's] denial due to his circumstances or circumstantial evidence regarding him.

If the magistrate of the grievance tribunal is someone of lofty status like the caliph, a delegated vizier, or a regional governor, when he brings forth the witnesses he should take into consideration the [status] of the two disputants, as good governance (*siyāsa*) requires.

31 Y has: *al-ḥukkām wa'l-quḍāt*.

If their standing is also high, he should attend to the case himself. If the parties are of middling standing, he should delegate this to his judge (*qāḍī*) [to be adjudicated] in the magistrate's presence. And, finally, if the parties are obscure, then the judge should adjudicate it at some distance from the magistrate.

It is said that al-Ma'mūn, may God be pleased with him, used to sit to hear grievances on Sundays. One day he rose from the session, and a woman wearing rags approached him, saying:

O best of those who are fair, one granted wisdom,
O leader by whom the land has been illuminated,
To you, pillar of dominion, now complains a widow,
Set upon by a lion she cannot resist
He has usurped from her lands that had once been secured her,
Since her kin and children have all parted ways.

Al-Ma'mūn looked down in thought, then raised his head and said:

By less than what you've recounted have patience and resilience been tested,
And the heart been afflicted with sadness and grief.
Now is the time of the noonday prayer, so go
And bring the opposing party on the appointed day.
Saturday's session will be devoted to us,
And I will give you justice, or else the session on Sunday.

So she departed and then came to the session on Sunday before anyone else. Al-Ma'mūn asked, "Where is your disputant?" She answered, "The person right beside you, the Commander of the Faithful's son, al-'Abbās." Al-Ma'mūn told his judge, Yaḥyā b. Aktham,[32] though it is also said that he spoke to his vizier Aḥmad b. Abī Khālid,[33] "Sit her and him [i.e., al-Ma'mūn's son] down and adjudicate between them." He sat them down and did so in the presence

32 A famous judge, jurist, and caliphal advisor, d. 242/857. He was appointed as the judge and then the *maẓālim* magistrate of the new capital of Samarra in 237/851–2; Ibn al-Jawzī, *Muntaẓam*, 11:250.

33 Aḥmad b. Abī Khālid al-Aḥwal, (d. 212/827–8).

of al-Ma'mūn, and her voice began to rise. One of the chamberlains rebuked her, so al-Ma'mūn said to him, "Leave her be, for truth has made her speak and falsehood has left him silent." And he ordered that her lands be returned to her. What al-Ma'mūn did in his procedure with these two, being in their presence but not taking up the case himself directly, is what was called for by good governance (*siyāsa*) in two ways. First, the ruling would either have been in favor of his son or against him. It is not permissible for him to rule in his son's favor, though it would be to rule against him. Second, the other disputant was a woman who was beneath being addressed by al-Ma'mūn, while his son was of too lofty a station for anyone other than [the caliph] to force him to relinquish her right. So he had the case heard in his presence by someone who was suitable to engage with the woman in addressing her claim and assessing proof, while al-Ma'mūn himself, may God be pleased with him, enforced the ruling and upheld her right.

The second situation regarding the strength of a claim is that it is accompanied by a written list of vetted witnesses, but they are not present. In such a case, what distinguishes the magistrate of the grievance tribunal [from the judge] are four things:

*First, he can intimidate the defendant and thus hasten his admission, since the magistrate has powers of intimidation [that the judge lacks], which obviates the need to hear direct testimony (*bayyina*).*

Second, he can proceed to having the witnesses brought to the court if he knows their location and if this does not cause them undue hardship.

*Third, he can have the defendant detained (*mulāzama*) for three days with the possibility of extending this period if he deems it appropriate in light of the strength of evidence and indications of truth.*

Fourth, he can examine the claim and, if the issue is financial, he can force the defendant to find a guarantor. And if the issue is some property, like land, he can place a freeze on it so that its ownership cannot be transferred, and he can turn over its use and yield to a trustworthy party who can oversee it. If time passes, and it seems unlikely that the witnesses will come, the magistrate of the grievance tribunal can renew his inquisition of the defendant regarding his properties or income. And Mālik b. Anas, may God be pleased with him, allowed asking the defendant about his involvement and claim of ownership in such cases, though al-Shāfiʿī and Abū Ḥanīfa did not allow it. The magistrate of the grievance tribunal can utilize what is permitted and is not restricted just to what is required. If the [defendant] responds in a way that terminates the dispute, the magistrate rules accordingly. **If not, he sorts it out between them based on what the Sacred Law (*sharʿ*) obliges.**

The third situation regarding the strength of a claim is that the document accompanying it contains [the names of] witnesses who are present but not vetted (*ghayr muʿaddalīn*) by the judge (*ḥākim*). In this case, what distinguishes the magistrate of the grievance tribunal is that he can immediately proceed to inquire into this by bringing the witnesses and examining their quality. He could find that they fall into one of three categories: either they are people of some standing and respectable conduct, in which case trusting their testimony is more compelling; they turn out to be, after examination, of poor standing (*ardhāl*), so they cannot be relied upon, though they could still function to intimidate the opposing party; or they are of a middle tier, in which case [the magistrate] can, after examining them, have them take oaths, either before or after he has heard their testimony, if he deems that appropriate.[34]

In the case of hearing the testimony of these two types [i.e., the first and the third], the magistrate has three courses of action available. Either he can hear their testimony himself and rule on that basis; he can turn hearing their testimony over to a judge (*qāḍī*), who would then pass this back to him, in which case ruling on that basis would depend on his [i.e., the magistrate's assessment], since the judge is only permitted to rule on the basis of the testimony of a witness he deems reliable; or he can turn hearing their [testimony] over to vetted witnesses [i.e., notaries]. If he charges them with transmitting the testimony to him, [those notaries] are not required to investigate the character of those [witnesses]. But if the magistrate tasked them with providing him whatever testimony of the witnesses proved sound and acceptable, then those notaries would be required to assess the

34 Y and one ms. of M have *akhlāq* instead of *aḥlāf*.

witnesses according to what would be required for their testimony to be accepted, such that they could offer up that testimony, its reliability having been established, and a ruling arrived at accordingly.

The fourth situation regarding the strength of a claim is that the document accompanying it contains the testimony of witnesses who are vetted and upstanding but deceased, but the document itself has been authenticated. In this case, what distinguishes the magistrate of the grievance tribunal is three items: firstly, intimidating the defendant in such a way that he is compelled to be truthful and admit the truth; secondly, he can ask [the defendant] how he came into control or possession [of the disputed property], since it is possible that his reply could help the truth become clear; and thirdly, uncovering the situation by [questioning] the neighbors of the [disputed] property or of the two disputants so that the magistrate can arrive at clarity regarding the truth and identify which party is in the right.[35]

If he is unable to arrive at a [resolution] via any of these three routes, he should turn the case over to respectable intermediaries who inspire obedience, are familiar with the two parties, have experience with the issue at dispute, and who can compel them, via repetition over an extended period, to both be truthful and reconcile.[36] Either this all results in [a ruling] for one of the parties,[37] **or the ruling is made according to the procedure of the judge (*ḥukm al-qaḍā'*).**

The fifth situation regarding the strength of a claim occurs when the plaintiff produces [a document] that concerns the contested issue in the defendant's handwriting. Here, the grievance tribunal requires the defendant be questioned regarding the handwriting. *If he is asked: "Is this your writing?" and he acknowledges it, he needs to be asked about the authenticity of the content. If he acknowledges the authenticity of its content, then he confirms [the accusation] and is then obliged to accept the resolution [based on his] admission. If he does not admit the authenticity of the content, some magistrates of the grievance tribunal would rule against him based on his writing if he had admitted it was his, even*

35 Y adds: and tell the rightful party from the false one.

36 Y has: truthful or to reconcile.

37 Thus Y and several mss of M, while one has: Either this results in mutual truthfulness and reconciliation...

if he did not admit the accuracy of the contents, seeing this as a type of circumstantial evidence according to prevailing conventions (wa-jaʿala dhālika min shawāhid al-ḥuqūq iʿtibāran bi'l-ʿurf). Scrupulous scholars and all the jurists among them,[38] however, argue that the magistrate is not allowed to rule on the basis of the writing alone (*mujarrad al-khaṭṭ*), unless [the accused] also acknowledges the document's contents, **because adjudicating in the grievance tribunal does not allow (*lā yubīḥu*) what the Sacred Law (*sharʿ*) forbids.**

In such a case, adjudicating in the grievance tribunal entails referring back to what [the defendant] recalls regarding his writing. If he says, "I wrote this so that he would offer a loan to me, but he never lent me anything," or "so that he would pay me a certain price regarding what I sold him, but he never paid." This is something people occasionally do. In such cases, the magistrate of the grievance tribunal should utilize what means of intimidation they have according to how they view the situation and what would strengthen evidence, and then the case should be handed off to intermediary [officials]. If it does not result in reconciliation and agreement, **then the judge (*qāḍī*) should arrive at a ruling for the two parties by having them swear oaths.**

If the [defendant] denies the handwriting, some magistrates of the grievance tribunal compare it to other examples of their writing, having them write out text repeatedly until it becomes impossible for them to feign or dissimulate [in their script]. Then the magistrate compares the two writing samples. If they resemble one another, he rules accordingly against the defendant. This is the position of those scholars who consider writing to be dispositive and rule on its basis. But the position of leading scholars (*muḥaqqiqūn*) is not to undertake this [comparison of writing] to arrive at a ruling directly but rather to intimidate the defendant. Indeed, the suspicion [of the defendant's guilt] is weaker when he has denied it is his writing than when he acknowledges it is his. And suspicion is removed altogether if the two scripts are totally unlike. [At this point], it is the plaintiff's turn to be intimidated. And then the two are handed over to

38 Y has: What had been held by a group – and they are the majority – is that....

intermediary [officials]. If it does not result in a ruling,[39] **then the judge (*qāḍī*) should arrive at a ruling for the two parties by oaths.**

The sixth situation regarding the strength of a claim is when an accounting ledger (*ḥisāb*) is produced regarding the contents of the claim, and this situation occurs in cases of financial and commercial transactions (*muʿāmalāt*). The accounts ledger can be one of two types. Either it is the accounts ledger of the plaintiff or that of the defendant. If it is the plaintiff's accounting ledger, then it merits less suspicion, and in such cases the grievance tribunal then examines how well ordered the ledger is. If it is disordered and likely that falsification occurred, then it is dispensed with. This suggests the claim is weak rather than strong. If it is well ordered and organized, however, and it has been carefully copied, then this inspires more trust. It follows that it should be used to intimidate [the other party] on the basis of what indications it contains. Then the two parties should be handed over to intermediary [officials], then, [if there is no resolution,] to a final ruling [i.e., by a judge].

If the accounts ledger is the defendant's, then it strengthens the claim even more. Either it is deemed to be his writing or that of his scribe. If it is alleged to be his writing, then the magistrate of the grievance tribunal should ask the defendant, "Is this your writing?" If he acknowledges it, he is asked, "Do you know what it is [i.e., its contents]?" If he admits he is familiar with it, he is asked, "Do you acknowledge its authenticity?" If he acknowledges its authenticity, then by these three admissions he has acknowledged the contents of the accounts ledger, and he is held accountable to that admission. But if he acknowledges that it is his writing yet denies familiarity with its contents and does not acknowledge its authenticity, then those magistrates of the grievance tribunal who accept ruling on the basis of writing [in documents] rule against him on the basis of his accounts ledger even if he does not admit its authenticity. [Such magistrates] consider trust in such [documents] to be stronger than confidence in unacknowledged written records (*al-khaṭṭ mursal*), since the delivery of an item will not be noted in an accounts ledger

39 Y has: result in reconciliation....

until it has been received. But the position of leading scholars (*muḥaqqiqūn*),[40] and it is the position of the jurists, is that [the defendant] is not ruled against on the basis of an accounts ledger the authenticity of whose contents he has not acknowledged. **Rather, it offers more use as a means of intimidation than an unacknowledged document would on the basis of the above-mentioned differences between the two types [of documents] in customary practice (*'urf*).** Then the two are referred to intermediary [officers, and, if there is no resolution,] then to a settlement by a judge (*qaḍā'*).

If the handwriting is attributed to the [defendant's] scribe, the defendant is asked concerning this before his scribe is. If he acknowledges the document's contents, he is held accountable for them. If he does not acknowledge them, his scribe is asked about them. If the scribe denies they are his, this weakens suspicion. If he is a dubious person, then the magistrate should intimidate him [into divulging something], though not if he is trusted. If he acknowledges the writing is his and acknowledges its contents, he becomes a witness against the defendant, who is ruled against on the basis of this testimony provided the scribe is upstanding (*'adl*) and provided [the magistrate] holds one can rule on the basis of one witness and the oath [of the plaintiff], either because of his school of law (*madhhab*) or out of political authority or policy concern (*siyāsatan*) called for by the circumstances of the case. For in the grievance tribunal the circumstances of cases can alter rulings. And in each case, there is a limit to what intimidation is used that cannot be exceeded, determined by the situations of each case.

§

Section on if the claim is accompanied by something that weakens it.

There are six situations in which it is accompanied by something that weakens it, which contrast with the situations in which it is strengthened and in which the intimidation [employed by the magistrate] shifts from being deployed against the defendant to being deployed against the plaintiff.

40 Y has: And the majority have held....

The first situation is that the claim is met with a document with witnesses who are available and whose testimony proves the falseness of the claim. And this can be of four sorts. Firstly, that they testify that what he claimed he had actually sold. Secondly, that they testify to his having admitted to having no basis for the claim he was making. Thirdly, that they testify that his father, whom he had claimed had transferred the property, admitted that there was no basis for the claim he was making. Fourth, that they testify for the defendant that he is the owner of what [the plaintiff] is claiming, testimony that proves false his claim and obliges[41] that he be disciplined in a manner appropriate to his status. If he says, as people occasionally do, that this testimony to the effect that the goods had been sold was actually [describing] the property being offered as collateral (*rahn*) or as a compelled sale (*iljā'*), then the book listing sales should be examined. If it notes that it was not a case of putting up collateral or a compelled sale, this casts doubt on the claim. And if the book does not include this, the claim is bolstered. And intimidation should be wielded against whichever of the two parties is appropriate considering the circumstances. [The magistrate] should also inquire from neighbors and those who have interacted with the parties. If something emerges that requires reinterpreting the contents of the document, the magistrate should do so. If nothing does, then the signature of the notaries to the sale is the most compelling evidence for a ruling.

On the question of asking the defendant to swear an oath that the sale really took place, not as offering security or under severe duress, jurists have disagreed on the permissibility of this due to it differing from what he had originally claimed. Abū Ḥanīfa, may God be pleased with him, along with part of the Shāfiʿī school, have held that having the defendant swear such an oath is permissible because what he has claimed is a possibility. Others from the Shāfiʿī school have not allowed it, since what he had previously acknowledged contradicts his later claim.[42] The judge (*qāḍī*) of the grievance tribunal should act in the laws (*qawānīn*) he applies according to the circumstances of the cases.

41 Y adds in here: of the grievance tribunal.

42 Y summarizes these arguments but does not attribute them to any school.

And along those lines, if the claim being made is for a debt that is owed, and the defendant produces a document exonerating himself from that, but the plaintiff states that he had signed to this effect before he had actually been paid but was then never paid, having the defendant swear an oath is as has been mentioned previously.

The second situation is that the document countering the claim being made has upstanding witnesses who are absent. This can be of two types.

First, that the denial it includes provides some explanation, such as "[The claimant] has no right to this property because I bought it from him and paid him its price. And this document notarizes this with witnesses." In this case, the defendant is making a claim based on a document whose witnesses are absent, which makes it like situations discussed above. [The magistrate] has more authority and increased leeway for action and the right to use [evidence], as the indication here is stronger and the circumstantial evidence (*shāhid al-ḥāl*) clearer. If ownership is not established by the document, [the magistrate] can intimidate either party according to what the circumstances entail. He should summon the witnesses if possible, setting an appointed time for them to appear, and he should refer the two parties to intermediary [officials]. If this results in a mutually agreed-upon settlement, then the case is finished. He can omit hearing the witnesses once they have arrived.

If the case is not concluded through reconciliation and settlement, [the magistrate] focuses on investigating the matter by consulting the two parties' neighbors and those living around the disputed property. At the time of such investigation, the magistrate of the grievance tribunal can choose one of three dispositions depending on what his reasoning leads him to on the basis of the indications and circumstantial evidence (*shawāhid al-ḥāl*); [first], he can remove the disputed property from the defendant's control and surrender it to the plaintiff until some direct evidence of a sale is produced; [second], he can place it in the care of a trustworthy administrator who can safeguard its productive use for the party with legal right to it; or, [third], he can affirm its belonging to the defendant but sequester it from him, assigning a trusted administrator to preserve its productive use. The magistrate of the grievance tribunal takes one of these three courses of action so long as one of two situations obtain, either the truth emerges through investigation or the witnesses come to present their testimony. If there is no hope of them doing so, then the case should be settled between the two parties. If the defendant asks for the plaintiff to be made to swear an oath, [the magistrate] should have him do so, and this would be dispositive for the matter between them.[43]

And the second type is when the [defendant's] denial includes no explanation, [such as] his saying, "This property is mine, and this claimant has no right to it." And the testimony [found in] the document against the claimant can be of two types, either to his admission that he has no right to it or to his admission that it is the property of the defendant. [In both cases], the property is affirmed as belonging to the defendant and cannot be stripped from him. As for sequestering the property from him, with its productive use and yield protected, for the duration of the investigation and [referring it to] intermediaries, this should be considered depending on the circumstantial evidence pertaining to the two parties and the reasoning of the magistrate of the grievance tribunal until a ruling is reached between the two parties.

As for the third situation, it is that the witnesses of the document opposing the claim are present but not vetted as upstanding, in which case the magistrate of the grievance tribunal deals with them in the manner we presented on the plaintiff's side in terms of their three possible situations. And he should take care to consider whether the denial includes an explanation or not. And the magistrate of the grievance tribunal acts according to what we described earlier, relying on his best judgment on the basis of circumstantial evidence (*shawāhid al-ḥāl*).

The fourth situation is that the document's witnesses are upstanding but deceased, so it provides no ruling except that it can be used to intimidate [a party] as called for by the investigation and then in

43 M: *battan baynahum* / Y: *banā'an baynahum.*

arriving at a final ruling on the basis of what the document contains in terms of explained or unexplained denial.

The fifth situation is that the defendant counters with a written document signed by the plaintiff and containing evidence that proves his falsehood in his claim, in which case the magistrate acts according to what we described earlier regarding signed documents. And [the use of the document] to intimidate is done after consideration of the circumstances of the case.

And the sixth situation is that an accounts ledger is produced regarding the claim, and it proves the falsity of the claim. In this case, the magistrate acts according to what we described earlier in relation to accounts ledgers. And intimidation, investigation, and continuation of the case should be done in consideration of the circumstances of the case. Then the ruling is made if there is no hope of another way to resolve the dispute.

§

Section: If the claim is not accompanied by anything strengthening or weakening it, then the magistrate of the grievance tribunal should take care to look into the condition and nature (*ḥāl*) of the two disputants and what seems more probable (*ghalabat al-ẓann*). The conditions of the two parties' [situations] must be one of three types: first, the preponderance of probability (*ghalabat al-ẓann*) favors the plaintiff; second, it favors the defendant; and, third, the two are equal in this regard. And what this preponderance of probability influences regarding one of the two parties is the intimidation used against them and the intensity of investigation. It is not the basis of a ruling on the case.

If the preponderance of probability lies with the plaintiff and doubt is directed at the defendant, this could be because of three reasons. First, that the plaintiff, though he lacks proof to produce, is weak and deemed pliant, while the defendant is influential and powerful. If [the plaintiff] has claimed that [the defendant] expropriated a house or property, in such cases it seems most probable that someone so docile and subordinated would not dare to launch a claim against someone so influential and strong [i.e., without good reason].

Second, that the plaintiff is a person well known for honesty and trustworthiness, while the defendant is well known for lying and betrayal. The preponderance of probability is thus that the plaintiff is truthful in his claim.

Third, that their circumstances and conditions are equivalent, except that it was known that the plaintiff had existing control or possession over [the disputed item], while there is no known reason for the defendant to have novel control or possession.

In these three situations, the magistrate of the grievance tribunal should pursue two courses of action. First, he should intimidate the defendant due to the suspicion that has been cast upon him. Second, he should ask him about how he came into a degree of possession and control over the disputed item. Mālik b. Anas, may God be pleased with him, allowed the judge to do this in his school of law if there is suspicion. So the magistrate of the grievance tribunal is even more enabled to do so.

And it may be the case that the defendant, if they are of high status, recoils at being placed on equal footing with his disputant in court and thus concedes the claim of his opponent without contest. Such is the story of [the Abbasid caliph] Mūsā al-Hādī. One day he sat for the grievance tribunal, with [the scribe] 'Umāra b. Ḥamza[44] standing beside him in a place of honor. A man among those who had come to present their grievances came forward, claiming that 'Umāra had expropriated land of his. Al-Hādī had 'Umāra sit with the man for a trial. ['Umāra] said, "O Commander of the Faithful, if the property is his, then I will not oppose him in the matter. If it is mine, then I grant it to him rather than sell off my place in the court of the Commander of the Faithful."

And it may be that the magistrate of the grievance tribunal subtly restore to the complainant their right while preserving the dignity of the party complained against[45] or that he arrange it indirectly so as to preserve someone's dignity from the accusation of prejudice or

44 'Umāra b. Ḥamza Ibn Maymūn, a well-known scribe and governor, d. 199/814.

45 Y's text is much clearer in meaning here, including the additional phrasing *al-mutaẓallam minhu*, which M omits. M instead includes what is likely a dittography of the word *maṭlūb*, which appears again several words later.

depriving people of their rights. Such a case is what ʿAwn b. Muḥammad reported regarding people from the Marghāb River by Basra. They brought a dispute regarding [the caliph] al-Mahdī to his judge, ʿUbaydallāh b. al-Ḥasan al-ʿAnbarī.[46] But neither the caliph nor al-Hādī after him surrendered [the disputed land] to them. Then [Hārūn] al-Rashīd came, and the people came to present the complaint to him. [His vizier] Jaʿfar b. Yaḥyā [al-Barmakī][47] was the magistrate of the grievance tribunal. But [the caliph] still did not return the land to them. So Jaʿfar b. Yaḥyā purchased it from al-Rashīd for twenty thousand dirhams and granted it to those people. He said, "I did this so that you would know that the Commander of the Faithful is obstinately unyielding in his right, so his slave purchased it and gifts it to you all." Ashjaʿ al-Sulamī[48] recited, regarding this incident:

> The floating comet rendered it with his own hands, while its people
> Were in the station of the Unarmed Star [i.e., Spica].
> They were certain they had lost it, that they would soon perish,
> Lost to fate on a day of predicament.
> He pried it away for them when they were,
> Held to their fate between the chest and throat.
> No one could have pried it away but him,
> The noble man alone can resolve the impossible.

It is possible that what Jaʿfar b. Yaḥyā did came from his own initiative in an effort to shield al-Rashīd from engaging in wrongdoing. Or al-Rashīd arranged this so that neither his father nor his brother would be associated with injustice, and this seems more likely. Whichever was the case, the people were restored their right, while dignity was preserved and humiliation spared.

If the preponderance of probability lies with the defendant, this could be because of three reasons. The first is that the plaintiff is well known for wrongdoing and betrayal, while the defendant is well

46 A famous judge, d. 168/785.
47 One of the famous Barmakid dynasty of viziers, d. 187/803.
48 A poet close to the Barmakids, d. *circa* 196/811.

known for fair dealing and trustworthiness. The second is that the plaintiff is a degenerate lowlife while the defendant is free from such vices and virtuous. In this case, he can be required to swear an oath due to his iniquity. The third is that there is an accepted reason for the defendant to have taken possession or control of the disputed item, while there is no evident reason for the plaintiff's control or possession.

In these three situations, the preponderance of probability lies with the defendant, while the plaintiff is the object of suspicion. The school of Mālik, may God have mercy on him, is that, in such cases, if the person's claim involves an existing item, the [judge] should not hear it until some reason is given explaining the claim. If the claim involves money that is owed,[49] the judge should not hear it until the plaintiff has provided direct evidence that he had engaged in commercial relations with the defendant. And al-Shāfiʿī and Abū Ḥanīfa, may God be pleased with them, did not hold this regarding judicial procedure.[50] **As for the procedure of the grievance tribunal, the subject is dealt with according to what is permissible, not what is required.** Such things are thus permitted when suspicion arises or due to obstinacy. And the magistrate can engage in more intensive investigation using those means that will arrive at the truth, while still respecting the defendant, according to the increased latitude in procedure. If the matter reaches the point of both sides swearing oaths, which is the final stage before arriving at a final ruling and which neither the judge nor the magistrate of the grievance tribunal can deny once one side has requested it despite threats and admonition, if the [plaintiff] chooses to separate his various claims and to swear oaths on some of them during different sessions due to his stubbornness and lowly conduct, what a judge's procedure would require would be not denying this separation of claims and oaths. The magistrate of the grievance tribunal, by contrast, can instruct the claimant to group all his

49 The Baghdādī edition has *māl al-ama*, which makes no sense, while the Enger edition and Y have *māl al-dhimma*.

50 Y lacks this sentence but includes, "and the likes of this have been reported from Aḥmad [b. Ḥanbal]."

claims together once his obstinacy becomes evident and have the disputant swear all their oaths in one instance.

If the two disputants are in equipoise, with corresponding direct evidence (*bayyina*), and no indication or probability makes the proof of one party preferrable to the other, then the magistrate must address each with moral admonition (*'iẓa*). This applies equally to the judge (*quḍāt*) and the magistrate of the grievance tribunal.[51] After such admonition, what distinguishes the magistrate of the grievance tribunal [from the judge] is the use of intimidation (*irhāb*) against the parties because of their equivalent arguments, then investigating the basis of the claim and how the property changed possession. If the investigation turns up which party is in the right, this dictates the ruling. If the investigation does not yield what settles the dispute, the magistrate should refer them to intermediary officials drawn from respected neighbors or clan elders. If they cannot succeed in resolving the dispute, **then it must be settled by a judge**. This is the final stage of their matter and is determined by what the magistrate sees as appropriate to settle the case originally brought before him.

§

It may be the case that the magistrate of the grievance tribunal is brought issues of particular legal difficulty or complexity, **and those present in the session and scholars there might guide him and elucidate the matter**. He should not condemn their initiative or be too haughty[52] to act on it in resolving the case.

Such is the case in what al-Zubayr b. Bakkār reported from Ibrāhīm al-Ḥarāmī, from[53] Muḥammad b. Ma'n al-Ghifārī, that a woman came to 'Umar b. al-Khaṭṭāb, may God be pleased with him, and said, "O Commander of the Faithful, my husband fasts all day and prays all night. I'd hate to complain about him if he is acting in obedience of God." 'Umar replied, "What an excellent

51 The word *quḍāt* is missing in the al-Baghdādī edition of M, but it is present in the Enger edition, and the sentence makes no sense without it.

52 M: *yastakthiru* / Y: *yastakbiru*.

53 The al-Baghdādī edition incorrectly has *bin* instead of *'an*, which is found in Enger.

husband you have." She repeated her complaint, but he merely repeated his reply. Then Kaʿb b. Sūr al-Asadī [sic; his actual name is al-Azdī][54] said to him, "O Commander of the Faithful, this woman is complaining to you about her husband being distant from her by night." ʿUmar, may God be pleased with him, replied to him, "As you have understood her words, judge you between them." Kaʿb said, "Bring me her husband," and he was brought forth. He said, "Your wife is complaining about you." The husband replied, "Regarding food or drink?" Kaʿb said, "Neither one." Then the wife recited:

O wise judge, guided by prudence,
His prayer mat has enticed my partner away from my bed,
His worship has rendered him an ascetic in the sheets,
He sleeps there neither by day nor night.
I give him no praise as pertains to ladies,
So render judgment, O Kaʿb, and do not hesitate.

The husband retorted:

Yes, I've been made an ascetic in her bed and bridal chamber,
But I'm a man dumbstruck by what was revealed
in the Chapter of the Bees and the Seven Long Suras.
The Book of God puts fear of weighty things in the heart.

Kaʿb answered:

She has rights over you, man,
Her share of four, which all reasonable folk know.
So give her all that, and leave off the excuses.

Then [Kaʿb] said to the man, "God has allowed two or three or four wives for you. So you have three days and nights for worshipping your Lord. And she gets a day and a night." ʿUmar said to Kaʿb, may

54 A Successor and judge, d. 36/656.

God be pleased with him, "I don't know which of your two accomplishments I'm more impressed by, that you understood her concerns or the ruling you rendered for them. Go now, for I've appointed you judge of Basra."

This ruling by Kaʿb and ʿUmar's enforcement was a ruling according to what was permissible rather than what was obligatory, since the husband was not strictly required to give his wife one night nor to respond to her enticements to bed provided that he had, at some point, consummated the marriage.[55] **This shows that the magistrate of the grievance tribunal should rule by what is permissible rather than what is strictly required.**

§

Section on the delegation (*tawqīʿāt*) of cases by the magistrate of the grievance tribunal:

If the magistrate of the grievance tribunal delegates cases brought before him by a complainant, the official to whom he delegates it can be one of two sorts: either he is authorized by his position (*wāliyan*) to rule on it or he is not.

If he already has a mandate authorized by his position, such as the case being assigned to a judge (*qāḍī*) to adjudicate, then this delegation can entail one of two possibilities: either it grants permission to render a ruling, or it grants permission to investigate the case and involve intermediary officials. If it grants permission to render a ruling, then ruling between the parties is permitted for the official on the basis of their original mandate (*wilāya*). The delegation merely emphasizes this, and this mandate to render a ruling would not be affected by any limitations in its phrasing even if it only granted

55 This is the main Shāfiʿī opinion on this issue, while the Ḥanbalī school requires the wife's sexual needs be met at least once every four months. The Mālikī school requires the husband to tend to his wife's needs unless there is some mitigating circumstance, otherwise a judge has grounds to end the marriage. The Ḥanafī school has no clear rule, only obliging sex frequently enough to maintain the wife's chastity. See Ibn Ḥajar, *Fatḥ al-bārī*, 9:373; Wahba al-Zuḥaylī, *Mawsūʿat al-fiqh al-islāmī* (Damascus: Dār al-Fikr, 2010), 8:318.

permission to engage in investigation in the form [of the dispute] or to mediate between the two disputants.

If, on the other hand, the delegation restricted the mandated official from ruling on the case, he should not render a ruling between the parties. [In this situation], the restriction has the effect of removing the official from [the position] of rendering a ruling between those two parties while leaving his authority intact for all other cases. This is because, since mandated authority (*wilāya*) can be of two types, general or specific, removal of such authority can also be general or specific.

If the magistrate's act of delegation did not prohibit the official delegated to from rendering a ruling on the case when[56] it tasked him with investigation,[57] then some have held that his procedure (*naẓar*)[58] remains as it generally would be in terms of permitting him to render a ruling between the parties. This is because being mandated to perform part of one's normal functions is not a prohibition from performing others. Others have held that it does entail such a prohibition. Still others have held that, rather, the official is prohibited from rendering a ruling and is restricted to what the delegation specified in terms of investigation and mediation on the basis of what is implied (*faḥwā*) by the delegation.

It is then determined whether the delegation mandated mediation or involving intermediaries. If it did, the official is not required to again take up the case after such mediation. If, however, the delegation mandated investigating the case, the official is required to follow up, since the delegation was a request for information regarding the case, and the official must provide a reply [to the magistrate]. These are the rules regarding a delegation to someone already holding a mandate of authority.

As for the second situation, namely that the magistrate delegates to an official who does not have an existing mandate of authority (*wilāya*), such as delegating a case to a jurist or expert witness (*shāhid*), then this delegation would be one of three types: first, to

56 The Baghdādī edition of M and Y both have *ḥīn* here (when), while Enger's M has *ghayr*, which seems to make no sense.
57 Y adds in *wa'l-wasāṭa* (and involving intermediaries) here.
58 Baghdādī's edition of M has *nadhar*, while Enger's M and Y have *naẓar*.

investigate the form (*ṣūra*) of the case; second, to engage in arbitration or involve intermediaries; or, third, to render a ruling.

If the official is delegated to investigate the form of the case, he should do so and conclude whether and what he could provide the magistrate as acceptable testimony to arrive at a ruling. If the official concludes that nothing of this sort exists, the evidence can still provide information that, **while not admissible as testimony, can be used in the grievance tribunal as the sort of evidence indicating that one of the two parties merits intimidation or further investigation.**

If the delegation is for arbitration or involving intermediaries, then the official should do so. And this does not strictly depend on what the delegation specified in terms of arbitration and mediation, since arbitration and involving intermediaries does not require official appointment (*taqlīd*) or mandated authority (*wilāya*). Rather, delegating mediation entails[59] appointing an intermediary chosen by the delegator and bringing the two parties before him of their own volition (*ikhtiyāran*).[60] If the arbitration or involvement of intermediaries results in a resolution between the two disputants, the official is not required to follow up. He would testify to this resolution if he were called to do so. If the arbitration and mediation does not result in a resolution, the official can testify to what both sides acknowledged in his presence and provide this to the magistrate of the grievance tribunal if the two parties again bring their case before it. He is not, however, required to provide this to the magistrate if the two parties do not return.

If the delegation is to render a ruling for the two parties, this is a mandate in which one must consider the specific language of the delegation, so that the official's actions will accord with what is required. In such a case, the delegation can be one of two forms.

59 M has *yufīdu*, while Y has *yuqayyadu* (is limited by), orthographically differing only in a dot. In both cases, the text could be read with a similar meaning.

60 While M has *ikhtiyāran*, Y has *ijbāran*, meaning by "by compulsion." The two words are orthographically similar, so it is not clear if this is al-Māwardī misreading Abū Ya'lā's text, al-Māwardī intentionally altering it, or if some change was introduced into one of the two texts by copyists. Of course, the meaning is dramatically different.

The first is that the official is charged with granting the disputant's request, in which case he should consider what he is asking regarding the wrong he claims, and the case is limited to that issue. If the disputant requests mediation or an investigation into the case, the mandate of delegation requires this of [the official] and is limited to that.

Regardless of whether the mandate of delegation takes the form of a command, like "Grant the disputant's request," or in a comment like, "What is your opinion on addressing his request?" this is an act of delegation. It does not entail authorization that would result in a binding ruling, so it is a less serious matter.

If the complainant requests a ruling on the issue of dispute, the disputant must be named and the issue of contention specified in order for the authority to rule on the matter to be competent. If the disputant is not identified or the issue of contention not specified, there is not competent authority to rule on the issue, since [the official in question] has neither a general mandate of authority to apply broadly nor a specific mandate, as the specifics are unknown. If the complainant names his disputant and specifies the issue of contention, the mandate of delegation should be referred to regarding granting the complainant's request. If the delegation took the form of a command and then the official acted to respond to the request and grant it, then the official's mandate of authority and his ruling on the case is valid. And if the delegation took the form of seeming only to ask the official to inquire into the case and consider granting the request, in governmental matters (*a'māl sulṭāniyya*) such a delegation has the effect of a command, as is well known in customary usage. As for rulings regarding religious obligations (*aḥkām dīniyya*), a party among the jurists have allowed this in light of custom and consider mandated authority to be legitimate in this case. Another group has not allowed it and does not consider mandated authority to be valid in this case without an explicit command accompanying it that specifies the empowerment of the official for this purpose.

If the complainant had requested a delegation of authority to issue a ruling for the disputants, and the magistrate charged the delegate with granting this request, those who consider custom definitive in this would consider the mandated authority valid, while those who only looked at the phrasing of the delegation would not,[61] because the party has asked for a delegation of authority to rule and not for the ruling itself.

The second situation for delegations of authority is that the official is charged with responding to the disputant by granting them what they had asked. So he takes the matter up anew according to its merits (*mā taḍammanahu*), and what the delegation contains or specifies is what defines the nature of the delegated authority. If this is the case, there can be three possible situations: a situation of full [authority], a situation of permissibility, and a situation that is neither of these two cases.[62]

As for the situation in which the delegation of mandated authority is full and total (*kamālan*), this includes two elements. The first is the mandate to take up the case. The second is the mandate to arrive at a ruling. It would involve [the magistrate] stating, "Look into this matter between the complainant and their disputant and issue a ruling for the two parties according to what is right (*al-ḥaqq*) and what the Sacred Law (*al-sharʿ*) requires." If this is the case, then this course of action is permitted, **since rulings must be according to what the Sacred Law obliges anyway.** This statement in acts of delegation is merely descriptive. It does not constitute a [new] condition. If the act of delegation includes both looking into the case and ruling on it, this is a full delegation that constitutes a legitimate appointment and authorization.

As for the situation in which the act of delegation is permissible (*jāʾiz*) while not reaching the level of being complete, this would be if it included the mandate to issue a ruling but not to look into the dispute, in which case [the magistrate] would state in his delegation, "Issue a ruling between the complainant and their disputant," or, "Judge between them." The mandate of authority would be considered legitimate in this situation, since judging and issuing a ruling

61 Y has the subjects in question approving (*ṣaḥḥaḥa*) the *wilāya* here, while M has the *wilāya* as the subject of the intransitive *ṣaḥḥat*. Y seems grammatically sounder in this context.

62 The Baghdādī edition of M has *yakhlū ʿan al-amrayn*, while Enger has *yakhruju ʿan al-amrayn*. Y has *takhlū ʿan al-amrayn*.

only take place after consideration of the case. So the mandate to issue a ruling implies a mandate to look into the case, since the former necessitates the latter.

As for the situation in which the delegation is neither complete nor permissible, this is if the magistrate states in his act of delegation, "Look into the issue between them." Such a delegation does not constitute an authorized mandate, because looking into a dispute might entail arbitration or involving intermediaries, which is permissible, or it might entail issuing a ruling that would follow on that. And both of these are equally possible [interpretations]. As a result of this ambiguity, this does not constitute an authorized mandate. But if the magistrate states, "Look into the issue with an aim of ascertaining the truth (*bi'l-ḥaqq*)," some hold that this would constitute an authorized mandate, since this truth or right is entailed in the statement. But others hold that no such mandate is constituted, since mutually agreed resolution (*ṣulḥ*) and mediation might also both be entailed, even if not necessarily. And God knows best.

Appendix III

Davānī's *Dīvān-e Maẓālem* – Edited Persian Text

NOTES ON PREPARING THIS CRITICAL EDITION

I have been able to locate eight manuscripts of this text. This edition is based on five of them, two in Istanbul, one in the Digital Library of the Āstān-e Qods-e Rezavī in Mashhad, and two at the University of Tehran.

There are two manuscripts in the Central Library of the University of Tehran, numbers 6/1021 (dated 939/1532) and 4/7265 (copy dated 1005/1598). These two manuscripts were used by Hossein Moderressi (as Ḥosayn Modarresī Ṭabāṭabā'ī) in an edition of the treatise published as "Dīvān-e Maẓālem," in *Farhang-e Īrānzamīn*, vol. 27 (Tehran: 1366/1988), 98–118 **(henceforth Ṭab.)**. Unfortunately, the editor does not provide any critical apparatus noting divergences in the manuscripts he used. At the time of writing, I have not been able to access these manuscripts directly. Reliance is therefore on Moderressi's published edition for their contents.

Another ms. is located in the Āstān-e Qods-e Rezavī Library in Mashhad (*thabt* #37368, 25b-31a, **henceforth Mash.**). This manuscript was copied in the 11th/17th century.

The first of the Istanbul manuscripts, Nuruosmaniye 4989, 59b-63a (**henceforth Nur.**) is held in the Nur Osmaniye Library and appears to be a nineteenth-century copy of an earlier copy and is included in an undated compendium (*majmū'a*). The other treatises in the compendium, which consists of 255 folios, deal primarily with different theological issues, such as cosmology and ontology. Some were written by well-known authors, such as al-Sharīf al-Jurjāni, Davānī, and Miskawayh.

The second Istanbul ms. (Mehmet Nuri Efendi 184–194 folios, **henceforth Mehm.**) is part of a compendium that probably dates from the mid nineteenth century, as it refers to *fatāwā* appearing in the *Bahjat al-fatāwā* of Yenişehirli Efendi (d. 1156/1743) and treatises by Ibn ʿĀbidīn (d. 1252/1836). The compendium includes primarily legal treatises, such as short works by Khayr al-Dīn al-Ramlī (d. 1081/1671), numerous treatises by Ibn ʿĀbidīn, and others by Anatolian scholars such as Ahmet Reşid Efendi Sıdkızade (d. 1250/1834).

Three other manuscripts are: Ms. 53/4862, University of Tehran; Ms. 6/101, Marashi Najafi Library in Qom; and Ms. 2/4 Shaykh ʿAlī Ḥaydar, Mashhad. I have not been able to access these.

In my opinion, the Mehm. ms. is the least reliable, since it adds in numerous pious formulas not found in either the Nur. or Mash. mss., includes several large lacunas where difficult sections would otherwise appear, and on several occasions fails the *lectio difficilior potior* test. The Nur. ms. includes a few grave copyist errors. The two manuscripts used in the Ṭab. edition are dated from within decades of the author's death, and they accord well with the Mash. ms. as well. We have thus favored the Ṭab. edition and the Mash. ms. in this critical edition.

After completing this critical edition of Davānī's treatise, I learned that an edition had previously been published by Dr. Ẓahīr al-Dīn Aḥmad in the Urdu-language journal *Majallah-yi Taḥqīq* under the title "*ʿAllāma Davānī kī fārisī rasāʾel*" (see *Majallah-yi Taḥqīq* 9 [1987]: 112–182, specifically 113–124). The editor does not mention which manuscripts he relied on, however, and he restricts himself to offering definitions for some technical terms and identifying some persons mentioned in the text.

CRITICAL APPARATUS:

- The proposition *beh* in the text is often joined with its object in the mss. When it functions as a Persian preposition it will be rendered as a separate word. When it is the Arabic preposition '*bi-*' in an Arabic construction it will be left attached.

- Indefinite *yā*'s in this text are often written as small *yā*'s similar to the *kesre'ye eḍāfe*. The text does not generally include markers of *eḍāfe* on the final *hā*'. The indefinite *yā*' will be rendered as '*ay*' after final *hā*'.
- Text that is drawn directly from al-Māwardī's *al-Aḥkām al-sulṭāniyya* or paraphrases it closely will be underlined.
- All paragraph separations are interpolations for help in reading.

[Ṭab, 106, Mash 25b, Nur 59b, Mehm 127b]

[ديوان المظالم للدواني][1]

بسم الله الرحمن الرحيم و به نستعين فی التتميم

[و له الحمد على افضاله العميم][2] و الصلاة على نبيه المبعوث لرفع معالم الدين القويم و دفع مظالم [الجيل][3] الذميم و على آله و صحبه المقتفين لأثره الكريم السالكين لصراط (sic) المستقيم.

[و بعد][4] اين بعض مسائل [ا]ست متعلق بديوان مظالم كه از كتب معتبره مثل أحكام سلطانی كه أقضی القضاة [امام][5] أبو الحسن ماوردی كه امام عصر خود بوده تصنيف كرده و معتبران ائمه اعتبار نموده اند و عمل به آن كرده و[از][6] ديگر كتب و قواعد استنباط می رود.

اميد كه واليان احكام كه ولاة اهل اسلام اند مطالعه نمايند و به آن عمل كنند تا مستحقّ ذكر جميل در دنيا و اجر جزيل در عقبی گردند و بوسيلهٔ ايشان حقوق مسلمانان ضايع نشود[7] و نظام مصالح بندگان خدای تعالی اختلال نيابد[:]

اولاً اين مسائل معروض حضرت سلطنت شعار مكرمت دِثار خلف الملوک الكبار و السلاطين ذوی الاقتدار ملاذ البريا من الضنک و الهلک نظام السلطنة و الدولة و الدين علاء الملک[8] ايده الله تعالى لتأييد الدين و وفقه لنظم مصالح المسلمين می گردد[،]

چه در اين ايام كه اين فقير از وطن مألوف و سكن معروف دور افتاده در خطهٔ لار پای افتقار در دامن انكسار كشيده اتفاق تلفيق [آ]ن افتاد ان شاء الله تعالى بمطالعهٔ

1 Sic in Mehm., not in Nur., Mash., or Ṭab.
2 Not in Ṭab.
3 Sic in Mash. and Nur. Ṭab. has the rare form خيل (*khayal/khayl*, vanity, pride), while Mehm. has حيل (*ḥiyal*, plural of dodge or scheme), which is not in agreement with the adjective الذميم.
4 Sic in Nur., not in Mehm, Mash. or Ṭab.
5 Sic in Ṭab., Nur. and Mehm., not in Mash.
6 Sic in Mehm., not in Ṭab., Nur. or Mash.
7 Sic in Ṭab., Mash. and Nur. Mehm. has نكردد.
8 Sultan Neẓām Malek ʿAlā' al-Molk of Lār. The exact dates of ʿAlā' al-Molk's reign are unclear. Zambaur has him ruling from 883/1478 onward, and his reign would have ended at some point between then and the death of his successor, Hārūn, which is reliably put at 927/1521; J. Aubin, "Références pour Lar medieval," *Journal Asiatique* (1955): 494.

آن [Mehm 128a] و عمل بر آن موفق [شوند][9] تا سبب رضای باری و [رفاهیت و رستگاری][10] باشد و [الموفق معان و الله المستعان][11].

نموده میشود که نظر در مظالم عبارت [ا]ست از یاری دادن مظلومان و دفع تعدی ظالمان[،]

پس حاکم دیوان مظالم باید که سیاست و مَهابت او بیش از قضاة باشد بلکه با قدری بزرگ و هیبتی عظیم و نفاذ حکم و ورع تمام باشد مثل سلطان یا امیر یا وزیر یا کسی که اهلیت یکی از این امور داشته باشد تا مردم از مهابت و جَلالت[12] او ترسان باشند و از تزویر و دروغ و حیله اجتناب نمایند تا حق ظاهر شود و مهمات مسلمانان [معوَّق][13] نماند چه قاضی[14] [Mash 26a] [دوافع][15] شرعیه که صورت مشروع داشته باشد و الحقیقه تزویر باشد می باید شنید[،] و به این سبب حقوق مردم در عقدهٔ تسویف و تعطیل می افتاد و صاحب دیوان مظالم بحسب رأی سدید و حدس صائب می تواند[16] که بعض از این امور مسموع ندارد و حکم نماید چنانچه بعد از این مفصلا معلوم خواهد شد[،]

و دیگر آنکه مهابت و سیاست صاحب دیوان مظالم مانع است آنکه به حیل و تزویر حقوق را اخفا کنند[،]

و بتوجه حاکم عادل صاحب دیوان مظالم بی [تأخیر و تعلُّل][17] حق ظاهر می شود و اموری که در محاکم چند سال [معوَّق می ماند][18] به یک مجلس که حاکم دیوان مظالم متوجه شود فیصل می یابد و حق ظاهر می شود[،] و اگر سلطان خود متوجه حکم دیوان مظالم نشود و کسی بجهة آن نصب نکند مقصّر [باشد][19] در حق رعایا.

و حضرت رسالة پناه مصطفی علیه افضل الصلوات و التحیات بنفس انفس خود نظر در مظالم فرموده [Nur 60a] و بطریق دیوان مظالم حکم کرده میان زبیر بن العوام و یکی

9 Not in Ṭab.
10 Inverted in Ṭab.
11 Mehm. has و الله المستعان و علیه التکلان.
12 Nur. has جلادت.
13 Mehm. alone has حقوق. This and below are instances of *lectio difficilior potior*, where the copyist has read the conventional word *ḥuqūq* instead of the rarer word *moʿavvaq*.
14 Nur. includes the word را here.
15 Mehm. alone has قاضي را وقايع.
16 Ṭab. has می تواند بود.
17 Inverted in Mehm.
18 Mehm. has حقوق می نماید.
19 Not in Mehm.

از انصار که میان ایشان در شرب آب [مناقشه][20] بود و بستان زبیر بالاتر [و اسبق][21] بود و حضرت حکم فرمود که «اسق یا زبیر ثم للانصاری» یعنی اول تو که زبیری آب ده بستان خود را بعد از آن انصاری آب دهد پس انصاری گفت «و انه ابن عمتک»[22] [Mehm 128b] یعنی از جهة آنکه او پسر عمه تواست پس حضرت رسالت پناه غضب فرمود و فرمود[23] «ای زبیر آب را [روان][24] کن تا زمانی که به هر دو کعب رسد بعد از آن رها کن».[25]

و قبل[26] از آن منقول است که سلیمان پیغمبر[27] حکم فرمود میان دو زن که دعوی فرزندی طفل[28] می کردند و هر یک می گفتند که فرزند من است[29] و سلیمان تحقیق حال به این وجه فرمود که گفت فرزند را به دو پاره کنم و هر یکی[30] را پارهٔ بدهم [،] آن کس که اجنبی بود اضطرابی ننمود و آن کس که فی الواقع مادر بود اضطراب بسیار نمود و گفت که از آن او باشد[،]

و قصهٔ یوسف [علیه السلام][31] که زلیخی نسبت به یوسف می کرد که قصد او کرده و حال آنکه امر بر عکس بود[32] و بر این وجه فیصل نمودند که ببیند که پیراهن یوسف از پیش دریده یا از قفا [Mash 26b] و چون دیدند که پیراهن یوسف از[33] قفا دریده معلوم کردند که زلیخی خلاف واقع می گوید و یوسف [علی نبینا و علیه الصلوة و السلام][34] صادق است چنانچه در قرآن مجید مذکور است[35] از این قبیل است که بقرینه حکم شده.

20 Sic in Nur., Ṭab. and Mash., Mehm. has منافسه.
21 Sic in Nur., Ṭab. and Mash., not in Mehm.
22 Ṭab. has لانه ابن عامتك.
23 Ṭab. has گفت.
24 Mehm. has رها.
25 Cf. al-Māwardī, *Aḥkām*, 102. See *Ṣaḥīḥ al-Bukhārī*: *kitāb al-musāqā*, *bāb shurb al-aʿlā qabl al-asfal*.
26 Ṭab. has مثل.
27 Mehm. and Ṭab. add *ʿalā nabīyinā wa ʿalayhi al-ṣalāt wa'l-salām*.
28 Ṭab. has طفل دعوی.
29 Sic in Nur. and Mehm. Ṭab. has از آن من است, while Mash. has آن من است.
30 Ṭab. has کدام.
31 Not in Nur., Ṭab. or Mehm.
32 Ṭab. adds the phrase که زلیخا قصد یوسف نموده بود.
33 Mash. includes an erased قصا here.
34 Only in Mash.
35 Quran 12:23-29.

و هیچ یک از خلفاء [چهارگانه][36] نظر در دیوان مظالم نکرده اند چه در زمان ایشان بی انصافی [آن سان][37] غالب نبود و بحکم قضا مخالفت مرتفع می شد[،][38] بعد از آن چون تزویر و زور[39] و تغلب و تطاول در میان مردم ظاهر شد عبد الملک [بن] مروان روزی تعیین کرد برای نظر در حال متظلمان و چون او را در مسأله اشکالی می شد از قاضی ابو ادریس ازدي[40] که مفتی آن زمان بود استفسار می کرد و چون جور حاکمان و متغلبان و تزویر مردم زیادت شد و احتیاج بزیادتي توجه بود عمر [بن][41] عبد العزیز بنفس خود به نظر در مظالم مشغول می شد تا مظالم بنی امیه باز می داد و در این امر با ایشان سختگیری می کرد تا بحدّی که با او گفتند که می ترسیم که در عاقبت این ره[42] خللی واقع شود در جواب گفت هر روز که از آن ترسم[43] کمتر از روز قیامت خواهد بود.[44]

پس از خلفاء عباس مهدی پس هادی پس رشید پس مأمون[45] به نفس خود به دیوان مظالم مشغول می شدند [Mehm 129a] و منقول است که مأمون در دیوان مظالم روز یکشنبه می نشست و فخر الدین رازی در مناقب شافعی می گوید که[46] هارون الرشید در آخر محمد بن حسن شیبانی حاکم دیوان مظالم[47] ساخته بود و ابو یوسف که هم شاگرد ابو حنیفة بود قاضی ساخته بود[،] درآخر خلفاء عباسي مهتدي[48] نیز به ولایت دیوان مظالم مشغول می شد[،][49]

و قبل از اینها ملوک عجم این معنی را از ارکان قواعد عدل و سلطنت دانستندی و در این باب اهتمام تمام به جای آوردندی و در جاهلیت قریش نیز همین طریق پیش گرفتند چنانچه عباس و ابو سفیان و رؤساء قریش در مکه سوگند یاد کردند و عهد بستند که به ردّ مظالم مشغول شوند و نگذارند که هیچ کس بر کسي [Mash 27a] ظلم کند [Nur 60b] و حضرت رسالت پناه علیه افضل الصلوات در آن وقت بیست و پنج ساله

---

36 Sic in Ṭab., Nur., and Mash., not in Mehm.
37 Sic in Ṭab. Nur. has ایشان; Mash. lacks this entirely.
38 Cf. al-Māwardī, *Aḥkām*, 103.
39 Mehm. adds غلبه.
40 Sic. in Nur. and Mehm. Ṭab. has ʿAwdī.
41 Not in Nur.
42 Ṭab. has مرد. Mash. has رو.
43 Mash. has ترسیم.
44 Cf. al-Māwardī, *Aḥkām*, 104.
45 Ṭab. adds ایشان here.
46 In Nur. a dittography of the word که occurs here.
47 Fakhr al-Dīn al-Rāzī, *Manāqib al-imām al-Shāfiʿī*, ed. Aḥmad Ḥijāzī al-Saqā (Cairo: Maktabat al-Kulliyyāt al-Azhariyya, 1406/1986), 71.
48 Nur. adds و here.
49 Cf. al-Māwardī, *Aḥkām*, 104.

بود[50] در خانه عبد الله بن جدعان و بعد از نبوت آن حضرت فرمود «ما يزيد الاسلام الا شدّة»[51] يعنی زياده نمی کند دين[52] اسلام بر اين امر الا سختی و محکمی يعنی دين اسلام ناسخ آن نيست بلکه آن را محکمتر[53] می سازد.[54]

و بايد که سلطان[55] يکروز برای نظر در اين ديوان معين گرداند[56] و اگر سلطان رجوع ولايت ديوان مظالم به شخصی ديگر کرده باشد بايد که هم روزه به اين امر اقدام نمايد و پادشاه عدالت پناه مؤيد من عند الله بمزيد النصرة و العدل و الاحسان السلطان بن السلطان بن السلطان ابو النصر حسن بيگ بهادر خان[57] انار الله برهانه در اين باب اعتنا و اهتمام تمام داشتند و ارکان دولت او که به ايالت ممالک موسوم می شدند[58] همين طريقه سلوک می نمودند و آن روز را روز ديوان بَزه مسکين نام نهاده اند و در هفتهٔ دو روز برای همين مهم می نشستند و الحق تا آن حضرت و اخلاف اشراف او بتخصيص پادشاه بزرگجاه انجم سپاه[59] يعقوب بيگ خان[60] اخلد الله فراديس الجنان در ميان بودند زمانه نورانی بود و کافهٔ عباد الله و بلاد الله هم در مهد امن و امان بودند و مَيامن و برکات[61] در حرث و نسل ظاهر بود[،][62] [Mehm 129b]

اميد که بميامن اصحاب القلوب رفاهيتی در ميان مسلمانان ظاهر شود و از اين ظلم و بلا و ضيق و غلا خلاص يابند ان شاء الله تعالی[،] و همان اين معنی که عادت [اسلاف اشراف سلاطين لار از قديم الايام باز با اين مستمر شده که در يک هفته دو روز در

50 Ṭab. adds و با ايشان بود.

51 Mash. has ما يزيده. For this Hadith, see *Musnad Aḥmad Ibn Ḥanbal*: 1:190 (Maymaniyya print).

52 Nur. has اين.

53 Nur. has محکم.

54 Cf. al-Māwardī, *Aḥkām*, 106. Davānī draws this ḥadīth directly from al-Māwardī's text. For an approximation of that maxim, see *Musnad Aḥmad Ibn Ḥanbal*: 2:180 (Maymaniyya print), where the Prophet says in a sermon after the recapture of Mecca that, "*mā kāna min ḥilf fī al-jāhiliyya fa-inna al-islām lam yazidhu illā shidda...*," and *Ṣaḥīḥ Muslim*: *kitāb faḍā'il al-ṣaḥāba, bāb mu'ākhāt al-Nabī ṣ bayn aṣḥābihi*, where the Prophet says, "*lā ḥilf fī al-islām wa ayyumā ḥilf kāna fī al-jāhiliyya lam yazidhu al-islām illā shidda.*"

55 Sic in Nur., Mash., and Mehm., inverted as و سلطان بايد in Ṭab.

56 Cf. al-Māwardī, *Aḥkām*, 106.

57 Ūzūn Ḥasan, the great leader of the Aqquyunlu (r. 851/1457–883/1478, died in Tabriz aged fifty-two); Woods, *Aqquyunlu*, 123. Mash. has خوان.

58 Sic in Nur., Mash. and Mehm. Ṭab. has می شوند.

59 Sic in Nur., Mash. and Mehm. Ṭab. has بزرگ جمجاه إسکندر سپاه.

60 Abū al-Muẓaffar Ya'qūb b. Ūzūn Ḥasan Bayandur (r. 1478-90); see Woods, *Aqquyunlu*, 128-47, 213.

61 Sic in Nur., Mash. and Mehm. Ṭab. lacks the و.

62 Cf. Qāḍī Ḥusayn Maybūdī, who wrote of his reign that "the people rest tranquil and carefree"; in Woods, 140.

بارگاه مجتمع می [شوند][63] و افاضل و][64] اصحاب وزارت و حجاب خود را در آن مجمع حاضر می کنند از این قبیل بوده[65] و چنانچه سابقاً نقل رفت روز یکشنبه که اول دیوان ایشان است موافق آن است که مأمون خلیفه تعیین کرده بود و در آن روز [فصل][66] قضایا دیوان مظالم می کرده.

پس باید که در آن مجلس بمقتضای احکام سلطانی عمل فرمایند و به نفس نفیس خود به غور معاملات و مهمات مردم رسند و بی پروای را دخل ندهند که خدای ندهند[67] که خدای تعالی از ایشان سؤال خواهد کرد و با آنکه حواله به دیگری کرده باشند از گردن ایشان ساقط نمی شود و اگر [Mash 27b] خللی واقع شود در امری[68] این خطاب با ایشان خواهد بود «یا راعی [السوء][69] شربت اللبن و اکلت اللحم و لم تجبر الکسیر[،]»[70] و باید که سهل الحجاب باشد[71] یعنی ارباب تظلم را به او راه باشد و در مجلس او حامیان و اعوان و قضاة و حکام و فقها[ء] و دبیران و گواهان و جمعی که اهل خبرت باشند حاضر باشند.

و نظر دیوان مظالم مشتمل است بر ده قسم[:][72]

اول نظر در تعدی حاکمان بر رعیت[،] پس باید که متفحص احوال حکّام باشد تا اگر ضعیف باشند قوة دهد و اگر ظالم باشند منع کند یا تبدیل[،] و عمر بن عبد العزیز در اول خلافت خطبه کرد و در آن گفت وصیت می کنم شما را به پرهیزکاری خدای تعالی غیر از آن فائده ندارد و رحم نمی کند خدای تعالی الا بر اهل آن و به خدای سوگند که اگر به سنّتی چند حق بودی که آن را می رانیده اند و من آن را زنده کردم [Nur 61a] و سنّتی چند باطل که زنده گردانیده بودند که من آن را می رانیده ام نخواستمی که قدر

63 Mehm. has شدند.

64 Bracketed section is missing from Mash.

65 Sic in Ṭab. Mehm. has the wording و افاضل و وزرا و حجاب. Omitted in Nur.

66 Nur. has فیصل.

67 Dittography has occurred in the Nur. ms, with the repetition of the phrase که خدای ندهد.

68 Mash. has در امری واقع شود.

69 Mehm. has *sinawwar.*

70 Cf. Mālik b. Dīnār's report: *qara'tu fī ba'ḍ al-kutub yujā'u bi-rā'ī al-sū' yawm al-qiyāma fa-yuqālu yā rā'ī sharibta al-laban wa akalta al-laḥm wa lam ta'wa al-ḍālla wa lam tajbur al-kasīr wa lam tar'ahā ḥaqq ra'āyatihā al-yawm antaqimu lahum minkum*; Abū Nu'aym al-Iṣbahānī, *Ḥilyat al-awliyā'*, 2:375.

71 Mash. has باشند.

72 In this list Davānī paraphrases and summarizes al-Māwardī's list, with the exception of the third item (see below). Cf. al-Māwardī, *Aḥkām*, 107-111.

یک فواق شتر زنده [باشم][73] آخرت خود را بصلاح آورید تا دنیای شما بصلاح آید[74]
[75]. [Mehm 130a]

دوم نظر در جور عاملان در تحصیل مال[،] تا اگر زیادتی گرفته باشند باز گردانند و اگر تسلیم [بیت المال][76] کرده باشند از آنجا باز دهند.

سوم نظر در محاسبات اهل دیوان[،] تا عدالت[77] ایشان در داد و ستد معلوم کند[،][78]

و در این سه قسم ا حتیاج به آن نیست که کسی از حاکم دیوان مظالم طلب کند بلکه می باید که خود بی طلب غیر به غور رسد.

چهارم نظر در تظلم ارباب وظائف و مواجب[79][،] تا اگر عمال بر ایشان حیف کرده باشند و حق ایشان کم کرده باشند اگر پیش عمال باشد از ایشان باز ستانند و به مستحقان رساند و اگر به بیت المال داده باشد از آنجا باز دهد[،] بعض از عاملان مأمون خلیفه به او نوشتند که لشکریان ظلم کردند و غارت کردند مأمون به او نوشت که اگر ترا عدل بودی ایشان ظلم نتوانستندی کردن و اگر ترا قوت بودی ایشان غارت نتوانستندی و او را عزل کرد.

پنجم نظر در مغصوبات[80][،] اگر در تصرف دیوان باشد و حاکم داند به أرباب آن رساند و اگر چه ایشان طلب نکنند[،] و اگر حاکم نداند هر گاه که خداوندان طلب کنند نظر در دفتر دیوان کنند اگر در آنجا ثبت باشد که فلان ملک از فلان مالک گرفته اند [Mash 28a] بمجرّد همین باز مالک رساند[81] و احتیاج به گواه و بیّنه نباشد[،] و اگر در تصرف دیگری باشد به یکی از چهار چیز از او باز توان گرفت[:] یا اقرار صاحب ید یا علم حاکم که خود داند که بغصب در دست[82] او است یا به بیّنهٔ مدّعی یا به استفاضت

73 Mehm. has بودمی.
74 Sic Nur. and Mash.; Ṭab. has آورند.
75 Davānī cuts out a short narrative clause from the Umayyad caliph's sermon; al-Māwardī, *Aḥkām*, 107.
76 Sic in Ṭab., Mash. and Mehm. Missing in Nur.
77 Sic in Ṭab. and Mehm. Nur. has عدل.
78 Here Davānī may be deviating from al-Māwardī's list, or he may be providing his own looser translation for al-Māwardī's *kuttāb al-dawāwīn* as the third group; cf. al-Māwardī, *Aḥkām*, 108-109.
79 For use of this term in administrative use, see Abū Bakr Tehrānī, *Ketāb-e Deyārbakreyye*, ed. Nejātī Lūghāl and Fārūq Sūdar, vol. 2 ([Tehran]: Chāpkhāne-ye Anjomān-e Tork, 1964), 529.
80 Sic Nur., Mash. and Mehm.; Ṭab. has در مغصوبات نظر کند.
81 Sic. in Ṭab. and Nur., Mash. has رسانند .
82 Sic in Ṭab. and Nur., Mash. has تصرف.

و شهرت زیرا که چون شهادت به استفاضه جائز است حکم حاکم به طریق اولی که جائز باشد.

ششم نظر در اوقاف[،] اگر وقف عام باشد رعایت شرط واقف نماید و به مقتضای آن عمل کند و در این صورة دفتر عاملان وقف یا عاملان سلطنت یا مکتوباتی که بر نفس حاکم صحت آن غالب باشد مثل پَروانجات سلاطین و حکام کافی است و اگر چه گواه نباشد و در این ماده احتیاج به طلب کسی نیست[،] و اگر وقف [Mehm 130b] خاص باشد و مستحق آن قومی[83] معیّن [باشند][84] موقوف بر طلب و تظلم ایشان باشد و بی طلب ایشان بر حاکم نظر در آن واجب نباشد مگر آنکه معلوم باشد که ایشان نمی دانند.[85]

هفتم تنفیذ حکمی که قاضی از تنفیذ آن عاجز باشد یا از جهت ضعف قاضی یا از جهت قوت و تعزز صاحب ید.

هشتم تنفیذ حکمی که محتسب از تنفیذ آن عاجز باشد.

نهم رعایت عبادات ظاهره و شعائر دین چون جمعه و عیدین و حجّ و عزا.[86]

دهم نظر میان خصمان و متنازعان تا حکم کند میان ایشان به وجه شرع در چیزی چند که قاضی را جائز نیست.

و فرق میان نظر حاکم مظالم و نظر قضاة از ده[87] وجه است[:][88]

اول آنکه می باید که شوکت و هیبت این حاکم بیش از قاضی باشد [Nur 61b] تا تواند که آن چه قاضی از آن عاجز است یا او را شرعاً جائز نیست به عمل آورد.

83 Sic in Ṭab and Nur., Mash. has قومی.

84 Sic in Ṭab., Mash. and Mehm. Not in Nur.

85 Interestingly, Davānī omits al-Māwardī's caveat that the *nāẓir* is not permitted to rule based on any private *waqf* documents that were not testified to (or notarized?) by upstanding witnesses. Cf. al-Māwardī, 111-112.

86 Davānī omits jihad from this list, an item mentioned by al-Māwardī.

87 Mehm. has دو.

88 Davānī's list tracks al-Māwardī's approximately, though it lacks point number eight on al-Māwardī's list, which addresses *maẓālim* rules on witnessing, and its points numbers seven and eight do not correspond to al-Māwardī's list. Note that Davānī's promised list of ten points only reaches nine.

دوم آنکه نظر این حاکم فراختر است از نظر قضاة چنانچه شرعاً او را چیزی چند جائز است که بر قاضی جائز نیست مثل آنکه در صورتی که او را شکّی باشد از[89] صاحب ید استفسار کند که چگونه به او رسیده تا حق و باطل آن[90] معلوم شود.

سوم آنکه می تواند که خصمان را بترساند[91] و بیم بسیار دهد و کشف اسرار و اسباب و امارات نماید تا حق ظاهر شود. [Mash 28b]

[چهارم][92] آنکه چون ظلم از کسی ظاهر شود او را تأدیب و زجر بلیغ نماید.

پنجم آنکه چون او را شکّ باشد با وجود آنکه بیّنه[93] اقامت کرده باشند حکم موقوف دارد تا وقتی که از قرائن و امارات و[94] اهل خبرت احوال نیکو تحقیق نماید و قاضی را در مثل این حال تاخیر حکم و موقوف داشتن نمی رسد مگر رضاء خصمان چنانچه[95] اگر بی رضای ایشان تأخیر کند آثم باشد.

ششم آنکه او را می رسد که حواله خصمان به متوسطان کند تا میان ایشان توسط کنند[96] و قاضی را نمی رسد الّا گاهی خصمان راضی باشند و اگر بی رضای ایشان کند خصمان را می رسد که [Mehm 131a] قبول نکنند و قاضی آثم باشد.

هفتم آنکه او را می رسد که گواهان را سوگند دهد چون او را شکّی باشد.[97]

هشتم آنکه او را می رسد که خصمان را سپارد و ملازمت فرماید تا زمانی که حقیقت حال ظاهر شود.[98]

نهم آنکه او را می رسد که گواهان را پیش خود طلبد و استماع شهادت ایشان کند و اگر [چه][99] دعوی محرّر چنانچه در محکمها معهود است نشده باشد بلکه عرض حال بر حاکم {کافی است چنانچه او معلوم کند که مقصود چیست.

89 Sic in Ṭab., Mash. and Mehm. Nur. has *ū*.
90 Mash. has او.
91 Ṭab. has ترسانیده.
92 Not in Mehm. From this point onward in this list, Mehm. omits the ordinal numbers.
93 Mehm. has را.
94 Mehm. has استفسار.
95 Ṭab. has که اگر.
96 Sic Ṭab., Mash. and Mehm. Nur. has میان توسط کند.
97 Cf. al-Māwardī, 112.
98 Sic in Nur. Mehm. has ظاهر کنند and Ṭab. has معلوم گردد. Mash. has ظاهر گردد. This item appears under point seven on al-Māwardī's list.
99 Missing from Mehm.

و قاضی را هیچ یک[100] از این امور نمی رسد[،] و چون مرافعه پیش} [101] حاکم دیوان مظالم برند اگر قرائن صدق مدّعی باشد مثل آنکه با او قبالهٔ مسجّل باشد به گواهان عدل مصلحت چنان باشد که یا گواهان را پیش خود خواهد و گواهی طلبد یا مدّعی علیه را انکار[102] و تخویف کند و اگر گواهان غائب باشند اول مدّعی علیه بترساند و تهدید و تخویف کند باشد که به قوت هیبت و سیاست مدّعی علیه اقرار نماید و از انکار باز آید و اگر نشود فرماید که گواهان را حاضر گردانند[103] اگر بر ایشان مشقتی زیاده نباشد و فرماید که مدّعی علیه را به موکل سپارند و کفیل از او بگیرند و اگر مصلحت در آن بیند ملک را بسپارد تا حقیقت معلوم شود[،] و اگر از گواهان گشاد نشود شاید که چنانچه مذهب مالک است از مدّعی علیه استفسار نماید که چگونه این ملک به دست او آمده و تخویف و تهدید بسیار بحسب مصلحت نماید و اگر چه مذهب شافعی و ابو حنیفه جائز نیست چه حاکم مظالم را می رسد که بحسب [Mash 29a] مصلحت عمل به آن چه جائز است نماید و لازم نیست که اقتصار بر واجب کند بخلاف قاضی که او را عمل بجواز جائز نیست و نظر او مخصوص به واجب است[،] و اگر عمل بغیر مذهب امام خود کند اصحّ آن است که او را روا نیست بخلاف حاکم مظالم که او را جائز است[،] و اگر گواهان حاضر باشند و تزکیه نرفته باشد باید که تفحص احوال ایشان نماید و اگر [مرده][104] باشند و معلوم الحال نباشند باید که تخویف مدّعی علیه نماید و از سبب ید [Nur 62a] باز پرسد و از همسایگان و نزدیکان و اهل خبرت تحقیق نماید و اگر خط مدّعی علیه [Mehm 131b] باشد مطابق دعوی مدّعی و مدّعی علیه معترف باشد که[105] خط او است بعض حکام[106] الزام او واجب دانسته اند چنانچه مذهب مالک است و بعض جائز نداشته اند و گفته اند الخط لا ینطق و تحقیق آن است که اگر حاکم مظالم عمل به آن نماید و الزام او کند این حکم منفّذ باشد و اگر گوید که این خط من است لیک هنوز مال به من نرسیده حواله به متوسطان و تخویف مناسب باشد و اگر گوید خط من نیست و امتحان کنند و مشابه خط او باشد بعض حکم بر او کنند و بعض جائز ندارند و لیکن محل تخویف

100 Sic Nur. and Mehm. Ṭab. has هیچ کدام.

101 This entire section was omitted from Mash. due to haplography on the phrase *ḥākim*.

102 Sic in all besides Mehm., which has تهدید. The copyist of Mehm. may have had a slipping of eye here since he moved the phrase تهدید و تخویف from the following line and put it here in place of انکار و تخویف.

103 Mehm. has کنند.

104 Sic in Ṭab., Mash. and Mehm., not in Nur. This section of Davānī's treatise digests several pages of complex material from al-Māwardī, eliding sometimes disconnected subjects while preserving an overall coherence. The situation of cases in which the witnesses who swore to the authenticity of documents being offered as evidence does appear, although in al-Māwardī the deceased witnesses have been established as upright; al-Māwardī, *Aḥkām*, 115.

105 Sic in Nur., Mash. and Tab., not in Mehm.

106 Sic in Nur., Mash. and Ṭab. Mehm. has علما.

و تهدید بلیغ باشد و اگر دفتر محاسبه مدّعی با[107] مدّعی علیه موافق دعوی باشد تخویف و ظن قوی لازم آید و اگر دفتر مدّعی علیه باشد و معترف شود که خط او است همان حکم اول دارد بلکه اعتماد و وثوق بر آن بیشتر باشد و اگر خط دیگری باشد که معتمد[108] بوده [به صحّت].[109]

و حقیقت آنکه بواسطهٔ نابودن دیوان مظالم بسی حقوق مسلمانان ضایع می شود و اهل تزویر استیلا بر حقوق و اموال مردم می کنند و چون [حال][110] بر قاضی عرض می کنند اولا عدول که اکثر غیر عدول اند در تحریر دعوی می پیچند و گاه هست که مدتی مدید بسبب آنکه می گویند که دعوی محرر نیست و حیله و تزویر بسیار می کنند به تعویق می افتد و بعد از آنکه [Mash 29b] از این مرتبه گذشت و گواه گذرانیدند در صیغه شهادت می پیچند و دقیقها[111] و حیلتها انگیز می کنند و استفتا[112] می کنند که این صیغه تمام نیست[113] و مدتی مدید در تاخیر و تسویف[114] می اندازند[،] و اگر از این ورطه خلاص حاصل شد در تزکیه می پیچند و مدتی مدید به آن مشغول اند[،] و در عبارت گواهی تزکیه همان حیل و تزویرات در کار است [،] و اگر از این نیز خلاص شدند دست در جرح می زنند و گواهان بر جرح می گذرانند و باز تزکیه گواهان جرح و جرح جرح و همچنین الی حیث لا یقف چنانچه گاه می باشد که جزوی مرافعه مدتها در میان است و فیصل [Mehm 132a] نمی یابد بمرتبه ای که متخاصمان ملول و بیزار می شوند[،] و اگر [خود][115] قضیه ای دعوی جنایتی باشد مقصود مطلقاً فوت می شود[،]

و این مفاسد همه بسبب عدم توجه حاکم دیوان مظالم است چه اگر حاکم عادل بی غرض بطریق احکام دیوان مظالم نظر کند اکثر آن است که به یک مجلس رفع خصومت می شود و حق ظاهر می گردد[،] و این فقیر بسیار از این جنس مشاهده کرده که مدتی مرافعه در محاکم معوّق[116] بوده و به یك لحظه[117] که بعض حکام صاحب احتشام متوجه شده اند مقطع[118] یافته و حق ظاهر شده زیرا که زمانه فاسد است و اکثر مردم خوف

107 Sic in all but Mehm., which has یا.
108 Sic in Ṭab and Nur. Mash. and Mehm. have معتمد او.
109 Sic in Nur. and Ṭab. Not in Mehm or Mash. At this point, Davānī's treatise diverges from al-Māwardī's text. Cf. al-Māwardī, 115.
110 Sic in Mehm. Not in Mash., Nur. or Ṭab.
111 Mehm. has دقتها.
112 Sic in Ṭab. Mash. and Mehm. Nur. has استعفا.
113 Mehm. has در تمام است یا بیست.
114 Mash. inverts these two terms.
115 Sic in Nur. and Mash. Not in Ṭab.
116 Mehm. has حقوق.
117 Mehm. adds در.
118 Mehm. has قطع.

خدای تعالی ندارند و لیکن از حاکم صاحب سیاست می ترسند و چون می دانند[119] که او متوجه به تحقیق حال است تزویر و حیل کمتر می کنند و حق ظاهر می شود.

در بعض کتب حنفیه مسطور است که عصام بن یوسف که یکی از ائمه حنفیه بوده در مجلس بعض حکام حاضر بود و شخص را[120] آوردند [Nur 62b] و نسبت دزدی به او می کردند و او منکر شد[،] [امام][121] مذکور حکم کرد که مدعی گواه بیاورد و اگر او را گواه نباشد سوگندی بر منکر باشد که این[122] دزد نکرده[،] آن حاکم قبول نکرد و گفت به حجاب و قِوام که تازیانه و عقّابین بیاوردند چون حاضر گردند و او را ده تازیانه زدند [Mash 30a] اقرار کرد [و رفت][123] و آن چیزها که دزدیده بود بعینها آورد و تسلیم مالک کرد[،] عصام [مذکور][124] منفعل شد و تعجب نمود[،]

و سرّ این است که حق سبحانه و تعالی چون زمام مصالح بعض از بندگان خود در کف کفایت بعض نهاد[125] و ایشان را حاکم ایشان ساخت[126] از آن جا که[127] کمال عنایت[128] او است بحکم ارباب الدول ملهمون[129] حکام را بالهامی مخصوص می دارد تا نظم مصالح آن طایفه بر دست و زبان ایشان جاری شود و از ایشان صورتهای غریب که از دیگری ظاهر نمی شود[130] مشاهده می گردد [امام][131] شافعی فرموده که سخن سلاطین را سهل ندانید[132] که سخن ایشان از زبان دولت صادر می شود[،]

119 Mehm. has بدانند.
120 Not in Mehm.
121 Sic in Nur. and Mehm. Ṭab. has ʿAṣām.
122 Not in Mehm.
123 Not in Mehm.
124 Sic in Mash., Nur. and Mehm. Not in Ṭab.
125 Mehm. has نهاده.
126 Mehm. has ساخته.
127 Nur. and Mehm lack the که.
128 Mehm. has.رحمت و عنایت
129 This saying seems to be quoted from the poetic biographical dictionary of the Khurasani migrant to India, Sadīd al-Dīn Muḥammad ʿAwfī (d. after 628/1230-31) (see Dekhodā, *Amthāl ū ḥekam*, 1:317). It appears in a near contemporaneous work to Davānī, namely that of the Ottoman scholar Ibn al-Khaṭīb Muḥammad b. Qāsim al-Amāsī (d. 940/1534), *Rawḍat al-akhyār al-muntakhab min Rabīʿ al-abrār*, ed. Maḥmūd Fākhūrī (Aleppo: Dār al-Qalam al-ʿArabī, 2003), 60. A very similar saying comes from Aḥmad b. Muḥammad al-Zardī al-Naysābūrī (d. 338/950), namely that God "aids with His inspiration" (*aʿānahu bi-ilhāmihi*) those whom He has put in political authority. He also quotes Ibn al-Muqaffaʿ as saying: "*tafaqqadū kalām mulūkikum idh hum muwaffaqūn li'l-ḥikma muyassarūn li'l-ijāba fa-in lam tuḥiṭ bihi ʿuqūlukum*)..."; Yāqūt al-Ḥamawī, *Muʿjam al-udabā'*, 1:463.
130 Mehm. adds in و.
131 Sic in Mehm. Not in Nur. or Ṭab. or Mash.
132 Sic in Ṭab., Mash. and Mehm. Nur. has ندانند.

و از جملهٔ آن چه این فقیر خود مشاهده کرده آن است که در بعض ولایت شیراز [حفت بالاعزاز][133] خونی[134] واقع شده بود [Mehm 132b] و این صورت را نوشته به دست شخص به عرض حاکم [شیراز که از امراء عظام بود][135] رسانیدند چون نظر حاکم بر آن شخص افتاد و بعض کلمات او استماع کرد در خاطر او در آمد که این شخص که این صورت باز نموده و این معنی[136] به عرض رسانیده قاتل است و این صورت از او صادر شده بعد از آن تحقیق کردند و همچنان بود که حاکم تحدس و تفرس کرده بود[،][137]

و همچنین در جوار این فقیر عورتی بود که قرض به مردم دادی و زنی را به او چیزی دادنی بوده و با او گفته که شخص ترا می خواهد که به نکاح در آورد او چنانچه رسم زنان باشد آن چه از حلی و البسه داشته پوشیده و شب به خانه آن زن رفته و او مردی را انگیز کرده بود که او را بکشد و خود و دختری که داشته اتفاق کرده اند و آن عورت را به قتل آورده و کسی بر این معنی مطلع نبود تا معلوم شد که در آن محله که آن زن می بوده [مرده ای را در چاه انداخته اند چون][138] تفحص نمودند ایشان منکر شدند بعد از آن مادر[139] و دختر [هر دو را در زندان سپردیم [Mash 30b] و جدا جدا طلبیدیم][140] و استفساری چند کردم تا معلوم شد که ایشان به شرکت مردی[141] کرده اند آن مرد بعد از طلب انکار بجدّ می کرد بعد از آنکه او را تخویف به تعذیب کردند بی آنکه بعمل آورند اقرار مفصل کرد چنانچه هیچ قید از آنچه می باید اهمال نکرد و به قصاص رسیدند[،]

دیگر شخص از حفاظ کازرون به بعض ولایات شیراز رفته بوده و چنانچه معهود این طایفه است به دریوزه و غیره چیزی چند حاصل کرده و در آخر روزی دو شخص را بکرایه گرفته که او را بر عیسوی[142] (?) سوارکنند و به شیراز رسانند بعد از آن چند روز گذشت و این شخص را پیدا نبود و[143] از این مکاریان تفحص می نمودند می گفتند

133 Sic in Nur., Mash. and Ṭab. Not in Mehm.

134 Mehm. ahd Mash. have خوفي.

135 Sic in Nur and Mash. Not in Mehm., which just has حاکم آنجا, or Ṭab., which has just حاکم شیراز.

136 Sic in Ṭab. and Mash. Nur. seems to have the word معضل.

137 Nur. lacks the word بود.

138 Sic in Ṭab. Mash. has. جامه Nur. has the word خانه instead of چاه. Section absent in Mehm., which instead has a half-line lacuna.

139 Mehm. has با زن instead of مادر.

140 Absent in Mehm., which has lacuna instead.

141 Sic in Nur. Mehm. adds این کار, and Ṭab. adds این فعل.

142 Sic in Nur. Mehm. has *beʿīsavī*, Ṭab. and Mash. have *bar ʿīsū-ye* or *ʿasū-ye*. One reading/interpretation could be *bar ʿayasawī*, on a light-tan colored camel, but the idiom of *kharr-e ʿĪsā* (Jesus' camel), or a reference to someone trying to appear or associate with something much greater than themselves, is the only meaning that seems to fit here. See Dekhodah, *Amthāl ū ḥekam*, 2:733.

143 Mehm. adds چون.

که ما او را به سربند امیر رسانیدیم و رها کردیم چه در آن جا مردم ساکن اند و شب [Nur 63a] هنگام بود و در آن جا ماند و نمی دانیم که به کجا رفت چون ایشان را به مجلس حاکم حاضر کردند بهمین طریق[144] تقریر می نمودند چون [Mehm 133a] حکم رفت که ایشان را تعذیب نمایند تا راست گویند یکی از ایشان که پیرتر بود بی تعذیب حقیقت حال باز نمود و اقرار مشروع کرد که ما هر دو باتّفاق این کار کردیم و آن یکی جوان بود انکار می کرد بعد از آنکه متوجه تعذیب او شدند و به اندک تعذیبی او نیز اقرار تفصیلی کرد چنانچه تمام قیود مرعی بود و به قصاص رسیدند[،]

و دزدان که در اول منکر بودند و آخر به اندک سیاستی که حاکم فرموده[145] حق ظاهر شده و مال باز داده اند بسیار است از جملهٔ در جَرون چیزی از کسی دزدیده بودند و در میان جمعی که متّهم بودند شخص بود که تمامت[146] رمضان به قراءة قرآن مشغول بود فقیر را در خاطر بود که از[147] او مثل این صورت صادر نشده باشد و در این باب رقعهٔ به عسسان نوشت که او را تعذیب [نکنند {Mash 31b} تا رقعه][148] رسیدن ظاهر شده بود که این کار او کرده و اکثر آنچه دزدیده بود باز پس آورد و سپرد.

غرض از تمهید این مقدمات آنکه حکم دیوان مظالم حکم شرع است و بر سلطان واجب است که یا خود متصدر آن شود چنانچه بعض خلفاء کرده اند یا آنکه رجوع به یکی از امراء صاحب سیاست عادل[149] بی طمع فرمایند و اگر تهاون در این نمایند آثم باشد و هر کس که گوید این نوع حکم مشروع نیست نامشروع[150] گفته باشد و نسبت اکابر ائمه به خطا [کرده باشد و][151] مستحق تعزیر بلیغ باشد بلکه خطر کفر چه به طریقی که [سابقاً مذکور شد این نوع][152] حکم از حضرت رسالت پناه [صلی الله علیه و سلم][153] و خلفاء و ائمه [رضا الله عنهم][154] منقول است و به ثبوت رسیده پس طعن در آن موجب کفر باشد نعوذ بالله [من الکفر و الطغیان][155] پس لایق آن است که حضرت سلطنت شعاری به نفس خود تحقیق احکام دیوان مظالم فرماید[156] و بی پروای را دخل ندهد و به حواله به دیگران

144 Sic. in Nur. Ṭab. has مضمون.
145 Mehm. has کرده.
146 Mehm. has the dittography of تمام تمام.
147 Sic in Mehm., Ṭab. and Mash. Nur. has رد.
148 Sic in Mash. Ṭab. has نکنند تا رسیدن رقعه. By contrast, Mehm. has بکنند تا رقعه رسیدن, and Nur. has just تعذیب رسیدن. This is a very confusing passage.
149 Sic in Nur., Mehm. and Mash. Ṭab. has inversion of امراي عادل صاحب سياست.
150 Sic in Ṭab., Mehm. and Mash. The Nur. ms. alone omits the words نیست نامشروع, leaving a nonsensical clause هر کسی که گود این حکم مشروع گفته باشد
151 Omitted in a lacuna in Mehm.
152 Omitted in a lacuna in Mehm.
153 Mehm. has علیه شرائف صلوات الله.
154 Sic in Nur., omitted in Mash. and Mehm.
155 Sic in Nur., Mehm. and Mash. Ṭab. has only منه.
156 Sic in Mash. and Ṭab. Nur has فرمایند and Mehm. has بفرماید.

اکتفا نفرماید که روز قیامت سؤال از آن حضرت خواهد بود و حواله به دیگران عذر نمی شود و این احکام را که [Mehm 133b] محض شرع است به عمل آورد و آن را مطموس نسازد و بعض ائمه کشف و تحقیق گفته اند که مهدی موعود مدار احکام بر آن خواهد نهاد.

اللهم[157] وفقه و سائر ولاة الاسلام لاجراء الاحکام و نظم مصالح الانام بحق محمد علیه و علی سائر الانبیاء و آل کل الصلاة و السلام تمت هذه الرساله المنسوبه الی المولی المحقق جلال المله و الدین الدوانی قدّس سرّه.

157 Mehm. adds in والله الموفق للخیر و السداد.

Select Bibliography

This bibliography is limited to sources referenced in the text.

SECONDARY SOURCES

Abbasi, Rushain. "Did Premodern Muslims Distinguish the Religious and Secular? The *Dīn–Dunyā* Binary in Medieval Islamic Thought." *Journal of Islamic Studies* 31, n. 2 (2020): 185–225.

—. "Islam and the Invention of Religion: A Study of Medieval Muslim Discourses on *Dīn*." *Studia Islamica* 116 (2021): 1–106.

—. "Beyond the Realm of Religion: The Idea of the Secular in Premodern Islam." PhD dissertation, Harvard, 2021.

Abū Fāris, Muḥammad ʿAbd al-Qādir. *Al-Qāḍī Abū Yaʿlā al-Farrāʾ wa kitābuhu al-Aḥkām al-sulṭāniyya*. Beirut: Muʾassasat al-Risāla, 1983.

Abu-Manneh, Butrus. "The Islamic Roots of the Gülhane Rescript." *Die Welt des Islams* 34, n. 2 (1994): 173–203.

Agmon, Iris. *Family & Court: Legal Culture and Modernity in Late Ottoman Palestine*. Syracuse: Syracuse University Press, 2006.

Ahmed, Shahab. *What Is Islam? The Importance of Being Islamic.* Princeton: Princeton University Press, 2015.

Akbar, Muhammad. *The Administration of Justice by the Mughals*. Lahore: Muhammad Ashraf, 1948.

Akgündüz, Ahmet. "Osmanlı Kanunnâmelerinin Şerʿî Sınırları." *Osmanlı*. V. 6. Ankara: Yeni Türkiye Yayınları, 1999.

—. *Islamic Public Law*. Rotterdam: IUR Press, 2011.

Akiba, Jun. "A New School for Qadis: Education of the Sharia Judges in the Late Ottoman Empire." *Turcica* 35 (2003): 125–163.

—. "*Sharīʿa* Judges in the Ottoman *Nizāmiye* Courts, 1864–1908." *Osmanlı Araştırmarları / Journal of Ottoman Studies* 51 (2018): 209–237.

Al-Attas, Syed Muhammad Naquib. *On Justice and the Nature of Man*. Kuala Lumpur: Taʾdib Intl., 2020.

Al-Jarbou, Ayoub M. "The Saudi Board of Grievances: Development and New Reforms." *Arab Law Quarterly* 25 (2011): 177–202.

Al-Azami, Usaama. "Legitimising Political Dissent: Islamist Salafi Discourses on Obedience to the Ruler and Rebellion after the Arab Revolutions." In *Salafi Social and Political Movements*. Ed. Masooda Bano, 61–85. Edinburgh: Edinburgh University Press, 2021.

Alam, Muzaffar. *The Languages of Political Islam: India 1200–1800*. Chicago: The University of Chicago Press, 2004.

Alhalalsheh, Ibrahim. "Ürdün Ahvâl-i Şahsiyye Kanununun Osmanlı Hukuk-ı Âile Kararnamesi İle Mukayesesi." PhD dissertation, Marmara University, 2009.

Allehbi, Mohammed. "'It is Permitted for the Amīr but not the Qāḍī': The Military-Administrative Genealogy of Coercion in Abbasid Criminal Justice." *Islamic Law and Society* 30, n. 1–2 (2023): 65–95.

Amedroz, H. F. "The Mazalim Jurisdiction in the Ahkam Sultaniyya of Mawardi." *Journal of the Royal Asiatic Society of Great Britain and Ireland* July (1911): 635–674.

Amitai-Preiss, Reuven and David O. Morgan, ed. *The Mongol Empire and its Legacy*. Leiden: Brill, 1999.

An-Na'im, Abdullahi. *Islam and the Secular State*. Cambridge, MA: Harvard University Press, 2007.

Anay, Mahmut. "Celâleddin Devvânî: Hayatı, Eserleri, Ahlâk ve Siyaset Düşüncesi." PhD Dissertation, Istanbul University, 1994.

Anderson, J.N.D. "Homicide in Islamic Law." *Bulletin of the School of Oriental and African Studies* 13, n. 4 (1951): 811–828.

Anjum, Ovamir. "Islam as a Discursive Tradition: Talal Asad and his Interlocutors." *Comparative Studies of South Asia, Africa, and the Middle East* 27, n. 3 (2007): 656–672.

—. *Politics, Law, and Community in Islamic Thought*. Cambridge: Cambridge University Press, 2012.

Anscombe, Frederick F. *State, Faith, and Nation in Ottoman and Post-Ottoman Lands*. Cambridge: Cambridge University Press, 2014.

Apellániz, Francisco. "Judging the Franks: Proofs, Justice, and Diversity in Late Medieval Alexandria and Damascus." *Comparative Studies in Society and History* 58, n. 2 (2016): 350–378.

Ardıç, Nurullah. *Islam and the Politics of Secularism*. London: Routledge, 2012.

Arjomand, Saïd Amir. "Political Ethic and Public Law in the Early Qajar Period." In *Religion and Society in Qajar Iran*. Ed. Robert Gleave, 21–40. London: Routledge, 2005.

Atçıl, Abudrrahman. *Scholars and Sultans in the Early Modern Ottoman Empire*. Cambridge: Cambridge University Press, 2017.

Aubin, Jean. "Études Safavides. I. Šāh Ismāʿīl et les Notables de l'Iraq Persan." *Journal of the Social and Economic History of the Orient* 2 (1959): 55–58.

Ayalon, David. "The Great Yasa of Chingiz Khan: A Reexamination (Part C2)." *Studia Islamica* 38 (1973): 107–156.

Aydın, Mehmet Âkif. *Osmanlı Devleti'nde Hukuk ve Adalet*. Istanbul: Klasik, 2014.

Aykan, Yavuz. "A Legal Concept in Motion: The 'Spreader of Corruption' (*sāʿī bi'l-fesād*) from Qarakhanid to Ottoman Jurisprudence." *Islamic Law and Society* 26, n. 3 (2019): 1–19.

Ayoub, Samy. "The Mecelle, Sharia, and the Ottoman State." *Journal of the Ottoman and Turkish Studies Association* (2015): 121–146.

—. "'The Sulṭān Says': State Authority in the Late Ḥanafī Tradition." *Islamic Law and Society* 23, no. 3 (2016): 239–278.

—. *Law, Empire, and the Sultan: Ottoman Imperial Authority in Late Ḥanafī Jurisprudence.* Oxford: Oxford University Press, 2019.

—. "A Theory of a State? How Civil Law Ended Legal Pluralism in Modern Egypt." *Journal of Law and Religion* (2022): 1–20.

Baer, Gabriel. "Tanzimat in Egypt – The Penal Code." *Bulletin of the School of Oriental and African Studies* 26, n. 1 (1963): 29–49.

Baldwin, James. *Islamic Law and Empire in Ottoman Cairo*. Edinburgh: Edinburgh University Press, 2017.

Barnes, Jamal. *A Genealogy of the Torture Taboo*. London: Routledge, 2017.

Bazzaz, Sahar. *Forgotten Saints: History, Power, and Politics in the Making of Modern Morocco*. Cambridge, MA: Harvard University Press, 2010.

Bdaiwi, Ahab. "Shiʿi Defenders of Avicenna: An Intellectual History of the Dashtakī Philosophers of Shiraz." PhD dissertation, University of Exeter, 2014.

—. "Philosophia Ottomanica: Jalāl al-Dīn Dawānī on Establishing the Existence of the Necessary Being." In *Empires of the Near East and India: Source Studies of the Safavid, Ottoman, and Mughal Literate Communities*. Ed. H. Khafipour, 319–335. New York: Columbia University Press, 2019.

—. *Jalāl al-Dīn Dawānī: An Avicennan Philosopher and Ashʿarī Theologian.* Cambridge: Cambridge University Press, forthcoming.

Bearman, Peri; Peters, Rudolph and Frank E. Vogel, eds. *The Islamic School of Law*. Cambridge, MA: Harvard University Press, 2005.

Bedir, Murteza. "*Fıkıh* to Law: Secularization through Curriculum." *Islamic Law and Society* 11, n. 3 (2004): 378–401.

Bein, Amit. *Ottoman Ulema, Turkish Republic: Agents of Change and Guardians of Tradition*. Palo Alto: Stanford University Press, 2011.

—. "'Ulama' and Political Activism in the Late Ottoman Empire: The Political Career of Şeyhülislâm Mustafa Sabri Efendi (1869–1954)." In *Guardians of Faith in Modern Times: 'Ulama in the Modern Middle East*. Ed. Meir Hatina, 67–90. Leiden: Brill, 2009.

Bektaş, Erhan. *Religious Reform in the Late Ottoman Empire*. London: IB Tauris, 2023.

Benton, Lauren A. *Law and Colonial Cultures: Local Regimes in World History, 1400–1900*. Cambridge: Cambridge University Press, 2002.

van Berkel, Maaike. "Abbasid *Maẓālim* between Theory and Practice." In *Le Pluralisme Judiciaire dan l'Islam Premoderne*. Ed. Mathieu Tillier, special issue. *Bulletin d'Études Orientales* 63 (2014): 229–242.

Berkes, Niyazi. *The Development of Secularism in Modern Turkey*. London: Hurst, 1964.

Bowen, Charles. "Progress in the Administration of Justice during the Victorian Period." In *Select Essays in Anglo-American Legal History*, 516–557. Boston: Little, Brown & Co., 1907.

Bouquet, Olivier. "Is it Time to Stop Speaking about Ottoman Modernization?" In *Order and Compromise: Government Practices in Turkey from the Late Ottoman Empire to the Early 21st Century*. Ed. Marc Aymes, Benjamin Gourisse and Élise Massicard, 45–67. Leiden: Brill, 2015.

Brack, Jonathan Z. "Mediating Sacred Kingship: Conversion and Sovereignty in Mongol Iran." PhD dissertation, University of Michigan, 2016.

Broadbridge, Anne. *Kingship and Ideology in the Islamic and Mongol Worlds*. Cambridge: Cambridge University Press, 2008.

Brockett, Gavin. *How Happy to Call Oneself a Turk*. Austin, TX: University of Texas Press, 2011.

Brockopp, Jonathan. *Muhammad's Heirs: The Rise of Muslim Scholarly Communities, 622–951*. Cambridge: Cambridge University Press, 2017.

Brunschvig, Robert. "Justice religieuse et justice laïque dans la Tunisie des Deys et des Beys: jusqu'au milieu du XIXe siècle." *Studia Islamica* 23 (1965): 27–70.

Burak, Guy. *The Second Formation of Islamic Law*. Cambridge: Cambridge University Press, 2015.

—. "Between the *Ḳānūn* of Qāytbāy and Ottoman *Yasaq*: A Note on the Ottomans' Dynastic Law." *Journal of Islamic Studies* 26, n. 1 (2015): 1–23.

—. "Evidentiary truth claims, imperial registers, and the Ottoman archive: contending legal views of archival and record-keeping practices in Ottoman Greater Syria (seventeenth-nineteenth centuries)." *Bulletin of the School of Oriental and African Studies* 79, n. 2 (2016): 233–254.

Busse, Heribert. "The Revival of Persian Kingship under the Būyids." In *Islamic Civilization 950–1150*. Ed. D.S. Richards, 250–304. London: Bruno Cassirer, 1973.

Cammack, Mark E. "Islam and Nationalism in Indonesia: Forging an Indonesian Madhhab." In *The Islamic School of Law*. Ed. Peri Bearman, Rudolph Peters, and Frank E. Vogel, 175–190. Cambridge, MA: Harvard University Press, 2005.

—, Donovan, Helen and Tim B. Heaton. "Islamic Divorce Law and Practice in Indonesia." In *Islamic Law in Contemporary Indonesia*. Ed. R. Michael Feener and Mark E. Cammack, 99–127. Cambridge, MA: Harvard University Press, 2007.

— and R. Michael Feener. "The Islamic Legal System in Indonesia." *Pacific Rim Law & Policy Journal* 21, n. 1 (2012): 13–42.

Catlos, Brian A. *Muslims of Medieval Latin Christendom, c. 1050–1614*. Cambridge: Cambridge University Press, 2014.

Chatterjee, Nandini. *Negotiating Mughal Law: A Family of Landlords across Three Indian Empires*. Cambridge: Cambridge University Press, 2020.

Chen, Edith. "An Unbeliever Can Rule *Dār al-Islām*: Ḥanafī Law in the Wake of the Mongol Invasion." *Islamic Law and Society* 30 (2023): 442–475.

Coulson, Noel J. *A History of Islamic Law*. Edinburgh: Edinburgh University Press, 2022, reprint of 1964 ed.

Da"ās, 'Izzat 'Ubayd. *Al-Qawā'id al-fiqhiyya*. Beirut: Dār al-Tirmidhī, 1409/1989.

Danishpazhouh, Mohammad-Taqi. "An Annotated Bibliography on Government and Statecraft." Trans. Andrew Newman. In *Authority and Political Culture in Shi'ism*. Ed. Saïd Amir Arjomand, 213–239. Albany: SUNY Press, 1988.

Darling, Linda T. *A History of Social Justice and Political Power in the Middle East: The Circle of Justice from Mesopotamia to Globalization*. London and New York: Routledge, 2013.

—. "*Mirrors for Princes* in Europe and the Middle East: A Case of Historiographical Incommensurability." In *East Meets West in the Middle Ages and Early Modern Times*. Ed. Albrecht Classen, 223–242. Berlin: De Gruyter, 2013.

Davānī, 'Alī. *Sharḥ-e zendegānī-ye Jalāl al-Dīn Davānī*. Qom: Chāpkhāne-ye Ḥekmat, [1955].

Dignas, Beate and Engelbert Winter. *Rome and Persia in Late Antiquity*. Cambridge: Cambridge University Press, 2007.

Elliot, H. M. and John Dawson, eds. *The History of India as Told by its Own Historians: The Muhammadan Period*. Vol. 7. New York: AMS Press, 1966.

El-Nahal, Galal H. *The Judicial Administration of Ottoman Egypt in the Seventeenth Century*. Minneapolis: Bibliotheca Islamica, 1979.

El Rouayheb, Khaled. *Relational Syllogisms and the History of Arab Logic, 900–1900*. Leiden: Brill, 2010.

—. *Islamic Intellectual History in the Seventeenth Century: Scholarly Currents in the Ottoman Empire and the Maghreb*. Cambridge: Cambridge University Press, 2015.

Emon, Anver. "*Ḥuqūq Allāh* and *Ḥuqūq al-'Ibād*: A Legal Heuristic for a Natural Rights Regime." *Islamic Law and Society* 13, n. 3 (2006): 325–391.

—. *Religious Pluralism and Islamic Law*. Oxford: Oxford University Press, 2012.

Ergene, Boğaç. "On Ottoman Justice: Interpretations in Conflict (1600–1800)." *Islamic Law and Society* 8, n. 1 (2001): 52–87.

—. "Evidence in Ottoman Courts: Oral and Written Documentation in Early-Modern Courts of Islamic Law." *Journal of the American Oriental Society* 124, no. 3 (2004): 471–491.

Esposito, John L., ed. *Voices of Resurgent Islam*. New York: Oxford University Press, 1983.

Fadel, Mohammad. "Islamic Law Reform: Between Reinterpretation and Democracy." *Yearbook of Islamic and Middle Eastern Law Online* 18, n. 1 (2017): 44–90.

Fatima, Haseeb. "Inheritance Rights of Orphaned Grandchildren under Section 4 of Muslim Family Law Ordinance, 1961 and its Alternative Solutions." *Law and Policy Review* 3, n 2 (2024): 22–42.

Feener, R. Michael and Mark E. Cammack, ed. *Islamic Law in Contemporary Indonesia*. Cambridge, MA: Harvard University Press, 2007.

Fleischer, Cornell. *Bureaucrat and Intellectual in the Ottoman Empire: The Historian Mustafa Ali (1541–1600)*. Princeton: Princeton University Press, 1986.

Floor, Willen. "The Secular Judicial System in Safavid Persia." *Studia Iranica* 29, no. 1 (2000): 9–60.

Fuess, Albrecht. "*Ẓulm* by *Maẓālim*? The Political Implications of the Use of *Maẓālim* Jurisdiction by the Mamluk Sultans." *Mamlūk Studies Review* 13, n. 1 (2009): 121–147.

Gaughan, Judy E. *Murder Was Not a Crime: Homicide and Power in the Roman Republic*. Austin: University of Texas Press, 2010.

Gerber, Haim. *State, Society, and Law in Islam*. Albany: State University of New York Press, 1994.

Gesinke, Indira Falk. *Islamic Reform and Conservatism: Al-Azhar and the Evolution of Modern Sunni Islam*. London: IB Tauris, 2010.

Gibb, H.A.R. "Al-Mawardi's Theory of the Caliphate." In *Studies on the Civilization of Islam*. Ed. Stanford Shaw and William Polk, 151–165. Princeton: Princeton University Press, 1962, originally published *Islamic Culture* 11, n. 3 (1937).

Gradeva, Rossitsa. "On Judicial Hierarchy in the Ottoman Empire: The Case of Sofia from the Seventeenth to the Beginning of the Eighteenth Century." In *Dispensing Justice in Islam: Qadis and their Judgments*. Ed. Muhammad Khalid Masud, Rudolph Peters and David Powers, 271–298. Leiden: Brill, 2005.

Hagen, Gottfried. "World Order and Legitimacy." In *Legitimizing the Order: The Ottoman Rhetoric of State Power*. Ed. Hasan Karateke and Maurus Reinkowski, 55–83. Leiden: Brill, 2005.

Hallaq, Wael B. *Shari'a: Theory, Practice, Transformations*. Cambridge: Cambridge University Press, 2009.

—. *The Impossible State: Islam, Politics, and Modernity's Moral Predicament*. New York: Columbia University Press, 2013.

Harvey, Ramon. *The Qur'an and the Just Society*. Edinburgh: Edinburgh University Press, 2018.

Ḥasan, ʿAmmār ʿAlī. *Al-Tanshi'a al-siyāsiyya li'l-ṭuruq al-ṣūfiyya fī miṣr*. Cairo: Dār al-ʿAyn, 1430/2009.

Hasan, Farhat. *State and Locality in Mughal India: Power Relations in Western India, c. 1572–1730*. Cambridge: Cambridge University Press, 2004.

Hassan, Mona. *Longing for the Lost Caliphate*. Princeton: Princeton University Press, 2016.

Hanioğlu, Şükrü. *A Brief History of the Late Ottoman Empire*. Princeton: Princeton University Press, 2008.

Hayes, Christine. *What's Divine about Divine Law? Early Perspectives*. Princeton: Princeton University Press, 2015.

van der Haven, Elisabeth Cornelia. "The Bey, the mufti and the scattered pearls: Shari'a and political leadership in Tunisia's Age of Reform – 1800–1864." PhD dissertation, University of Leiden, 2006.

Heinzelmann, Tobias. "The Ruler's Monologue: The Rhetoric of the Ottoman Penal Code of 1858." *Die Welt des Islams* 54 (2014): 292–321.

Hendrickson, Jocelyn. *Leaving Iberia: Islamic Law and Christian Conquest in North West Africa*. Cambridge, MA: Harvard University Press, 2021.

Heyd, Uriel. *Studies in Old Ottoman Criminal Law*. Ed. V.L. Ménage. Oxford: Clarendon, 1973.

Hill, Enid. "The Place and Significance of Islamic Law in the Life and Work of 'Abd al-Razzaq Ahmad al-Sanhuri, Egyptian Jurist and Scholar, 1895–1971 [Part I]." *Arab Law Quarterly* 3, n. 1 (1988): 33–64.

—. "Al-Sanhuri and Islamic Law... [Part II]." *Arab Law Quarterly* 3, n. 2 (1988): 182–218.

Hodgson, Marshall. *The Venture of Islam*. 3 vols. Chicago: University of Chicago Press, 1974.

Hoexter, Miriam. "*Ḥuqūq Allāh* and *Ḥuqūq al-'Ibād* as Reflected in the *Waqf* Institution." *Jerusalem Studies in Arabic and Islam* 19 (1995): 133–156.

Holt, P.M. *The Age of the Crusades*. London: Longman, 1986.

Hurvitz, Nimrod. *Competing Texts: The Relationship Between al-Mawardi's and Abu Ya'la's* al-Ahkam al-sultaniyya. Cambridge, MA: Harvard Islamic Legal Studies Program, 2007.

—. "The Contribution of Early Islamic Rulers to Adjudication and Legislation: The Case of the *Mazalim* Tribunals." In *Law and Empire: Ideas, Practices, Actors*. Ed. Jeroen Duindam et al., 135–166. Leiden: Brill, 2013.

Hussin, Iza R. *The Politics of Islamic Law*. Chicago: University of Chicago Press, 2016.

Ibrahim, Ahmed Fekry. *Pragmatism in Islamic Law*. Syracuse: Syracuse University Press, 2015.

Imber, Colin. "Law and Legislation under Süleymân I." In *The Battle for Central Europe: The Siege of Szigetvár and the Death of Süleyman the Magnificent and Nicholas Zrínyi*. Ed. Pál Fodor, 93–114. Leiden: Brill, 2018.

Inalcik, Halil. *The Ottoman Empire*. London: Phoenix, 1973.

Ion, Theodore P. "Roman Law and Mohammedan Jurisprudence: II." *Michigan Law Review* 6, no. 3 (1908): 197–214.

Irwin, Robert. "Privatization of 'Justice' under the Circassian Mamluks." *Mamlūk Studies Review* 6 (2005): 63–70.

Jackson, Sherman A. *Islamic Law and the State: The Constitutional Jurisprudence of Shihāb al-Dīn al-Qarāfī*. Leiden: Brill, 1996.

—. *The Islamic Secular*. Oxford: Oxford University Press, 2024.

Jeffery, Arthur. *The Foreign Vocabulary of the Qur'ān*. Leiden: Brill, 2007.

Jennings, Ronald C. "Kadi, Court, and Legal Procedure in 17th C. Ottoman Kayseri: The Kadi and the Legal System." *Studia Islamica* 48 (1978): 133–172.

Johansen, Baber. "Secular and religious elements in Hanafite law. Function and limits of the absolute character of government authority." In *Islam et Politique au Maghreb*. Ed. E. Gellner et J.C. Vatin, 189–218. Aix: Table ronde du CRESM, 1979.

—. "Formes de langage et fonctions publiques: Stéréotypes, témoins et offices dans la preuve par l'écrit en droit musulman." *Arabica* 44, no. 3 (1997): 333–376.

—. *Contingency in a Sacred Law: Legal and Ethical Norms in the Muslim Fiqh*. Leiden: Brill, 1999.

—. "Signs as Evidence: The Doctrine of Ibn Taymiyya (1263–1328) and Ibn Qayyim al-Jawziyya (d. 1351) on Proof." *Islamic Law and Society* 9, no. 2 (2002): 168–193.

—. "Vérité et torture: *ius commune* et droit musulman entre le xe et le xiiie siècle." In *De La Violence*. Ed. Françoise Héritier, 124–168. Paris: Odile Jacob, 2005.

Judd, Steven. *Religious Scholars and the Umayyads*. New York: Routledge, 2014.

—. "The Jurisdictional Limits of the *Qāḍī* Courts during the Umayyad Period." *Bulletin d'études orientales* 16 (2014): 43–56.

Kaicker, Abhishek. "Petitions and Local Politics in the Late Mughal Empire: The view from Kol, 1741." *Modern Asian Studies* 53, n. 1 (2019): 21–51.

Kamola, Stefan T. "Rashīd al-Dīn and the Making of History in Mongol Iran." PhD dissertation, University of Washington, 2013.

Kara, Ismail. "Turban and fez: Ulema as opposition." In *Late Ottoman Society: The Intellectual Legacy*. Ed. Elisabeth Özdolga, 162–200. London: Routledge Curzon, 2005.

Kennedy, Hugh. *Muslim Spain and Portugal*. London: Routledge, 1996.

Khadduri, Majid. *The Islamic Conception of Justice*. Baltimore: Johns Hopkins University Press, 1984.

Khan, Shafaat Ahmad. *John Marshall in India: Notes and Observations in Bengal 1668–1672*. Oxford: Oxford University Press, 1927.

Kinross, Patrick. *Atatürk: A Biography of Mustafa Kemal*. New York: W. Morrow, 1965.

Lambton, Ann K.S. "Quis custodiet custodes: Some Reflections on the Persian Theory of Government." *Studia Islamica* 5 (1956): 125–148.

—. *State and Government in Medieval Islam*. Oxford: Oxford University Press, 1981.

Landau-Tasseron, Ella. "The 'Cyclical Reform': A Study of the *Mujaddid* Tradition." *Studia Islamica* 70 (1989): 79–117.

Langbein, John H. *Torture and the Law of Proof*. Chicago: University of Chicago Press, 1976.

Lange, Christian. *Justice, Punishment, and the Medieval Muslim Imagination*. Cambridge: Cambridge University Press, 2008.

Laoust, Henri. "La pensée et l'action politiques d'al-Māwardī." *Revue des études islamiques* 36 (1968): 11–92.

Lassner, Jacob. *The Topography of Baghdad in the Early Middle Ages*. Detroit: Wayne State University Press, 1970.

Lee, Dana Elizabeth. "At the Limits of Law: Necessity in Islamic Legal History, Second/Eighth through Tenth/Sixteenth Centuries." PhD dissertation, Princeton University, 2019.

Lev, Yaacov. *State and Society in Fatimid Egypt*. Leiden: Brill, 1991.

—. *The Administration of Justice in Medieval Egypt*. Edinburgh: Edinburgh University Press, 2021.

Levanoni, Amalia. "*Takfīr* in Egypt and Syria during the Mamlūk Period." In *Accusations of Unbelief in Islam*. Ed. Camilla Adang et al., 155–188. Leiden: Brill, 2016.

Lewis, Bernard. *The Emergence of Modern Turkey*. London: Oxford University Press, 1961.

Lingwood, Chad. *Politics, Poetry, and Sufism in Medieval Iran: New Perspectives on Jami's Salaman va Absal*. Leiden: Brill, 2014.

Little, Donald. "A New Look at *al-Aḥkām al-Sulṭāniyya*." *Muslim World* 64, n. 1 (1974): 1–15.

Lockwood, Oliver and Joan O'Donovan, eds. *From Irenaeus to Grotius: a Sourcebook in Christian Political Thought*. Grand Rapids: W.B. Eerdmans, 1999.

Lombardi, Clark. *State Law as Islamic Law in Modern Egypt*. Leiden: Brill, 2006.

— and Nathan Brown. "Do Constitutions Requiring Adherence to *Shari'a* Threaten Human Rights? How Egypt's Constitutional Court Reconciles Islamic Law with the Liberal Rule of Law." *American University Intl. Law Review* 21, n. 3 (2006): 379–435.

—. "The Supreme Constitutional Court of Egypt on Islamic Law, Veiling and Civil Rights." *American University Journal of International Law* 21, n. 3 (2006): 437–460.

—. "Designing Islamic constitutions: Past trends and options for a democratic future." *I-con (International Journal of Constitutional Law)* 11, n. 3 (2013): 615–645.

Long, David E. "The Board of Grievances in Saudi Arabia." *Middle East Journal* 27, n. 1 (1973): 71–75.

Loughlin, Martin. *Foundations of Public Law*. Oxford: Oxford University Press, 2010.

Lydon, Ghislaine. *On Trans-Saharan Trails: Islamic Law, Trade Networks, and Cross-Cultural Exchange in Nineteenth-Century Western Africa*. Cambridge: Cambridge University Press, 2009.

—. "A Paper Economy of Faith without Faith in Paper: A Reflection on Islamic Institutional History." *Journal of Economic Behavior & Organization* 71, n. 3 (2009): 647–659.

MacIntyre, Alasdair. *Whose Justice? Which Rationality?* Notre Dame: University of Notre Dame Press, 1988.

Madelung, Wilferd. "The Assumption of the Title of Shāhānshāh by the Būyids and the 'Reign of the Daylam (*Dawlat al-Daylam*)'." *Journal of Near Eastern Studies* 28, n. 3 (1969): 168–183.

Maitland, Frederic W. *Equity*. Cambridge: Cambridge University Press, 1920.
Makdisi, George. *Ibn ʿAqīl et la résurgence de l'Islam traditionaliste au xie siècle*. Damascus: Institut Français de Damas, 1963.
Mansfield, Peter. *The British in Egypt*. New York: Holt, Rinehart & Winston, 1971.
March, Andrew. *Islam and Liberal Citizenship*. Oxford: Oxford University Press, 2009.
Mardin, Ebül'ula. *Medeni Hukuk Cephesinden Ahmet Cevdet Paşa*. Ankara: Türkiye Diyanet Vakfı, 2009.
Mardin, Şerif. "The Just and the Unjust." *Daedalus* 120, n. 3 (1991): 113–129.
Marglin, Jessica. "In the Court of the Nations: Jews, Muslims and Legal Pluralism in Nineteenth-Century Morocco." PhD dissertation, Princeton, 2013.
Markiewicz, Christopher Andrew. "The Crisis of Rule in Late Medieval Islam: A Study of Idrīs Bidlīsī (861–926/1457–1520) and Kingship at the Turn of the Sixteenth Century." PhD dissertation, University of Chicago, 2015.
—. *The Crisis of Kingship in Late Medieval Islam: Persian Emigres and the Making of Ottoman Sovereignty*. Cambridge: Cambridge University Press, 2019.
Marlow, Louise. "Difference and encyclopaedism in tenth-century Eastern Iran." *Jerusalem Studies in Arabic and Islam* 40 (2013): 195–244.
—. "Abū Zayd al-Balkhī and the *Naṣīḥat al-mulūk* of Pseudo-Māwardī." *Der Islam* 93, n. 1 (2016): 35–64.
Marsot, Afaf Lutfi. *Women and Men in Late Eighteenth-Century Egypt*. Austin: University of Texas Press, 1995.
Massell, Gregory J. *The Surrogate Proletariat: Moslem Women and Revolutionary Strategies in Soviet Central Asia, 1919–1929*. Princeton: Princeton University Press, 1974.
Massignon, Louis. *The Passion of al-Hallaj*. Trans. Herbert Mason. Princeton: Princeton University Press, 1982.
Masud, Muhammad Khaled. *Shari'a Today: Essays on Contemporary Issues and Debates in Muslim Societies*. Islamabad: National Book Foundation, 2013.
—, Peters, Rudolph; and David Stephan Powers, eds. *Dispensing Justice in Islam: Qāḍīs and Their Judgments*. Leiden: Brill, 2006.
Meijer, Roel, ed. *Global Salafism: Islam's New Religious Movement*. New York: Columbia University Press, 2009.
Melchert, Christopher. "Māwardī, Abū Ya'lá and the Sunni Revival." In *Prosperity and Stagnation: Some Cultural and Social Aspects of the Abbasid Period (750–1258)*. Ed. Krzystof Koscielniak, 37–61. Krakow: UNUM, 2010.
— "Māwardī's Legal Thinking." *Al-ʿUṣūr al-Wusṭā* 23 (2015): 68–86.
Melville, Charles. "From Adam to Abaqa: Qāḍī Baiḍāwī's Rearrangement of History." *Studia Iranica* 30, n. 1 (2001): 67–86.
Meshal, Reem. "Antagonistic *Sharīʿa*s and the Construction of Orthodoxy in Sixteenth-Century Cairo." *Journal of Islamic Studies* 21, no. 2 (2010): 182–212.

Messick, Brinkley. *The Calligraphic State: State Textual Domination and History in a Muslim Society*. Berkeley: University of California Press, 1993.

Mikhail, Hanna. *Politics and Revelation: Māwardī and After*. Edinburgh: Edinburgh University Press, 1995.

Miller, Ruth A. *Legislating Authority: Sin and Crime in the Ottoman Empire and Turkey*. New York: Routledge, 2005.

Minorsky, Vladimir. "A Civil and Military Review in Fārs in 881/1476." *Bulletin of the School of Oriental [and African] Studies* 10, no. 1 (1939): 141–178.

Morgan, David. "The 'Great Yasa of Chinggis Khan' Revisited." In *Mongols, Turks, and Others: Eurasian Nomads and the Sedentary World*. Ed. Reuven Amitai and Michal Biran, 291–308. Leiden: Brill, 2005.

Motoyoshi, A. Sumi. *Description in Classical Arabic Poetry*. Leiden: Brill, 2004.

Müller, Christian. "Écrire pour établir la preuve orale en Islam: la practique d'un tribunal à Jérusalem au xive siècle." In *Les Outils de la pensée,* 63–97. Paris: Maison des Sciences de l'Homme, 2010.

—. "Redressing Injustice: *Maẓālim* jurisdictions at the Umayyad court of Córdoba (eighth-eleventh centuries CE)." In *Court Cultures in the Muslim World*. Ed. Albrecht Fuess and Jan-Peter Hartung, 93–104. New York: Routledge, 2011.

Murphey, Rhoads. "Hybridity in Ottoman legal tradition as a source of flexibility in governing the empire: An overview with particular reference to the application of the ruler's executive judicial or *örfi* powers." In *Imperial Lineages and Legacies in the Eastern Mediterranean*. Ed. Rhoads Murphey, 35–48. Oxford: Routledge, 2016.

Mūs, al-Ḥusayn. *Mudawwanat al-usra fī ḍaw' taqyīd al-mubāḥ*. Casablanca: Abdulla Abdulghani Foundation, 2015.

Mutafakkir, Aḥmad. *Min a'lām al-fatwā bi-murrākush 'abr al-'uṣūr*. Marrakesh: Mu'assasat Āfāq li'l-Dirāsāt wa'l-Nashr wa'l-Ittiṣāl, 2014.

Nakissa, Aria. "An Epistemic Shift in Islamic Law: Educational Reform at al-Azhar and Dār al-'Ulūm." *Islamic Law and Society* 21, n. 3 (2014): 209–251.

Naqqāsh, Rajā'. *Al-Imām al-Marāghī: ḥayātuhu wa afkāruhu*. Cairo: Dār al-Shurūq, 2007.

Neumann, Christoph K. *Das indirekte Argument: Ein Plädoyer für die Tanzimat vermittels der Historie*. Hamburg: Lit Verlag, 1994.

— "Whom did Ahmed Cevdet Represent?" In *Late Ottoman Society: The Intellectual Legacy*. Ed. Elisabeth Özdalga, 117–134. London: Routledge Curzon, 2005.

Nicholas, Barry. *An Introduction to Roman Law*. Oxford: Oxford University Press, 1962.

Nielsen, Jørgen. *Secular Justice in an Islamic State*: *Maẓālim under the Baḥrī Mamlūks, 662/1264–789/1387*. [Leiden]: Nederlands Historisch-Archaeologisch Instituut te Istanbul, 1985.

Nizami, Farhan. "Madrasahs, Scholars and Saints: Muslim Responses to the British Presence in Delhi and the Upper Doab 1803–1857." PhD dissertation, Oxford University, 1983.

Nurlaelawati, Euis. *Modernization, Tradition and Identity: The Kompilasi Hukum Islam and Legal Practice in the Indonesian Religious Courts.* Amsterdam: Amsterdam University Press, 2010.

Opwis, Felicitas. Maṣlaḥa *and the Purpose of the Law.* Leiden: Brill, 2010.

Peletz, Michael. "Are Women Getting (More) Justice? Malaysia's *Sharia* Courts in Ethnographic and Historical Perspective." *Law & Society Review* 52, n. 3 (2018): 652–684.

Peters, Rudolph. "The Codification of Criminal Law in Nineteenth Century [sic] Egypt: Tradition or Modernization." In *Law, Society, and National Identity in Africa.* Ed. J.M. Abu-Nasr, Ulrich Spellenberg and Ulrike Wanitzek, 211–225. Hamburg: H. Buske, 1990.

—. *Crime and Punishment in Islamic Law.* Cambridge: Cambridge University Press, 2005.

—. "What Does it Mean to be an Official Madhhab? Hanafism and the Ottoman Empire." In *The Islamic School of Law.* Ed. Peri Bearman, R. Peters and Frank Vogel, 147–158. Cambridge, MA: Harvard University Press, 2005.

Petry, Carl F. "'Quis Custodiet Custodes?' Revisited: The Prosecution of Crime in the Late Mamluk Sultanate." *Mamlūk Studies Review* 3 (1999): 13–30.

Pfeiffer, Judith. "Teaching the Learned: Jalāl al-Dīn al-Dawānī's *Ijāza* to Mu'ayyadzāda 'Abd al-Raḥmān Efendi and the Circulation of Knowledge between Fārs and the Ottoman Empire at the Turn of the Sixteenth Century." In *The Heritage of Arabo-Islamic Learning: Studies Presented to Wadad Kadi.* Ed. Maurice Pomerantz and Aram Shahin, 284–332. Leiden: Brill, 2016.

Pourjavady, Reza. "Ketābshenāsī-ye āthār-e Jalāl al-Dīn Davānī." *Ma'āref* 15, n. 1–2 (1377/1998): 81–138.

—. *Philosophy in Early Safavid Iran.* Leiden: Brill, 2011.

Powell, Avril A. "Old Books in New Bindings: Ethics and Education in Colonial India." In *Knowledge Production, Pedagogy, and Institutions in Colonial India.* Ed. Indra Sengupta and Daud Ali, 199–226. New York: Palgrave Macmillan, 2011.

Powers, David. "On Judicial Review in Islamic Law." *Law and Society Review* 26, no. 2 (1992): 315–342.

—. "Four Cases Relating to Women and Divorce in Al-Andalus and the Maghrib, 1100–1500." In *Dispensing Justice in Islam: Qadis and their Judgments.* Ed. Muhammad Khalid Masud, Rudolph Peters and David Powers, 383–409. Leiden: Brill, 2006.

Quraishi, Asifa. "The Separation of Powers in the Tradition of Muslim Governments." In *Constitutionalism in Islamic Countries.* Ed. Rainer Grote and Tilmann Röder, 63–74. Oxford: Oxford University Press, 2012.

Rabbat, Nasser. "The Ideological Significance of the Dar al-Adl in the Medieval Islamic Orient." *International Journal of Middle East Studies* 27, no. 1 (1995): 3–28.

Rapoport, Yossef. "Legal Diversity in the Age of *Taqlīd*: The Four Chief *Qāḍīs* under the Mamluks." *Islamic Law and Society* 10, n. 2 (2003): 210–228.

—. *Marriage, Money and Divorce in Medieval Islamic Society*. Cambridge: Cambridge University Press, 2005.

—. "Royal Justice and Religious Law: Siyāsah and Shari'ah under the Mamluks." *Mamlūk Studies Review* 16 (2012): 71–102.

Rebstock, Ulrich. "A Qāḍī's Errors." *Islamic Law and Society* 6, n. 1 (1999): 1–37.

Repp, Richard C. "Qānūn and Sharī'a in the Ottoman Context." In *Islamic Law: Social and Historical Contexts*. Ed. Aziz Al-Azmeh, 124–145. Oxford: Taylor & Francis, 2013.

Rezakhany, Hassan John. "Jalāl ad-Dīn ad-Dawānī's Solution to the Liar Paradox and Its Reception in Qāḍī Mubārak and Mullā Mubīn." *Journal of South Asian Intellectual History* 1, n. 2 (2018): 183–220.

Robinson, Francis. "Ottomans-Safavids-Mughals: Shared Knowledge and Connective Systems." *Journal of Islamic Studies* 8, no. 2 (1997): 151–184.

Rosenthal, Franz. *The Muslim Concept of Freedom prior to the Nineteenth Century*. Leiden: Brill, 1960.

Rubin, Avi. "Legal borrowing and its impact on Ottoman legal culture in the late nineteenth century." *Continuity and Change* 22, n. 2 (2007): 279–303.

—. *Ottoman* Nizamiye *Courts: Law and Modernity*. New York: Palgrave MacMillan, 2011.

—. "Modernity as Code: The Ottoman Empire and the Global Movement of Codification." *Journal of the Social and Economic History of the Orient* 59, n. 5 (2016): 829–856.

Rudolph, Ulrich. *Al-Māturīdī and the Development of Sunnī Theology in Samarqand*. Trans. Rodrigo Adem. Leiden: Brill, 2015.

Rustow, Marina. *The Lost Archive: Traces of a Caliphate in a Cairo Synagogue*. Princeton: Princeton University Press, 2020.

Salvatore, Armando. "After the State: Islamic reform and the 'implosion' of *shari'a*." In *Muslim Traditions and Modern Techniques of Power*. Ed. Armando Salvatore, 123–140. Münster: Lit, 2001.

Sarkar, Jadunath. *Mughal Administration*. Calcutta: MC Sarkar & Sons, 1963.

Sbaï, Jalila. *La politique musalmane de la France*. Paris: CNRS Editions, 2018.

Schacht, Joseph. *An Introduction to Islamic Law*. Oxford: Clarendon, 1964.

Schauer, Frederick. "Formalism." *Yale Law Journal* 97, n. 4 (1988): 509–548.

Schneider, Irene. "Imprisonment in Pre-Classical and Classical Islamic Law." *Islamic Law and Society* 2, n. 2 (1995): 157–173.

—. "Religious and State Jurisdiction During Nasir al-Din Shah's Reign." *Religion and Society in Qajar Iran*. Ed. Robert Gleave, 84–110. London: Routledge, 2005.

—. *The Petitioning System in Iran: State, Society and Power Relations in the Late 19th Century*. Wiesbaden: Harrassowitz Verlag, 2006.

Schull, Kent F. *Prisons in the Late Ottoman Empire*. Edinburgh: Edinburgh University Press, 2014.

Scott, Rachel M. *Recasting Islamic Law: Religion and the Nation State in Egyptian Constitution Making*. Ithaca: Cornell University Press, 2021.

Shabana, Ayman. *Custom in Islamic Law and Legal Theory*. London: Palgrave, 2010.

Shahawy, Hassaan. "How Subjectivity Became Wrong: Early Hanafism and the Scandal of *Istiḥsān* in the Formative Period of Islamic Law (750–1000 CE)." PhD dissertation, Oxford, 2019.

Shareef, Umar. "*Taqyīd al-Mubāḥ* and Tobacco: Between Administrative and Legislative Authority." *Islamic Law and Society* 30, n. 3 (2023): 1–30.

—. "*Siyāsa* As a Part of the *Sharīʿa*: Tracing the Genealogy of the Ruler's Right to 'Restrict the Permissible' (*Taqyīd al-Mubāḥ*)." PhD dissertation, Georgetown University, 2025.

Siddiqi, Noman Ahmad. "The *Faujdar* and *Faujdari* Under the Mughals." In *The Mughal State: 1526–1750*. Ed. Muzaffar Alam and Sanjay Subrahmanyam, 234–251. Delhi: Oxford University Press, 1998.

Silverstein, Brian. *Islam and Modernity in Turkey*. London: Palgrave Macmillan, 2010.

Simonsohn, Uriel I. *A Common Justice: The Legal Alliance of Christians and Jews under Early Islam*. Philadelphia: University of Pennsylvania Press, 2011.

Sinani, Besnik. *Sufism in Saudi Arabia Since 1979: The Politics of Orthodoxy in Contemporary Islam*. Leiden: Brill, forthcoming.

Singha, Radhika. *A Despotism of Law: Crime and Justice in Early Colonial Law*. Delhi: Oxford University Press, 1998.

Skovgaard-Petersen, Jakob. *Defining Islam for the Egyptian State*. Leiden: Brill, 1997.

Smith, Henry E. "Equity as Meta-Law." *Yale Law Journal* 130 (2021): 1051–1144.

Solum, Lawrence B. "Procedural Justice." *Southern California Law Review* 78, n. 1 (2004): 181–321.

Spuler, Bertold. *Iran in the Early Islamic Period*. Trans. Gwendolin Goldbloom and Berenike Walburg. Ed. Robert Hoyland. Leiden Brill, 2015.

Stilt, Kristen. *Islamic Law in Action: Authority, Discretion and Everyday Experiences in Mamluk Egypt*. Oxford: Oxford University Press, 2011.

Subrin, Stephen N. "How Equity Conquered Common Law: The Federal Rules of Civil Procedure in Historical Perspective." *University of Pennsylvania Law Review* 135 (1987): 910–1002.

Subtelny, Maria E. *Timurids in Transition*. Leiden: Brill, 2007.

Suleiman, Farid. "A Note on al-Bayḍāwī's Years of Birth and Death." *Journal of Qur'anic Studies* 22, n. 2 (2020): 105–115.

Tareen, SherAli. *Perilous Intimacies: Debating Hindu-Muslim Friendship After Empire*. New York: Columbia University Press, 2023.

Terzioğlu, Derin. "Ibn Taymiyya, *al-Siyāsa al-Sharʿiyya*, and the Early Modern Ottomans." In *Historicizing Sunni Islam in the Ottoman Empire, c. 1450–1750*. Ed. Tijana Krstić and Derin Terzioğlu, 101–154. Leiden: Brill, 2021.

Tetlow, Elisabeth Meier. *Women, Crime, and Punishment in Ancient Law and Society: Volume I –The Ancient Near East*. New York: Continuum, 2004.

Tezcan, Baki. *The Second Ottoman Empire*. Cambridge: Cambridge University Press, 2010.

Tillier, Mathieu. "*Qāḍīs* and the political use of the *maẓālim* under the 'Abbāsids." In *Public Violence in Islamic Societies*. Ed. Christian Lange and Maribel Fierro, 42–66. Edinburgh: Edinburgh University Press, 2009.

—. "The Qadis' Justice according to Papyrological Sources (Seventh to Tenth Centuries CE)." In *Legal Documents as Sources for the History of Muslim Societies: Studies in Honour of Rudolph Peters*. Ed. Maaike van Berkel, Léon Buskens, and Petra Sijpesteijn, 39–60. Leiden: Brill, 2017.

—. "Mazalim in historiography." In *The Oxford Handbook of Islamic Law*. Ed. Rumee Ahmed and Anver Emon, 357–380. Oxford: Oxford University Press, 2018.

—. "The Umayyads and the Formation of Islamic Judgeship." In *The Umayyad World*. Ed. Andrew Marsham, 168–182. London: Routledge, 2020.

Topal, Alp Eren. "Political Reforms as Religious Revival: Conceptual Foundations of *Tanzimat*." *Oriente Moderno* 101 (2021): 153–180.

Travers, Robert. *Empires of Complaints: Mughal Law and the Making of British India, 1765–1793*. Cambridge: Cambridge University Press, 2022.

Tyan, Emile. *Le Notariat et le régime de la preuve par écrit dans la pratique du droit musulman*. 2nd ed. Beirut: Faculté de Droit de Beyrouth, 1959.

—. *Histoire de l'organisation judiciaire en pays d'islam*. 2nd ed. Leiden: Brill, 1960.

Ursinus, Michael. *Grievance Administration (*Şikayet*) in an Ottoman Province: The Kaymakam of Rumelia's 'Record Book of Complaints' of 1781–1783*. London: Routledge Curzon, 2005.

Vikør, Knut. *Between God and the Sultan: A History of Islamic Law*. London: Oxford University Press, 2005.

Vogel, Frank. *Islamic Law and Legal System*. Leiden: Brill, 2000.

Walton, Jeremy F. *Muslim Civil Society and the Politics of Religious Freedom in Turkey*. New York: Oxford University Press, 2017.

Weismann, Itzchak. *The Naqshbandiyya*. London: Routledge, 2007.

Weiss, Bernard. *The Spirit of Islamic Law*. Athens, GA: University of Georgia Press, 1998.

Wittmann, Richard. "Before Qadi and Grand Vizier: Intra-Communal Dispute Resolution and Legal Transactions Among Christians and Jews in the Plural Society of Seventeenth Century Istanbul." PhD dissertation, Harvard University, 2008.

Wood, Leonard. *Islamic Legal Revival*. Oxford: Oxford University Press, 1916.

Woods, John E. "Timur's Genealogy." In *Intellectual Studies on Islam: Essays Written in Honor of Martin B. Dickson*. Ed. Michel Mazzaoui and Vera Moreen, 85–126. Salt Lake City: University of Utah Press, 1990.

—. *The Aqquyunlu: Clan, Confederation, Empire*. Revised ed. Salt Lake City: University of Utah Press, 1999.

Wright, Zachary. *Realizing Islam: The Tijaniyya in North Africa and the Eighteenth-Century Muslim World*. Chapel Hill: University of North Carolina Press, 2020.

Yanagihashi, Hiroyuki. "The Judicial Functions of the *Sulṭān* in Civil Cases according to the Mālikīs up to the Sixth/Twelfth Century." *Islamic Law and Society* 3, n. 1 (1996): 41–74.

Yavari, Neguin. *Advice for the Sultan: Prophetic Voices and Secular Politics in Medieval Islam.* London: Hurst, 2014.

Yılmaz, Hüseyin. "The Sultan and the Sultanate: Envisioning Rulership in the Age of Süleyman the Lawgiver (1520–1566)." PhD dissertation, Harvard University, 2005.

Yūsuffīrād, Murtaḍā. *Andīsha-yi siyāsī Jalāl al-Dīn Davānī.* Qom: n.p., 1378/2008.

Zebiri, Kate. *Maḥmūd Shaltūt and Islamic Modernism.* Oxford: Clarendon Press, 1993.

Zeghal, Malika. *The Making of the Modern Muslim State.* Princeton: Princeton University Press, 2024.

Zürcher, Erik J. *Turkey: A Modern History.* London: IB Tauris, 1997.

PRIMARY SOURCES

ʿAbbās, Iḥsān. Ed. *ʿAhd Ardishīr.* Beirut: Dār Ṣādir, 1967.

Ābī, Ṣāliḥ ʿAbd al-Salām. *Al-Thamar al-dānī fī taqrīb al-maʿānī Ḥāshiyat Risālat Ibn Abī Zayd al-Qayrawānī.* 2nd ed. Cairo: Muṣṭafā al-Bābī al-Ḥalabī, 1944.

ʿĀbidīnī, Ayman Diyāb. *Manhaj al-salaf al-qawīm fī al-ʿalāqa bayn al-ḥukkām wa'l-maḥkūmīn.* 3rd ed. Cairo: Mu'assasat Sabīl al-Mu'minīn, 2009.

Abū Yaʿlā Ibn al-Farrā', al-Qāḍī Muḥammad b. al-Ḥusayn. *Kitāb al-Muʿtamad fī uṣūl al-dīn.* Ed. Wadi Z. Haddad. Beirut: Dar El-Machreq, 1986.

—. *Al-Aḥkām al-sulṭāniyya.* Ed. Muḥammad Ḥāmid al-Fiqī. Beirut: Dār al-Kutub al-ʿIlmiyya, 1421/2000.

Abū Yūsuf, Yaʿqūb b. Ibrāhīm. *Taxation in Islām Volume III: Abū Yūsuf's Kitāb al-Kharāj.* Trans. A. Ben Shemesh. Leiden: Brill, 1969.

—. *Kitāb al-Kharāj.* Beirut: Dār al-Maʿrifa, 1979.

—. *Kitāb al-Kharāj.* Ed. Maḥmūd al-Bājī. Tunis: Dār Bū Salāma, 1984.

ʿAjlān, Fahd Ṣāliḥ. *Al-Taḥrīm wa'l-tajrīm fī bayān al-ʿalāqa bayn al-taḥrīm al-sharʿī wa'l-tajrīm al-qānūnī.* [Riyadh]: Markaz al-Bayān li'l-Buḥūth wa'l-Dirāsāt, 2017.

Africanus, Leo. *The History and General Description of Africa.* Trans. John Pory. Ed. Robert Brown. 3 vols. London: Hakluyt Society, 1896.

Albānī, Muḥammad Nāṣir al-Dīn. *Fatāwā al-Shaykh al-Albānī.* Ed. ʿUkāsha ʿAbd al-Mannān al-Ṭayyibī. Cairo: Maktabat al-Turāth al-Islāmī, 1994.

Amāsī, Muḥammad b. Qāsim. *Rawḍat al-akhyār al-muntakhab min Rabīʿ al-abrār.* Ed. Maḥmūd Fākhūrī. Aleppo: Dār al-Qalam al-ʿArabī, 2003.

ʿAṭṭār, Farīd al-Dīn. *Tadhkerat al-awleyā'.* Ed. Moḥammad Esteʿlāmī. Tehran: Zovvār, 1346/1968.

ʿAydarūs, ʿAbd al-Qādir b. ʿAbdallāh. *Al-Nūr al-sāfir fī akhbār al-qarn al-ʿāshir*. Ed. Aḥmad Ḥālū, Maḥmūd al-Arnāʾūṭ and Akram al-Būshī. Beirut: Dār Ṣādir, 2001.

Azrārī, Taqī al-Dīn Ibn Ḥijja al-Ḥamawī. *Kitāb Qahwat al-inshāʾ*. Beirut: Klaus Schwarz, 2005.

Bābānī, Ismāʿīl. *Hadiyyat al-ʿārifīn asmāʾ al-muʾallifīn wa āthār al-muṣannifīn min kashf al-ẓunūn*. Ed. Muḥammad ʿAbd al-Qādir ʿAṭā. 2 vols. Beirut: Dār al-Kutub al-ʿIlmiyya, 1429/2008.

Badāʾūnī, ʿAbd al-Qādir. *Muntakhab al-tavārīkh*. Ed. Aḥmad ʿAlī Ṣāḥeb. Tehran: Anjoman-e Āthār va Mafākher-e Farhangī, 1380/2002.

Bayhaqī, Abū Bakr Aḥmad. *Dalāʾil al-nubuwwa*. Ed. ʿAbd al-Muʿṭī Qalʿajī. 7 vols. Beirut: Dār al-Kutub al-ʿIlmiyya, 1408/1988.

—. *Al-Sunan al-kubrā*. Ed. Muḥammad ʿAbd al-Qādir ʿAṭā. 11 vols. Beirut: Dār al-Kutub al-ʿIlmiyya, 1999.

Bayjūrī, Burhān al-Dīn Ibrāhīm. *Ḥāshiyat al-imām al-Bayjūrī ʿalā Jawharat al-tawḥīd*. Ed. ʿAlī Jumʿa. Cairo: Dār al-Salām, 2006.

Bazzāzī, Muḥammad b. Muḥammad b. Shihāb. *Al-Fatāwā al-Bazzāziyya*. Printed in the margins of *al-Fatāwā al-Hindiyya*. 6 vols. Cairo: al-Maṭbaʿa al-Amīriyya, 1310/1892–3.

Bernier, François. *Travels in the Mogul Empire*. Trans. Archibald Constable. Oxford: Oxford University Press, 1914.

Bilmen, Ömer Nasuhi. *Hukûk-i Islâmiyye ve Istılâhât-ı Fikhiyye Kamusu*. 8 vols. Istanbul: Ravza Yayınları, 2013.

Buhūtī, Manṣūr b. Yūnus. *Al-Rawḍ al-murbiʿ*. Ed. Bashīr Muḥammad ʿUyūn. Damascus: Maktabat Dār al-Bayān, 1999.

Burhāmī, Yāsir. *Al-Minna sharḥ iʿtiqād ahl al-sunna*. 2nd ed. Alexandria: Dār al-Khulafāʾ al-Rāshidīn, 1431/2010.

Cevdet Paşa, Ahmed. *Tezâkir*. Ed. Cavid Baysun. 4 vols. Ankara: Türk Tarih Kurumu, 1991.

Dabūsī, Abū Zayd. *Taqwīm al-adilla*. Ed. Khalīl Muḥyī al-Dīn al-Mays. Beirut: Dār al-Kutub al-ʿIlmiyya, 2001.

Davānī, Jalāl al-Dīn Muḥammad b. Asʿad. *Akhlāq-i Jalālī*. Ed. Naṣīr al-Dīn. Lahore: Maṭbaʿ Karīmī, 1923.

—. "Celâleddin ed-Devvânî ve Tafsîr-u 'Kul yâ eyyuhel Kâfirûn' (Edisyon Kritik)." Cevdet Akbay, ed. MA thesis, Marmara University, 1987.

—. "Risāla-yi ʿadālat." Ed. Najīb Māyil Haravī. In *Majmūʿe-ye rasāʾel-e haṭṭ-e farsī* 1 (1989–90): 60–72.

—. *Thalāth rasāʾil min muṣannafāt al-ʿallāma al-muḥaqqiq Muḥammad b. Asʿad al-Dawānī*. Ed. Aḥmad Tūysirkānī. Mashhad: Majmaʿ al-Buḥūth al-Islāmiyya, 1411/[1990].

—. *Ḥaqīqat al-insān wa'l-rūḥ al-jawwāl fī al-ʿawālim*. Ed. Muḥammad Zāhid al-Kawtharī. Cairo: al-Maktaba al-Azhariyya, 2006.

—. "Dīvān-e Maẓālem." Ed. Hossein Modarressi. In *Farhang-e Īrān zamīn* 27 (1366/1988): 98–118.

—. —. Ms. #37368, Āstān-i Qods-i Rezavī Library, Mashhad, 25b-31a.

—. —. Ms. 4989, Nur Osmaniye Library, Istanbul, 59b-63a.
—. —. Ms. 184, Mehmed Nuri Efendi Library, Istanbul.
—. *Risāla fī afʿāl al-ʿibād*. Ms. 2681, Jāmiʿat al-Malik Suʿūd.
—. *Risāla fī ithbāt al-qadīm*. Ms. 369, Jāmiʿat al-Malik Suʿūd.
—. *Al-Zawrāʾ*. Ms. 3453, Jāmiʿat al-Malik Suʿūd.
Daylamī, Shīrawayh b. Shahrudār. *Al-Firdaws bi-maʾthūr al-khiṭāb*. 2 vols. Beirut: Dār al-Fikr, 1418/1997.
Dede Efendi, Ibrāhīm b. Yaḥyā Khalīfa. *Al-Siyāsa al-sharʿiyya*. Ed. Fuʾād ʿAbd al-Munʿim. Alexandria: Muʾassasat Shabāb al-Jāmiʿa, n.d.
Dhahabī, Shams al-Dīn Muḥammad b. Aḥmad. *Mīzān al-iʿtidāl fī naqd al-rijāl*. Ed. ʿAlī Muḥammad al-Bijāwī. 4 vols. Beirut: Dār al-Maʿrifa, n.d., reprint of 1963–4 Cairo ʿĪsā al-Bābī al-Ḥalabī edition.
—. *Tārīkh al-islām*. Ed. ʿUmar ʿAbd al-Salām Tadmurī. 52 vols. Beirut: Dār al-Kitāb al-ʿArabī, 1987.
—. *Siyar aʿlām al-nubalāʾ*. Ed. Shuʿayb al-Arnāʾūṭ et al. 3rd ed. 25 vols. Beirut: Muʾassasat al-Risāla, 1992–98.
Ḍirār b. ʿAmr. *Kitāb al-Taḥrīsh*. Ed. Ḥusayn Khānṣū and Muḥammad Kaskīn. Istanbul: Sharikat Dār al-Irshād, 2014.
Fang, Liaw Yock, ed. and trans. *Undang-Undang Melaka: The Laws of Melaka*. The Hague: Martinus Nijhoff, 1976.
Ghazālī, Abū Ḥāmid. *Al-Mustaṣfā*. Ed. Muḥammad ʿAbd al-Salām ʿAbd al-Shāfī. Beirut: Dār al-Kutub al-ʿIlmiyya, 1413/1992.
—. *Iḥyāʾ ʿulūm al-dīn*. Ed. Muḥammad Wahbī Sulaymān and Usāma ʿAmmūra. 5 vols. Damascus: Dār al-Fikr, 1427/2006.
—. *Miʿyār al-ʿilm*. Cairo: Maṭbaʿat al-ʿArabiyya, n.d.
— (attributed). *Al-Tibr al-masbūk fī naṣīḥat al-mulūk*. Ed. Aḥmad Shams al-Dīn. Beirut: Dār al-Kutub al-ʿIlmiyya, 1988.
Ghazzī, Najm al-Dīn. *Al-Kawākib al-sāʾira bi-aʿyān al-miʾa al-ʿāshira*. Ed. Jibrāʾīl Jabbūr. 3 vols. Beirut: Dār al-Āfāq al-Jadīda, 1979.
Ghumārī, Aḥmad. *Masālik al-dilāla ʿalā masāʾil matn al-Risāla*. Cairo: Maktabat al-Qāhira, 1415/1995.
—. *Al-Baḥr al-ʿamīq fī marwiyāt Ibn al-Ṣiddīq*. 2 vols. Cairo: Dār al-Kutubī, 2007.
Gomaa, Ali (ʿAlī Jumʿa). *Al-Bayān li-mā yashghalu al-adhhān*. Cairo: Muqaṭṭam, 1425/2005.
—. *Al-Tajruba al-miṣriyya*. Cairo: Nahḍat Miṣr, 2008.
Ḥājjī Khalīfa Muṣṭafā Kātib Chelebī. *Kashf al-ẓunūn ʿan asāmī al-kutub wa al-funūn*. Ed. Muḥammad ʿAbd al-Qādir ʿAṭā. 7 vols. Beirut: Dār al-Kutub al-ʿIlmiyya, 1429/2008.
Ḥarīrī, al-Qāsim b. ʿAlī. *Maqāmāt al-Ḥarīrī*. Beirut: Dār Bayrūt, 1985.
Ḥasanī, ʿAbd al-Ḥayy. *Nuzhat al-khawāṭir wa bahjat al-masāmiʿ waʾl-nawāẓir*. 2nd ed. 8 vols. Hyderabad: Dāʾirat al-Maʿārif al-ʿUthmāniyya, 1431/2010.
Ḥaṭṭāb al-Ruʿaynī, Muḥammad b. ʿAbd al-Raḥmān. *Mawāhib al-Jalīl fī sharḥ Mukhtaṣar Khalīl*. 6 vols. Beirut: Dār al-Fikr, 1398/1977.

Ḥaydar, ʿAlī. *Durar al-ḥukkām sharḥ Majallat al-aḥkām*. 4 vols. Riyadh: Dār ʿĀlam al-Kutub; Beirut: Dār al-Jīl, 1423/2003.

Haytamī, Ibn Ḥajar Aḥmad. *Al-Fatāwā al-kubrā al-fiqhiyya*. Cairo: ʿAbd al-Ḥamīd Aḥmad al-Ḥanafī, n.d.

—. *Ḥawāshī Tuḥfat al-muḥtāj bi-sharḥ al-Minhāj*. 10 vols. Cairo: Maṭbaʿat Muṣṭafā Muḥammad, 1937.

—. *Al-Zawājir ʿan iqtirāf al-kabāʾir*. Ed. ʿImād Zakī al-Bārūdī. 2 vols. Cairo: al-Maktaba al-Tawfīqiyya, 2003.

Hunwick, John, ed. *Sharīʿa in Songhay: The Replies of al-Maghīlī to the Questions of Askia al-Ḥājj Muḥammad*. London: Oxford University Press, 1985.

Ibn al-Abbār, Muḥammad b. ʿAbdallāh Quḍāʿī. *Al-Takmila li-kitāb al-Ṣila*. Ed. ʿAbd al-Salām al-Harrās. 4 vols. Beirut: Dār al-Fikr, 1995.

Ibn ʿAbd al-Ḥakam, ʿAbdallāh. *Sīrat ʿUmar b. ʿAbd al-ʿAzīz*. Ed. Aḥmad ʿUbayd. Cairo: Maktabat Wahba, [1954].

Ibn Abī al-ʿIzz al-Ḥanafī, ʿAlī b. ʿAlī. *Al-Tanbīh ʿalā mushkilāt al-Hidāya*. Ed. ʿAbd al-Ḥakīm Muḥammad Shākir and Anwar Ṣāliḥ Abū Zayd. 6 vols. Riyadh: Maktabat al-Rushd, 1414/2003.

Ibn ʿAbd al-Salām, ʿIzz al-Dīn. *Kitāb al-Fatāwā*. Beirut: Dār al-Maʿrifa, n.d.

—. *Al-Qawāʿid al-kubrā*. Ed. Nazīr Kamāl Ḥammād and ʿUthmān Jumʿa. 2 vols. Damascus: Dār al-Qalam, 1421/2000.

Ibn Abī al-Wafāʾ, ʿAbd al-Qādir. *Al-Jawāhir muḍiyya fī ṭabaqāt al-ḥanafiyya*. Ed. ʿAbd al-Fattāḥ Muḥammad al-Ḥuluw. 5 vols. Giza: Muʾassasat al-Risāla, 1978–88.

Ibn Abī Yaʿlā, Muḥammad. *Ṭabaqāt al-ḥanābila*. Ed. Muḥammad Ḥāmid al-Fiqī. 2 vols. Cairo: Maṭbaʿat al-Sunna al-Muḥammadiyya, 1371/1952.

Ibn ʿĀbidīn, Muḥammad Amīn. *Radd al-muḥtār ʿalā al-Durr al-mukhtār*. 5 vols. Cairo: Dār al-Ṭibāʿa al-Miṣriyya 1272/1856.

—. *Majmūʿat Rasāʾil Ibn ʿĀbidīn*. 2 vols. Damascus: [Muḥammad Hāshim al-Kutubī, 1907].

—. *Ḥāshiyat Ibn ʿĀbidīn*. 8 vols. Beirut: Dār al-Fikr, 1421/2000.

Ibn ʿAqīl, ʿAlī al-Ḥanbalī. *Kitāb al-Funūn*. Ed. George Makdisi. 2 vols. Beirut: Dar El-Machreq, 1970.

Ibn ʿAsākir, Abū al-Qāsim ʿAlī b. al-Ḥasan. *Tārīkh madīnat Dimashq*. Ed. Muḥibb al-Dīn ʿUmar al-ʿAmrawī. 80 vols. Beirut: Dār al-Fikr, 1418/1997.

Ibn ʿĀshūr, Muḥammad al-Ṭāhir. *Tafsīr al-taḥrīr wa'l-tanwīr*. 17 vols. Tunis: al-Dār al-Tūnisiyya, 1984.

Ibn Bashkuwāl, Khalaf b. ʿAbd al-Malik. *Al-Ṣila*. Ed. Ibrāhīm al-Abyārī. 3 vols. Cairo: Dār al-Kitāb al-Miṣrī, 1990.

Ibn Baṭṭāl, ʿAlī b. Khalaf. *Sharḥ Ṣaḥīḥ al-Bukhārī*. Ed. Abū Tamīm Yāsir Ibrāhīm. 10 vols. Riyadh: Maktabat al-Rushd, 2000.

Ibn Ḍuwayyān, Ibrāhīm. *Manār al-sabīl fī sharḥ al-Dalīl*. Ed. Zuhayr al-Shāwīsh. 2 vols. Damascus: al-Maktab al-Islāmī, 1989.

Ibn Fahd, Jārallāh b. al-ʿIzz. *Kitāb Nayl al-munā bi-dhayl bulūgh al-qurā li-takmilat itḥāf al-warā*. Ed. Muḥammad Ḥabīb al-Hayla. 2 vols. Beirut: Muʾassasat al-Furqān and Dār al-Gharb al-Islāmī, 1420/2000.

Ibn Farḥūn, Burhān al-Dīn Ibrāhīm. *Tabṣirat al-ḥukkām fī uṣūl al-aqḍiya wa manāhij al-aḥkām*. Ed. Jamāl al-Marʿashlī. 2 vols. Riyadh: Dār ʿĀlam al-Kutub, 1423/2003.

Ibn Firkāḥ, ʿAbd al-Raḥmān b. Ibrāhīm. *Mas'alat al-ghanā'im*. Ed. ʿAbd al-Sattār Abū Ghudda. Beirut: Dār al-Bashā'ir al-Islāmiyya, 1427/2006.

Ibn Fūrak, Abū Bakr. *Maqālāt al-shaykh Abī al-Ḥasan al-Ashʿarī*. Ed. Aḥmad ʿAbd al-Raḥīm al-Sāyiḥ. Beirut: Maktabat al-Thaqāfa wa'l-Dīniyya, 2005.

Ibn Ḥajar al-ʿAsqalānī, Aḥmad. *Inbā' al-ghumar bi-abnā' al-ʿumar*. 8 vols. Hyderabad: Dā'irat al-Maʿārif al-ʿUthmāniyya, 1968.

—. *Rafʿ al-iṣr ʿan quḍāt miṣr*. Ed. ʿAlī Muḥammad ʿUmar. Cairo: Maktabat al-Khānjī, 1988.

—. *Fatḥ al-bārī sharḥ Ṣaḥīḥ al-Bukhārī*. Ed. ʿAbd al-ʿAzīz b. ʿAbdallāh b. Bāz and Muḥammad Fu'ād ʿAbd al-Bāqī. 16 vols. Beirut: Dār al-Kutub al-ʿIlmiyya, 1997.

Ibn Ḥāmid, al-Ḥasan al-Baghdādī al-Ḥanbalī. *Tahdhīb al-ajwiba*. Ed. ʿAbd al-ʿAzīz Muḥammad al-Qāyidī. 2 vols. Maktabat al-ʿUlūm wa'l-Ḥikam, 1425/2005.

Ibn Ḥanbal, Aḥmad Abū ʿAbdallāh. *Musnad*. Cited to the Maymaniyya printing.

Ibn al-ʿImād, ʿAbd al-Ḥayy b. Aḥmad. *Shadharāt al-dhahab fī akhbār man dhahab*. Ed. ʿAbd al-Qādir al-Arnā'ūṭ and Maḥmūd al-Arnā'ūṭ. 11 vols. Damascus: Dār Ibn Kathīr, 1414/1993.

Ibn Jamāʿa, Muḥammad b. Ibrāhīm. *Taḥrīr al-aḥkām fī tadbīr ahl al-Islām*. Riyadh: Maktabat Dār al-Minhāj, 2012.

Ibn al-Jawzī, ʿAbd al-Raḥmān. *Al-Muntaẓam fī tārīkh al-mulūk wa'l-umam*. Ed. Muḥammad ʿAbd al-Qādir ʿAṭā and Muṣṭafā ʿAbd al-Qādir ʿAṭā. 18 vols. Beirut: Dār al-Kutub al-ʿIlmiyya, 1999.

—. *Ṣayd al-khāṭir*. Ed. Ṭāriq ʿAwaḍallāh. Riyadh: Madār al-Waṭan, 1437/2016.

—. *Naqd al-ʿilm wa'l-ʿulamā' aw Talbīs Iblīs*. Cairo: Maṭbaʿat Muḥammad ʿAlī Ṣubayḥī, n.d.

Ibn Maryam, Muḥammad b. Muḥammad al-Tilimsānī. *Al-Bustān fī dhikr al-ʿulamā' wa'l-awliyā' bi-tilimsān*. Ed. ʿAbd al-Qādir al-Būbāya. Beirut: Dār al-Kutub al-ʿIlmiyya, 2014.

Ibn al-Muqaffaʿ, ʿAbdallāh. *Kalīla wa dimna*. Ed. Louis Cheikho. Beirut: Maṭbaʿat al-Abā' al-Yasūʿīyīn, 1922.

Ibn Qayyim al-Jawziyya, Muḥammad b. Abī Bakr. *Iʿlām al-muwaqqiʿīn*. Ed. Muḥammad ʿIzz al-Dīn Khaṭṭāb. 5 vols. Beirut: Dār Iḥyā' al-Turāth al-ʿArabī, 2001.

—. *Al-Ṭuruq al-ḥukmiyya fī al-siyāsa al-sharʿiyya*. Ed. Nāyif Aḥmad al-Ḥamad. 2 vols. Mecca: Dār ʿĀlam al-Fawā'id, 2011.

Ibn Qudāma, Muwaffaq al-Dīn. *Taḥrīm al-naẓar fī kutub ahl al-kalām*. Ed. George Maqkdisi. London: Luzac, 1962.

—. *Al-Mughnī*. Ed. ʿAbdallāh al-Turkī and ʿAbd al-Fattāḥ al-Ḥuluw. 12 vols. Cairo: Hujr, 1986.

Ibn Rushd, Abū al-Walīd Muḥammad. *The Distinguished Jurist's Primer*. Trans. Imran Ahsan Khan Nyazee. 2 vols. Reading: Garnet, 2000.

Ibn Sa'd, Muḥammad. *Al-Ṭabaqāt al-kubrā*. Ed. 'Alī Muḥammad 'Umar. 11 vols. Cairo: Maktabat al-Khānjī, 1421/2001.

Ibn al-Ṣalāḥ, Abū 'Amr al-Shahrazūrī. *Fatāwā wa masā'il Ibn al-Ṣalāḥ*. Ed. 'Abd al-Mu'ṭī Amīn Qal'ajī. 2 vols. Beirut: Dār al-Ma'rifa, 1986.

Ibn Taymiyya, Taqī al-Dīn Aḥmad. *Majmū'at al-fatāwā*. Ed. Sayyid Ḥusayn al-'Affānī and Khayrī Sa'īd. 35 vols. Cairo: al-Maktaba al-Tawfīqiyya, [n.d.].

—. *Public Duties in Islam: The Institution of the Ḥisba*. Trans. Muhtar Holland. Leicester: Islamic Foundation, 1982.

—. *Al-Siyāsa al-shar'iyya fī iṣlāḥ al-rā'ī wa'l-ra'iyya*. Ed. Ibrāhīm Ramaḍān. Beirut: Dār al-Fikr al-Lubnānī, 1992.

Ibn al-Ṭiqṭaqā, Muḥammad b. 'Alī. *Al-Fakhrī fī al-ādāb al-sulṭāniyya*. Beirut: Dār Ṣādir, [n.d.].

Ibn Wahb al-Kātib, Isḥāq b. Ibrāhīm. *Al-Burhān fī wujūh al-bayān*. Ed. Aḥmad Maṭlūb and Khadīja al-Ḥadīthī. Baghdad: Maṭba'at al-'Ānī, 1967.

Al-Idrīsī, Muḥammad b. Muḥammad. *Nuzhat al-mushtāq fī ikhtirāq al-āfāq*. 2 vols. Cairo: Maktabat al-Thaqāfa al-Dīniyya, 1422/2002.

Iṣbahānī, Abū Nu'aym. *Dhikr akhbār Iṣbahān*. Ed. Sayyid Khusrawī Ḥasan. 2 vols. Beirut: Dār al-Kutub al-'Ilmiyya, 1990.

—. *Ḥilyat al-awliyā'*. 10 vols. Cairo: Maktabat al-Khānjī, 1996.

Iṣfahānī, Abū al-Faraj. *Al-Aghānī*. Ed. 'Alī Muhannā and Samīr Jābir. 24 vols. Beirut: Dār al-Fikr, n.d.

Jadhabtī, Muḥammad b. Ismā'īl al-Jīzī. *Al-Durra al-gharrā' fī naṣā'iḥ al-mulūk wa'l-wuzarā'*. Cairo: Maktabat Nizār Muṣṭafā al-Bāz, 1996.

Jāḥiẓ, 'Amr b. Baḥr. *Kitāb al-Ḥayawān*. Ed. 'Abd al-Salām Hārūn. 8 vols. Beirut: Dār al-Jīl, 1996.

Jaṣṣāṣ, Aḥmad b. 'Alī. *Aḥkām al-Qur'ān*. 3 vols. Beirut: Dār al-Kitāb al-'Arabī, n.d., reprint of Istanbul: Maṭba'at al-Awqāf al-Islāmiyya, 1335/1917.

Jazā'irī, 'Abd al-Mālik Ramaḍānī. *Mudrik al-naẓar fī al-siyāsa bayn al-taṭbīqāt al-shar'iyya wa al-infi'ālāt al-ḥamāsiyya*. 9th ed. Cairo: Dār al-Furqān, 2009.

Juwaynī, Imām al-Ḥaramayn 'Abd al-Malik. *Al-Burhān fī uṣūl al-fiqh*. Ed. 'Abd al-'Aẓīm al-Dīb. 2 vols. Cairo: Dār al-Anṣār, 1400/1980.

—. *Nihāyat al-maṭlab fī dirāyat al-madhhab*. Ed. 'Abd al-'Aẓīm Maḥmūd al-Dīb. 20 vols. Jeddah: Dār al-Minhāj, 1428/2007.

Kamāl Pāshā-zāde, Aḥmad b. Sulaymān. *Rasā'il Ibn Kamāl*. Istanbul: Asetane, [2015], reprint of Istanbul: Maṭba'at Iqdām, 1316/1898.

Kattānī, Muḥammad b. Ja'far. *Salwat al-anfās wa muḥādathat al-akyās mimman uqbira min al-'ulamā' wa'l-ṣulaḥā' bi-fās*. Ed. 'Abdallāh al-Kāmil al-Kattānī et al. 4 vols. Casablanca: Dār al-Thaqāfa, 2004.

Kawākibī, 'Abd al-Raḥmān. *'Abd al-Raḥmān al-Kawākibī: al-a'māl al-kāmila*. Ed. Muḥammad 'Umāra. Cairo: Dār al-Shurūq, 2009.

Khādimī, Muḥammad b. Muḥammad. *Ḥāshiyat al-Khādimī 'alā al-Durar wa'l-ghurar*. Cairo: Dār al-Ṭibā'a al-'Āmira, 1268/1853.

Khalīl b. Isḥāq al-Mālikī. *Mukhtaṣar Khalīl*. Ed. al-Ṭāhir Aḥmad al-Zāwī. 2nd ed. Beirut: Dār al-Madār al-Islāmī, 2004.

Khān, ʿAlī Muḥammad. *Mirat-i-Ahmadi: A Persian History of Gujarat.* Trans. M.F. Lokhandwala. Baroda: Oriental Institute, 1965.

Khaṣṣāf, Abū Bakr. *Adab al-qāḍī.* Ed. Farhat Ziadeh. Cairo: Maṭbaʿat Jablāwī, 1979.

Khaṭīb al-Baghdādī, Aḥmad b. ʿAlī. *Tārīkh Baghdād.* Ed. Muṣṭafā ʿAbd al-Qādir ʿAṭā. 24 vols. Beirut: Dār al-Kutub al-ʿIlmiyya, 1417/1998.

Khaṭṭābī, Abū Sulaymān Ḥamd. *Maʿālim al-sunan.* 3rd ed. 4 vols. Beirut: al-Maktaba al-ʿIlmiyya, 1981.

Khwānsārī, Muḥammad Bāqir. *Rawḍat al-jannāt fī aḥwāl al-ʿulamāʾ waʾl-sādāt.* 7 vols. Tehran: Maktabeh-ye Ismāʿīliyān, [1962–1972].

Kindī, Muḥammad b. Yūsuf. *Kitāb al-Wulāt wa Kitāb al-Quḍāt.* Ed. Rhuvon Guest. Beirut: al-Ābā, 1908 and Leiden: Brill, 1912.

Kınalızade Ali Çelebi. *Ahlâk-ı Alâ'î.* Ed. Mustafa Koç. Istanbul: Klasik, 2007.

Lāhījī, Quṭb al-Dīn Muḥammad ʿAlī Ishkavarī. *Maḥbūb al-qulūb.* Ed. Ḥāmid al-Dībājī. 2 vols. Tehran: Daftar-e Nashr-e Mīrāt-e Maktūb, 1382/2003.

Laknawī, ʿAbd al-Ḥayy al-Farangī Maḥallī. *Al-Fawāʾid al-bahiyya fī tarājim al-ḥanafiyya.* Karachi: Qadīmī Kutub-khāne, n.d.

Maḥmūd, ʿAbd al-Ḥalīm. *Fatāwā al-imām ʿAbd al-Ḥalīm Maḥmūd.* 5th ed. 2 vols. Cairo: Dār al-Maʿārif, 2002.

Makkī, Abū Ṭālib Muḥammad b. ʿAlī. *Qūt al-qulūb.* 2 vols. in 1. Cairo: Maṭbaʿat al-Anwār al-Muḥammadiyya, 1405/1985.

Manucci, Niccolao. *Storia do Mogor, or Mogul India 1653–1708.* Trans. William Irvine. 3 vols. London: John Murray, 1907.

Maqdisī, Abū Shāma. *Al-Rawḍatayn fī akhbār al-dawlatayn al-nūriyya wa al-ṣalāḥiyya.* Ed. Ibrāhīm al-Zubayq. 5 vols. Beirut: Muʾassasat al-Risāla, 1997.

Maqrīzī, Taqī al-Dīn Aḥmad. *Al-Mawāʿiẓ waʾl-iʿtibār bi-dhikr al-khiṭat waʾl-āthar.* Ed. Muḥammad Zaynhum and Madīḥat al-Sharqāwī. 3 vols. Cairo: Maktabat al-Madbūlī, 1997.

Marghīnānī, Burhān al-Dīn ʿAlī. *Al-Hidāya.* 4 vols. Lahore: Maktaba Raḥmāniyya, n.d.

Masʿūdī, ʿAlī b. al-Ḥusayn. *Murūj al-dhahāb.* 2nd ed. 2 vols. N.p.: al-Sharika al-ʿĀlamiyya, 1990.

Māturīdī, Abū Manṣūr Muḥammad. *Taʾwīlāt al-Qurʾān.* Ed. Bekir Topaloğlu et al. 17 vols. Istanbul: Dār al-Mīzān, 2006.

Māwardī, Abū al-Ḥasan ʿAlī b. Ḥabīb. *Maverdii: Constitutiones Politicae.* Ed. Maximilian Enger. Bonn: Adolphum Marcum, 1853.

—. *Adab al-qāḍī.* Ed. Muḥyī Hilāl al-Sarḥān. 2 vols. Baghdad: Maṭbaʿat al-ʿĀnī, 1392/1972.

—. *Qawānīn al-wizāra wa siyāsat al-mulūk.* Ed. Riḍwān al-Sayyid. Beirut: Dār al-Ṭalīʿa, 1979.

—. *Naṣīḥat al-mulūk.* Ed. Khaḍir Muḥammad Khaḍir. Kuwait: Maktabat al-Falāḥ, 1403/1983.

—. *Al-Aḥkām al-sulṭāniyya waʾl-wilāyāt al-dīniyya.* Ed. Aḥmad Mubārak al-Baghdādī. Kuwait: Maktabat Dār Ibn Qutayba, 1409/1989.

—. *Kitāb Durar al-sulūk fī siyāsat al-mulūk*. Ed. Fu'ād 'Abd al-Mun'im Aḥmad. Riyadh: Dār al-Waṭan, 1417/1997.

—. *Al-Amthāl wa'l-ḥikam*. Ed. Fu'ād 'Abd al-Mun'im Aḥmad. Riyadh: Dār al-Waṭan, 1420/1999.

—. *Al-Ḥāwī al-kabīr*. Ed. 'Alī Muḥammad Mu'awwaḍ and 'Ādil Aḥmad 'Abd al-Mawjūd. 19 vols. Beirut: Dār al-Kutub al-'Ilmiyya, 1999.

—. *Adab al-dunyā wa'l-dīn*. Ed. Muḥammad Ḥasan Sulaymān. Cairo: Dār al-Fārūq, 2008.

—. *Tashīl al-naẓar wa ta'jīl al-ẓafar*. Ed. Riḍwān al-Sayyid. 2nd ed. Beirut: Ibn al-Azraq Center for Political Heritage Studies, 1432/2012.

Miskawayh, Aḥmad b. Muḥammad. *Tajārub al-umam*. Cairo: al-Maṭba'a al-Amīriyya, n.d.

Mullā Hüsrev, Muḥammad b. Farāmurz. *Durar al-ḥukkām sharḥ Ghurar al-aḥkām*. Ed. Aḥmad Rif'at al-Qarah-Ḥiṣārī. 2 vols. Istanbul: Fazilet Neşriyat, 2015, reprint of 1308/1890 Istanbul edition.

Munāwī, 'Abd al-Ra'ūf. *Fayḍ al-qadīr sharḥ al-Jāmi' al-ṣaghīr*. Ed. Ḥamdī al-Damardāsh Muḥammad. 13 vols. Mecca: Maktabat Nizār Muṣṭafā al-Bāz, 1998.

—. *Al-Jawāhir al-muḍiyya fī bayān al-ādāb al-sulṭāniyya*. Ed. 'Abdallāh Ibrāhīm al-Nāṣir. Riyadh: Jāmi'at al-Malik Su'ūd, 1424/2013.

Muzanī, Ismā'īl b. Yaḥyā. *Mukhtaṣar*. Ed. 'Abd al-Qādir Shāhīn. Beirut: Dār al-Kutub al-'Ilmiyya, 1998.

Nabhānī, Yūsuf. *Jāmi' karamāt al-awliyā'*. Ed. 'Abd al-Wārith Muḥammad 'Alī. 2 vols. Beirut: Dār al-Kutub al-'Ilmiyya, 1422/2002.

Nābulusī, 'Abd al-Ghanī. *Al-Ḥadīqa al-nadiya sharḥ al-Tarīqa al-muḥammadiyya*. 2 vols. Istanbul: Asetane, reprint of 1295/1878 Maṭba'at 'Āmira edition.

Nawawī, Muḥyī al-Dīn Yaḥyā. *Sharḥ Ṣaḥīḥ Muslim*. 15 vols. Beirut: Dār al-Qalam, 1987.

—. *Minhāj al-ṭālibīn*. Ed. Muḥammad Ṭāhir Sha'bān. Jeddah: Dār al-Minhāj, 2000.

Nubāhī, Abū al-Ḥasan. *Tārīkh quḍāt al-Andalus*. Ed. Maryam Qāsim Ṭawīl. Beirut: Dār al-Kutub al-'Ilmiyya, 1415/1995.

Nūr al-Ḥasan b. Ṣiddīq Ḥasan Khān. *Al-Ṭarīqa al-muthlā fī al-irshād ilā tark al-taqlīd wa ittibā' mā huwa al-awlā*. Ed. Sa'īd Mi'shāsha. Beirut: Dār Ibn Ḥazm, 1421/2000.

Qāḍīkhān, al-Ḥasan b. Manṣūr. *Fatāwā Qāḍīkhān*. Ed. Sālim Muṣṭafā al-Badrī. 3 vols. Beirut: Dār al-Kutub al-'Ilmiyya, 1988.

Qāḍī 'Iyāḍ b. Mūsā. *Tartīb al-madārik*. Ed. Muḥammad Sālim Hāshim. 2 vols. Beirut: Dār al-Kutub al-'Ilmiyya, 1998.

—. *Kitāb al-Shifā*. Beirut: Dār Ibn Ḥazm, 2000.

Qaffāl al-Shāshī, Muḥammad b. 'Alī. *Maḥāsin al-sharī'a*. Ed. Muḥammad 'Alī Samak. Beirut: Dār al-Kutub al-'Ilmiyya, 2007.

Qalqashandī, Aḥmad. *Ṣubḥ al-'ashā*. 14 vols. Cairo: Dār al-Kutub al-Miṣriyya, 1340/1922.

Qarāfī, Shihāb al-Dīn Aḥmad. *Al-Furūq*. Ed. Khalīl Manṣūr. Beirut: Dār al-Kutub al-'Ilmiyya, 1998.

—. *Al-Dhakhīra*. Ed. Muḥammad al-Ḥajjī. 14 vols. Beirut: Dār al-Gharb, 1994.
—. *The Criterion for Distinguishing Legal Opinions from Judicial Rulings and the Administrative Acts of Judges and Rulers*. Trans. Mohammad Fadel. New Haven: Yale University Press, 2017.
Qudūrī, Aḥmad b. Muḥammad. *Mukhtaṣar*. Trans. Ṭāhir Maḥmood Kiānī. London: Ta-Ha Publishers, 2010.
Al-Qurṭubī, Muḥammad b. Aḥmad. *Al-Jāmiʿ li-aḥkām al-Qur'ān*. Ed. Muḥammad Ibrāhīm al-Ḥifnāwī and Maḥmūd Ḥamīd ʿUthmān. 20 vols. in 10. Cairo: Dār al-Ḥadīth, 1994.
Rāzī, Fakhr al-Dīn Muḥammad. *Manāqib al-imām al-Shāfiʿī*. Ed. Aḥmad Ḥijāzī al-Saqā. Cairo: Maktabat al-Kulliyyāt al-Azhariyya, 1406/1986.
Rūdhrāwarī, Ẓahīr al-Dīn. *Dhayl Kitāb Tajārib al-umam*. Published in Miskawayh, *Tajārib al-umum*. Ed. Abū al-Qāsim Imāmī, 8 vols. Tehran: Sorūsh, 2001.
Ṣābī, al-Hilāl b. Muḥsin. *Al-Wuzarā' aw Tuḥfat al-umarā' fī tārīkh al-wuzarā'*. Ed. ʿAbd al-Sattār Aḥmad Farāj. [Cairo]: Dār Iḥyā' al-Kutub al-ʿArabī, 1958.
Sahmī, Ḥamza b. Yūsuf. *Tārīkh Jurjān*. Hyderabad: Dā'irat al-Maʿārif al-ʿUthmāniyya, 1950.
Saḥnūn ʿAbd al-Salām b. Saʿīd al-Tanūkhī. *Al-Mudawwana al-kubrā*. Ed. ʿĀmir al-Jazzār and ʿAbdallāh al-Minshāwī. 5 vols. Cairo: Dār al-Ḥadīth, 1426/2005.
Sakhāwī, Shams al-Dīn Muḥammad. *Al-Ḍaw' al-lāmiʿ li-ahl al-qarn al-tāsiʿ*. 12 vols. in 6. Beirut: Dār al-Jīl, 1992.
Samʿānī, ʿAbd al-Karīm b. Muḥammad. *Al-Ansāb*. Ed. ʿAbdallāh ʿUmar al-Bārūdī. Beirut: Dār al-Jinān, 1988.
Ṣanʿānī, Muḥammad b. Ismāʿīl Ibn al-Amīr. *Majmūʿ fīhi sabaʿ rasā'il li'l-imām al-muḥaqqiq Muḥammad b. Ismāʿīl al-Amīr al-Ṣanʿānī*. Ed. Muḥammad Aṣghar al-Muqaṭṭirī. Beirut: Dār Ibn Ḥazm, 2004.
Sarakhsī, Muḥammad b. Aḥmad. *Al-Mabsūṭ*. 30 vols. Beirut: Dār al-Maʿrifa, n.d.
Ṣāwī, Aḥmad. *Bulghat al-sālik li-aqrab al-masālik ʿalā al-Sharḥ al-ṣaghīr li-Aḥmad al-Dardīr*. 4 vols. Beirut: Dār al-Kutub al-ʿIlmiyya, 1415/1995.
Ṣayrafī, ʿAlī b. Dāwūd. *Nuzhat al-nufūs wa'l-abdān fī tawārīkh al-zamān*. Ed. Ḥasan Ḥabashī. 3 vols. Cairo: Maṭbaʿat Dār al-Kutub, 1970.
Shāfiʿī, Muḥammad b. Idrīs. *Kitāb al-Umm*. 8 vols. Beirut: Dār al-Maʿrifa, 1393/1973.
Shāh Walī Allāh al-Dihlawī. *Ḥujjat Allāh al-bāligha*. Ed. Saʿīd Aḥmad Palanpūrī. 2 vols. Deoband: Maktabat Ḥijāz, 2010.
Shākir, Aḥmad. *Jamharat maqālāt al-ʿallāma al-shaykh Aḥmad Muḥammad Shākir*. Ed. ʿAbd al-Raḥmān ʿAbd al-ʿAzīz. 2 vols. Giza: Dār al-Riyāḍ, 1426/2005.
Shaltūt, Maḥmūd. *Fatāwā*. Cairo: Dār al-Shurūq, 1408/1983.
—. *Al-Islām: ʿaqīda wa sharīʿa*. 17th ed. Cairo: Dār al-Shurūq, 1411/1991.
Shaʿrānī, ʿAbd al-Wahhāb. *Al-Mīzān al-kubrā*. 2 vols in 1. Cairo: Maktabat Zahrān [no date]. Reprint of Cairo: Maktabat al-Kastiliyya, 1862.
Shāṭibī, Abū Isḥāq Ibrāhīm. *Kitāb al-Iʿtiṣām*. Cairo: al-Maktaba al-Tijāriyya al-Kubrā, 1914.

—. *Fatāwā al-imām al-Shāṭibī*. Ed. Muḥammad Abū al-ʿAjfān. 2nd ed. Tunis: n.p., 1985.

Shawkānī, Muḥammad b. ʿAlī. *Al-Rasāʾil al-fiqhiyya liʾl-imām al-Shawkānī*. Ed. Aḥmad Farīd al-Mazīdī. Beirut: Dār al-Kutub al-ʿIlmiyya, 2005.

Shīrāzī, Abū Isḥāq Ibrāhīm. *Al-Muhadhdhab*. 2 vols. Beirut: Dār al-Fikr, n.d.

Shirbīnī, Muḥammad b. al-Khaṭīb. *Mughnī al-Muḥtāj*. Ed. Muḥammad Khalīl Aytānī. 4 vols. Beirut: Dār al-Maʿrifa, 1998.

Shūshtarī, Qāḍī Nūr Allāh. *Majālis al-muʾminīn*. 2 vols. Tehran: Ketābkhorūshī-ye Eslāmī, 1377/1998.

Subki, Tāj al-Dīn ʿAbd al-Wahhāb. *Muʿīd al-niʿam wa mubīd al-niqam*. Ed. Muḥammad ʿAlī al-Najjār et al. Cairo: Dār al-Kitāb al-ʿArabī, 1948.

—. *Ṭabaqāt al-shāfiʿiyya al-kubrā*. Ed. ʿAbd al-Fattāḥ Muḥammad al-Ḥuluw and Maḥmūd Muḥammad al-Ṭanāḥī, 2nd edn. 9 vols. Cairo: Hujr, 1992.

Subkī, Taqī al-Dīn ʿAlī. *Fatāwā al-Subkī*. 2 vols. Beirut: Dār al-Maʿrifa, n.d.

Suyūṭī, Jalāl al-Dīn ʿAbd al-Raḥmān. *Bughyat al-wuʿāt*. Ed. Muḥammad Abū al-Faḍl Ibrāhīm. 2 vols. Beirut: Maktabat al-ʿAṣriyya, n.d.

—. *Al-Bāhir fī ḥukm al-Nabī ṣallā Allāhu ʿalayhi wa sallama biʾl-bāṭin waʾl-ẓāhir*. Ed. Mehmet Hayri Kıbaşoğlu. Cairo: Dār al-Salām, 1407/1987.

—. *Al-Ashbāh waʾl-naẓāʾir*. Ed. Muḥammad al-Muʿtaṣim al-Baghdādī. Beirut: Dār al-Kitāb al-ʿArabī, 1414/1993.

Ṭabarī, Muḥammad b. Jarīr. *Tārīkh al-Ṭabarī*. 6 vols. Beirut: Dār al-Kutub al-ʿIlmiyya, 2003.

Ṭaḥāwī, Abū Jaʿfar Aḥmad. *Sharḥ maʿānī al-āthār*. Ed. Muḥammad Sayyid Jād al-Ḥaqq, Muḥammad Zuhrī al-Najjār and Yūsuf ʿAbd al-Raḥmān al-Marʿashlī. 4 vols. Beirut: ʿĀlam al-Kutub, 1414/1994.

—. *Sharḥ mushkil al-āthār*. Ed. Shuʿayb al-Arnāʾūṭ. 16 vols. Beirut: Muʾassasat al-Risāla, 1994.

Taftāzānī, Saʿd al-Dīn Muḥammad. *Sharḥ al-Arbaʿīn liʾl-Nawawī*. Istanbul: Asetane, reprint of the 1316/1898 ʿĀmiriyya print.

Tanūkhī, al-Muḥsin b. ʿAlī. *Nishwār al-muḥāḍara wa akhbār al-mudhākara*. Ed. ʿAbbūd al-Shālijī. 8 vols. Beirut: Dār Ṣādir, 1971.

Ṭarābulusī, ʿAlāʾ al-Dīn ʿAlī b. Khalīl. *Muʿīn al-ḥukkām fīmā yataraddadu bayn al-khaṣmayn min al-aḥkām*. Cairo: al-Maṭbaʿa al-Maymaniyya, 1310/1892.

Ṭāshkubrīzāda (Taşköprüzade), Aḥmad b. Muṣṭafā. *Al-Shaqāʾiq al-nuʿmāniyya fī ʿulamāʾ al-dawla al-ʿUthmāniyya*. Istanbul: Jāmiʿat Istānbūl, Markaz al-Dirāsāt al-Sharqīyya, 1985.

Tehrānī, Abū Bakr. *Ketāb-e Deyārbakreyye*. Ed. Nejātī Lūghāl and Fārūq Sūdar. [Tehran]: Chāpkhāne-ye Anjomān-e Tork, 1964.

ʿUmarī, Aḥmad b. Yaḥyā. *Masālik al-abṣār fī mamālik al-amṣār*. Ed. Kāmil Muslimān al-Jabūrī. 15 vols. Beirut: Dār al-Kutub al-ʿIlmiyya, 2010.

ʿUqbānī, Muḥammad b. Aḥmad. *Tuḥfat al-nāẓir wa ghunyat al-dhākir fī ḥifẓ al-shaʿāʾir wa taghyīr al-manākir*. Ed. ʿAlī al-Shanūfī. Damascus: al-Maʿhad al-Thaqāfī al-Fransī, 1967.

Wādiʿī, Muqbil bin Hādī. *Al-Makhraj min al-fitna*. 3rd ed. Ṣaʿda: Maktabat Ṣanʿāʾ al-Athariyya, 2002.

Wakīʿ Muḥammad b. Khalaf. *Akhbār al-quḍāt*. Ed. Saʿīd Muḥammad al-Laḥḥām. Riyadh: ʿĀlam al-Kutub, n.d.

Wazzānī, Abū ʿĪsā Sīdī al-Mahdī b. Muḥammad. *Al-Nawāzil al-jadīda al-kubrā fī-mā li-ahl Fās wa ghayrihim min al-badū wa'l-qurā / al-Miʿyār al-jadīd al-jāmiʿ al-muʿrib ʿan fatāwā al-muta'akhkhirīn min ʿulamā' al-maghrib*. Ed. ʿUmar ʿImād. 12 vols. Casablanca: Maṭbaʿat al-Faḍāla, 1418/1997.

—. *Al-Nawāzil al-ṣughrā*. Ed. Muḥammad al-Sayyid ʿUthmān. 4 vols. Beirut: Dār al-Kutub al-ʿIlmiyya, 1435/2014.

Yaʿqūbī, Abū al-ʿAbbās Aḥmad. *Tārīkh al-Yaʿqūbī*. Ed. M.Th. Houtsma. 2 vols. Leiden: Brill, 1883.

Yāqūt al-Ḥamawī. *Muʿjam al-udabā'*. Ed. Iḥsān ʿAbbās. 7 vols. Beirut: Dār al-Gharb al-Islāmī, 1993.

Zarqā, Muṣṭafā Aḥmad. *Al-Madkhal al-fiqhī al-ʿāmm*. 3rd ed. 2 vols. Damascus: Dār al-Qalam, 1433/2012, originally published 1945.

Zabīdī, Murtaḍa. *Itḥāf al-sāda al-muttaqīn bi-sharḥ Iḥyā' ʿulūm al-dīn*. 10 vols. Beirut: Mu'assasat al-Tārīkh al-ʿArabī, 1414/1994, reprint of 1311/1894 Cairo Maymaniyya print.

Notes

INTRODUCTION: WHEN LAW AND JUSTICE DON'T MATCH

1. Indira Falk Gesinke, *Islamic Reform and Conservatism: Al-Azhar and the Evolution of Modern Sunni Islam* (London: IB Tauris, 2010), 7.
2. For this Hadith and its uses, see *Sunan* of Abū Dāwūd: *kitāb al-malāḥim, bāb mā yudhkaru fī qarn al-mi'a*; Ella Landau-Tasseron, "The 'Cyclical Reform': A Study of the *Mujaddid* Tradition," *Studia Islamica* 70 (1989): 79–117; John O. Voll, "Renewal and Reform in Islamic History: *Tajdid* and *Islah*," in *Voices of Resurgent Islam*, ed. John L. Esposito (New York: Oxford University Press, 1983), 32–47.
3. 'Alawī b. Aḥmad al-Saqqāf, "Mukhtaṣar al-Fawā'id al-Makkiyya," in *Majmū'at sab'a kutub mufīda* (Cairo: Muṣṭafā al-Bābī al-Ḥalabī, 1940), 104.
4. Rashīd Riḍā, *Tafsīr al-Qu'rān al-ḥakīm al-mashhūr bi-tafsīr al-Manār*, ed. Ibrāhīm Shams al-Dīn (Beirut: Dār al-Kutub al-'Ilmiyya, 1999), 3:105. For an interpretation similar to 'Abduh's but not as daring as Shaltūt's, i.e., recognizing that a woman's testimony is accepted alone in matters inaccessible to men, like childbirth, but not arguing that witness rules overall should change and not citing Ibn al-Qayyim, see Yūsuf al-Qaraḍāwī, *Kayfa nata'āmalu ma'a al-Qur'ān al-'aẓīm*, 3rd ed. (Cairo: Dār al-Shurūq, 1421/2000), 101. Shaykh Muḥammad al-Ghazālī, usually a more progressive voice, concludes that the two-women-for-one-man rule regarding testimony exists because women's menstrual cycle has an effect on their memory; Muḥammad al-Ghazālī, *al-Sunna al-nabawiyya bayn ahl al-fiqh wa ahl al-ḥadīth*, 11th ed. (Cairo: Dār al-Shurūq, 1996), 66.
5. Kate Zebiri, *Maḥmūd Shaltūt and Islamic Modernism* (Oxford: Clarendon Press, 1993), 23.
6. Maḥmūd Shaltūt, *al-Islām: 'aqīda wa sharī'a*, 17th ed. (Cairo: Dār al-Shurūq, 1411/1991), 239–240; Ibn Qayyim al-Jawziyya, *I'lām al-muwaqqi'īn 'an rabb al-'ālamīn*, ed. Muḥammad 'Izz al-Dīn Khaṭṭāb, 5 vols. (Beirut: Dār Iḥyā' al-Turāth al-'Arabī, 2001), 1:94–96.
7. For examples of uses of this verse in Islamophobic discourse, see Ayaan Hirsi Ali, *Heretic* (New York: Harper, 2015), 145; Glenn Beck, *It is about Islam* (New York: Threshold Editions, 2015), 164.
8. Asma Barlas, *"Believing Women" in Islam* (Austin: University of Texas Press, 2002), 105; Irshad Manji, *Allah, Liberty and Love* (New York: Free Press, 2011), 196. The two-women-for-one-man issue has long featured in Islam/

West polemics around women's rights. It is referred to in an account of an 1801 debate between the Indian Muslim traveler in Britain, Mīrzā Abū Ṭālib, and an English woman on the topic of who enjoyed more liberties, English or "Asiatic" women. Abū Ṭālib responds to the point by stating that the ratio has to do with women's lack of expertise and "the fickleness of their disposition"; Mīrzā Abū Ṭālib, *Westward Bound: Travels of Mirza Abu Taleb*, ed. Mushirul Hasan, trans. Charles Stewart (New Delhi: Oxford University Press, 2005), 300–1.

9. For a charitable version of this, see Gary Wills, *What the Qur'an Meant and Why it Matters* (New York: Viking Press, 2017), 187.
10. See, for example, Martin Sheen's President lecturing a TV host who cites the Bible to prove the abomination of homosexuality by asking her if people should also be put to death for working on the sabbath and sell their children into slavery; *The West Wing*, "The Midterms," S2, E3, NBC, Oct. 18, 2000.
11. *Agatha Christie's Poirot*, "Murder on the Orient Express," ITV, Oct. 7, 2010.
12. Michel Foucault, *Les mots et les choses* (Paris: Éditions Gallimard, 1966), 179.
13. Max Weber, *The Sociology of Religion*, trans. Ephraim Fischoff (London: Metheun & Co., 1965), 125. For a fascinating example of how this was reflected in Britain in changes in how judicial oath-breaking and perjury were viewed and punished, with other-worldly threats replaced by worldly punishment and assumptions of self-interest, see Keith Thomas, *Religion and the Decline of Magic: Studies in Popular Beliefs in Sixteenth and Seventeenth-Century England* (New York: Oxford University Press, 1971), 68.
14. Murteza Bedir, "*Fıkıh* to Law: Secularization through Curriculum," *Islamic Law and Society* 11, n. 3 (2004): 386.
15. Mottahedeh wrote that "Ulamalogy is a noble science – at least we have to think so, because it is almost all the Islamic social history we will ever have..."; cited from R. Stephen Humphreys, *Islamic History: A Framework for Inquiry*, rev. ed. (Princeton: Princeton University Press, 1991), 187. Jonathan Brockopp proposes an alternative historiography that views the ulama's centrality as not inevitable and the early administrative tradition as a competing lettered tradition. See Jonathan Brockopp, *Muhammad's Heirs: The Rise of Muslim Scholarly Communities, 622–951* (Cambridge: Cambridge University Press, 2017).
16. See Talal Asad, *The Idea of an Anthropology of Islam* (Washington, DC: Occasional Paper of the Center for Contemporary Arab Studies, Georgetown University, 1986), 14. For an excellent discussion of the impact of Asad's contribution and its background, see Ovamir Anjum, "Islam as a Discursive Tradition: Talal Asad and his Interlocutors," *Comparative Studies of South Asia, Africa, and the Middle East* 27, n. 3 (2007): 656–72.
17. See Jonathan Brown, *Hadith: Muhammad's Legacy in the Medieval and Modern World*, 2nd ed. (London: Oneworld, 2017), 71 ff., 99–104.
18. Unattributed in *Ṣaḥīḥ al-Bukhārī*: *kitāb al-ʿilm, bāb al-ʿilm qabla al-qawl wa'l-ʿamal* but cited as a Hadith in *Sunan* of Abū Dāwūd: *kitāb al-ʿilm, bāb al-ḥathth ʿalā ṭalab al-ʿilm*, generally noted for its weakness but deemed *ḥasan li-ghayrihi* by al-Arnā'ūṭ, ed., *Musnad al-imām Aḥmad Ibn Ḥanbal*, ed. Shuʿayb al-Arnā'ūṭ et al. (Beirut: Mu'assasat al-Risāla, 1416/1995–1421/2001), 36:46.
19. H. F. Amedroz, "The Mazalim Jurisdiction in the Ahkam Sultaniyya of Mawardi," *Journal of the Royal Asiatic Society of Great Britain and Ireland* July (1911): 635–674; Şerif Mardin, "The Just and the Unjust," *Daedalus* 120, no. 3 (1991): 115; Joseph Schacht, *An Introduction to Islamic Law* (Oxford:

Clarendon, 1964), 51; Wael B. Hallaq, *Sharīʿa: Theory, Practice, Transformations* (Cambridge: Cambridge University Press, 2009), 55, 208; Jørgen Nielsen, *Secular Justice in an Islamic State: Maẓālim under the Baḥrī Mamlūks, 662/1264–789/1387* ([Leiden]: Nederlands Historisch-Archeologisch Instituut te Istanbul, 1985), 85–90; Christian Müller, "Redressing Injustice: *Maẓālim* jurisdictions at the Umayyad court of Córdoba (eighth-eleventh centuries CE)," in *Court Cultures in the Muslim World*, ed. Albrecht Fuess and Jan-Peter Hartung (New York: Routledge, 2011), 93–104; Mathieu Tillier, "Maẓālim courts," in *Encyclopaedia of Islam THREE* (Leiden: Brill, 2007–present).

20. The similarity between the English equity court and the *maẓālim* tribunal has been discussed by Khadduri, Coulson, and others. See Majid Khadduri, *The Islamic Conception of Justice* (Baltimore: Johns Hopkins University Press, 1984), 156; Noel J. Coulson, *A History of Islamic Law* (Edinburgh: Edinburgh University Press, 2022, reprint of 1964 ed.), 131. The courts of equity in England emerged from the court of the Exchequer (the government department handling fiscal matters) and the Chancery (the department handling secretarial matters) in the late thirteenth and early fourteenth centuries and formed under the person of the Chancellor, the king's grand vizier who oversaw both departments. Part of the Chancellor's legal authority was that he could invent new writs if he were petitioned regarding some unusual offense, but these could later be quashed by the common law courts if they went against the common law of the land. More importantly, the Chancellor was the 'conscience of the king' and the representation of his royal justice, to which all could in theory bring a plea. Since at times one could not sue the king or his representatives in the courts of law, the Chancellor was the source of redress for wrongs done by the state. The Chancellor was also the official to petition if the courts of law either offered no remedy or if such a remedy was realistically infeasible due to the wealth or power of the defendant. The new courts of equity borrowed much procedure and rules from ecclesiastical courts (Chancellors were bishops through the sixteenth century). But, by the sixteenth century, they were using their own growing body of 'the rules of equity and good conscience.' This was not so different from the common law of the land, and the judges of the equity courts often consulted common law judges and lawyers and, early on, the Chancellor would send questions of fact to the common law Court of the King's Bench for answer by a jury. But the courts of equity also acquired jurisdiction where the common law lapsed. See F.W. Maitland, *Equity* (Cambridge: Cambridge University Press, 1920), 2–11.
21. For this connection, see Ulrich Rebstock, "A Qāḍī's Errors," *Islamic Law and Society* 6, n. 1 (1999): 13–14.
22. Maaike van Berkel, "Abbasid *Maẓālim* between Theory and Practice," in *Le Pluralisme Judiciaire dan l'Islam Premoderne*, ed. Mathieu Tillier, special issue, *Bulletin d'Études Orientales* 63 (2014): 239.
23. For a different perspective on the areas of *maẓālim* competency, see Emile Tyan, *Histoire de l'organisation judiciaire en pays d'islam*, 2nd ed. (Leiden: Brill, 1960), 452–473; Hallaq, *Sharīʿa*, 201–216.
24. For a summary of scholarship on this issue, see Nimrod Hurvitz, "The Contribution of Early Islamic Rulers to Adjudication and Legislation: The

Case of the *Mazalim* Tribunals," in *Law and Empire: Ideas, Practices, Actors*, ed. Jeroen Duindam et al. (Leiden: Brill, 2013), 135–155.

25. The Ḥanbalī Ibn ʿAqīl (d. 513/1119) defines *siyāsa* as what promotes wellbeing (*ṣalāḥ*) among the people and wards off harm, even if neither God nor the Prophet commanded it; cited from Ibn ʿAqīl, *Kitāb al-Funūn*, apud Ibn Qayyim al-Jawziyya, *al-Ṭuruq al-ḥukmiyya fī al-siyāsa al-sharʿiyya*, ed. Nāyif Aḥmad al-Ḥamad, 2 vols. (Mecca: Dār ʿĀlam al-Fawāʾid, 2011), 1:29 (I was not able to find this in Makdisi's Dar El-Machreq edition of the *Kitāb al-Funūn*, but 1. the original was allegedly much larger and 2. another, much larger manuscript of the book has recently been discovered). Al-Ghazālī (d. 505/1111) defines *siyāsa* at its broadest as serving the aims of "bringing into accord, congregating and cooperating for, and managing well, the means of common livelihood (*li'l-ta'līf wa'l-ijtimāʿ wa'l-taʿāwun ʿalā asbāb al-maʿīsha wa ḍabṭihā*); al-Ghazālī, *Iḥyāʾ ʿulūm al-dīn*, ed. Muḥammad Wahbī Sulaymān and Usāma ʿAmmūra, 5 vols. (Damascus: Dār al-Fikr, 1427/2006), 1:60. For al-Māwardī, *siyāsa* is "good governance." For example, he calls firing a vizier for no reason "outside of *siyāsa*" (*khārij ʿan al-siyāsa*) because in an effective state actions must have causes and not be disordered; al-Māwardī, *Qawānīn al-wizāra wa siyāsat al-mulūk*, ed. Riḍwān al-Sayyid (Beirut: Dār al-Ṭalīʿa, 1979), 195–196. Baber Johansen translates *siyāsa* as "political function"; Baber Johansen, "Signs as Evidence: The Doctrine of Ibn Taymiyya (1263–1328) and Ibn Qayyim al-Jawziyya (d.1351) on Proof," *Islamic Law and Society* 9, no. 2 (2002): 181. For excellent overviews of various perspectives on *siyāsa* by Muslim jurists, see Muhammad Khaled Masud, *Shari'a Today: Essays on Contemporary Issues and Debates in Muslim Societies* (Islamabad: National Book Foundation, 2013), 248–279; Omar Gebril, "Recasting *al-Siyāsa al-Sharʿiyya* in 1920s Egypt: Formulating a Theory of an Islamic Modern State," *Journal of Islamic Law* 5, n. 1 (2024): 106–140. See also Christian Lange, *Justice, Punishment, and the Medieval Muslim Imagination* (Cambridge: Cambridge University Press, 2008), 14; Kristen Stilt, *Islamic Law in Action: Authority, Discretion and Everyday Experiences in Mamluk Egypt* (Oxford: Oxford University Press, 2011).

26. ʿAlāʾ al-Dīn ʿAlī b. Khalīl al-Ṭarābulusī, *Muʿīn al-ḥukkām fīmā yataraddadu bayn al-khaṣmayn min al-aḥkām* (Cairo: al-Maṭbaʿa al-Maymaniyya, 1310/1892), 207. For this I am grateful to Guy Burak's yet to be published *Kânûn: A Genealogy of Law in Ottoman and Post-Ottoman Middle East*.

27. This 'criminal law' public law element is particularly obvious in the Ḥanafī school of law. See Samy Ayoub, "'The Sulṭān Says': State Authority in the Late Ḥanafī Tradition," *Islamic Law and Society* 23, no. 3 (2016): 244.

28. Asifa Quraishi, "The Separation of Powers in the Tradition of Muslim Governments," in *Constitutionalism in Islamic Countries*, ed. Rainer Grote and Tilmann Röder (Oxford: Oxford University Press, 2012), 63–74.

29. Mohammad Fadel, "Islamic Law Reform: Between Reinterpretation and Democracy," *Yearbook of Islamic and Middle Eastern Law Online* 18, n. 1 (2017): 70.

30. Zayn al-Dīn Ibrāhīm Ibn Nujaym, *al-Baḥr al-rāʾiq sharḥ Kanz al-daqāʾiq* (Cairo: Dār al-Kitāb al-Islāmī, n.d.), 5:76; Ibn ʿĀbidīn, *Ḥāshiyat Ibn ʿĀbidīn*, 6 vols. (Beirut: Dār al-Fikr, 1421/2000, reprint of 1966 Cairo Muṣṭafā al-Bābī al-Ḥalabī edition), 4:15. See Samy Ayoub, *Law, Empire, and the Sultan:*

Ottoman Imperial Authority in Late Ḥanafī Jurisprudence (Oxford: Oxford University Press, 2019), 54. Ibn Nujaym's wording is that *siyāsa* is "an action undertaken by the ruler (*ḥākim*) for what he sees as the common good (*maṣlaḥa*) even if no particular evidence appeared regarding that."

31. In common law, public law is generally understood as covering the legal foundations of state institutions as well as the relationship between the government and individuals, including the fields of constitutional law, administrative law, criminal law, and tax law. Private law deals with the relationship between individuals, includes contracts, torts, and property law. Of course, there is also overlap; Alon Harel, "Public and Private Law," in *The Oxford Handbook of Criminal Law*, ed. Markus D. Dubber and Tatjana Hörnle (Oxford: Oxford University Press, 2014), 1040–1063. Here I am not using public law in the sense of fundamental law. See Martin Loughlin, *Foundations of Public Law* (Oxford: Oxford University Press, 2010).
32. For very useful overviews of the questions of Islamic public and criminal law, see Mohammed Fadel, "Public and Private Law in Islamic Law," under "Public Law," and Silvia Tellenbach, "Crime and Punishment in Islamic Law," in *Oxford International Encyclopedia of Legal History*, 2:277–280, and 5:19–20. See also Bernard Weiss, *The Spirit of Islamic Law* (Athens, GA: University of Georgia Press, 1998), 175–185. Regarding the relatively late development of this public aspect of 'criminal law,' Gaughan has shown that, roughly until 100 BCE, there was no crime of murder in Roman law. This was because such matters were not handled by the state in what was still a very decentralized society and polity. For centuries, wrongful, intentionally killing was dealt with through vendetta, arbitration, or within families. See Judy E. Gaughan, *Murder Was Not a Crime: Homicide and Power in the Roman Republic* (Austin: University of Texas Press, 2010), 5 (thanks to Rami Koujah for suggesting this source).
33. Uriel Heyd, *Studies in Old Ottoman Criminal Law*, ed. V.L. Ménage (Oxford: Clarendon, 1973), 1.
34. Judd observes that available evidence suggests that the *qāḍī*'s jurisdiction did not include political issues like division of spoils, dealing with rebels or heretics, and that the lack of mention of major issues like homicide strongly suggests these were also not part of his jurisdiction; Steven Judd, "The Jurisdictional Limits of the *Qāḍī* Courts during the Umayyad Period," *Bulletin d'études orientales* 16 (2014): 52–53.
35. Haim Gerber, *State, Society, and Law in Islam* (Albany: State University of New York Press, 1994), 68–69, 73, 76–77; Galal H. El-Nahal, *The Judicial Administration of Ottoman Egypt in the Seventeenth Century* (Minneapolis: Bibliotheca Islamica, 1979), 25, 34.
36. Heyd, *Studies in Old Ottoman Criminal Law*, 218.
37. Gerber, *State, Society, and Law in Islam*, 76–77.
38. James Baldwin, *Islamic Law and Empire in Ottoman Cairo* (Edinburgh: Edinburgh University Press, 2017), 71.
39. Gerber, *State, Society, and Law in Islam*, 68–69.
40. See Awrangzīb's 1672 edict to Gujarat; Jadunath Sarkar, *Mughal Administration*, 5th ed. (Calcutta: MC Sarkar & Sons, 1963), 109–115; Muhammad Akbar, *The Administration of Justice by the Mughals* (Lahore: Muhammad Ashraf, 1948), 54–61; Radhika Singha, *A Despotism of Law: Crime and Justice in Early*

Colonial Law (Delhi: Oxford University Press, 1998), 7–8; Robert Travers, *Empires of Complaints: Mughal Law and the Making of British India, 1765–1793* (Cambridge: Cambridge University Press, 2022), 53.

41. Akbar, *The Administration of Justice by the Mughals*, 54–61. For the translation of this edict, see ʿAlī Muḥammad Khān, *Mirat-i-Ahmadi: A Persian History of Gujarat*, trans. M.F. Lokhandwala (Baroda [Vadodara], India: Oriental Institute, 1965), 248–252. See also Singha, *A Despotism of Law*, 15.
42. Noman Ahmad Siddiqi, "The *Faujdar* and *Faujdari* under the Mughals," in *The Mughal State: 1526–1750*, ed. Muzaffar Alam and Sanjay Subrahmanyam (Delhi: Oxford University Press, 1998), 248–249. See Travers, *Empires of Complaints*, 49, 52–53.
43. Müller, "Redressing injustice," 97–99.
44. See, for example, Schacht, *An Introduction to Islamic Law*, 54; Nielsen, 31; Khadduri, *Islamic Conception of Justice*, 156–157; Knut Vikør, *Between God and the Sultan: A History of Islamic Law* (London: Oxford University Press, 2005), 190; Hurvitz, "The Contribution of Early Islamic Rulers to Adjudication and Legislation," 150; Ronald C. Jennings, "Kadi, Court, and Legal Procedure in 17th C. Ottoman Kayseri: The Kadi and the Legal System," *Studia Islamica* 48 (1978): 148. Coulson offers that the *maẓālim/qāḍī*-court distinction was as close to secular/religious as one could get given that "all the functions of the Islamic state were theoretically religious in nature"; Coulson, *A History of Islamic Law*, 128.
45. Schacht, *An Introduction to Islamic Law*, 50–51, 54.
46. Nielsen, 32, 95.
47. The authority and its use are labeled *qānūn*, as opposed to *siyāsa*, in the Ottoman context; Richard C. Repp, "Qānūn and Sharīʿa in the Ottoman Context," in *Islamic Law: Social and Historical Contexts*, ed. Aziz Al-Azmeh (Oxford: Routledge, 2013), 124–125.
48. Jennings, "Kadi, Court, and Legal Procedure in 17th C. Ottoman Kayseri," 148.
49. See Jacques Berlinerblau, *Secularism: The Basics*, 2nd ed. (London: Routledge, 2025); José Casanova, "The Secular and Secularisms," *Social Research* 76, n. 4 (2009): 1049–1066; Talal Asad, *Formations of the Secular: Islam, Christianity and Modernity* (Palo Alto: Stanford University Press, 2003); Charles Taylor, *A Secular Age* (Cambridge, MA: Harvard University Press, 2007); Owen Chadwick, *The Secularization of the European Mind in the Nineteenth Century* (London: Cambridge University Press, 1975). For an excellent review of scholarship on the secular, see Rachel M. Scott, *Recasting Islamic Law: Religion and the Nation State in Egyptian Constitution Making* (Ithaca: Cornell University Press, 2021), 16–28.
50. Rushain Abbasi, "Did Premodern Muslims Distinguish the Religious and Secular? The *Dīn-Dunyā* Binary in Medieval Islamic Thought," *Journal of Islamic Studies* 31, n. 2 (2020): 220–221, 225; Sherman A. Jackson, *The Islamic Secular* (Oxford: Oxford University Press, 2024), 38, 41, 50. In the 500s CE the East Syrian Church referred to non-ecclesiastical courts as 'secular' (*ʿālāmāye*) in the 'worldly' sense; Uriel Simonsohn, *A Common Justice: The Legal Alliance of Christians and Jews under Early Islam* (Philadelphia: University of Pennsylvania Press, 2011), 57.
51. Khadduri, *Islamic Conception of Justice*, 156–157.

52. Anjum points out the fallacy in earlier scholarship that had identified a putative eleventh- and twelfth-century CE "supplanting of the Sharīʿa by secular law or politics"; Anjum, *Politics, Law, and Community in Islamic Thought* (Cambridge: Cambridge University Press, 2012), 101. For a general treatment of *siyāsa* as inherent in and authorized by the Shariah, see Asifa Quraishi-Landes, "The Separation of Powers in the Tradition of Muslim Governments," 63–74; Baber Johansen, *Contingency in a Sacred Law: Legal and Ethical Norms in the Muslim Fiqh* (Leiden: Brill, 1999), 216–217. Focusing on the *ḥisba* in the Mamluk era, Stilt notes the error of categorizing *siyāsa* as secular; Kristen Stilt, *Islamic Law in Action*, 35, and see Yossef Rapoport, "Royal Justice and Religious Law: Siyāsah and Shariʿah under the Mamluks," *Mamlūk Studies Review* 16 (2012): 75, 101. For nineteenth-century Egypt, see Khaled Fahmy, *In Quest of Justice: Islamic Law and Forensic Medicine in Modern Egypt* (Oakland: University of California Press, 2018), 123, 128. And, overall, for the *maẓālim*, see Mohammad Hashim Kamali, *Citizenship and Accountability of Government: An Islamic Perspective* (Cambridge: Islamic Texts Society, 2011), 263; Hurvitz, "The Contribution of Early Islamic Rulers to Adjudication and Legislation," 138–139; Albrecht Fuess, "*Ẓulm* by *Maẓālim*? The Political Implications of the Use of *Maẓālim* Jurisdiction by the Mamluk Sultans," *Mamlūk Studies Review* 13, n. 1 (2009): 132. Yaacov Lev includes his chapter on *maẓālim* within a section titled "Judicial Institutions outside the Pale of Islamic Law"; Yaacov Lev, *The Administration of Justice in Medieval Egypt* (Edinburgh: Edinburgh University Press, 2021). For tensions involved, see Malika Zeghal, *The Making of the Modern Muslim State* (Princeton: Princeton University Press, 2024), 55–57. Hallaq's scholarship on this topic is among the most sophisticated and nuanced, but at times it still suggests that he views *siyāsa* as outside of the Shariah. He notes that "the exercise of the powers of *siyāsa* was not only permitted, but in fact insisted upon by *sharʿī* juristic theory and judicial practice. Such powers were not only consistent with the dictates of religious law, but could in no way constitute an infringement thereof if properly exercised." Yet he also refers to *siyāsa* and Shariah as two distinct legal streams and, in the Ottoman context, refers to *qānūn* rules specifying punishments for banditry and other crimes as "extra-Shariah"; Hallaq, *Sharīʿa*, 200, 203, 214, cf. idem, *The Impossible State: Islam, Politics, and Modernity's Moral Predicament* (New York: Columbia University Press, 2013), 64–69. Scholars like Sherman Jackson differ in that they see *siyāsa* as authorized by the Shariah but then as lying outside it. Even for Jackson, while he sees the *maẓālim* as "extra-*sharʿī* in substance," it is still "Islamic law," constrained within a Shariah framework and not secular in the Western sense; Jackson, *The Islamic Secular*, 142, 145–146. Rachel Scott summarizes Jackson's view as "sharia itself established the possibility of state law existing outside it"; Scott, *Recasting Islamic Law*, 36.
53. Nandini Chatterjee, *Negotiating Mughal Law: A Family of Landlords across Three Indian Empires* (Cambridge: Cambridge University Press, 2020), 39–40; Farhat Hasan, *State and Locality in Mughal India* (Cambridge: Cambridge University Press, 2004), 76. See also Travers, quoting a high-ranking official in Murshidabad in the 1760s describing the different judicial organs and their functioning but how all were based on the Shariah; Travers, *Empires of Complaints*, 52.

54. Jackson, *The Islamic Secular*, 88.
55. Jackson, *The Islamic Secular*, 69.
56. Jackson, *The Islamic Secular*, 3, 5, 8, 10, 57, 60, 73, 77, 85–86, 108, 113, 115, 130–132, 142–143, 158, 165.

1. A HISTORY OF *MAẒĀLIM* TRIBUNALS

1. Shāh Walī Allāh, *Ḥujjat Allāh al-bāligha,* ed. Saʿīd Aḥmad Palanpūrī, 2 vols. (Deoband: Maktabat Ḥijāz, 2010), 2:463.
2. For example, al-Māwardī, who provides us with the earliest systematic description of the institution of the *maẓālim* tribunal in his *al-Aḥkām al-sulṭāniyya,* repeatedly speaks of the ruler's duty to alleviate injustices (*maẓālim*) in the abstract sense in his Mirrors for Princes works, such as the *Tashīl al-naẓar*; Abū al-Ḥasan al-Māwardī, *Tashīl al-naẓar wa taʿjīl al-ẓafar*, ed. Riḍwān al-Sayyid, 2nd ed. (Beirut: Ibn al-Azraq Center for Political Heritage Studies, 1432/2012), 360–361. See also Ibn al-Muqaffaʿ, *Kalīla wa dimna*, ed. Louis Cheikho (Beirut: Maṭbaʿat al-Abā' al-Yasūʿīyīn, 1922), 13; ʿAbdallāh b. ʿAbd al-Ḥakam, *Sīrat ʿUmar b. ʿAbd al-ʿAzīz*, ed. Aḥmad ʿUbayd (Cairo: Maktabat Wahba, [1954]), 36, 49, 106–107, 125–129; Muḥammad b. Aḥmad al-ʿUqbānī, *Tuḥfat al-nāẓir wa ghunyat al-dhākir fī ḥifẓ al-shaʿā'ir wa taghyīr al-manākir*, ed. ʿAlī al-Shanūfī (Damascus: al-Maʿhad al-Thaqāfī al-Fransī, 1967), 97; ʿAbd al-Ḥayy al-Ḥasanī, *Nuzhat al-khawāṭir wa bahjat al-masāmiʿ wa'l-nawāẓir,* 3nd ed. (Hyderabad: Dā'irat al-Maʿārif al-ʿUthmāniyya, 1408/1988), 3:122.
3. See Appendix I: Maẓālim – An Annotated Bibliography.
4. As Tillier observes, this was the result of Nielsen's otherwise excellent study of Mamluk-era *maẓālim* assuming that issues not mentioned as playing out in other fora were *maẓālim* cases; Tillier, "Mazalim in historiography," 357–380.
5. See Hiroyuki Yanagihashi, "The Judicial Functions of the *Sulṭān* in Civil Cases according to the Mālikīs up to the Sixth/Twelfth Century," *Islamic Law and Society* 3, n. 1 (1996): 41–43.
6. Ludwig Wittgenstein, *Philosophical Investigations*, trans. G.E.M. Anscombe, 2nd ed. (Oxford: Wiley Blackwell, 1953), 31–32 (§66).
7. See Tyan, *Histoire*, 446–451.
8. See Mohammed Allehbi, "'It is Permitted for the Amīr but not the Qāḍī': The Military-Administrative Genealogy of Coercion in Abbasid Criminal Justice," *Islamic Law and Society* 30, n. 1–2 (2023): 65–95; Siddiqi, "The *Faujdar* and *Faujdari* Under the Mughals." For an excellent review of scholarship on the *shurṭa* in the early and early-middle Islamic periods, see Lev, *The Administration of Justice in Medieval Egypt*, 161 ff.
9. See al-Māwardī, *Kitāb al-Aḥkām al-sulṭāniyya wa'l-wilāyāt al-dīniyya*, ed. Aḥmad Mubārak al-Baghdādī (Kuwait: Maktabat Dār Ibn Qutayba, 1409/1989), 285–290.
10. Bertold Spuler, *Iran in the Early Islamic Period*, trans. Gwendolin Goldbloom and Berenike Walburg, ed. Robert Hoyland (Leiden Brill, 2015), 361; Van Berkel, 234–235. Much more common is the phrase *aṣḥāb al-jarā'im* being

used for criminals. In his reports on the year 206/821–22, the Abbasid governor Ṭāhir b. al-Ḥusayn writes a letter to his son with political advice admonishing him to, amongst other duties, implement the Hudud on the *aṣḥāb al-jarā'im*. The people sprung from the Bāb al-Shām prison in Baghdad in 255/868–9 are referred to as *aṣḥāb al-jarā'im;* Muḥammad b. Jarīr al-Ṭabarī, *Tārīkh al-Ṭabarī*, 6 vols. (Beirut: Dār al-Kutub al-'Ilmiyya, 2003), 5:157, 437; Tyan, *Histoire*, 594–609.

11. Wakī' Muḥammad b. Khalaf, *Akhbār al-quḍāt*, ed. Sa'īd Muḥammad al-Laḥḥām (Riyadh: 'Ālam al-Kutub, n.d.), 237, 567. Al-Kindī describes how, during the reign of Mu'āwiya, someone took up both posts of *shurṭa* and *qāḍī* at the same time; Muḥammad b. Yūsuf al-Kindī, *Kitāb al-Wulāt wa Kitāb al-Quḍāt*, ed. Rhuvon Guest (Beirut: al-Ābā, 1908 and Leiden: Brill, 1912), 311. See Allehbi, "'It is Permitted for the Amīr but not the Qāḍī,'" 65–95. Tillier suggests that there is not much evidence of judges having their own bailiffs or guards assigned to the court prior to the Abbasids; Tillier, "The Umayyads and the Formation of Islamic Judgeship," in *The Umayyad World*, ed. Andrew Marsham (London: Routledge, 2020), 175.
12. Yaakov Lev, *State and Society in Fatimid Egypt* (Leiden: Brill, 1991), 156–157. See also Lange, *Justice, Punishment*, 42.
13. See Ibn Taymiyya, *Public Duties in Islam: The Institution of the Ḥisba*, trans. Muhtar Holland (Leicester: Islamic Foundation, 1982), 24–5; Faḍlallāh b. Rūzbahān Khunjī, *Sulūk al-mulūk* (Tehran: Enteshārāt-e Khvārazmī, 1984), 227–229 and Davānī's *maẓālim* treatise translated in Chapter Three.
14. This is the *Kânûnnâme* of Nişâncı 'Abdürrahman Paşa; Heyd, *Studies in Old Ottoman Criminal Law*, 209.
15. Jennings, "Kadi, Court, and Legal Procedure in 17th C. Ottoman Kayseri," 159.
16. Gerber, *State, Society, and Law in Islam*; 68–69, 73, 76–77.
17. See Baldwin, *Islamic Law and Empire in Ottoman Cairo*.
18. '*segala yang teraniaya*'; Liaw Yock Fang, ed. and trans., *Undang-Undang Melaka: The Laws of Melaka* (The Hague: Martinus Nijhoff, 1976), 64–5.
19. This *qāḍī* was 'Abdallāh b. Muḥammad b. Khaḍrā' al-Salāwī (d. 1906 CE); Aḥmad Mutafakkir, *Min a'lām al-fatwā bi-murrākush 'abr al-'uṣūr* (Marrakesh: Mu'assasat Āfāq li'l-Dirāsāt wa'l-Nashr wa'l-Ittiṣāl, 2014), 59.
20. David Powers, "Four Cases Relating to Women and Divorce in Al-Andalus and the Maghrib, 1100–1500," in *Dispensing Justice in Islam: Qadis and their Judgments*, ed. Muhammad Khalid Masud, Rudolph Peters, and David Powers (Leiden: Brill, 2006), 388. In one case described by Powers, it may be that the second judge to whom the plaintiff (a mother) appealed was a *maẓālim* judge, since the mother is described as coming to him "with a complaint of having been wronged (*mutaẓallima*)"; Aḥmad b. Yaḥyā al-Wansharīsī, *al-Mi'yār al-mu'rib*, ed. Muḥammad Ḥajjī et al. (Beirut: Dār al-Gharb al-Islāmī, 1981–1983), 3:33. We also find a remarkable entanglement of judge, mufti, and executive authority. In nineteenth-century Marrakesh, a scholar who repeatedly criticized the rulings of the *qāḍī* found himself imprisoned by this judge. Only the direct intervention of sultan 'Abd al-Raḥmān freed him; Mutafakkir, *Min a'lām al-fatwā bi-murrākush*, 81–82, 90.
21. Powers, "On Judicial Review in Islamic Law," *Law and Society Review* 26, no. 2 (1992): 315–342.

22. Leo Africanus, *The History and General Description of Africa*, trans. John Pory, ed. Robert Brown, 3 vols. (London: Hakluyt Society, 1896), 2:444–445.
23. Rossitsa Gradeva, "On Judicial Hierarchy in the Ottoman Empire: The Case of Sofia from the Seventeenth to the Beginning of the Eighteenth Century," in *Dispensing Justice in Islam*, ed. David Powers et al., 296.
24. Elisabeth Meier Tetlow, *Women, Crime, and Punishment in Ancient Law and Society: Volume I – The Ancient Near East* (New York: Continuum, 2004), 54–55.
25. Al-Ya'qūbī translates the Sassanid office of *shāhrīst* as *ṣāḥib al-maẓālim*; al-Ya'qūbī, *Tārīkh al-Ya'qūbī* (Leiden: Brill, 1883), 1:203. See Tyan, *Histoire*, 519–521; Nielsen, 1–2.
26. Ibn 'Abd al-Ḥakam, *Sīrat 'Umar b. 'Abd al-'Azīz*, 36, 49, 106–107, 125–129.
27. Abū Ṭālib Muḥammad b. 'Alī al-Makkī, *Qūt al-qulūb*, 2 vols. in 1 (Cairo: Maṭba'at al-Anwār al-Muḥammadiyya, 1405/1985), 1:132.
28. See the case of Egypt's judge Khayr b. Nu'aym al-Ḥaḍramī in 120/738; al-Kindī, *Kitāb al-Wulāt wa Kitāb al-Quḍāt*, 348, and also 427. Another case is a fascinating proto-*maẓālim* case: a group from the tribe of Banū 'Abd Kulūl protested before the judge Abū Khuzayma Ibrāhīm al-Ru'aynī (d. 154/771) that a man had married one of their women, but that they, as her kinsmen (*awliyā'*), objected. The judge responds that he would not prohibit what God had allowed and that, if the woman's guardian (*walī*) had married her off, then the marriage stood. The men appealed the case to the governor, Yazīd b. Ḥātim, who ordered the judge to annul the marriage. He refused, but the governor then separated the couple; al-Kindī, 367; Abū al-Faraj al-Iṣfahānī, *al-Aghānī*, ed. 'Alī Muhannā and Samīr Jābir, 24 vols. (Beirut: Dār al-Fikr, [n.d.]), 2:342. See also Ibn al-Jawzī, *al-Muntaẓam fī tārīkh al-umam wa'l-mulūk*, ed. Muḥammad 'Abd al-Qādir 'Aṭā and Muṣṭafā 'Abd al-Qādir 'Aṭā, 19 vols. (Beirut: Dār al-Kutub al-'Ilmiyya, 1412/1992), 8:186. The *Akhbār al-quḍāt* of Wakī' (d. 306/918–19) describes the appointment of Ibn Shubruma (d. 144/761) to the *maẓālim* of Kufa right after the Abbasid revolution; Wakī', *Akhbār al-quḍāt*, 570.
29. Al-Khaṭīb al-Baghdādī, *Tārīkh Baghdād*, ed. Muṣṭafā 'Abd al-Qādir 'Aṭā, 14 vols. (Beirut: Dār al-Kutub al-'Ilmiyya, 1997), 10:306.
30. Abū Yūsuf, *Taxation in Islām Volume III: Abū Yūsuf's Kitāb al-Kharāj*, trans. A. Ben Shemesh (Leiden: Brill, 1969), 107. This does not appear in all editions of this book. Thanks to Sohaira Siddiqui for alerting me to this.
31. Van Berkel, "Abbasid Maẓālim," 229–242.
32. Van Berkel, 234-5.
33. The issue of Fars came under the caliph al-Muqtadir (r. 908–932 CE) and the Sawād under al-Muhtadī; Amedroz, "The Mazalim Jurisdiction in the Ahkam Sultaniyya of Mawardi," 639, 656, 659.
34. Van Berkel, 233, 236.
35. This was heard by the judge Aḥmad b. Isḥāq Ibn al-Bahlūl (d. 318/930); al-Muḥsin b. 'Alī al-Tanūkhī, *Nishwār al-muḥāḍara wa akhbār al-mudhākara*, ed. 'Abbūd al-Shālijī, 8 vols. (Beirut: Dār Ṣādir, 1971), 2:167–168.
36. Al-Khaṭīb al-Baghdādī, *Tārīkh Baghdād*, 10:222 ('Abd al-Raḥmān b. Thābit b. Thawbān); 10:306 ('Ubaydallāh b. Muḥammad al-Jumaḥī). See also Nielsen, 4.
37. Al-Ṭabarī, *Tārīkh*, 4:524.
38. Ibn al-Jawzī, *Muntaẓam*, 8:309; al-Mas'ūdī, *Murūj al-dhahāb*, 2nd ed., 2 vols. ([n.p.]: al-Sharika al-'Ālamiyya, 1990), 2:557.

39. Al-Hilāl b. Muḥsin al-Ṣābī, *al-Wuzarā' aw Tuḥfat al-umarā' fī tārīkh al-wuzarā'*, ed. 'Abd al-Sattār Aḥmad Farāj ([Cairo]: Dār Iḥyā' al-Kutub al-'Arabī, 1958), 373. See also Jacob Lassner, *The Topography of Baghdad in the Early Middle Ages* (Detroit: Wayne State University Press, 1970), 256.
40. Tillier, "*Qāḍīs* and the political use of the *maẓālim* under the 'Abbāsids," 52; Nielsen, 5. It is difficult to know what to make of a reference that al-Ṭabarī makes to the head of the *maẓālim*, Yūsuf b. Ya'qūb, urging anyone to come forward who had a grievance against the Abbasid prince al-Nāṣir li'l-Dīn Allāh b. al-Mutawakkil in 277/890; al-Ṭabarī, *Tārīkh*, 5:598.
41. Ḥamza b. Yūsuf al-Sahmī, *Tārīkh Jurjān* (Hyderabad: Dā'irat al-Ma'ārif al-'Uthmāniyya, 1950), 191; Shams al-Dīn al-Dhahabī, *Tārīkh al-islām*, ed. 'Umar 'Abd al-Salām Tadmurī, 52 vols. (Beirut: Dār al-Kitāb al-'Arabī, 1987), 17:285; 23:58; al-Iṣfahānī, *al-Aghānī*, 14:132; Ibn 'Asākir, *Tārīkh Madīnat Dimashq*, ed. Muḥibb al-Dīn 'Umar al-'Amrawī, 80 vols. (Beirut: Dār al-Fikr, 1418/1997), 5:342; al-Ḥarīrī, *Maqāmāt al-Ḥarīrī* (Beirut: Dār Bayrūt, 1985), 208.
42. Jalāl al-Dīn al-Suyūṭī, *Bughyat al-wu'āt*, ed. Muḥammad Abū al-Faḍl Ibrāhīm, 2 vols. (Beirut: Maktabat al-'Aṣriyya, n.d.), 1:75. Thanks to Rana Mikati for her help on this.
43. Abū Nu'aym al-Iṣbahānī, *Dhikr akhbār Iṣbahān*, ed. Sayyid Khusrawī Ḥasan, 2 vols. (Beirut: Dār al-Kutub al-'Ilmiyya, 1990), 1:114.
44. Tillier, "*Qāḍīs* and the political use of the *maẓālim* under the 'Abbāsids," 46, 49–50.
45. Al-Khaṭīb al-Baghdādī, *Tārīkh Baghdād*, 4:87.
46. C.E. Bosworth, "The Ṭāhirids and the Ṣaffārids," and idem, "The Early Ghaznavids," in *The Cambridge History of Iran*, vol. 4, *The Period from the Arab Invasion to the Saljuqs*, ed. R.N. Frye (Cambridge: Cambridge University Press, 1975), 127, 184.
47. Marina Rustow, *The Lost Archive: Traces of a Caliphate in a Cairo Synagogue* (Princeton: Princeton University Press, 2020), 215, 218, 221.
48. Ibn Ḥajar al-'Asqalānī, *Raf' al-iṣr 'an quḍāt miṣr*, ed. 'Alī Muḥammad 'Umar (Cairo: Maktabat al-Khānjī, 1988), 198, 333; Nielsen, 9.
49. Ibn Ḥajar, *Raf' al-iṣr*, 56.
50. Tillier, "*Qāḍīs* and the political use of the *maẓālim* under the 'Abbāsids," 57; Nielsen, 5.
51. Ibn al-Jawzī, *Muntaẓam*, 9:225. Yaḥyā b. Aktham was appointed as the judge and then the *maẓālim* magistrate of the new capital of Samarra in 237/851–2; ibid., 11:250.
52. Al-Dhahabī, *Mīzān al-i'tidāl fī naqd al-rijāl*, ed. 'Alī Muḥammad al-Bijāwī, 4 vols. (Beirut: Dār al-Ma'rifa, n.d.), 2:309.
53. Al-Khaṭīb al-Baghdādī, *Tārīkh Baghdād*, 5:40. The use of the word *ḥukm* here instead of issue (*mas'ala*) or case (*qaḍiyya*) is interesting. It could be a reference to the *maẓālim* as an appeals forum for a ruling already made by a *qāḍī*.
54. Ibn al-Jawzī, *Muntaẓam*, 9:224, 226.
55. 'Abd al-Karīm b. Muḥammad al-Sam'ānī, *al-Ansāb*, ed. 'Abdallāh 'Umar al-Bārūdī (Beirut: Dār al-Jinān, 1988), 3:423.
56. Ibn al-Jawzī, *Muntaẓam*, 13:180–1. For more on Thumal's qualifications and strict application of rules, see Amedroz, 657; Ibn Ḥajar, *Raf' al-iṣr*, 177–178.
57. Nielsen, 6.

58. Ẓahīr al-Dīn al-Rūdhrāwarī, *Dhayl Kitāb Tajārib al-umam*, published in Miskawayh, *Tajārib al-umum*, ed. Abū al-Qāsim Imāmī, 8 vols. (Tehran: Sorūsh, 2001), 7:68–69.
59. Al-Ṣābī, *al-Wuzarā'*, 342; al-Qalqashandī, *Ṣubḥ al-a'shā'*, 14 vols. (Cairo: al-Maṭba'a al-Amīriyya, 1334/1916), 10:247, 252.
60. C.E. Bosworth, "The Political and Dynastic History of the Iranians World (AD 1000–1217)" and A.K.S. Lambton, "The Internal Structure of the Saljuq Empire," in *The Cambridge History of Iran,* vol. 5, *The Saljuq and Mongol Periods*, ed. J.A. Boyle (Cambridge: Cambridge University Press, 1968), 23, 213, 227–228.
61. Nielsen, 8.
62. Yavuz Aykan argues that the Turkic Qarakhanid realm in the eleventh century CE was a crucial moment for Ḥanafī jurists articulating the ruler's role in criminal law; Yavuz Aykan, "A Legal Concept in Motion: The 'Spreader of Corruption' (*sā'ī bi'l-fesād*) from Qarakhanid to Ottoman Jurisprudence," *Islamic Law and Society* 26, n. 3 (2019): 3.
63. Spuler, *Iran in the Early Islamic Period*, 361.
64. Al-Ṭabarī, *Tārīkh*, 5:598.
65. Al-Ḥarīrī, *Maqāmāt al-Ḥarīrī*, 208; Amedroz, 663.
66. Beyond what overlaps with his discussion of the *maẓālim*, al-Māwardī lists other powers the criminal court enjoys that the judges do not. For example, the criminal court can imprison repeat, unreformed offenders to life in prison to protect the public from them; al-Māwardī, *al-Aḥkām al-sulṭāniyya*, 219–20.
67. For a remarkably concise and clear study of this period, see Yaacov Lev, *The Administration of Justice in Medieval Egypt*, 202–228.
68. Al-Kindī, *Kitāb al-Wulāt*, 602.
69. Ibn Ḥajar, *Raf' al-iṣr 'an quḍāt miṣr*, 328. Abū Ṭāhir Muḥammad b. Aḥmad al-Dhuhlī had served as judge in southern Iraq, Baghdad, Damascus, and Egypt.
70. Rustow, *The Lost Archive*, 219 and more generally 207–244.
71. Heyd notes that Ottoman *dîvân*s and *maẓālim* tribunals in general were approached via written petition; Heyd, *Studies in Old Ottoman Criminal Law*, 226.
72. Nielsen, 9–13.
73. Lev, *The Administration of Justice*, 212, 220–221, 224. The assertion here about non-Muslim populations is based on Richard Bulliet, *Conversion to Islam in the Medieval Period* (Cambridge, MA: Harvard University Press, 1979), 23, 102, 109.
74. Rustow, 240.
75. Nielsen, 10–12.
76. Nasser Rabbat, "The Ideological Significance of the Dar al- Adl in the Medieval Islamic Orient," *International Journal of Middle East Studies* 27, no. 1 (1995): 3, 6–7; Abū Shāma al-Maqdisī, *al-Rawḍatayn fī akhbār al-dawlatayn al-nūriyya wa al-ṣalāḥiyya*, ed. Ibrāhīm al-Zubayq, 5 vols. (Beirut: Mu'assasat al-Risāla, 1997), 4:344.
77. Rabbat, 7.
78. Nielsen, 43, 82.
79. Taqī al-Dīn Ibn Ḥijja al-Ḥamawī al-Azrārī, *Kitāb Qahwat al-inshā'* (Beirut: Klaus Schwarz, 2005), 112–113.

80. Before the solidification of Mamluk rule under al-Ẓāhir Baybars, Mu'izz al-Dīn Aybak held his *maẓālim* in the Ṣāliḥiyya madrasa college; Sherman A. Jackson, *Islamic Law and the State* (Leiden: Brill, 1996), 14.
81. Rabbat, 13–15.
82. Nielsen, 91–92.
83. Rabbat, 18.
84. Fuess, "*Ẓulm* by *Maẓālim*?" 126.
85. David Ayalon, "The Great Yasa of Chingiz Khan: A Reexamination (Part C2)," *Studia Islamica* 38 (1973): 120.
86. Nielsen, 32, 95.
87. Robert Irwin, "Privatization of 'Justice' under the Circassian Mamluks," *Mamlūk Studies Review* 6 (2005): 63–70.
88. Hallaq, *Sharī'a*, 201.
89. Rapoport, *Marriage, Money and Divorce in Medieval Islamic Society* (Cambridge: Cambridge University Press, 2005), 79.
90. Rapoport, "Royal Justice and Religious Law: Siyāsah and Shari'ah under the Mamluks," 75, 101.
91. Ibn Taymiyya describes the cases taken up by the military courts that would normally fall under the *qāḍī*'s subject matter jurisdiction as those involving "claims based on suspicion without documentary evidence or witnesses"; Ibn Taymiyya, *Public Duties in Islam*, 24–5; Nielsen, 39.
92. Rapoport, "Royal Justice and Religious Law," 80–1.
93. H.A.R. Gibb, trans., *The Travels of Ibn Battuta*, 3 vols. (New Delhi: Munshiram Manoharlal, 2004), 1:57.
94. Nielsen, 75.
95. Nielsen, 102.
96. Rapoport, "Royal Justice and Religious Law," 84, 85, 88. For a summary of legal positions on whether a ruler or judge should retain a chamberlain, see Ibn Ḥajar, *Fatḥ al-bārī sharḥ Ṣaḥīḥ al-Bukhārī*, ed. 'Abd al-'Azīz b. 'Abdallāh b. Bāz and Muḥammad Fu'ād 'Abd al-Bāqī, 16 vols. (Beirut: Dār al-Kutub al-'Ilmiyya, 1997), 13:166. On the role of these courts in adjudicating commercial lawsuits between Muslim and non-Muslim merchants in Alexandria and Damascus in that time period, see Francisco Apellániz, "Judging the Franks: Proofs, Justice, and Diversity in Late Medieval Alexandria and Damascus," *Comparative Studies in Society and History* 58, n. 2 (2016): 350–378.
97. Nielsen, 36 ff.
98. Fuess, 138.
99. Rapoport, *Marriage, Money and Divorce*, 78–81.
100. Rapoport, "Royal Justice and Religious Law," 97–98.
101. Carl F. Petry, "'Quis Custodiet Custodes?' Revisited: The Prosecution of Crime in the Late Mamluk Sultanate," *Mamlūk Studies Review* 3 (1999): 17.
102. See Qāḍī 'Iyāḍ b. Mūsā, *Tartīb al-madārik*, ed. Muḥammad Sālim Hāshim, 2 vols. (Beirut: Dār al-Kutub al-'Ilmiyya, 1998), 2:259–260.
103. Ibn Bashkuwāl, *al-Ṣila*, ed. Ibrāhīm al-Abyārī, 3 vols. (Cairo: Dār al-Kitāb al-Miṣrī, 1990), 2:459; Muḥammad b. 'Abdallāh al-Quḍā'ī Ibn al-Abbār, *al-Takmila li-kitāb al-Ṣila*, ed. 'Abd al-Salām al-Harrās, 4 vols. (Beirut: Dār al-Fikr, 1995), 1:102.
104. Tyan, *Histoire*, 522–524.
105. Müller, "Redressing Injustice," 95.

106. Müller, "Redressing Injustice," 95, 97, 99.
107. Leo Africanus, *The History and General Description of Africa*, 2:444–445.
108. Abū al-Ḥasan al-Nubāhī, *Tārīkh quḍāt al-Andalus*, ed. Maryam Qāsim Ṭawīl (Beirut: Dār al-Kutub al-ʿIlmiyya, 1415/1995), 20.
109. Al-Idrīsī, *Nuzhat al-mushtāq fī ikhtirāq al-āfāq*, 2 vols. (Cairo: Maktabat al-Thaqāfa al-Dīniyya, 1422/2002), 1:23.
110. Aḥmad b. Yaḥyā al-ʿUmarī, *Masālik al-abṣār fī mamālik al-amṣār*, ed. Kāmil Muslimān al-Jabūrī, 15 vols. (Beirut: Dār al-Kutub al-ʿIlmiyya, 2010), 4:52.
111. ʿAbdallāh dan Fodio, "Ḍiyāʾ al-ḥukkām fīmā lahum wa ʿalayhim min al-aḥkām," in *Mukhtārāt al-Shaykh ʿAbdallāh bin Fūdī*, ed. Sulaymān Mūsā Atthāʾī (Gusau, Nigeria: Iqraʾ, 2013), 125–127.
112. Guy Burak, *The Second Formation of Islamic Law* (Cambridge: Cambridge University Press, 2015), 207–223.
113. See Burak, "Between the *Ḳānūn* of Qāytbāy and Ottoman *Yasaq*: A Note on the Ottomans' Dynastic Law," *Journal of Islamic Studies* 26, n. 1 (2015): 6–7, 18; Ayoub, *Law, Empire, and the Sultan*.
114. Anne Broadbridge, *Kingship and Ideology in the Islamic and Mongol Worlds* (Cambridge: Cambridge University Press, 2008); John Woods, *The Aqquyunlu: Clan, Confederation, Empire* (Salt Lake City: University of Utah Press, 1999); Burak, *The Second Formation of Islamic Law*, 207–223; idem, "Narrating Change," *Islamic Law Blog*, 10/13/2022, https://web.archive.org/web/20240808205415/https://islamiclaw.blog/2022/10/13/narrating-change/#_ftnref5. The late Halil Inalcik also laid the groundwork for the argument by locating the notion of a dynastic law in the pre-Chinggisid, pre-Islamic Turkic tradition; Halil Inalcik, *The Ottoman Empire* (London: Phoenix, 1973), 66–67.
115. Marshall Hodgson, *The Venture of Islam* (Chicago: University of Chicago Press, 1974), 2:392 ff. See also Broadbridge, *Kingship and Ideology*; Woods, *The Aqquyunlu*; Burak, *The Second Formation of Islamic Law*, 207–223.
116. For debates about what the Yasa was, if it was anything, see David Morgan, "The 'Great Yasa of Chinggis Khan' Revisited," in *Mongols, Turks, and Others: Eurasian Nomads and the Sedentary World*, ed. Reuven Amitai and Michal Biran (Leiden: Brill, 2005), 291–308.
117. For an examination of these changes see Jonathan Z. Brack, "Mediating Sacred Kingship: Conversion and Sovereignty in Mongol Iran," (University of Michigan, PhD dissertation, 2016); Stefan T. Kamola, "Rashid al-Din and the Making of History in Mongol Iran," (University of Washington, PhD dissertation, 2013); Burak, *The Second Formation of Islamic Law*; idem, "Narrating Change"; Ayoub, *Law, Empire, and the Sultan*.
118. Burak, *Second Formation of Islamic Law*, 220.
119. Burak, *Kânûn: A Genealogy of Law in Ottoman and Post-Ottoman Middle East*, forthcoming.
120. Burak, "Between the *Ḳānūn* of Qāytbāy and Ottoman *Yasaq*," 6–7, 18.
121. Ann Lambton, "Quis custodiet custodes: Some Reflections on the Persian Theory of Government," *Studia Islamica* 5 (1956): 144–145.
122. This amir's name was Qūtlūdumūr; Ibn Baṭṭūṭa, *The Travels of Ibn Battuta*, 3:543, 545.
123. Gibb, *The Travels of Ibn Battuta*, 2:378.
124. Maria E. Subtelny, *Timurids in Transition* (Leiden: Brill, 2007), 11.

125. Subtelny, 15–16.
126. Subtelny, 24; John Woods, "Timur's Genealogy," in *Intellectual Studies on Islam: Essays Written in Honor of Martin B. Dickson*, ed. Michel Mazzaoui and Vera Moreen (Salt Lake City: University of Utah Press, 1990), 101. Ibn ʿArabshāh's (d. 854/1450) early and first-hand but polemical description of Yasa/*töre* mentions that the accused were guilty until proven innocent, slave-girls and boys could bear witness against the free, and that the judge had no authority to grant clemency; Robert Irwin, "What the Partridge Told the Eagle: A Neglected Arabic Source on Chinggis Khan and the Early History of the Mongols," in *The Mongol Empire and its Legacy*, ed. Reuven Amitai-Preiss and David O. Morgan (Leiden: Brill, 1999), 8–9.
127. Subtelny, 25.
128. Woods, *Aqquyunlu*, 17.
129. Woods, *Aqquyunlu*, 109. For the Ottoman appreciation of this ruler, see Burak, "Between the *Ḳānūn* of Qāytbāy and Ottoman *Yasaq*," 9.
130. Khunjī, *Sulūk al-mulūk*, 227–229. For a study of Khunjī, see Ann Lambton, *State and Government in Medieval Islam* (Oxford: Oxford University Press, 1981), 178–200. Thanks to Guy Burak for drawing my attention to this study.
131. On the centrality of the notion of justice in the Ottoman self-perception see Linda T. Darling, *A History of Social Justice and Political Power in the Middle East: The Circle of Justice from Mesopotamia to Globalization* (London and New York: Routledge, 2013); Boğaç Ergene, "On Ottoman Justice: Interpretations in Conflict (1600–1800)," *Islamic Law and Society* 8, n. 1 (2001): 52–87.
132. Derin Terzioğlu, "Ibn Taymiyya, *al-Siyāsa al-Sharʿiyya*, and the Early Modern Ottomans," in *Historicizing Sunni Islam in the Ottoman Empire, c. 1450–1750*, ed. Tijana Krstić and Derin Terzioğlu (Leiden: Brill, 2021), 101–154.
133. Bernard Lewis, *The Emergence of Modern Turkey* (London: Oxford University Press, 1961), 107; Gerber, *State, Society, and Islam*, 69 (he asserts that nothing even had its function under the Ottomans); Hallaq, *Sharīʿa*, 208. Heyd says that, in light of the function of the *dîvân*, this observation "needs to be modified"; Heyd, 225.
134. Gerber, *State, Society, and Law in Islam*, 69 ff.; Hallaq, *Sharīʿa*, 208.
135. James Baldwin, *Islamic Law and Empire in Ottoman Cairo*. For the claim being rebutted, see Gerber, 69.
136. Michael Ursinus, *Grievance Administration (*Şikayet*) in an Ottoman Province: The Kaymakam of Rumelia's 'Record Book of Complaints' of 1781–1783* (London: Routledge Curzon, 2005), 3, 4, 18, 33. For a comparable but less granular view of forums for justice in Ottoman Tunis, see Robert Brunschvig, "Justice religieuse et justice laïque dans la Tunisie des Deys et des Beys: jusqu'au milieu du XIXe siècle," *Studia Islamica* 23 (1965): 27–70.
137. Ursinus, 8. Wittman observes that "the aim of the *divan*'s activities was the establishment of a lawful condition in circumstances in which the law was misused or applied falsely, or access to the law was denied to a complainant"; Richard Wittmann, "Before Qadi and Grand Vizier: Intra-Communal Dispute Resolution and Legal Transactions among Christians and Jews in the Plural Society of Seventeenth-Century Istanbul," (PhD dissertation, Harvard University, 2008), 143.
138. Gerber, *State, Society, and Law*, 76–77.
139. Heyd, 209.

140. Ursinus, 30–32.
141. Baldwin, *Islamic Law and Empire in Ottoman Cairo*, 66–67.
142. Ursinus, 27, 29.
143. Baldwin, *Islamic Law and Empire in Ottoman Cairo*, 65–67.
144. Gerber, *Shariah, State, Society, and Law in Islam*, 71; Ursinus, 34–36.
145. Heyd, 209; Ursinus, 5.
146. Nahal, *The Judicial Administration of Ottoman Egypt*, 15–16, 91–2; Baldwin, *Islamic Law and Empire in Ottoman Cairo*, 46.
147. Baldwin, *Islamic Law and Empire in Ottoman Cairo*, 65–67, 69–70.
148. Baldwin, *Islamic Law and Empire in Ottoman Cairo*, 58, 61–62.
149. Wittman, "Before Qadi and Grand Vizier," 188, 201, 205.
150. Willen Floor, "The Secular Judicial System in Safavid Persia," *Studia Iranica* 29, no. 1 (2000): 9–60. Evliya Chelebi (d. *circa* 1095/1684) objects to the use of torture and other severe punishments in the Safavid court at Tabriz, calling them criminal and against the Shariah; Evliya Chelebi, *At Ottoman Traveler: Selections from the* Book of Travels *by Evliya Çelebi*, trans. Robert Dankoff and Sooyang Kim (London: Eland, 2010), 67.
151. Irene Schneider, "Religious and State Jurisdiction During Nasir al-Din Shah's Reign," in *Religion and Society in Qajar Iran*, ed. Robert Gleave (London: Routledge, 2005), 84.
152. Schneider, 84–110. See also Saïd Amir Arjomand, "Political Ethic and Public Law in the Early Qajar Period," in *Religion and Society in Qajar Iran*, 21–40; and Irene Schneider, *The Petitioning System in Iran: State, Society and Power Relations in the Late 19th Century* (Wiesbaden: Harrassowitz Verlag, 2006).
153. Gibb, *The Travels of Ibn Battuta*, 3:694–695; al-Ḥasanī, *Nuzhat al-khawāṭir*, 2:129.
154. Al-Ḥasanī, *Nuzhat al-khawāṭir*, 4:30.
155. Nandini Chatterjee describes law in Mughal India as emanating from several sources: royal and sub-royal decrees, Islamic jurisprudence, and local custom. But the whole system was seen as Shariah, an order based on Islam and "royal grace" (i.e., *siyāsa*); Chatterjee, *Negotiating Mughal Law*, 39–40.
156. Akbar, *The Administration of Justice by the Mughals*, 15, 27; al-Ḥasanī, *Nuzhat al-khawāṭir*, 4:283; Travers, *Empires of Complaints*, 37–8.
157. H. M. Elliot and John Dawson, ed. *The History of India as Told by its Own Historians: The Muhammadan Period*, vol. 7. (New York: AMS Press, 1966), 171–172.
158. Niccolao Manucci, *Storia do Mogor, or Mogul India 1653–1708*, trans. William Irvine, 3 vols. (London: John Murray, 1907), 1:203–204.
159. François Bernier, *Travels in the Mogul Empire*, trans. Archibald Constable (Oxford: Oxford University Press, 1914), 263, 360; Akbar, *Administration of Justice by the Mughals*, 39, 45, 48; Sarkar, *Mughal Administration*, 94. See also al-Ḥasanī, *Nuzhat al-khawāṭir*, 6:161, 167.
160. Abhishek Kaicker, "Petitions and Local Politics in the Late Mughal Empire: The view from Kol, 1741," *Modern Asian Studies* 53, n. 1 (2019): 28, 31–33.
161. Scott, *Recasting Islamic Law*.
162. Ayoub M. Al-Jarbou, "The Saudi Board of Grievances: Development and New Reforms," *Arab Law Quarterly* 25 (2011): 188. Thanks to Manar Almuwarraee for her help on this.

163. Al-Jarbou, "The Saudi Board of Grievances: Development and New Reforms," 187–188, 194.
164. I was told this by Saudi legal scholars who did not feel comfortable speaking on the record.
165. 'Alī b. Sulaymān al-Sa'wī, "Qaḍā' al-maẓālim wa niẓāmuhu fī al-mamlaka al-'arabiyya al-su'ūdiyya," *Majallat Dīwān al-Maẓālim* 1, n. 1 (1441/2020): 30. There is some question here. Though the Board's website lists "examining requests regarding the enforcement of foreign rulings" as an area of its jurisdiction, as of 2012 the Enforcement Courts assumed jurisdiction over the execution of foreign judgments and awards. In theory, the Board of Grievances retains only jurisdiction over foreign judgments and arbitration awards *in which the government's administrative agency is a party*. There is also some question as to whether the Board's competence regarding "rulings regarding crimes specified by the administrative decree on the boycott of Israel" only applies to government actors violating this boycott or to private subjects and companies as well.

2. FROM BAGHDAD TO ISTANBUL: THE GENEALOGY OF A *MAẒĀLIM* TREATISE

1. For the most thorough overall studies on al-Māwardī, see H.A.R. Gibb, "Al-Mawardi's Theory of the Caliphate," in *Studies on the Civilization of Islam*, ed. Stanford Shaw and William Polk (Princeton: Princeton University Press, 1962, originally published *Islamic Culture* 11, n. 3 [1937]), 151–165; Henri Laoust, "La pensée et l'action politiques d'al-Māwardī," *Revue des études islamiques* 36 (1968): 11–92; Donald Little, "A New Look at *al-Aḥkām al-Sulṭāniyya*," *Muslim World* 64, n. 1 (1974): 1–15; Hanna Mikhail, *Politics and Revelation: Māwardī and After* (Edinburgh: Edinburgh University Press, 1995), 65–68; Christopher Melchert, "Māwardī's Legal Thinking," *al-'Uṣūr al-Wusṭā* 23 (2015): 68–86; idem, "Māwardī, Abū Ya'lá and the Sunni Revival," in *Prosperity and Stagnation: Some Cultural and Social Aspects of the Abbasid Period (750–1258)*, ed. Krzystof Koscielniak (Krakow: UNUM, 2010), 37–61; Tāj al-Dīn al-Subki, *Ṭabaqāt al-shāfi'iyya al-kubrā*, ed. 'Abd al-Fattāḥ Muḥammad al-Ḥuluw and Maḥmūd Muḥammad al-Ṭanāḥī, 2nd edn., 9 vols. (Cairo: Hujr, 1992), 3:339. For the accusation that al-Māwardī held some Mu'tazilite views, see Dhahabī, *Mīzān al-i'tidāl*, 3:155.
2. Al-Khaṭīb al-Baghdādī, *Tārīkh Baghdād*, 5:252.
3. Al-Khaṭīb, *Tārīkh Baghdād*, 1:76. He must have visited the city before 398/1007, when he was in his early thirties, since he studied in Baghdad with the grammarian 'Abdallāh al-Bāfī, who died that year; Tāj al-Dīn al-Subkī, *Ṭabaqāt al-shāfi'iyya al-kubrā*, 3:317.
4. We know that he was in the southern Iraqi city of Wāsiṭ several years later, in 421/1030, when it is recorded that he read his book *Adab al-dunyā wa'l-dīn* to students in the city's mosque; Mikhail, *Politics and Revelation*, 83, (based on Maximilian Enger, ed., *Maverdii: Constitutiones Politicae* [Bonn: Adolphum Marcum, 1853], iv).

5. Ibn al-Najjār and Ibn al-Jawzī report that al-Māwardī's son, 'Abd al-Wahhāb (d. 441/1049), who predeceased him, came with him from Basra and was given the honor of being accepted as a witness by the chief judge of Baghdad, Ibn Mākūlā, in 430/1039, despite his youth. Since he had to have been at least pubescent to have his testimony accepted, that would place 'Abd al-Wahhāb's birth in Basra no later than 415/1024; Ibn al-Jawzī, *al-Muntaẓam*, 15:322; Ibn al-Najjār, *Dhayl Tārīkh Baghdād*, published with al-Khaṭīb, *Tārīkh Baghdād*, 16:218–19.
6. Among those who assumed this are Majid Khadduri, *The Islamic Conception of Justice*, 132; Allehbi, "'It is Permitted for the Amīr but not the Qāḍī'," 4. The chief judgeship in Baghdad was held by Ibn al-Akfānī (d. 405/1014), then by Ibn Abī al-Shawārib until his death in 417/1026, followed by a three-year interim in which no one held the position, then by the Shāfi'ī Ibn Mākūlā (d. 447/1055), then by the Ḥanafī al-Dāmaghānī, who held it until his death in 478/1085; al-Khaṭīb, *Tārīkh Baghdād*, 5:251–252, 8:79, 10:140; Ibn Abī al-Wafā', *al-Jawāhir muḍiyya, fī ṭabaqāt al-ḥanafiyya*, ed. 'Abd al-Fattāḥ Muḥammad al-Ḥuluw, 5 vols. (Giza: Mu'assasat al-Risāla, 1978–1988), 3:269–271; Ibn al-Jawzī, *al-Muntaẓam*, 16:251.
7. See Tāj al-Dīn al-Subkī, *al-Ṭabaqāt al-shāfi'iyya al-kubrā*, 5:262.
8. Al-Khaṭīb, *Tārīkh Baghdād*, 12:102.
9. Gibb, "Al-Mawardi's Theory of the Caliphate," 152.
10. Ibn al-Jawzī, *Muntaẓam*, 15:225, 285–286.
11. This comes from the history of Muḥammad b. 'Abd al-Malik al-Hamadhānī. Ibn al-Jawzī proffers that, while these other scholars had used analogy to come to their conclusions, al-Māwardī had recalled the Hadith in which the title *malik al-amlāk* is disparaged; Ibn al-Jawzī, *al-Muntaẓam*, 15:264–265; *Ṣaḥīḥ al-Bukhārī*: *kitāb al-adab, bāb abghaḍ al-asmā' ilā Allāh, taḥrīm al-tasammī bi-malik al-amlāk wa malik al-mulūk*. See also Heribert Busse, "The Revival of Persian Kingship under the Būyids," in *Islamic Civilization 950–1150*, ed. D.S. Richards (London: Bruno Cassirer, 1973), 62, 64–65 and an excellent discussion by the late Wilferd Madelung, "The Assumption of the Title of Shāhānshāh by the Būyids and the 'Reign of the Daylam (*Dawlat al-Daylam*)'," *Journal of Near Eastern Studies* 28, n. 3 (1969): 180–183.
12. Ibn al-Jawzī, *Muntaẓam*, 15:289, 16:85.
13. Ibn al-Jawzī, *Muntaẓam*, 16:4.
14. This book, the *Iqnā'*, did not prove of lasting influence in the school, though Abū Shujā' al-Iṣbahānī (d. *circa* 500/1105) wrote a commentary on it; Tāj al-Dīn al-Subkī, *Ṭabaqāt*, 6:15.
15. 'Izz al-Dīn Ibn 'Abd al-Salām (d. 660/1262) attempted to reconcile the two books in his *al-Jam' bayn al-Ḥāwī wa'l-Nihāya* but did not complete it; Tāj al-Dīn al-Subkī, *Ṭabaqāt*, 8:248. Al-Māwardī's opinions were particularly interesting to the Khurasani scholar 'Abd al-Wāḥid al-Rūyānī (d. 502/1108), whose *Baḥr* was based on the *Ḥāwī* and was later cited extensively by influential Shāfi'ī writers like the Egyptian Najm al-Dīn Ibn Rif'a (d. 710/1310); Tāj al-Dīn al-Subkī, *Ṭabaqāt*, 7:195.
16. Qāḍī 'Iyāḍ b. Mūsā, *Kitāb al-Shifā* (Beirut: Dār Ibn Ḥazm, 2000), 118.
17. For an excellent overview, see Neguin Yavari, *Advice for the Sultan: Prophetic Voices and Secular Politics in Medieval Islam* (London: Hurst, 2014).

18. This is admirably argued by Fu'ād 'Abd al-Mun'im Aḥmad, who edited the work; al-Māwardī, *Durar al-sulūk fī siyāsat al-mulūk*, ed. Fu'ād 'Abd al-Mun'im Aḥmad (Riyadh: Dār al-Waṭan, 1417/1997), 36–40.
19. See Riḍwān al-Sayyid's introduction to al-Māwardī, *Tashīl al-naẓar wa ta'jīl al-ẓafar*, ed. Riḍwān al-Sayyid, 2nd ed. (Beirut: Ibn al-Azraq Center for Political Heritage Studies, 1432/2012), 101–103; al-Māwardī, *Qawānīn al-wizāra wa siyāsat al-mulūk*, ed. Riḍwān al-Sayyid (Beirut: Dār al-Ṭalī'a, 1979), 239; idem, *Kitāb Durar al-sulūk*, 35, 36 54. For a dismissal of al-Māwardī's authorship of the *Naṣīḥat al-mulūk*, see Louise Marlow, "Difference and encyclopaedism in tenth-century Eastern Iran," *Jerusalem Studies in Arabic and Islam* 40 (2013): 195–244; idem, "Abū Zayd al-Balkhī and the *Naṣīḥat al-mulūk* of Pseudo-Māwardī," *Der Islam* 93, n. 1 (2016): 35–64. Mikhail defends the attribution on stylistic and other grounds but argues the work has been mistitled; Mikhail, *Politics and Revelation*, 65–68.
20. That it was quite possible for al-Māwardī to have written works of such disparate style and contents is clear in his *Amthāl wa'l-ḥikam*, which consists of a thematic list of Prophetic Hadiths followed by maxims and sayings of various ancient figures. It is quite literally an Islamic and Near-Eastern diptych, marrying Near-Eastern heritage to a genre of very Sunni books on Hadiths that had become maxims, such as the *Kitāb Amthāl al-ḥadīth* of Abū al-Shaykh al-Iṣbahānī (d. 369/979).
21. Al-Māwardī, *Kitāb al-Aḥkām al-sulṭāniyya*, 1.
22. Gibb, "Al-Mawardi's Theory of the caliphate," 152; Sayyid's introduction to al-Māwardī, *Tashīl*, 101–103.
23. Melchert, "Māwardī's Legal Thinking," 66, 70.
24. For Abū Ya'lā Ibn al-Farrā's biography, see the massive biography of him by his son Ibn Abī Ya'lā, *Ṭabaqāt al-ḥanābila*, ed. Muḥammad Ḥāmid al-Fiqī, 2 vols. (Cairo: Maṭba'at al-Sunna al-Muḥammadiyya, 1371/1952), 2:193–231, and for modern studies: George Makdisi, *lbn 'Aqīl et la résurgence de l'Islam traditionaliste au xie siècle* (Damascus: Institut Français de Damas, 1963), 232–237; Muḥammad 'Abd al-Qādir Abū Fāris, *al-Qāḍī Abū Ya'lā al-Farrā' wa kitābuhu al-Aḥkām al-sulṭāniyya* (Beirut: Mu'assasat al-Risāla, 1983) (thanks to Christopher Melchert for alerting me to this source); the late Wadi Z. Haddad's introduction to Ibn al-Farrā', *Kitāb al-Mu'tamad fī uṣūl al-dīn*, ed. Wadi Z. Haddad (Beirut: Dar El-Machreq, 1986), 16–28.
25. See Haddad, ed., *Kitāb al-Mu'tamad*, 13.
26. Ibn al-Farrā', *al-Aḥkām al-sulṭāniyya*, ed. Muḥammad Ḥāmid al-Fiqī (Beirut: Dār al-Kutub al-'Ilmiyya, 1421/2000, based on Cairo edition), 19.
27. Those who have concluded that Abū Ya'lā's book was first include Sherman Jackson and Christopher Melchert. Many more have argued or assumed that al-Māwardī's was earlier, including Muḥammad 'Abd al-Qādir Abū Fāris, Henri Laoust (raising the possibility of a common model as well), Claude Cahen, Wilferd Madelung, and Ovamir Anjum. Others have confessed their agnosticism on the matter. Melchert and Donald Little provide reviews of scholarship on this question. See Melchert, "Māwardī, Abū Ya'lá and the Sunni Revival," 37–61; Little, 7–8; Anjum, *Politics, Law, and Community in Islamic Thought*, 118; Abū Fāris, *al-Qāḍī Abū Ya'lā al-Farrā'*, 544. See also Nimrod Hurvitz, *Competing Texts: The Relationship Between al-Mawardi's and Abu Ya'la's* al-Ahkam al-sultaniyya (Cambridge, MA: Harvard Islamic Legal Studies Program, 2007).

28. The best analysis on this comes from Little, "A New Look...," 10–15 and Melchert, "Māwardī, Abū Ya'lá and the Sunni Revival."
29. Melchert, "Māwardī, Abū Ya'lá and Sunni Revival," 50.
30. Anjum, *Politics, Law, and Community in Islamic Thought*, 118–121.
31. See Little, 5.
32. Al-Māwardī, *Aḥkām*, 116.
33. Al-Māwardī, *Aḥkām*, 115; Ibn al-Farrā', 81. This is *pace* Rushain Abbasi's assessment that al-Māwardī viewing the powers that the *maẓālim* magistrate enjoyed, such as admitting circumstantial evidence, as beyond the judge's range meant they were "extra-*shar'ī*." They were simply taken from different *madhhab*s. In addition, as will be discussed in Chapter Four, al-Māwardī had a very restricted view of the judge's powers compared to later Sunni scholars. See Rushain Abbasi, "Beyond the Realm of Religion: The Idea of the Secular in Premodern Islam," (PhD dissertation, Harvard, 2021), 560–561.
34. See editors' introduction to Isḥāq b. Ibrāhīm Ibn Wahb al-Kātib, *al-Burhān fī wujūh al-bayān*, ed. Aḥmad Maṭlūb and Khadīja al-Ḥadīthī (Baghdad: Maṭba'at al-'Ānī, 1967), 40. Thanks to Mohammed Allehbi for drawing my attention to this source.
35. Al-Māwardī, *al-Aḥkām*, 110.
36. Al-Māwardī, *al-Aḥkām*, 116, 122.
37. Ibn Wahb, *al-Burhān fī wujūh al-bayān*, 375.
38. For the proper vowelling of Davān, which also appears in the less soundly attested forms Duvvān and Davvān, see 'Alī Davānī, *Sharḥ-e zendegānī-ye Jalāl al-Dīn Davānī* (Qom: Chāpkhāne-ye Ḥekmat, [1955]), 47.
39. The birth date follows Lambton and Newman. We know that he was born between 1424 and 1434 based on al-Sakhāwī's statement that he was in his seventies in 897/1491–2. The most up-to-date studies on Davānī are Ahab Bdaiwi, "Shi'i Defenders of Avicenna: An Intellectual History of the Dashtakī Philosophers of Shiraz," (PhD dissertation, University of Exeter, 2014), 44–48; Bdaiwi's forthcoming *Jalāl al-Dīn Dawānī: An Avicennan Philosopher and Ash'arī Theologian* (Cambridge: Cambridge University Press, forthcoming); Reza Pourjavady, *Philosophy in Early Safavid Iran* (Leiden: Brill, 2011), 4–14; Mahmut Anay, "Celâleddin Devvânî: Hayatı, Eserleri, Ahlâk ve Siyaset Düşüncesi," (PhD Dissertation, Istanbul University, 1994); Christopher Andrew Markiewicz, "The Crisis of Rule in Late Medieval Islam: A Study of Idrīs Bidlīsī (861–926/1457–1520) and Kingship at the Turn of the Sixteenth Century," (PhD Dissertation, University of Chicago, 2015) and idem, *The Crisis of Kingship in Late Medieval Islam: Persian Emigres and the Making of Ottoman Sovereignty* (Cambridge: Cambridge University Press, 2019). For early and representative biographies, see (writing about Davānī during his lifetime in 897 AH) Shams al-Dīn al-Sakhāwī, *al-Ḍaw' al-lāmi'*, 12 vols. in 6 (Beirut: Dār al-Jīl, 1992), 4:133; writing several decades later with uniquely detailed information, Qāḍī Nūr Allāh Shūshtarī (d. 1019/1610), *Majālis al-mu'minīn*, 2 vols. (Tehran: Ketābkhorūshī-ye Eslāmī, 1377/1998), 2:221–230; Quṭb al-Dīn Muḥammad 'Alī Ishkavarī Lāhījī, *Maḥbūb al-qulūb*, ed. Ḥāmid al-Dībājī, 2 vols. (Tehran: Daftar-e Nashr-e Mīrāt-e Maktūb, 1382/2003), 2:463–467; 'Abd al-Qādir b. 'Abdallāh al-'Aydarūs, *al-Nūr al-sāfir fī akhbār al-qarn al-'āshir*, ed. Aḥmad Ḥālū, Maḥmūd al-Arnā'ūṭ and Akram al-Būshī (Beirut: Dār Ṣādir, 2001), 190; Ibn al-'Imād, *Shadharāt al-dhahab*, ed.

ʿAbd al-Qādir al-Arnāʾūṭ and Maḥmūd al-Arnāʾūṭ, 11 vols. (Damascus: Dār Ibn Kathīr, 1414/1993), 10:221; Muḥammad Bāqir Khwānsārī, *Rawḍat al-jannāt fī aḥwāl al-ʿulamāʾ waʾl-sādāt*, 7 vols. (Tehran: Maktabeh-ye Esmāʿīleyān, [1962–1972]), 2:239–45; ʿAbd al-Ḥayy al-Laknawī, *al-Fawāʾid al-bahiyya fī tarājim al-ḥanafiyya* (Karachi: Qadīmī Kutubkhāne, n.d.), 89–90. Other secondary-source studies include ʿAlī Davānī, *Sharḥ-e zendegānī-ye Jalāl al-Dīn Davānī*; Ann Lambton, c.v., *Encyclopaedia of Islam* (Brill); Andrew Newman, c.v., *Encyclopaedia Iranica*; Judith Pfeiffer, "Teaching the Learned: Jalāl al-Dīn al-Dawānī's *Ijāza* to Muʾayyadzāda ʿAbd al-Raḥmān Efendi and the Circulation of Knowledge between Fārs and the Ottoman Empire at the Turn of the Sixteenth Century," in *The Heritage of Arabo-Islamic Learning: Studies Presented to Wadad Kadi*, ed. Maurice Pomerantz and Aram Shahin (Leiden: Brill, 2016), 284–332. See also Jean Aubin, "Études Safavides. I. Šāh Ismāʿīl et les Notables de l'Iraq Persan," *Journal of the Social and Economic History of the Orient* 2 (1959): 55–58. For an extensive list Davānī's works, see Shūshtarī, *Majālis al-muʾminīn*, 2:225–229; Reza Pourjavady, "Ketābshenāsī-ye āthār-e Jalāl al-Dīn Davānī," *Maʿāref* 15, no. 1–2 (1377/1998): 81–138, and Ismāʿīl al-Bābānī, *Hadiyat al-ʿārifīn asmāʾ al-muʾallifīn wa āthār al-muṣannifīn min Kashf al-ẓunūn*, ed. Muḥammad ʿAbd al-Qādir ʿAṭā (Beirut: Dār al-Kutub al-ʿIlmiyya, 1429/2008), 7:201.

40. Davānī, "Risālat Unmūdhaj al-ʿulūm," in *Thalāth rasāʾil min muṣannafāt al-ʿallāma al-muḥaqqiq Muḥammad b. Asʿad al-Dawānī*, ed. Aḥmad Tūysirkānī (Mashhad: Majmaʿ al-Buḥūth al-Islāmiyya, 1411/1990), 275–279; al-Laknawī, 90.
41. This comes from his student Abū al-Qāsim Naṣr al-Bayān al-Kāzirūnī in his *Sullam al-samawāt*; Khwānsārī, *Rawḍat al-jannāt*, 2:243 and al-Laknawī, 90.
42. Najm al-Dīn al-Ghazzī, *al-Kawākib al-sāʾira bi-aʿyān al-miʾa al-ʿāshira*, ed. Jibrāʾīl Jabbūr, 3 vols. (Beirut: Dār al-Āfāq al-Jadīda, 1979), 2:148.
43. Pfeiffer, "Teaching the Learned," 323. For a full biography of Abū Isḥāq al-Kāzerūnī, see Farīd al-Dīn ʿAṭṭār, *Tadhkerat al-awleyāʾ*, ed. Moḥammad Esteʿlāmī (Tehran: Zovvār, 1346/1968), 763–776.
44. Davānī, "Unmūdhaj al-ʿulūm," 280–281; Jonathan Brown, "Even If It's not True It's True: Using Unreliable Ḥadīths in Sunni Islam," *Islamic Law and Society* 18, no. 1 (2011): 25–27.
45. Davānī's political writings have most recently been discussed by Murtaḍā Yūsuffīrād, *Andīshe-ye siyāsī-ye Jalāl al-Dīn Davānī* (Qom, 1378/2008); Markiewicz, *The Crisis of Kingship in Late Medieval Islam.*
46. Davānī dates the completion of *al-Zawrāʾ* to *Jumādī al-thānī*, 872 AH in Tabriz; idem, *al-Zawrāʾ*, Ms. #3453, King Saud University, 11a. He notes that he writes from Kashan in his *Risāla fī afʿāl al-ʿibād*, Ms. 2681 King Saud University, 20b; ʿAlī Davānī, *Sharḥ-e Zendegānī-ye Jalāl al-Dīn Davānī*, 79–84.
47. Woods, *The Aqquyunlu*, 104–105.
48. See Woods, *The Aqquyunlu*, 145.
49. Ann Lambton, "Quis custodiet custodes: Some Reflections on the Persian Theory of Government," *Studia Islamica* 5 (1956): 146.
50. See Davānī's extensive encomium for Sultan Maḥmūd, in Davānī, *Thalāth rasāʾil*, 271–273. For his exchange with Beyazid II, see ʿAbd al-Ḥusayn Navāʾī, *Asnād va mukātabāt-e tārīkh-e Īrān, az Taymūr tā Shāh Esmāʿīl* (Tehran: s.n., 1963), 448–455; Ahab Bdaiwi, "Philosophia Ottomanica: Jalāl al-Dīn Dawānī

on Establishing the Existence of the Necessary Being," in *Empires of the Near East and India: Source Studies of the Safavid, Ottoman, and Mughal Literate Communities*, ed. H. Khafipour (New York: Columbia University Press, 2019), 321; al-Ḥasanī, *Nuzhat al-khawāṭir*, 5:309–310; Markiewicz, *The Crisis of Kingship in Late Medieval Islam*, 67.

51. See Woods, *The Aqquyunlu*, 157; ʿAlī Davānī, *Sharḥ-e zendegānī*, 191–193.
52. Ḥājjī Khalīfa Muṣṭafā Kātib Chelebī, *Kashf al-ẓunūn ʿan asāmī al-kutub wa al-funūn*, ed. Muḥammad ʿAbd al-Qādir ʿAṭā (Beirut: Dār al-Kutub al-ʿIlmiyya, 1429/2008), 2:406. Kātib Chelebī is probably relying on Davānī's small *tafsīr* on *sūrat al-Kāfirūn*, which he introduces as having been written in Jarūn in 905 AH. See Cevdet Akbay, "Celâleddin ed-Devvânî ve Tafsîr-u 'Kul yâ eyyuhel Kâfirûn' (Edisyon Kritik)," (MA thesis, Marmara University, 1987), 2.
53. Shūshtarī, *Majālis*, 2:225; ʿAlī Davānī, 150.
54. Al-Ḥasanī, *Nuzhat al-khawāṭir*, 4:340.
55. See Bdaiwi, "Philosophia Ottomanica," 319–335.
56. See Francis Robinson, "Ottomans-Safavids-Mughals: Shared Knowledge and Connective Systems," *Journal of Islamic Studies* 8, no. 2 (1997): 151–184; Khaled El Rouayheb, *Islamic Intellectual History in the Seventeenth Century: Scholarly Currents in the Ottoman Empire and the Maghreb* (Cambridge: Cambridge University Press, 2015), 39–41; Bdaiwi, "Philosophia Ottomanica."
57. Chelebī, *Kashf al-ẓunūn*, 1:116, 1:376–377; 2:406; 2:367. For a discussion of an issue disputed by the two scholars regarding relational syllogism, see Khaled El-Rouyaheb, *Relational Syllogisms and the History of Arab Logic*, 900–1900 (Leiden: Brill, 2010), 92–94.
58. Kātib Chelebī, *Kashf*, 3:199.
59. See al-Laknawī, 90.
60. Al-Ḥasanī, *Nuzhat al-khawāṭir*, 4:10–11, 68, 101, 260, 280–282.
61. See al-Ḥasanī, *Nuzhat al-khawāṭir*, 6:28, 39, 191, 249, 295, 312, 354, 398. It was apparently one al-Amīr Fatḥ Allāh al-Shīrāzī (d. 997/1588–9) and one Muḥammad b. Maḥmūd al-Ṭārimī (d. 941/1534–5) who brought Davānī's books to India; al-Ḥasanī, *Nuzhat al-khawāṭir*, 4:225, 280–2. See also Hassan John Rezakhany, "Jalāl ad-Dīn ad-Dawānī's Solution to the Liar Paradox and Its Reception in Qāḍī Mubārak and Mullā Mubīn," *Journal of South Asian Intellectual History* 1, n. 2 (2018): 183–220.
62. Aḥmad b. Muṣṭafā Ṭāshkubrīzāda (Taşköprüzade), *al-Shaqāʾiq al-nuʿmāniyya fī ʿulamāʾ al-dawla al-ʿUthmāniyya* (Istanbul: Jāmiʿat Istānbūl, Markaz al-Dirāsāt al-Sharqīyya, 1985), 137, 149, 292, 329, 330–331, 356, 469, 472.
63. On Davānī's influence on Ottoman political thought of the sixteenth century see: Hüseyin Yılmaz, "The Sultan and the Sultanate: Envisioning Rulership in the Age of Süleyman the Lawgiver (1520–1566)," (PhD dissertation, Harvard, 2005), 44–45. On the importance of his *Akhlāq-i Jalālī* throughout the post-Mongol Persianate world see, for example, Chad Lingwood, *Politics, Poetry, and Sufism in Medieval Iran: New Perspectives on Jami's Salaman va Absal* (Leiden: Brill, 2014), 86–89; Avril A. Powell, "Old Books in New Bindings: Ethics and Education in Colonial India," in *Knowledge Production, Pedagogy, and Institutions in Colonial India*, ed. Indra Sengupta and Daud Ali (New York: Palgrave Macmillan, 2011), 199–226; Muzaffar Alam, *The Languages of Political Islam* (Chicago: The University of Chicago Press, 2004), 50, 60, 130, 151; Zahra Ayubi, *Gendered Morality* (New York: Columbia University Press, 2019).

64. Shūshtarī, *Majālis*, 2:222.
65. Al-Khwānsārī, *Rawḍat al-jannāt*, 2:239. We know this because Kātib Chelebī tells us that he completed this after the death of his opponent, Ṣadr al-Dīn al-Shīrāzī, who died in 903/1498.
66. Shūshtarī, 2:223.
67. Aubin, "études Safavides," 58.
68. See ʿAlī Ḥaydar, *Durar al-ḥukkām sharḥ Majallat al-aḥkām*, 4 vols. (Riyadh: Dār ʿĀlam al-Kutub; Beirut: Dār al-Jīl, 1423/2003), 1:12; Bedir, "*Fıkıh* to Law," 385–389.
69. For biographies of Ahmet Cevdet Paşa, see Yusuf Halaçoğlu and Mehmet Âkif Aydin, "Cevdet Paşa," in *Islâm Ansiklopedisi*, available at https://islamansiklopedisi.org.tr/cevdet-pasa; Christoph K. Neumann, *Das indirekte Argument: Ein Plädoyer für die Tanzimat vermittels der Historie* (Hamburg: Lit Verlag, 1994); idem, "Whom did Ahmed Cevdet Represent?" in *Late Ottoman Society: The Intellectual Legacy*, ed. Elisabeth Özdalga (London: Routledge Curzon, 2005), 117–134 (especially p. 129 for a full bibliography of Turkish-language studies on Cevdet); Richard L. Chambers, "The Education of a Nineteenth-Century Ottoman Âlim, Ahmed Cevdet Paşa," *International Journal of Middle East Studies* 4, n. 4 (1973): 440–464; Hulusi Yavuz, "Ahmed Cevdet Paşa and the Ulema of His Time," *Islam Tetkikleri Enstitüsü Dergisi* 7, n. 3–4 (1979): 178–198; Fatma Aliye, *Ahmed Cevdet Paşa ve Zamanı* (Istanbul: Pınar Yayınları, 1994); Mustafa Gündüz, *Ahmed Cevdet Paşa* (Ankara: Doğu Batı, 2012); Mustafa Oğuz, *Ahmed Cevdet Paşa ve Tarihçiliği* (Konya: Kömen Yayınları, 2014); Ahmed Zeki İzgöer, *Müsülman, Osmanlı ve Modern: Ahmed Cevdet Paşa* (Istanbul: İz Yayınevi, 2014).
70. Yılmaz, "The Sultan and the Sultanate," 26. For one instance it was referred to, Dede Cöngī's (d. 975/1567) *al-Risāla fī al-siyāsa al-sharʿiyya*, see Derin Terzioğlu, "Ibn Taymiyya, *al-Siyāsa al-Sharʿiyya*, and the Early Modern Ottomans," in *Historicizing Sunni Islam in the Ottoman Empire, c. 1450–1750*, ed. Tijana Krstić and Derin Terzioğlu (Leiden: Brill, 2021), 101–154.
71. Neumann, "Whom did Ahmed Cevdet represent?" 123.
72. Avi Rubin, *Ottoman* Nizamiye *Courts: Law and Modernity* (New York: Palgrave MacMillan, 2011), 28–34, 53, 63–64; idem, "Legal borrowing and its impact on Ottoman legal culture in the late nineteenth century," *Continuity and Change* 22, n. 2 (2007): 285.
73. Rubin, "Legal borrowing," 282, 284.
74. Ahmed Cevdet Paşa, *Tezâkir*, ed. Cavid Baysun, 4 vols. (Ankara: Türk Tarih Kurumu, 1991), 4:85.
75. To see which sections Cevdet translated and which he did not, see the translation of Davānī's treatise in the next chapter.
76. Cevdet, *Tezâkir*, 4:90. I thank Guy Burak, Yakoob Ahmed, Murteza Bedir and Abdurrahman Atçıl for helping me with this translation.
77. Cevdet also planned to print and publish the treatise, but he was prevented from doing so by the Grand Vizier Ali Paşa; Cevdet, *Tezâkir*, 4:91.
78. Roderic H. Davison, *Essays in Ottoman and Turkish History, 1774–1923: The Impact of the West* (Austin: University of Texas Press, 1990), 123–124; Mehmet Yıldız, "1856 Islahat Fermamına Giden Yolda Meşruiyet Arayışları (Uluslararası Baskılar ve Cizye Sorununa Bulunan Çözümün İslâmî Temelleri)," *Türk Kültürü İncelemeleri Dergisi* 7 (2002): 75–114.

79. This is actually reported in early Christian Syriac sources, which attribute this ruling to the Umayyad caliph Yazīd II (d. 105/724), along with the ruling that a non-Muslim's *diya* was half that of a Muslim; Tillier, "The Umayyads and the Formation of Islamic Judgeship," 178–180. Interestingly, into the 1200s CE Muslims living under Christian rule in Iberia were accepted as equal to Christians as witnesses, but then their standing quickly eroded; Brian Catlos, *Muslims of Medieval Latin Christendom, c. 1050–1614* (Cambridge: Cambridge University Press, 2014), 359. Jewish and Christian courts in Iraq in the 900s–1000s CE allowed Muslims to serve as notary witnesses in their courts in part because the rabbis approved of their accuracy with documentation and there were no Christians available; Simonsohn, *A Common Justice*, 163, 185–187.

80. Niyazi Berkes, *The Development of Secularism in Modern Turkey* (London: Hurst, 1964), 168; Ebul'ula Mardin, *Medeni Hukuk Cephesinden Ahmet Cevdet Paşa* (Ankara: Türkiye Diyanet Vakfı, 2009), 61, 63–64. Although I know of no insight into Cevdet's reasoning behind this statement, it may refer to legal opinions based on Quran 5:106, which seems to allow Muslims who are traveling to have non-Muslims bear witness to their wills if no Muslims are available. Though many scholars interpret the verse as meaning people outside one's tribe or local community, the non-Muslim interpretation was affirmed by several schools of law. For example, the Ḥanafī al-Jaṣṣāṣ affirmed that non-Muslim notaries were allowed to witness bequests (*waṣiyya*). And, though al-Māturīdī rejects this permissibility, he notes that it was reported from Saʿīd b. Jubayr and Ibn Masʿūd; al-Jaṣṣāṣ, *Aḥkām al-Qur'ān*, 3 vols. (Beirut: Dār al-Kitāb al-ʿArabī, n.d., reprint of Istanbul: Maṭbaʿat al-Awqāf al-Islāmiyya, 1335/1917), 2:490; Abū Manṣūr al-Māturīdī, *Ta'wīlāt al-Qur'ān*, ed. Bekir Topaloglu et al., 17 vols. (Istanbul: Dār al-Mīzān, 2006), 4:361–364. For others permitting this, see Manṣūr b. Yūnus al-Buhūtī, *al-Rawḍ al-murbiʿ*, ed. Bashīr Muḥammad ʿUyūn (Damascus: Maktabat Dār al-Bayān, 1999), 502; Muḥammad al-Nawawī al-Jāwī, *Qūt al-ḥabīb al-gharīb* (Cairo: Maṭbaʿat Muṣṭafā al-Bābī al-Ḥalabī, 1938), 289; Mullā Hüsrev, *Durar al-ḥukkām sharḥ Ghurar al-aḥkām*, ed. Aḥmad Rifʿat al-Qarah-Ḥiṣārī, 2 vols. (Istanbul: Fazilet Neşriyat, 2015, reprint of 1308/1890 Istanbul edition), 2:378; Ṣāliḥ ʿAbd al-Salām al-Ābī, *al-Thamar al-dānī fī taqrīb al-maʿānī*, 2nd ed. (Cairo: Muṣṭafā al-Bābī al-Ḥalabī, 1944), 448.

3. A POST-MONGOL TREATISE ON THE GRIEVANCE TRIBUNAL: A TRANSLATION OF JALĀL AL-DĪN DAVĀNĪ'S *RESĀLE DAR DĪVĀN-E MAẒĀLEM*

1. Unlike his teacher, Khunjī includes an essentially verbatim Persian rendering of al-Māwardī's exhaustive instructions on legal procedure. Also unlike Davānī, Khunjī introduces this dry material with extensive historical reports about early pious Muslim rulers, in particular ʿUmar b. ʿAbd al-ʿAzīz, drawing on sources much more varied than Davānī. Interestingly, Khunjī's vignettes suggest a pro-Alid theme; Faḍlallāh b. Rūzbahān Khunjī, *Sulūk al-mulūk*

(Tehran: Enteshārāt-e Khvārazmī, 1984), 214–227. On Khunjī, see Matthew Melvin-Koushki, "Khunji, Fazl Allah b. Ruzbihan (1455–1521)," in Gerhard Bowering et al, eds., *Princeton Encyclopedia of Islamic Political Thought* (Princeton: Princeton University Press, 2012), 297–298.

2. Shūshtarī, *Majālis al-mu'minīn*, 2:228; 'Alī Davānī, *Sharḥ-e zendegānī-ye Jalāl al-Dīn Davānī*, 170. The famous Persian bibliographer Mohammad-Taqi Danishpazhouh concurred; Mohammad-Taqi Danishpazhouh, "An Annotated Bibliography on Government and Statecraft," trans. Andrew Newman, in *Authority and Political Culture in Shi'ism*, ed. Said Amir Arjomand (Albany: SUNY Press, 1988), 221. The exact dates of 'Alā' al-Mulk's reign are not clear. Zambaur has him ruling from 883/1478 onward, and his reign would have ended at some point between then and the death of his successor, Hārūn, which is reliably put at 927/1521; J. Aubin, "Références pour Lar medieval," *Journal Asiatique* (1955): 494; E. de Zambaur, *Manuel de Généalogie et de Chronologie pour l'Histoire de l'Islam* (Hannover: Orient-Buchhandlung Heinz Lafaire, 1955, originally printed, 1927), 260.
3. The honorific *aqḍā al-quḍāt* was coined for al-Māwardī in 429/1037–8 according to Yāqūt; Yāqūt al-Ḥamawī, *Mu'jam al-udabā'*, ed. Iḥsān 'Abbās, 7 vols. (Beirut: Dār al-Gharb al-Islāmī, 1993), 5:1955. The title was also bestowed on a contemporary as well, one Muḥammad b. 'Abd al-Raḥmān (d. 478/1085); Ziriklī, *A'lām*, 6:191.
4. This is Sultan Neẓām Malek 'Alā' al-Molk of Lar (r. 883/1478 – early 900s/1500s); Aubin, "Références pour Lar medieval," 494.
5. The famous Companion (d. 36/656), his mother was the Prophet's paternal aunt.
6. See *Ṣaḥīḥ al-Bukhārī*: *kitāb al-musāqā, bāb shurb al-a'lā qabl al-asfal*. This instance raises the question of whether the Prophet issued this ruling out of anger, which contradicts his command that judges not rule when angry. The general response of Muslim commentators is that this would be impossible for the Prophet due to his infallibility (*'iṣma*). In his *Sunan* (*al-Mujtabā*), al-Nasā'ī places this Hadith under the chapter title of 'License for the Trustworthy Judge to Rule when Angry.' Another argument, mentioned by al-Khaṭṭābī, was that the Anṣārī man had committed apostasy by speaking to the Prophet as he did and had therefore invalidated his property right. The Prophet thus was treating him gently; Ibn Ḥajar, *Fatḥ al-Bārī*, 5:49; Abū Sulaymān al-Khaṭṭābī, *Ma'ālim al-sunan*, 3rd ed., 4 vols. (Beirut: al-Maktaba al-'Ilmiyya, 1981), 4:182.
7. Introducing the story of Solomon, not found explicitly in al-Māwardī (who references it but as a ruling made by 'Alī), fits with the comparison of the Aqquyunlu ruler Ūzūn Ḥasan with that prophetic king. See Abū Bakr Tehrānī, *Ketāb-e Deyārbakreyye*, ed. Nejātī Lūghāl and Fārūq Sūdar, vol. 2 ([Tehran]: Chāpkhāne-ye Anjomān-e Tork, 1964), 527.
8. Quran 12:23–29.
9. The Umayyad caliph, r. 65/685–86/705.
10. 'Ābid Allāh (or 'Ā'idh Allāh) b. 'Abdallāh al-Khawlānī (d. 80/699) served as a judge from 684–699 CE. The *nisba* al-Azdī may be a mistake here. Al-Māwardī and Abū Ya'lā have al-Awdī. These latter two may have confused him with 'Abdallāh b. Idrīs al-Awdī of Kufa (d. 192/808), a famous Hadith transmitter about whose death date many erred; Wakī', *Akhbār al-quḍāt*, 618; Ibn Sa'd,

al-Ṭabaqāt al-kubrā, ed. ʿAlī Muḥammad ʿUmar, 11 vols. (Cairo: Maktabat al-Khānjī, 1421/2001), 9:451; Steven Judd, *Religious Scholars and the Umayyads* (New York: Routledge, 2014), 106; al-Dhahabī, *Siyar aʿlām al-nubalāʾ*, 9:42–44.

11. The famously pious Umayyad caliph, r. 99/717–101/720.
12. R. 158/775–169/785.
13. R. 169/785–170/786.
14. R. 170/786–193/809.
15. R. 189/813–218/833.
16. The famous Central Asian Shāfiʿī jurist, theologian and philosopher, d. 606/1209.
17. One of Abū Ḥanīfa's leading pupils and the compiler of the formative texts of the Ḥanafī school, he moved from Kufa to serve the Abbasids in Baghdad, d. 189/805.
18. Another of the leading architects of the Ḥanafī school, Abū Ḥanīfa's main acolyte and al-Shaybānī's main teacher, d. 182/798.
19. Fakhr al-Dīn al-Rāzī, *Manāqib al-imām al-Shāfiʿī*, ed. Aḥmad Ḥijāzī al-Saqā (Cairo: Maktabat al-Kulliyyāt al-Azhariyya, 1406/1986), 71.
20. R. 255/869–256/870.
21. In Cevdet's translation, this paragraph appears earlier, after the Joseph and Zulaykha reference. Regarding the Hadith cited here, Davānī draws it directly from al-Māwardī's text. For this Hadith, see *Musnad Aḥmad Ibn Ḥanbal*: 1:190 (Maymaniyya print). For other approximations of that maxim, see ibid., 2:180, where the Prophet says in a sermon after the recapture of Mecca that, "*mā kāna min ḥilf fī al-jāhiliyya fa-inna al-islām lam yazidhu illā shidda...*," and *Ṣaḥīḥ Muslim*: *kitāb faḍāʾil al-ṣaḥāba, bāb muʾākhāt al-Nabī ṣ bayn aṣḥābihi*, where the Prophet says, "*lā ḥilf fī al-islām wa ayyumā ḥilf kāna fī al-jāhiliyya lam yazidhu al-islām illā shidda.*"
22. I.e., Ūzūn Ḥasan, the great leader of the Aqquyunlu (d. in Tabriz in 1478, aged fifty-two); Woods, *The Aqquyunlu*, 123.
23. For a description of Ūzūn Ḥasan's *maẓālim*, see Woods, *The Aqquyunlu*, 109.
24. Abū al-Muẓaffar Yaʿqūb b. Ūzūn Ḥasan Bayandur (r. 1478–1490); see Woods, The *Aqquyunlu*, 128–147, 213.
25. Cf. Qāḍī Ḥusayn Maybūdī, who wrote of his reign that "the people rest tranquil and carefree"; in Woods, *The Aqquyunlu*, 140.
26. This likely refers to the idea, which had grown in prevalence since the tenth century CE, that the true 'rulers' of the realm were the Sufi saints, or 'the friends of God.' For example, see Abū Nuʿaym al-Iṣbahānī, *Ḥilyat al-awliyāʾ*, 10 vols. (Cairo: Maktabat al-Khānjī, 1996), 10:173–174.
27. Cf. Mālik b. Dīnār's report: *qaraʾtu fī baʿḍ al-kutub yujāʾu bi-rāʿī al-sūʾ yawm al-qiyāma fa-yuqālu yā rāʿī sharibta al-laban wa akalta al-laḥm wa lam taʾwa al-ḍālla wa lam tajbur al-kasīr wa lam tarʿahā ḥaqq raʿāyatihā al-yawm antaqimu lahum minkum*; Abū Nuʿaym, *Ḥilyat al-awliyāʾ*, 2:375.
28. In this list Davānī paraphrases and summarizes al-Māwardī's list, with the exception of the third item (see below). Cf. al-Māwardī, *Aḥkām*, 107–111.
29. Davānī translates al-Māwardī's phrase *al-wulāt* as *ḥākemān*/*ḥokkām*.
30. Davānī cuts out a short narrative clause from the Umayyad caliph's sermon; al-Māwardī, *Aḥkām*, 107.

31. This would seem to be the council (*dīvān*) primarily charged with finance and revenues. For this understanding, see V. Minorsky, "A Civil and Military Review in Fārs in 881/1476," *Bulletin of the School of Oriental [and African] Studies* 10, no. 1 (1939): 162.
32. Here Davānī may be deviating from al-Māwardī's list, or he may be providing his own looser translation for al-Māwardī's *kuttāb al-dawāwīn* as the third group. Cf. al-Māwardī, *Aḥkām*, 107–111.
33. This section represents a significant summarizing of al-Māwardī's more elaborate discussion.
34. Interestingly, Davānī omits al-Māwardī's caveat that the magistrate is not permitted to rule based on any private *waqf* documents that were not testified to (or notarized) by upstanding witnesses. Cf. al-Māwardī, *Aḥkām*, 111–112.
35. Here Davānī replaces jihad from al-Māwardī's items with mourning.
36. Here Davānī's text diverges from al-Māwardī's. While the latter stresses that the *nāẓir* should not rule on a dispute in any manner that differs from that of the judge and that this poses a risk of the *nāẓir* disposing of the case unjustly, Davānī introduces the phrase – a common theme in his treatise – that the *nāẓir* should handle disputes on which the Sacred Law does not permit the judge to rule; al-Māwardī, 111.
37. Davānī's list tracks al-Māwardī's approximately, though it lacks point number eight on al-Māwardī's list, which addresses *maẓālim* rules on witnessing: "Eighth, he can hear the testimony of witnesses of unsure standing, in a manner beyond the custom of judges (*quḍāt*) and the testimony of upstanding witnesses." And its points numbers seven and eight do not correspond to al-Māwardī's list. Note that Davānī's promised list of ten points only reaches nine.
38. Again, Davānī introduces the notion that the magistrate rules on matters in which the Sacred Law for some reason restricts the judge from achieving justice.
39. I.e., he can commence an investigation without a complaint being brought by a plaintiff, which would be required for the judge to adjudicate a case.
40. Again, without a complaint by a plaintiff, which would be required for a judge to act.
41. Here Davānī introduces an idea totally absent in al-Māwardī's text, namely that the magistrate can delay his ruling even after the formalistic direct evidence (*bayyeneh*) had been provided.
42. This item seems closer to item number nine on al-Māwardī's list. It could be considered no more than an attenuated paraphrase of item number eight on al-Māwardī's list, which describes in much more detail the more flexible rules of witnessing in the tribunal, namely that its judge can "listen to the testimony of witnesses of unclear credibility (*mastūrīn*)... or unaccredited (*muʿaddalīn*)" who would not be allowed to testify before a *qāḍī*; al-Māwardī, *Aḥkām*, 112.
43. This appears under point seven on al-Māwardī's list. Davānī's exact intended meaning in this point is unclear to me. He uses some of the same technical terms as al-Māwardī (e.g., *mulāzama*), but the context suggests subtle difference from al-Māwardī's text.
44. In al-Māwardī's text, this discussion forms part of a more organized list of possible situations in which various types of claims and evidence come before the tribunal. Cf. al-Māwardī, *Aḥkām*, 112–116. For more on the Mālikī position as opposed to the Shāfiʿī and Ḥanafī ones, see al-Māwardī, *Aḥkām*, 114.

45. This clause is an addition by Davānī to al-Māwardī's discussion. The latter only mentions that the judge is restricted to what is required procedurally, while the magistrate can act according to what is permitted. See al-Māwardī, *Aḥkām*, 111, 114.
46. Here Davānī takes a lengthy discussion on how the magistrate can use the defendant's admission that a document is written in his hand to intimidate him into a confession and reduces it to the principle that the magistrate can use the document as evidence if he chooses once the defendant has admitted it is in his hand. Also gone is any trace of al-Māwardī's assertion that "the master scholars and all the jurists among them hold that it is not permitted for the magistrate to rule based only on writing (*khaṭṭ*)" as well the important caveat that "adjudicating grievances does not render permissible rulings forbidden by the Sacred Law"; al-Māwardī, *Aḥkām*, 115.
47. Here the author, following al-Māwardī, means that some hold that the comparison of writing styles is only a means of frightening the defendant into confessing his guilt. It cannot be an independent act of evidence.
48. From this point on, Davānī's treatise diverges from al-Māwardī's text.
49. I.e., the purpose of providing compensation or reciprocatory justice.
50. This is redolent of the saying, sometimes errantly cited as a Hadith or from the caliph 'Uthmān, found sprinkled throughout the Islamicate heritage, "Those not restrained by the Quran will be restrained by the sultan"; *inna Allāh la-yaza'u bi'l-sulṭān akthar mimmā yaza'u bi'l-qur'ān/man lā yuza'u bi'l-qur'ān yuza'u bi'l-sulṭān/man yaza'u al-sulṭān akthar mimman yaza'u al-qur'ān*, etc.; al-Jāḥiẓ, *Rasā'il al-Jāḥiẓ*, ed. 'Abd al-Salām Hārūn, 4 vols. (Cairo: Maktabat al-Khānjī, 1384/1964), 1:313; al-Māwardī, *Adab al-dunyā wa'l-dīn*, ed. Muḥammad Ḥasan Sulaymān (Cairo: Dār al-Fārūq, 2008), 185; 'Ammār 'Alī Ḥasan, *al-Tanshi'a al-siyāsiyya li'l-ṭuruq al-ṣūfiyya fī miṣr* (Cairo: Dār al-'Ayn, 1430/2009), 100. As Ibn Fāris (d. 395/1004) and Abū 'Ubayd al-Harawī (d. 401/1011) explain, this means that people will refrain from sins more out of fear of the ruler than out of fear of God; Ibn Fāris, *Maqāyīs al-lugha*, ed. 'Abd al-Salām Hārūn, 6 vols. (Beirut: Dār al-Jīl, 1991), 6:106; Abū 'Ubayd al-Harawī, *Kitāb al-Gharībayn fī al-Qur'ān wa'l-ḥadīth*, ed. Aḥmad Farīd al-Mazīdī, 6 vols. (Mecca: Maktabat Nizār Muṣṭafā al-Bāz, 1419/1999), 6:1995.
51. Abū 'Iṣma 'Aṣām b. Yūsuf al-Balkhī (d. 210/825–6 or 215/830–1); see Ibn Abī al-Wafā', *al-Jawāhir al-muḍiyya fī ṭabaqāt al-ḥanafiyya*, 2:527–238.
52. The term for lashes here, *tāzeyāne*, refers to strokes given with a small whip, similar to a riding crop and a symbol associated with political authority; Christian Lange, *Justice, Punishment, and the Medieval Muslim Imagination*, 79.
53. According to Ibn 'Ābidīn, this story also appeared in the *Wāqi'āt* fatwa manual of Aḥmad b. Muḥammad al-Nāṭifī of Rayy (d. 446/1054–5) as well as other main fatwa works of the Ḥanafī school, such as the *Fatāwā al-Bazzāziyya*. In the full version, 'Aṣām reacts by saying "I have not seen injustice (*jawr*) more resembling justice"; Ibn 'Ābidīn, *Ḥāshiyat Ibn 'Ābidīn*, 8 vols. (Beirut: Dār al-Fikr, 1421/2000), 4:87–88; idem, *Radd al-muḥtār 'alā al-Durr al-mukhtār*, 5 vols. (Cairo: Dār al-Ṭibā'a al-Miṣriyya 1272/1856), 3:195–196; Muḥammad b. Muḥammad b. Shihāb al-Bazzāzī, *al-Fatāwā al-Bazzāziyya*, printed in the margins of *al-Fatāwā al-Hindiyya*, 6 vols. (Cairo: al-Maṭba'a al-Amīriyya, 1310/1892–3), 6:430.

54. This saying seems to be quoted from the poetic biographical dictionary of the Khurasani migrant to India, Sadīd al-Dīn Muḥammad ʿAwfī (d. after 628/1230–1231); Dekhodā, *Amthāl ū ḥekam*, 1:317. It appears in a near contemporaneous work to Davānī, namely that of the Ottoman scholar Ibn al-Khaṭīb Muḥammad b. Qāsim al-Amāsī (d. 940/1534), *Rawḍat al-akhyār al-muntakhab min Rabīʿ al-abrār*, ed. Maḥmūd Fākhūrī (Aleppo: Dār al-Qalam al-ʿArabī, 2003), 60. A very similar saying comes from Aḥmad b. Muḥammad al-Zardī al-Naysābūrī (d. 338/950), namely that God "aids with His inspiration" (*aʿānahu bi-ilhāmihi*) those whom He has put in political authority. He also quotes Ibn al-Muqaffaʿ as saying: "*tafaqqadū kalām mulūkikum idh hum muwaffaqūn li'l-ḥikma muyassarūn li'l-ijāba fa-in lam tuḥiṭ bihi ʿuqūlukum*)..."; Yāqūt al-Ḥamawī, *Muʿjam al-udabāʾ*, 1:463.
55. This could also be *bar ʿayasawī*, on a light-tan colored camel. But the idiom of *kharr-e ʿĪsā* (Jesus' donkey, i.e., the donkey Jesus rode into Jerusalem), or a reference to someone trying to appear or associate with something much greater than themselves, is the only meaning that seems to fit here. See Dekhodā, *Amthāl ū ḥekam*, 2:733.
56. Jarūn was a region near Hormuz where the Safavids would later build Bandar Abbas. In one of his many notes on Davānī's works and career, Kātib Chelebī reports that it is said the last work he penned was the *Sharḥ ʿAqāʾid al-ʿAḍudiyya*, completed in 905 Rabīʿ al-Awwal / October 1499 while in the locality of Jarūn (*jīrūn*); *Kashf al-ẓunūn*, 2:406. NB: Kātib Chelebī also has Davānī writing his *Risāla fī afʿāl Allāh* in 913 AH (sic); ibid., 2:173.

4. *MAẒĀLIM* AND QUESTIONS OF PROCEDURE AND SUBSTANTIVE LAW

1. The judge's name was Aḥmad b. Muḥammad Qāṭin al-Thilāʾī (d. 1200/1785), and he was writing to the famous scholar Muḥammad b. Ismāʿīl al-Amīr al-Ṣanʿānī (d. 1182/1768), "al-Masāʾil al-muhimma fīmā taʿummu bihi al-balwā ḥukkām al-umma," in *Majmūʿ fīhi sabaʿ rasāʾil li'l-imām al-muḥaqqiq Muḥammad b. Ismāʿīl al-Amīr al-Ṣanʿānī*, ed. Muḥammad Aṣghar al-Muqaṭṭirī (Beirut: Dār Ibn Ḥazm, 2004), 40–77. See also Muḥammad b. ʿAlī al-Shawkānī, *al-Badr al-ṭāliʿ*, ed. Khalīl al-Manṣūr, 2 vols. (Beirut: Dār al-Kutub al-ʿIlmiyya, 1998), 1:78–79.
2. Tillier reviews the speculative answers to this in his "Mazalim in Historiography."
3. Hurvitz, "The Contribution of Early Islamic Rulers to Adjudication and Legislation," 155.
4. Ibn Farḥūn, *Tabṣirat al-ḥukkām*, ed. Jamāl al-Marʿashlī, 2 vols. (Riyadh: Dār ʿĀlam al-Kutub, 1423/2003), 2:121 ff.; al-Ṭarābulusī, *Muʿīn al-ḥukkām*, 145–146, 212, 215–216; Shihāb al-Dīn al-Qarāfī, *al-Dhakhīra*, ed. Muḥammad al-Ḥajjī, 14 vols. (Beirut: Dār al-Gharb, 1994), 10:45–46; Ibrāhīm b. Yaḥyā Khalīfa Dede Efendi, *al-Siyāsa al-sharʿiyya*, ed. Fuʾād ʿAbd al-Munʿim (Alexandria: Muʾassasat Shabāb al-Jāmiʿa, n.d.); Derin Terzioğlu, "Ibn Taymiyya, *al-Siyāsa al-Sharʿiyya*, and the Early Modern Ottomans," 114–115;

Muḥammad b. Ḥusayn al-Bayram, "Risāla fi'l-Siyāsat al-Shar'iyya," in Elisabeth Cornelia van der Haven, "The Bey, the mufti and the scattered pearls: Shari'a and political leadership in Tunisia's Age of Reform – 1800–1864," (PhD dissertation, University of Leiden, 2006), 133, 136, 147. We should recognize Mohammed Fadel's observation, however, that al-Qarāfī was not "superseding" the doctrine of al-Māwardī but rather building on it. Perhaps we could say building on and adjusting it. See Mohammad Fadel, "Translator's Introduction," in Shihāb al-Dīn al-Qarāfī, *The Criterion for Distinguishing Legal Opinions from Judicial Rulings and the Administrative Acts of Judges and Rulers*, trans. Mohammad Fadel (New Haven: Yale University Press, 2017), 44.

5. Ibn Qayyim al-Jawziyya, *al-Ṭuruq al-ḥukmiyya*, 1:246; Ibn Taymiyya, *al-Siyāsa al-shar'iyya fī iṣlāḥ al-rā'ī wa'l-ra'iyya*, ed. Ibrāhīm Ramaḍān (Beirut: Dār al-Fikr al-Lubnānī, 1992), 23.
6. Christine Hayes, *What's Divine about Divine Law? Early Perspectives* (Princeton: Princeton University Press, 2015).
7. This comparative law observation is usually originally attributed to J.N.D. Anderson, who does note that Islamic law treats homicide "more as a tort than as a crime." Weiss echoes this in his statement that homicide and bodily harm "acquire a tortlike character" in Islamic law. Hallaq and Vikør term homicide "a private wrong" or place it under "private law." But Anderson's early and still valuable study immediately delves into the ways in which Islamic law on homicide expanded to include a state/corporate criminal law character. Weiss and Hallaq less explicitly treat this dimension as well. It seems that the 'In Islamic law, murder is a tort, not a crime' thesis is more a strawman, or at least an incomplete sentence, than a real claim. See J.N.D. Anderson, "Homicide in Islamic Law," *Bulletin of the School of Oriental and African Studies* 13, n. 4 (1951): 811–818; Weiss, *The Spirit of Islamic Law*, 182; Hallaq, *Sharī'a*, 320; Vikør, *Between God and the Sultan*, 282–283; Heyd, *Studies in Old Ottoman Criminal Law*, 1.
8. Schacht asserted that there exists "*no general concept of penal law* in Islam" (his emphasis). Following Anderson, Hallaq, Weiss, and others, I feel that such a strong statement fails to take into consideration clear parallels that do appear in Islamic law. Peters offers that comparative criminal law is not useful for understanding Islamic law, but I suggest that Western scholars' ineluctable references to 'criminal' law – not itself a term indigenous to the Shariah – means that comparisons are natural. See Schacht, 187; Rudolph Peters, *Crime and Punishment in Classical Islamic Law* (Cambridge: Cambridge University Press, 2005), 2. For very useful overviews of the questions of Islamic public and criminal law, see Mohammed Fadel, "Public and Private Law in Islamic Law," under "Public Law," and Silvia Tellenbach, "Crime and Punishment in Islamic Law," in *The Oxford International Encyclopedia of Legal History*, ed. Stanley Katz (Oxford: Oxford University Press, 2005), 2:277–280, and 5:19–20. See also Weiss, *The Spirit of Islamic Law*, 175–185.
9. Ibn 'Abd al-Salām, *Kitāb al-Fatāwā* (Beirut: Dār al-Ma'rifa, n.d.), 37–38. See also Fadel, "Islamic Law Reform," 68.
10. For a fascinating and well-researched comparison of Roman and Islamic legal conceptions of liable kinship groups (*'āqila*), including the observation that common traits do not entail one tradition copying another, see Theodore P. Ion, "Roman Law and Mohammedan Jurisprudence: II," *Michigan Law Review* 6, no. 3 (1908): 197–214. It has been observed that Roman law has

been at its most influential in leading non-Roman law systems to adopt its categories. See Alan Watson, *The Making of the Civil Law* (Cambridge, MA: Harvard University Pres, 1981).

11. As Nicholas observes, "It is a common generalization that in primitive law the criminal sanction develops later than the delictal..."; Barry Nicholas, *An Introduction to Roman Law* (Oxford: Oxford University Press, 1962), 208. For most of the Republican period (roughly until 100 BCE) there was no crime of murder, not even a word for murder, or even for crime. This was because such matters were not handled by the state in what was still a very decentralized society and polity. For centuries wrongful, intentionally killing was dealt with through vendetta, mediation, or within families. See Gaughan, *Murder Was Not a Crime*, 5.
12. *Aeneid* 6:854.
13. O.F. Robinson, "Criminal Law: The Roman Republic, The Roman Empire," in *The Oxford International Encyclopedia of Legal History*, 2:268–274.
14. Nicholas, 208, 210.
15. Ibn ʿAbd al-Salām, *Kitāb al-Fatāwā*, 37–38.
16. *Musnad* of Ibn Ḥanbal, 6:47.
17. *Musnad* of Ibn Ḥanbal, 4:133 (The Hadith reads ʻ*man taraka mālan fa-li-warathatihi wa man taraka daynan aw ḍayʻatan fa-ilayya wa anā walī man lā walī lahu afukku ʻanhu wa arithuhu mālahu wa'l-khāl wārith man lā wārith lahu yafukku ʻanhu wa yarithu mālahu*). See Anderson, "Homicide in Islamic Law," 814. Mohammad Fadel argues convincingly that Sunni jurists theorized the caliphate and governance as a contractual arrangement in which the Muslim community delegates to the ruler the right to act for its best interests in matters of administration and public law, basing this on the fiduciary principles of agency and guardianship taken from Islamic private law. See Fadel, "Islamic Law Reform," 70.
18. *Musnad* of Ibn Ḥanbal, 4:131 (The Hadith reads ʻ*man taraka kallan fa-ilā Allāh wa rasūlihi wa rubbamā qāla fa-ilaynā wa man taraka mālan fa-li-wārithihi wa'l-khāl wārith man lā wārith lahu wa anā wārith man lā wārith lahu arithuhu wa aʻqilu ʻanhu*).
19. An interesting test case was the Prophet leaving Ibn Umm Maktūm, who was blind, "in [charge] in his stead" (*istakhlafa*) in Medina on two occasions. Al-Khaṭṭābī stresses that this must be understood as placing him in charge of leading prayer only, since a blind person cannot serve as a judge, etc.; al-Khaṭṭābī, *Maʻālim al-sunan*, 3:3.
20. *Musnad* of Ibn Ḥanbal, 6:47.
21. As Ibn Taymiyya acknowledges, the legal category of Hudud offenses was a conventional category (*ʻurf ḥādith*) developed by early Muslim jurists to include those offenses for which the Quran and Sunna had prescribed set punishments. The Quran mentions the "limits of God" several times, warning Muslims of the sin of transgressing them and that they should not even approach them (Quran 2:187). Ibn Taymiyya sees the Quranic usage of *ḥadd* as the distinction between licit (*ḥalāl*) and illicit (*ḥarām*). But nowhere does the phrase appear in the clear context of labeling certain crimes (see Quran, 2:229, 4:14, 58:4, 65:1, though 4:14 is followed by a discussion of sexual impropriety). The Hadith corpus includes clear mentions of Hudud crimes. See Ibn Taymiyya, *al-Siyāsa al-sharʻiyya*, 86.

22. Mālik, *al-Muwaṭṭa'*: *kitāb al-ḥudūd, bāb mā jā'a fī al-rajm; bāb tark al-shafā'a li'l-sāriq idhā balagha al-sulṭān*. For an instructive example, see Miskawayh's praise for the Hamdanid ruler Nāṣir al-Dawla (d. 358/969), who is described as personally overseeing the prosecution of criminal cases (*jināyāt*); Aḥmad b. Muḥammad Miskawayh, *Tajārub al-umam* (Cairo: al-Maṭba'a al-Amīriyya, n.d.), 2:38.
23. Aykan, "A Legal Concept in Motion: The 'Spreader of Corruption' (*sā'ī bi'l-fesād*) from Qarakhanid to Ottoman Jurisprudence," 3. Even in Mughal India, banditry and rebellion were associated terms; Singha, *A Despotism of Law*, 7.
24. The Mālikī school differed in this regard only in that it granted the right to pass judgment in such cases to the *qāḍī* himself. A major position in the Ḥanafī school allowed the ruler to execute a serial sodomite or repeat-offending thief on the basis of *siyāsa* if that decision fit under the basic premises (*qawā'id*) of the Shariah; Ibn 'Ābidīn, *Radd al-muḥtār*, 3:147–148; Muḥammad Anwar Shāh Kashmīrī and Aḥmad 'Alī al-Sahāranpūrī, *Jāmi' al-Tirmidhī al-muḥashshā* (Karachi: Qadīmī Kutubkhāne, n.d.), 338; Baber Johansen, "Vérité et torture: *ius commune* et droit musulman entre le xe et le xiiie siècle," in *De La Violence*, ed. Françoise Héritier (Paris: Odile Jacob, 2005), 164. See also Samy Ayoub, *Law, Empire and the Sultan*.
25. Al-Māwardī, *Aḥkām*, 285–288.
26. Shams al-A'imma al-Sarakhsī, *al-Mabsūṭ*, 30 vols. (Beirut: Dār al-Ma'rifa, n.d.), 26:124.
27. Al-Māwardī, *al-Ḥāwī*, 12:192. See also *Ṣaḥīḥ al-Bukhārī*: *kitāb al-aḥkām, bāb al-ḥākim yaḥkumu bi'l-qatl 'alā man wajaba 'alayhi dūn al-imām alladhī fawqahu*.
28. Ibn Qudāma, *al-Mughnī*, ed. 'Abdallāh al-Turkī and 'Abd al-Fattāḥ al-Ḥuluw, 12 vols. (Cairo: Hujr, 1986), 10:147; al-Buhūtī, *al-Rawḍ al-murbi'*, 462; Muḥammad b. al-Khaṭīb al-Shirbīnī, *Mughnī al-muḥtāj*, ed. Muḥammad Khalīl Aytānī, 4 vols. (Beirut: Dār al-Ma'rifa, 1998), 4:55; Wahba al-Zuḥaylī, *Mawsū'at al-fiqh al-Islāmī*, 14 vols. (Damascus: Dār al-Fikr, 2010), 6:267.
29. This is one Sulaym b. 'Itr. As described by al-Kindī, the injured party would come to the judge with his *bayyina*, and the judge would write up a complaint (*qiṣṣa*) about that injury and send it to the *'āqila* (agnatic relatives, who share responsibility for compensation for injuries committed by a relative if the amount rises above one third of the full *diya*, according to a ruling by Ibn 'Umar) of the defendant while also informing the governor. When the *'aṭā'* stipend came in, compensation would be subtracted from perpetrators' family shares until it was all paid over a three-year period; al-Kindī, *Kitāb al-Wulāt wa Kitāb al-Quḍāt*, 309. Mālik also refers to this approach; *Muwaṭṭa'*: *kitāb al-'uqūl, bāb jāmi' al-'aql*. For the Companion rulings on which this is based, see Ibrāhīm Ibn Ḍuwayyān, *Manār al-sabīl fī sharḥ al-Dalīl*, ed. Zuhayr al-Shāwīsh, 2 vols. (Damascus: al-Maktab al-Islāmī, 1989), 2:354–356.
30. Abū Bakr al-Khaṣṣāf, *Adab al-qāḍī*, ed. Farhat Ziadeh (Cairo: Maṭba'at Jablāwī, 1979), 247. Jurists sometimes seemed to glory in the hypothetical predicaments that the private-wrongs conception of assaults might create. Peters describes the legal riddle of how a man could get away with murdering his mother-in-law: kill his wife as well, since the talion right to justice for both deaths would fall to the couple's children, whom *qiṣāṣ* laws prevented from demanding their own father's death. See Peters, *Crime and Punishment*

in Islamic Law, 48. The possibility that a family relationship or, more commonly, the decision of the victim's heirs to accept compensation (*diya*) instead of asking that the killer be executed proved hugely vexing for British East India Company officials, who took over the administration of Islamic law in areas the Company controlled. As a result, they worked with their Muslim 'law officer' consultants to issue a 1794 decree that, even if some family relationship blocked a demand for execution in *qiṣāṣ*, the magistrate could execute the culprit via *siyāsa* authority. He could even punish a killer who had paid the victim's family the *diya*, but this punishment could not extend to execution; Singha, 61. The novel criminal codes of the Ottoman Empire (1858) and Egypt (1875) both asserted the state's right to execute a murderer regardless of the preferences of the victim's family; Gabriel Baer, "Tanzimat in Egypt – The Penal Code," *Bulletin of the School of Oriental and African Studies* 26, n. 1 (1963): 46. The idea that criminal injury or homicide bears both a private wrong (*ḥaqq khāṣṣ*) and public wrong (*ḥaqq ʿāmm*) and that, even if the victim's family accepts compensation, the ruler still has the discretion to punish the attacker for the *ḥaqq ʿāmm* is advocated by the Syrian Muslim jurist Muṣṭafā Aḥmad al-Zarqā, *al-Madkhal al-fiqhī al-ʿāmm*, 3rd ed., 2 vols. (Damascus: Dār al-Qalam, 1433/2012, originally published 1945), 2:685.

31. Al-Shāfiʿī, *Kitāb al-Umm*, 8 vols. (Beirut: Dār al-Maʿrifa, 1393/1973), 6:21; See also Ibn Qudāma, *al-Mughnī*, 9:476.
32. Al-Sarakhsī, *al-Mabsūṭ*, 10:219. For the Hadith, see *Sunan* of Abū Dāwūd: *kitāb al-nikāḥ, bāb fī al-walī*; also *Sunan Ibn Mājah*, *Jāmiʿ al-Tirmidhī*, and others.
33. See Ibn Qudāma, *al-Mughnī*, 10:9, 22; al-Buhūtī, *al-Rawḍ al-murbiʿ*, 461; Aḥmad b. Muḥammad al-Qudūrī, *The Mukhtaṣar*, trans. Ṭāhir Maḥmood Kiānī (London: Ta-Ha Publishers, 2010), 530–531.
34. Jonathan AC Brown, "Qasāmah," in *Oxford Encyclopedia of the Islamic World: Digital Collection*, Oxford University Press, https://www.oxfordreference.com/view/10.1093/acref/9780197669419.001.0001/acref-9780197669419-e-336.
35. Nielsen, 47, 146.
36. *Mā yakhtaṣṣu bi-ḍabṭ al-bayḍa min iʿdād al-juyūsh wa jibāyat al-kharāj*; al-Nawawī, *Sharḥ Ṣaḥīḥ Muslim*, 15 vols. (Beirut: Dār al-Qalam, 1987), 11/12: 450. Al-Ṭarābulusī and al-Qarāfī concur; al-Ṭarābulusī, *Muʿīn al-ḥukkām*, 13–14; al-Qarāfī, *al-Furūq*, ed. Khalīl Manṣūr (Beirut: Dār al-Kutub al-ʿIlmiyya, 1998), 1:358. Al-Nawawī may have derived this language from the Andalusian Qāḍī ʿIyāḍ (d. 544/1149), see al-Nubāhī, *Tārīkh quḍāt al-andalus*, 21. This line of thinking can be traced back to the judge ʿUbaydallāh b. al-Ḥasan al-ʿAnbarī's (d. 168/785) letter to the caliph al-Mahdī; Wakīʿ, *Akhbār al-quḍāt*, 295–302. For the most extensive list of the duties of a ruler, see ʿAbd al-Raʾūf al-Munāwī, *al-Jawāhir al-muḍiyya fī bayān al-ādāb al-sulṭāniyya*, ed. ʿAbdallāh Ibrāhīm al-Nāṣir (Riyadh: Jāmiʿat al-Malik Suʿūd, 1424/2013), 65–83. The Yemeni Salafi al-Wādiʿī (d. 2001) affirmed one should pay taxes even if they are illegal because determining taxes is the state's prerogative; Laurent Bonnefoy, "How Transnational is Salafism in Yemen?" in *Global Salafism*, ed. Roel Meijer (New York: Columbia University Press, 2009), 326.
37. Al-Ṭarābulusī, *Muʿīn al-ḥukkām*, 12.

38. Taqī al-Dīn al-Subkī, *Fatāwā al-Subkī*, 2 vols. (Beirut: Dār al-Maʿrifa, n.d.), 2:419. See also Apellániz, "Judging the Franks: Proof, Justice and Diversity in Late Medieval Alexandria and Damascus," 350–378.
39. Aḥmad al-Qalqashandī, *Ṣubḥ al-ʿashā*, 14 vols. (Cairo: Dār al-Kutub al-Miṣriyya, 1340/1922), 7:197.
40. Nielsen, 102.
41. The question of Shariah-legitimate vs. illegitimate taxation is complicated in both theory and historical practice. The Prophet condemned the collection of the *maks*, the taboo term used by Muslim scholars for taxes with no basis in God's law, in no uncertain terms. But even the early Muslim community understood the Prophet's reference to *maks* as meaning the pre-Islamic *ʿushr* (10%) market tax, which the Muslim state soon repurposed anyway as a customs duty during the reign of ʿUmar (634–644 CE). This practice became accepted by the ulama provided it did not exceed the rates set by ʿUmar, but the imposition of any number of different taxes was common in Islamicate civilization. Rulers sometimes abolished excessive customs duties or other taxes as acts of piety, as in the case of Saladin, that of the Delhi Sultan Ibn Tughluq removing a 25% import tax and levying nothing more than scripturally mandated taxes after receiving recognition from the Abbasid caliph in the mid-1300s, and that of the Mangit Dynasty of Bukhara (1785–1920). Terminology in matters of taxation differed greatly. *Maks* could mean only customs duties, but it was often used to mean any tax other than the zakat, *ʿushr*, *kharāj*, and *jizya*. In the early 20th century, for example, the ulama of Fez listed as conditions for their support of a candidate for sultan in Morocco that he 1) impose no *maks* tax, but 2) that the descendants of the Prophet be exempted from tax collection, a combination that suggests that *maks* here was understood only as excessive or capricious taxation. Some more doctrinaire scholars could call for eliminating all taxes other than the *zakat*, the *kharāj*, the *ʿushr*, and the *jizya* as a condition for valid rule by the Shariah (for example, al-Maghīlī [d. 909–910/1503–6] in Songhai), but the more realistic position was exemplified by the Ḥanafī scholar Abū Jaʿfar al-Balkhī (d. 362/972–3), who said that anything that the sultan imposes as tax for the good of his subjects (*maṣlaḥat al-raʿiyya*) becomes an obliged debt to pay, and the Mālikī scholar al-Shāṭibī (d. 790/1388), who argued that a ruler could levy moderate taxes for the benefit of his realm. Of course, Ibn Qayyim al-Jawziyya notes that rulers often use terms like 'the law of the royal council' (*sharʿ al-dīwān*) to euphemize oppressive and illegitimate taxation. See Attiya Waris, "Taxation," in *The [Oxford] Encyclopedia of Islam and Law, Oxford Islamic Studies Online*, http://www.oxfordislamicstudies.com/article/opr/t349/e0127 (accessed 23-Jun-2016); *Sunan* of Abū Dāwūd: *kitāb al-kharāj wa'l-imāra wa'l-fay', bāb fī al-siʿāya ʿalā al-ṣadaqa*; Ibn Ḥajar Haytamī, *al-Zawājir ʿan iqtirāf al-kabā'ir*, ed. ʿImād Zakī al-Bārūdī, 2 vols. (Cairo: al-Maktaba al-Tawfīqiyya, 2003), 1:394–400; ʿAbd al-Ghanī al-Nābulusī, *al-Ḥadīqa al-nadiya sharḥ al-Ṭarīqa al-muḥammadiyya*, 2 vols. (Istanbul: Asetane, reprint of 1295/1878 Maṭbaʿat ʿĀmira edition), 2:741; Ibn Abī al-Wafā', *al-Jawāhir al-muḍiyya*, 4:31–32; Abū Isḥāq al-Shāṭibī, *Kitāb al-Iʿtiṣām* (Cairo: al-Maktaba al-Tijāriyya al-Kubrā, 1914), 2:121; H.A.R. Gibb, trans., *The Travels of Ibn Battuta*, 3:605; John Hunwick, ed., *Sharīʿa in Songhay: The Replies of al-Maghīlī to the Questions of Askia al-Ḥājj Muḥammad* (London: Oxford University Press, 1985), 82; Sahar

Bazzaz, *Forgotten Saints: History, Power, and Politics in the Making of Modern Morocco* (Cambridge, MA: Harvard University Press, 2010), 130; Itzchak Weismann, *The Naqshbandiyya* (London: Routledge, 2007), 79; Ibn Qayyim al-Jawziyya, *I'lām al-muwaqqi'īn,* 3:103.

42. Al-Māwardī, *al-Aḥkām al-sulṭāniyya*, 123, 125.
43. Al-Māwardī, *Aḥkām*, 117, 121; idem, *Adab al-qāḍī*, ed. Muḥyī al-Hilāl Sarḥān, 2 vols. (Baghdad: Maṭba'at al-Irshād, 1971), 185–186. See Appendix II.
44. Al-Māwardī, *Aḥkām*, 117; Abū Ya'lā Ibn al-Farrā', *al-Aḥkām al-sulṭāniyya*, 83. In an interesting remark, al-Māwardī refers to the rules that the magistrate is selecting from within the *madhhabs* as *qawānīn*; ibid., 118.
45. Abū Ya'lā Ibn al-Farrā' agrees; al-Māwardī, *Adab al-qāḍī*, 184–185; Ibn al-Farrā', *al-Aḥkām al-sulṭāniyya*, 63.
46. Ḍirār b. 'Amr (d. *circa* 200/815), *Kitāb al-Taḥrīsh*, ed. Ḥusayn Khānṣū and Muḥammad Kaskīn (Istanbul: Sharikat Dār al-Irshād, 2014), 127. Ḍirār's cynical jurist says that "disagreement is mercy, so whichever of those [jurists' opinions] you take, this is permitted for you, for the religion is wide."
47. Ibn Ḥajar, *Raf' al-iṣr*, 273. A report from the Shāfi'ī judge of Qom, Abū Sa'īd al-Iṣṭakhrī (d. 328/940), also suggests non-*mujtahid* judges were acknowledged; Tāj al-Dīn al-Subkī, *Ṭabaqāt al-shāfi'iyya al-kubrā*, 3:234.
48. Al-Māwardī, *Adab al-qāḍī*, 185–186. The text is identical in his *Ḥāwī*; idem, *al-Ḥāwī al-kabīr*, ed. 'Alī Muḥammad Mu'awwaḍ and 'Ādil Aḥmad 'Abd al-Mawjūd, 19 vols. (Beirut: Dār al-Kutub al-'Ilmiyya, 1999), 16:24, and 16:161. Al-Ghazālī seconds this observation, as does a Damascus Shāfi'ī scholar, al-Fazārī, in 1264 CE, with the comment that this restriction comes from *siyāsa* and not God's law; Ahmed Fekry Ibrahim, *Pragmatism in Islamic Law* (Syracuse: Syracuse University Press, 2015), 36; Rapoport, "Royal Justice," 77. A case from tenth-century Cairo is instructive. A Christian woman converted to Islam, but her husband did not. The long-serving judge, a Mālikī scholar named Abū Ṭāhir al-Dhuhlī (d. 368/979), ruled that, though the mother wanted the couple's young son to be considered Muslim, he would still remain Christian. The "people" were angered by this and voiced their displeasure. When it was mentioned that the opinion of the Shāfi'ī and Shiite schools was that the child could be declared Muslim, the judge changed his ruling. "So the people prayed for him, and his ruling pleased them"; Ibn Ḥajar, *Raf' al-iṣr*, 330.
49. I thank Mathieu Tillier for this insight.
50. Qāḍī 'Iyāḍ, *Tartīb al-madārik*, 1:347. Thanks to Mohammad Fadel for alerting me to this.
51. Al-Kindī, *Kitāb al-Wulāt wa Kitāb al-Quḍāt*, 584, 590.
52. Tāj al-Dīn al-Subkī, *Ṭabaqāt al-shāfi'iyya al-kubrā*, 5:77.
53. Al-Kindī, 584. It was reported that the judge Abū Ṭāhir al-Dhuhlī (d. 368/979) did not accept as direct evidence the oath of the plaintiff along with one witness' testimony (*shāhid wa'l-yamīn*), in contrast to the main position of the Mālikī school, which did accept *shāhid wa'l-yamīn* in matters of property/contracts. Al-Dhuhlī claimed that he was following his father and the early Mālikī judge of Baghdad, Ismā'īl al-Qāḍī (d. 282/895–896). The Andalusian judge Abū Ziyād al-Ru'aynī agreed, saying that many Andalusian judges broke with the Mālikī school's main position and rejected accepting *shāhid wa'l-yamīn* because it was being abused by corrupt people; al-Nubāhī, *Tārīkh quḍāt al-Andalus*, 71.

54. Al-Khaṭīb, *Tārīkh Baghdād*, 10:463–464.
55. Rapaport, "Legal Diversity in the Age of *Taqlīd*: The Four Chief *Qāḍīs* under the Mamluks," *Islamic Law and Society* 10, n. 2 (2003): 214. See also Jackson, *Islamic Law and the State*, 78–79, 152–159.
56. Ibn Ḥajar al-Haytamī et al., *Ḥawāshī Tuḥfat al-muḥtāj bi-sharḥ al-Minhāj*, 10 vols. (Cairo: Maṭba'at Muṣṭafā Muḥammad, 1937), 10:109–111. Cf. idem, *al-Fatāwā al-kubrā al-fiqhiyya* (Cairo: 'Abd al-Ḥamīd Aḥmad al-Ḥanafī, n.d.), 4:304–5, 307; 'Abd al-Wahhāb al-Sha'rānī, *al-Mīzān al-kubrā*, 2 vols in 1 (Cairo: Maktabat Zahrān [no date], reprint of Cairo: Maktabat al-Kastiliyya, 1862), 2:213.
57. David Powers, "Four Cases Relating to Women and Divorce in Al-Andalus and the Maghrib, 1100–1500," 383–409. In one instance in Cairo in 1524 CE, a Mālikī judge in the Ottoman Empire fell into conflict with the chief judge (Ḥanafī) overseeing him because the chief judge insisted that his junior rule by the principal ruling (*mashhūr*) of his school while the latter insisted on his right as a senior scholar to choose among the Mālikī school's rulings on an issue; Reem Meshal, "Antagonistic *Sharī'as* and the Construction of Orthodoxy in Sixteenth-Century Cairo," *Journal of Islamic Studies* 21, no. 2 (2010): 200. Shaykh Sīdī Ibrāhīm Ibn Hilāl of Sijilmas (d. 903/1497–8) affirmed fiercely that "it is not permissible to give fatwas except by the *mashhūr* ruling, and there is no acting except by the *mashhūr*"; Abū 'Īsā Sīdī al-Mahdī b. Muḥammad al-Wazzānī (also al-Wāzzānī) (d. 1342/1923–4), *al-Nawāzil al-jadīda al-kubrā fi-mā li-ahl Fās wa ghayrihim min al-badū wa'l-qurā / al-Mi'yār al-jadīd al-jāmi' al-mu'rib 'an fatāwā al-muta'akhkhirīn min 'ulamā' al-maghrib*, ed. 'Umar 'Imād, 12 vols. (Casablanca: Maṭba'at al-Faḍāla, 1418/1997), 4:16; al-Bazzāzī, *al-Fatāwā al-Bazzāziyya*, 5:134. On issues in which the Mālikī school had more than one opinion, al-Shāṭibī (d. 790/1388) allowed taking the non-preferred (*marjūḥ*) one if it had become widely accepted among the population so as not to confuse them; al-Shāṭibī, *Fatāwā al-imām al-Shāṭibī*, ed. Muḥammad Abū al-'Ajfān, 2nd ed. (Tunis: n.p., 1985), 150. In Fez, an eighteenth-century CE mufti upbraided other Mālikī judges and muftis for rulings not according to the *mashhūr* of the school; Muḥammad b. Ja'far al-Kattānī, *Salwat al-anfās wa muḥādathat al-akyās mimman uqbira min al-'ulamā' wa'l-ṣulaḥā' bi-fās*, ed. 'Abdallāh al-Kāmil al-Kattānī et al., 4 vols. (Casablanca: Dār al-Thaqāfa, 2004), 3:257.
58. 'Alī b. Dāwūd al-Ṣayrafī, *Nuzhat al-nufūs wa'l-abdān fī tawārīkh al-zamān*, ed. Ḥasan Ḥabashī, 3 vols. (Cairo: Maṭba'at Dār al-Kutub, 1970), 1:97. The Mālikī judge who escaped firing was criticized for passing the death sentence on a group of Christian villagers who had forcibly silenced a *mu'adhdhin* who disturbed their wedding celebration with the call to prayer; Ibn Ḥajar al-'Asqalānī, *Inbā' al-ghumar bi-abnā' al-'umar*, 8 vols. (Hyderabad: Dā'irat al-Ma'ārif al-'Uthmāniyya, 1968), 2:127; Amalia Levanoni, "*Takfīr* in Egypt and Syria during the Mamlūk Period," in *Accusations of Unbelief in Islam*, ed. Camilla Adang et al. (Leiden: Brill, 2016), 166. The criticism from fellow Mālikī scholars was probably due to the fact that the main Mālikī position on non-Muslims insulting Islam is that they are only punished by death if the gravity of their insult exceeds the *kufr* inherent in their religious beliefs. Since they were only objecting to the Muslim call to prayer interrupting their wedding, no such insult took place. See Aḥmad al-Ghumārī, *Masālik al-dilāla 'alā masā'il matn al-Risāla* (Cairo: Maktabat al-Qāhira, 1415/1995), 300.

59. Al-Ṭarābulsī, *Muʿīn al-ḥukkām*, 30.
60. This Mālikī judge was Abū al-Dhikr Muḥammad b. Yaḥyā al-Aswānī (d. 400/1010); Ibn Ḥajar, *Rafʿ al-iṣr ʿan quḍāt miṣr*, published in al-Kindī, *Kitāb al-Wulāt wa Kitāb al-Quḍāt*, 533, 561.
61. Taqī al-Dīn al-Subkī, *Fatāwā al-Subkī*, 2:13.
62. Al-Haytamī, *al-Fatāwā al-kubrā*, 4:331. In the mid 900s CE, the Fatimid vizier in Cairo appointed the Shāfiʿī judge al-Ḥasan b. Khalīl to the judgeship on the condition that he rule by the Ismāʿīlī school of law; Ibn Ḥajar, *Rafʿ al-iṣr*, published in al-Kindī, *Kitāb al-Wulāt wa Kitāb al-Quḍāt*, 590. A dissenting opinion comes from a leading Egyptian Shāfiʿī scholar of the generation of al-Haytamī's students, ʿAbd al-Raʾūf al-Munāwī (d. 1031/1622), who states that the ruler should not weigh in on which *madhhab* or position should be applied, since, as the saying has it, 'Disagreement within my nation is a mercy'; al-Munāwī, *al-Jawāhir al-muḍiyya*, 67. The Islamic legal revivalist scholar Muṣṭafā al-Zarqā (d. 1420/1999) wrote that the judge must rule by the *madhhab* he is appointed to because "*al-qaḍāʾ fī al-aṣl sharʿan min ḥaqq al-imām*"; al-Zarqā, *al-Madkhal al-fiqhī al-ʿāmm*, 1:317.
63. Al-Māwardī, *Aḥkām*, 111; Ibn al-Farrāʾ, 79.
64. Van Berkel, 233–234; Nielsen; 36, 44.
65. Van Berkel, 233–234.
66. Ibn Ḥajar, *Rafʿ al-iṣr*, 177–178.
67. Al-Laknawī, *al-Fawāʾid al-bahiyya fī tarājim al-ḥanafiyya*, 36. See also al-Tanūkhī, *Nishwār al-muḥāḍara*, 2:167–168.
68. Al-Wazzānī, *al-Nawāzil al-jadīda*, 10:319.
69. Nielsen 96–97, see also 102.
70. Sarkar, *Mughal Administration*, 96.
71. Nielsen, 47, 146.
72. Nielsen, 76.
73. Nielsen, 150. See also Levanoni, "*Takfīr* in Egypt and Syria," 157 (for the conviction at the *Dār al-ʿAdl* of someone claiming to be a prophet in 1260 CE), 164.
74. Al-Ṭabarī, 5:295.
75. Louis Massignon, *The Passion of al-Hallaj*, trans. Herbert Mason (Princeton: Princeton University Press, 1982), 180–204, 231; Ibn al-Jawzī, *Muntaẓam*, 13:304–305.
76. Al-Khaṭīb, *Tārīkh Baghdād*, 1:296.
77. Nielsen, 74; Tyan, *Histoire*, 445. See also Khadduri, *The Islamic Conception of Justice*, 156.
78. Muḥammad b. Aḥmad al-Qurṭubī, *al-Jāmiʿ li-aḥkām al-Qurʾān*, ed. Muḥammad Ibrāhīm al-Ḥifnāwī and Maḥmūd Ḥamīd ʿUthmān, 20 vols. in 10 (Cairo: Dār al-Ḥadīth, 1994), 4:456. The Shāfiʿī/Mālikī jurist al-Dīrīnī (d. 694/1295) states that a Muslim is allowed to accompany a Christian to court to aid him in "removing a harm (*maẓlima*)" because the Quran enjoins virtuous conduct towards non-Muslims; ʿAbd al-ʿAzīz b. Aḥmad al-Dīrīnī, "al-Durar al-multaqaṭa fī al-masāʾil al-mukhtalaṭa," (Ms. 1/622, Jāmiʿat al-Malik Suʿūd), 127b.
79. Tyan points out that the list of all the different types of people who have to be present at the *maẓālim* shows that it is meant to deal with any kind of legal problem and to have all those resources to draw on, with the magistrate there to make the decision that is most equitable; Tyan, *Histoire*, 496.

80. In describing the coexistence of equity and common law in the eighteenth and nineteenth centuries, Charles Bowen writes, "The two jurisdictions had no common historical origin, and the principles on which they administered justice were unlike. The remedies they afforded to the suitor were different; their procedure was irreconcilable; they applied diverse rules of right and wrong to the same matters." Maitland, however, contended that the two systems were intertwined from the start, with equity drawing on ecclesiastical law as well as common law; Charles Bowen, "Progress in the Administration of Justice during the Victorian Period," in *Select Essays in Anglo-American Legal History*, 3 vols. (Boston: Little, Brown & Co., 1907), 517; Maitland, *Equity*, 8–9. For the maxims of equity, see Richard Francis, *Maxims of Equity* (London: Nutt & Gosling, 1889).

81. Henry E. Smith, "Equity as Meta-Law," *Yale Law Journal* 130 (2021): 1115.

82. Tillier, "*Qāḍīs* and the political use of the *maẓālim*," 52.

83. It is problematic to use the word torture to translate *taʿdhīb* (torture, infliction of pain or punishment), *ʿadhāb* (punishment, pain or suffering inflicted), or *ḍarb* (beating, lashing), which are the terms usually used by our sources, since torture conjures images of the rack or iron maiden. The sources, however, seem to use these terms with relative equanimity. Discussions of inflicting pain on suspected thieves usually use the term *ḍarb*. In the case of Davānī's treatise, the device used for beating was the *tāziyāne*, which Lange says was not as serious as some whips but was rather like a riding crop. See Lange, *Justice, Punishment, and the Medieval Muslim Imagination*, 73–74, 79; Mohammad Fadel, "Torture: Islamic Law," in *Oxford Intl. Encyclopedia of Legal History*, 5:486–488.

84. The pro-judicial-torture camp in the Shariah was substantially mirrored in West/Central Europe from the thirteenth to seventeenth centuries. This changed dramatically in the eighteenth century, however. *Philosophes* like Voltaire condemned torture and states like the U.S. (1791) and Prussia (1754) prohibited it. Langbein argued that this resulted from legal change. Medieval Roman law had required total certainty to convict suspects in cases punishable by death or severe corporal punishment, and Roman law required either two witnesses to the crime or confession. When none of this was forthcoming, in cases in which there was, in effect, probable cause, judges authorized torture like thumb screws. If this resulted in the suspect confessing and admitting information that only the guilty party could have known, then the confession was considered valid. In the seventeenth century, however, legal change resulted in numerous other, lesser forms of punishment, such as galley slavery or transportation, so the requirement for certainty that legitimated torture was no longer as relevant. Other scholars have added that the Christianity-dominated view of pain as tied to sin and admission of guilt gave way increasingly to new views that pain was damaging. Along with Enlightenment critique of unjustified state power and the challenge this presented to inflicting pain on a person who was still innocent, this led to growing rejection of torture as tyrannical and unjust. See John H. Langbein, *Torture and the Law of Proof* (Chicago: University of Chicago Press, 1976), 4–5, 27–44, 59–60; Jamal Barnes, *A Genealogy of the Torture Taboo* (London: Routledge, 2017), 34, 36–40. Thanks to Rami Koujah for suggesting these sources.

85. Ibn Taymiyya, *Majmū'at al-fatāwā*, ed. Sayyid Ḥusayn al-'Affānī and Khayrī Sa'īd, 35 vols. (Cairo: al-Maktaba al-Tawfīqiyya, [n.d.]), 35:247–249. Like most scholars, al-Māwardī does not allow confessions or admission (*iqrār*) under duress (*ikrāh*) and specifically prohibits *ta'dhīb* in a subchapter on methods of execution (*qawad*), citing the Prophet prohibiting the infliction of pain on animals (*nahā 'an ta'dhīb al-bahā'im*). *A fortiori*, one cannot inflict gratuitous pain on humans; al-Māwardī, *al-Ḥāwī al-kabīr*, 7:5; 12:110; idem, *Aḥkām*, 286.

86. As for a defendant who is known to be withholding some property or right (*ḥaqq*) due another, or who refuses to produce someone who has been ordered before the court, Ibn Taymiyya and the ninth-century Ḥanafī al-Khaṣṣāf know of no scholar who would not allow punishing the person until they comply. This can be accomplished by beating according to the Mālikīs, Shāfi'īs, and Ḥanbalīs, claims Ibn Taymiyya. Ibn Taymiyya and al-Khaṣṣāf root this in a Hadith that "The delay of one finding [the means] renders licit his honor and punishment (*layyu al-wājid yuḥillu 'irḍahu wa 'uqūbatahu*)"; Ibn Taymiyya, *Fatāwā*, 35:249; al-Khaṣṣāf, *Adab al-qāḍī*, 253–254. For the Hadith, see *Sunan* of Abū Dāwūd: *kitāb al-aqḍiya, bāb fī al-ḥabs fī al-dayn wa ghayrihi*; *Sunan al-Nasā'ī*: *kitāb al-buyū'*, *bāb maṭl al-ghanī*.

87. Although Mālikīs and many Shāfi'īs did allow the confession if the accused reaffirmed it after the duress ended; al-Zuḥaylī, *Mawsū'at al-fiqh al-Islāmī*, 6:361; al-Māwardī, *Aḥkām*, 220. See also Ibn Qudāma, *al-Mughnī*, 5:272. Interestingly, in the Ḥanbalī school, if the accused claims he has been tortured and that this is why he confessed, he has to provide *bayyina* of this, since the presumption (*aṣl*) is the absence of compulsion. But if there is circumstantial evidence (jail time, manacles, etc.), then he only has to swear an oath. Al-Shirbīnī includes an informative discussion of how the appearance of external evidence of guilt via the confession removes the problematic nature of forced confession; al-Shirbīnī, *Mughnī al-muḥtāj*, 2:311; Burhān al-Dīn 'Alī al-Marghīnānī, *al-Hidāya* (Lahore: Maktaba Raḥmāniyya, n.d.), 3:346.

88. Allehbi, "'It is Permitted for the Amīr but not the Qāḍī,'" 8. See Abū Yūsuf, *Kitāb al-Kharāj*, ed. Maḥmūd al-Bājī (Tunis: Dār Bū Salāma, 1984), 152–153.

89. *Sunan* of Abū Dāwūd: *kitāb al-aqḍiya, bāb fī al-ḥabs fī al-dayn wa ghayrihi*; *Sunan al-Nasā'ī*: *kitāb qaṭ' al-sāriq, bāb imtiḥān al-sāriq bi'l-ḍarb wa'l-ḥabs*.

90. *Sunan* of Abū Dāwūd: *kitāb al-ḥudūd, bāb al-imtiḥān bi'l-ḍarb*; *Sunan al-Nasā'ī*: *kitāb qaṭ' al-sāriq, bāb imtiḥān al-sāriq bi'l-ḍarb wa'l-ḥabs*. In one of his few comments in his *Sunan*, Abū Dāwūd concludes from this Hadith that beating to assess guilt was only meant as a threat to scare the accused and that actual beating is only allowed as a punishment after a thief has confessed. The only Hadith with explicit mention of the Prophet having the 'accused' beaten prior to the establishment of guilt is rare and involves a man beaten to reveal the location of spoils in a newly conquered town. It appears in the *Ṣaḥīḥ* of Ibn Ḥibbān (d. 354/965) and two books of al-Bayhaqī (d. 458/1066). Ratings of its reliability are rare, though al-Albānī considered it *ṣaḥīḥ*; Ibn Ḥibbān al-Bustī, *Ṣaḥīḥ Ibn Ḥibbān*, ed. Mehmet Ali Sönmez and Halis Aydemir, 8 vols. (Beirut: Dār Ibn Ḥazm, 1433/2012), 3:133–135; Abū Bakr al-Bayhaqī, *Dalā'il al-nubuwwa*, ed. 'Abd al-Mu'ṭī Qal'ajī, 7 vols. (Beirut: Dār al-Kutub al-'Ilmiyya, 1408/1988), 4:229–230; idem, *al-Sunan al-kubrā*, ed. Muḥammad 'Abd al-Qādir 'Aṭā, 11 vols. (Beirut: Dār al-Kutub al-'Ilmiyya, 1999), 9:231–232;

Muḥammad Nāṣir al-Dīn al-Albānī, *Ṣaḥīḥ Mawārid al-ẓam'ān ilā zawā'id Ibn Ḥibbān*, 2 vols. (Riyadh: Dār al-Ṣumayʿī, 1422/2002), 2:144.

91. Ibn Taymiyya reports two positions amongst scholars. Some accept the confession if "the person's truthfulness is evident (*ẓahara ṣidquhu*)," as in cases where a confessed thief produces the stolen items after a beating. He attributes this position to al-Māwardī and Abū Yaʿlā. Other scholars did not accept the confession at all, a stance held by many Shāfiʿīs, Ḥanbalīs, and Mālikīs according to Ibn Taymiyya; Ibn Taymiyya, *Fatāwā*, 35:250; Peters, *Crime and Punishment in Islamic Law*, 82.

92. Al-Nawawī, *Minhāj al-ṭālibīn*, ed. Muḥammad Ṭāhir Shaʿbān (Jeddah: Dār al-Minhāj, 2000), 416; al-Qurṭubī, *al-Jāmiʿ li-aḥkām al-Qur'ān*, 5:535. Ibrāhīm al-Nakhaʿī, however, is quoted by al-Qurṭubī as saying "shackles are duress and prison is duress" (*al-qayd ikrāh wa al-sijn ikrāh*); ibid. Mullā Hüsrev notes that what constitutes *ikrāh* is ultimately determined by the judge who hears the complaint of it occurring; Mullā Hüsrev, *Durar al-ḥukkām*, 2:270.

93. One limit was what was determined to be the upper limit of discretionary punishment (*taʿzīr*). The Mālikī school set no clear limit on *taʿzīr*, the Ḥanafīs generally set it at 39 lashes (based on a Hadith in which the Prophet had someone who drank wine lashed 20 times with a two-headed lash, then on a Companion ruling adding 40 lashes to the Hudud punishment for drinking), Ḥanbalīs limited it to 10 lashes based on an explicit Hadith stating that non-Hudud punishments could not exceed that, and the Shāfiʿī school wavered between 10 and 40, with 20 for a slave based on analogy; al-Qudūrī, *The Mukhtaṣar*, 550–551; Ibrāhīm al-Ḍuwayyān, *Manār al-sabīl*, 2:382; al-Nawawī, *al-Minhāj*, 514; Abū Bakr al-Bayhaqī, *al-Sunan al-kubrā: kitāb al-ashriba, bāb mā jā'a fī al-taʿzir...*; *Ṣaḥīḥ Muslim: kitāb al-ḥudūd, bāb ḥadd al-khamr; bāb qadr aswāṭ al-taʿzīr*.

94. Ibn ʿĀbidīn, *Ḥāshiyat Ibn ʿĀbidīn*, 4:76; 5:299; idem, *Radd al-Muḥtār*, 3:188.

95. Al-Ṭarābulusī, *Muʿīn al-ḥukkām*, 218.

96. Al-Qurṭubī, *al-Jāmiʿ li-aḥkām al-Qur'ān*, 3:678.

97. See Lange, *Justice, Punishment, and the Medieval Muslim Imagination*, 74; Johansen, "Vérité et torture," 144–145.

98. Al-Māwardī, *Aḥkām*, 286. Ottoman criminal law also allowed the judge, in more complicated cases, to put the defendant in prison for a few weeks while the plaintiff gathered evidence or witnesses provided that the defendant had a bad reputation or if there were signs of his guilt; Peters, *Crime and Punishment*, 81–82. For more on prisons in Islamic legal history, see Irene Schneider, "Imprisonment in Pre-Classical and Classical Islamic Law," *Islamic Law and Society* 2, n. 2 (1995): 157–173; Franz Rosenthal, *The Muslim Concept of Freedom prior to the Nineteenth Century* (Leiden: Brill, 1960), 35–68; Kent F. Schull, *Prisons in the Late Ottoman Empire* (Edinburgh: Edinburgh University Press, 2014).

99. For example, Aḥmad al-Ṣāwī (d. 1825 CE), *Bulghat al-sālik li-aqrab al-masālik ʿalā al-Sharḥ al-ṣaghīr li-Aḥmad al-Dardīr*, 4 vols. (Beirut: Dār al-Kutub al-ʿIlmiyya, 1415/1995), 4:256–257 (NB: beating or imprisoning a suspected thief removes the Hudud element because it introduces a doubt [*shubha*]). The prominent Ottoman Ḥanafī jurist Muḥammad al-Khādimī (d. 1763 CE) admits the disagreement within his school but states that "later" Ḥanafī scholars allowed judges to beat suspected thieves or murderers to extract

confessions; Muḥammad b. Muḥammad al-Khādimī, *Ḥāshiyat al-Khādimī ʿalā al-Durar wa'l-ghurar* (Cairo: Dār al-Ṭibāʿa al-ʿĀmira, 1268/1853), 402–403. In fact, even Ibn Taymiyya gives a fatwa that a judge can beat someone accused of murder to elicit a confession if there is circumstantial evidence of guilt (*lawth wa huwa mā yaghlibu ʿalā al-ẓann annahu qatalahu... qarāʾin*); Ibn Taymiyya, *Fatāwā*, 34:97.

100. Peters, *Crime and Punishment in Islamic Law*, 81–83.
101. Ibn Qayyim al-Jawziyya, *al-Ṭuruq al-ḥukmiyya*, 1:32. The version of the Hadith cited by Ibn al-Qayyim and others who followed him (see al-Ṭarābulusī, *Muʿīn al-ḥukkām*, 209), which includes the essential detail of the Prophet ordering al-Zubayr to inflict pain on the suspect (*ʿadhdhibhu*) is actually very rare. See Ibn Ḥibbān, *Ṣaḥīḥ Ibn Ḥibbān*, 3:133–135; al-Bayhaqī, *Dalāʾil al-nubuwwa*, 4:229–230. In fact, a number of the Hadiths that al-Ṭarābulusī relies on in his justification of inflicting pain on suspects are not to be found in any known collection of Hadiths, let alone the collections to which al-Ṭarābulusī cites them. See, for example, the story of the two men from the Ghifār tribe in *Muʿīn al-ḥukkām* (page 209), which the author cites to the *Muwaṭṭaʾ*, and the story of the Prophet beating a servant girl in the affair of the Lie regarding Aisha (ibid., 210).
102. Ṣadr al-Dīn ʿAlī b. ʿAlī Ibn Abī al-ʿIzz, *al-Tanbīh ʿalā mushkilāt al-Hidāya*, ed. ʿAbd al-Ḥakīm Muḥammad Shākir and Anwar Ṣāliḥ Abū Zayd, 6 vols. (Riyadh: Maktabat al-Rushd, 1414/2003), 4:455–456.
103. Ibn Abī al-ʿIzz, *al-Tanbīh ʿalā mushkilāt al-Hidāya*, 4:455–456; Ibn ʿĀbidīn, *Ḥāshiyat Ibn ʿĀbidīn*, 4:87–88; idem, *Radd al-muḥtār*, 3:195–196.
104. Ibn Qayyim, *al-Ṭuruq al-ḥukmiyya*, 1:32.
105. *Sunan* of Abū Dāwūd: *kitāb al-ḥudūd, bāb fī al-imtiḥān bi'l-ḍarb*.
106. Al-Shirbīnī, *Mughnī al-muḥtāj*, 2:311.
107. Johansen, "Signs as Evidence," 138. *Qāḍī al-quḍāt* Saʿd al-Dīn Saʿd b. Muḥammad al-Dayrī (d. 867/1462) of Cairo is noted as having written a fatwa on imprisonment based on accusation; al-Laknawī, *al-Jawāhir al-bahiyya*, 80.
108. Al-Khaṣṣāf, *Adab al-qāḍī*, 264–265.
109. This name has also been vowelled al-Quhustānī.
110. Ibn ʿĀbidīn reproduces al-Quhistānī's text, which stated that the story about ʿAṣām and the amīr had appeared in the *Wāqiʿāt* of Aḥmad b. Muḥammad al-Nāṭifī of Rayy (d. 446/1054–5) and the *Dhakhīra*; Ibn ʿĀbidīn, *Ḥāshiyat Ibn ʿĀbidīn*, 4:87–88; idem, *Radd al-muḥtār*, 3:195–196; al-Bazzāzī, *al-Fatāwā al-Bazzāziyya*, 6:430, al-Ṭarābulusī, *Muʿīn al-ḥukkām*, 215.
111. Johansen, "Vérité et torture," 132–133.
112. Ibn ʿĀbidīn, *Ḥāshiyat Ibn ʿĀbidīn*, 4:76; 5:299; idem, *Radd al-Muḥtār*, 3:188.
113. *Sunan* of Abū Dāwūd: *kitāb al-ḥudūd, bāb fī al-imtiḥān bi'l-ḍarb*.
114. Al-Qudūrī, *Mukhtaṣar*, 551; Ibn Qudāma, *Mughnī*, 10:349. An exception in Ottoman law was if the number of lashes exceeded one hundred in *taʿzīr*. Then the state was liable for half the decedent's *diya*; Peters, *Crime and Punishment*, 99.
115. The incident cited as precedent for this comes in the famous *Fatāwā al-ẓahīriyya* of Ẓahīr al-Dīn Muḥammad b. Aḥmad of Bukhara (d. 619/1222–1223): A is accused of theft (*sariqa*), so he is brought to the sultan to be beaten until he confesses. A is beaten once or twice and then put in jail (*ḥabs*). He is so afraid of being beaten again that he escapes onto

the roof but then falls and dies. Meanwhile, it emerges that B actually committed the theft. Ẓahīr al-Dīn held that A's inheritors should receive the *diya* from the plaintiff as well as any fine (*gharāma*) that the sultan levied on the accuser for his wrongdoing. See al-Ṭarābulusī, *Mu'īn al-ḥukkām*, 193; Kātib Chelebī, *Kashf al-ẓunūn*, 2:473; al-Laknawī, *al-Fawā'id al-bahiyya*, 156–157. See also Ibn 'Ābidīn, *Radd al-muḥtār*, 3:196; idem, *Ḥāshiyat Ibn 'Ābidīn*, 4:87–88.

116. If the ruler had someone beaten unjustly (*ẓulm*), then either he or the lasher was liable; al-Māwardī, *al-Ḥāwī*, 13:415–420, 424; al-Nawawī, *Sharḥ Ṣaḥīḥ Muslim*, 11/12:233; Ibn Ḥajar, *Fatḥ*, 12:80. The evidence for these positions is 'Alī's statement that he only felt guilt at deaths that resulted from the Companions' punishment for drinking, since it had not originated in the Prophet's ruling (*Ṣaḥīḥ al-Bukhārī: kitāb al-ḥudūd, bāb al-ḍarb bi'l-jarīd wa'l-ni'āl*), and 'Umar's decision that his family was liable for the *diya* of a woman who had a miscarriage out of fear upon receiving a summons from him; al-Bayhaqī, *al-Sunan al-kubrā*, 8:558; al-Sha'rānī, *al-Mīzān al-kubrā*, 2:194.

117. Gerber, *State, Society, and Law in Islam*, 64.

118. Joseph Schacht, *An Introduction to Islamic Law*, 193; Hallaq, *Sharī'a*, 350. For a comprehensive survey of the Ḥanafī tradition's approach to the written word, see Baber Johansen, "Formes de langage et fonctions publiques: Stéréotypes, témoins et offices dans la preuve par l'écrit en droit musulman," *Arabica* 44, no. 3 (1997): 333–76. For an overall discussion, with a focus on the practice of a fourteenth-century Shāfi'ī judge, see Christian Müller, "Écrire pour établir la preuve orale en Islam: la practique d'un tribunal à Jérusalem au xive siècle," in *Les Outils de la pensée* (Paris: Maison des Sciences de l'Homme, 2010), 63–97. For a general study on the use of documentary evidence, especially in the Mālikī school, see Emile Tyan, *Le Notariat et le régime de la preuve par écrit dans la pratique du droit musulman*, 2nd ed. (Beirut: Faculté de Droit de Beyrouth, 1959). For a general survey of the *adab al-qāḍī* literature, see Muhammad Khalid Masud, "Adab al-qāḍī," *Encyclopaedia of Islam THREE*; Muhammad Khalid Masud, Rudolph Peters, and David Stephan Powers, "Qāḍīs and Their Courts: An Historical Survey," in *Dispensing Justice in Islam: Qāḍīs and Their Judgments*, ed. Muhammad Khalid Masud, Rudolph Peters, and David Stephan Powers (Leiden: Brill, 2006), 16–19. For the use of documents in other Sunni schools of law, see Brinkley Messick, *The Calligraphic State: State Textual Domination and History in a Muslim Society* (Berkeley: University of California Press, 1993); Ghislaine Lydon, *On Trans-Saharan Trails: Islamic Law, Trade Networks, and Cross-Cultural Exchange in Nineteenth-Century Western Africa* (Cambridge and New York: Cambridge University Press, 2009), esp. ch. 6. For a surprisingly expansive review of different positions and practices on the use of documentary evidence within the Mālikī school in the Islamic West, written by a fourteenth-century scholar, see al-Nubāhī, *Tārīkh quḍāt al-Andalus*, 171, 224, 239–248.

119. Ibn Baṭṭāl, *Sharḥ Ṣaḥīḥ al-Bukhārī*, ed. Abū Tamīm Yāsir Ibrāhīm, 10 vols. (Riyadh: Maktabat al-Rushd, 2000), 8:231. For Muḥammad b. al-Ḥarīth's biography, see Qāḍī 'Iyāḍ, *Tartīb al-madārik*, 2:167–168.

120. See Tyan, *Notoriat*. For notes on court archives in Fatimid Egypt, see Rustow, *The Lost Archive: Traces of a Caliphate in a Cairo Synagogue*, 67–68.

121. For an in-depth discussion of this issue, see Ibn Baṭṭāl, *Sharḥ Ṣaḥīḥ al-Bukhārī*, 8:230–234; Ibn Ḥajar, *Fatḥ al-bārī*, 13:180–181.
122. See, for instance, Ghislaine Lydon, "A Paper Economy of Faith without Faith in Paper: A Reflection on Islamic Institutional History," *Journal of Economic Behavior & Organization* 71, n. 3 (2009): 647–659.
123. Müller, "Écrire pour établir," 74, 79 83–84 et passim. Al-Kindī reports that Sulaym b. ʿItr (fl. 160s/770s) was the first judge in Egypt to make a record of his rulings after disputants in an inheritance case came back to him disputing the case again after he had already made the ruling once; al-Kindī, *Kitāb al-Wulāt*, 310. NB: Ibn Abī al-ʿAwwām (d. 418/1027) was a Ḥanbalī judge in Egypt who was first to move court records to the mosque, whereas before they were kept in the judge's house; al-Ziriklī, *Aʿlām*, 1:211.
124. Boğaç Ergene, "Evidence in Ottoman Courts: Oral and Written Documentation in Early-Modern Courts of Islamic Law," *Journal of the American Oriental Society* 124, no. 3 (2004): 471–491.
125. Jessica Marglin, "In the Court of the Nations: Jews, Muslims and Legal Pluralism in Nineteenth-Century Morocco," (PhD dissertation, Princeton, 2013), 71, 81.
126. Tyan, *Notariat*, 91.
127. Johansen, "Formes de langage," 342, 366–9. See also Tyan, *Notariat*, 9, n. 2.
128. The treatise was copied from al-Ḥaṣkafī's autograph, *ra'aytu bi-khaṭṭ shaykhinā shaykh al-Islām ʿAlā' al-Dīn Afandī*. It was copied in Ṣafar AH 1114/July 1702 by Muḥammad Saʿdī al-Ṣādiqī (Fatih Library, Istanbul, MS 2382), 7b.
129. Guy Burak, "Evidentiary truth claims, imperial registers, and the Ottoman archive: contending legal views of archival and record-keeping practices in Ottoman Greater Syria (seventeenth-nineteenth centuries)," *Bulletin of the School of Oriental and African Studies* 79, n. 2 (2016): 240.
130. *Mecelle*, Book 15, Title 2. See W.E. Grigsby, trans., *The Medjelle* (London: Stevens and Sons, 1895), 388.
131. Ömer Nasuhi Bilmen, *Hukûk-i Islâmiyye ve Istılâhât-ı Fikhiyye Kamusu* (Istanbul: Ravza Yayınları, 2013), 8:175. See Said Salih Kaymakcı, "The Sultan's Entrepreneurs, the Entrepreneurs' Sultan: Beratlı Avrupa Tüccarı and Institutional Change in the Nineteenth-Century Ottoman Empire (1835–1868)," (MA Thesis, Boğaziçi University, 2013).
132. Abū Yaʿla Ibn al-Farrā's *Ordinances* has "What had been held by a group – and they are the majority – is that...."
133. Al-Māwardī, *Aḥkām*, 115–116.
134. Al-Māwardī, *Aḥkām*, 116.
135. Al-Māwardī, *al-Ḥāwī*, 16:206.
136. For a Mālikī affirmation of al-Māwardī's discussion of how that school differs from others on procedure, see al-Qarāfī, *al-Dhakhīra*, 10:39–40.
137. Al-Ṭarābulusī, *Muʿīn al-ḥukkām*, 158. An example of necessity is a judge acting on a written request for the implementation of a ruling from another judge even if the messenger was not reliable, provided the document was sealed; al-Ṭarābulusī, *Muʿīn al-ḥukkām*, 116, 158. An example of custom is, among Central Asian Ḥanafī scholars, accepting the claim of a merchant that a debt is owed to him based on such a record appearing in his ledgers (*fī bādkārī*, perhaps *yādkārī*?); ibid., 157.
138. Taqī al-Dīn al-Subkī, *Fatāwā*, 2:445.

139. Ibrahim identifies this in 21/1001 cases examined; Ibrahim, *Pragmatism in Islamic Law*, 152–153.
140. Burak, "Evidentiary truth claims, imperial registers, and the Ottoman archive," 242 ff.

5. CAN GOD'S LAW BE UNJUST? EQUITY AND THE RIGHTS OF GOD'S SERVANTS

1. During the Mamluk period, leading Cairo scholars of the Shāfiʿī school also ruled that the judge could imprison a defendant claiming bankruptcy if that preserved the rights of the Muslims and because the default assumption was solvency. The Mālikī school also allowed this, also with the *maṣlaḥa* aim of protecting people's rights; al-Suyūṭī, *al-Ashbāh wa'l-naẓā'ir*, ed. Muḥammad al-Muʿtaṣim al-Baghdādī (Beirut: Dār al-Kitāb al-ʿArabī, 1414/1993), 748; Ibn Rushd, *The Distinguished Jurist's Primer*, trans. Imran Ahsan Khan Nyazee, 2 vols. (Reading: Garnet, 2000), 2:351.
2. Rapoport, "Royal Justice and Religious Law," 83–84.
3. *Ṣaḥīḥ al-Bukhārī*: *kitāb al-aḥkām, bāb al-shahādat takūnu ʿind al-ḥākim fī wilāyat al-qaḍā' aw qabla dhālika li'l-khaṣm*; Ibn Ḥajar, *Fatḥ al-bārī*, 13:199–200; al-Khaṣṣāf, *Adab al-qāḍī*, 333. The defendant also enjoyed a privilege in the epistemology of burden of proof. See also Johansen, "Signs as Evidence," 179.
4. Al-Qurṭubī, *al-Jāmiʿ li-aḥkām al-Qur'ān*, 1:194–195 (Quran 2:10); Saḥnūn, *al-Mudawwana al-kubrā*, ed. ʿĀmir al-Jazzār and ʿAbdallāh al-Minshāwī, 5 vols. (Cairo: Dār al-Ḥadīth, 1426/2005), 5:146–147; al-Suyūṭī, *al-Bāhir fī ḥukm al-Nabī ṣallā Allāhu ʿalayhi wa sallama bi'l-bāṭin wa'l-ẓāhir*, ed. Mehmet Hayri Kıbaşoğlu (Cairo: Dār al-Salām, 1407/1987), 27. Ibn Ḥajar al-ʿAsqalānī, a Shāfiʿī scholar himself, was skeptical of this rule in eras as corrupted as he felt his was; Ibn Ḥajar, *Fatḥ al-bārī*, 13:200; al-Khaṭṭābī, *Maʿālim al-sunan*, 4:20.
5. Abū Yūsuf, *Kitāb al-Kharāj* (Beirut: Dār al-Maʿrifa, 1979), 65–66.
6. Numerous Hadiths described the Prophet telling litigants before him that he did not know the truth or falsehood of their claims, but that a litigant who convinced him of a falsehood would find punishment in the afterlife (see *Ṣaḥīḥ al-Bukhārī*: *kitāb al-aḥkām, bāb mawʿiẓat al-imām li'l-khuṣūm*). Al-Khaṣṣāf incorporates a phrase from ʿUmar's letter to Abū Mūsā al-Ashʿarī: "For indeed God has assumed the hearts of the believers, and He has protected you all with *al-bayyināt*" (*fa'inna allāh tawallā min al-ʿibād al-sarā'ir wa dara'a ʿankum bi'l-bayyināt*); al-Khaṣṣāf, *Adab al-qāḍī*, 45.
7. Al-Khaṭṭābī, *Maʿālim al-sunan*, 4:14–15. As Shāh Walī Allāh describes, the plaintiff/claimant (*muddaʿī*) is the party claiming something other than what is evident and an addition to the status quo (*khilāf al-ẓāhir wa yuthbitu al-ziyāda*). The defendant (*muddaʿī ʿalayhi*), however, is claiming mere continuity of the status quo (*istiṣḥāb al-aṣl... al-mutamassik bi'l-ẓāhir*); Shāh Walī Allāh, *Ḥujjat Allāh al-bāligha*, 2:507.
8. Johansen, "Signs as Evidence," 173, 179 and *passim*. Despite its often-pejorative connotation, formalism is an essential feature for confidence in a legal

system's equal application and predictability. As Schauer puts it, formalism is "decisionmaking according to *rule*." It is the way in which "rules achieve their 'ruleness' precisely by doing what is supposed to be the failing of formalism: screening off from a decisionmaker factors that a sensitive decisionmaker would otherwise take into account." See Frederick Schauer, "Formalism," *Yale Law Journal* 97, n. 4 (1988): 509. For a broader and more international (civil law) perspective on the term, see "Formalisme," in *Dictionnaire encyclopédique de théorie et de sociologie du droit*, ed. André-Jean Arnaud et al. (Paris: Librairie Générale, 1988), 163–165.

9. Al-Māwardī, *al-Ḥāwī*, 17:306–307. See Quran 2:282; 65:2.
10. For example, Taqī al-Dīn al-Subkī allowed ruling by circumstantial evidence (*makhāyil*) in an instance in which a wife said she had been coerced by her husband into agreeing to a negotiated exit from her marriage (*khul'*). She provided no evidence (*bayyina*), but the judge (al-Subkī) was convinced by the circumstances: the husband had brought the governor's standard bearers (*janādira*) with him to the meeting; Taqī al-Dīn al-Subkī, *Fatāwā*, 2:197.
11. Tillier, "The Umayyads and the Formation of Islamic Judgeship," 177–178.
12. This was Ibn Ḥujayra (d. 188/803); al-Kindī, *Kitāb al-Wulāt*, 318.
13. Ibn Ḥajar, *Fatḥ al-bārī*, 5:355.
14. This was based on a Hadith in which the Prophet instructed the finder to hand the item over to a person who could accurately describe it. The Shāfi'ī and Ḥanafī schools required the claimant to provide *bayyina*. See Ibn Qudāma, *al-Mughnī*, 6:336–337; *Sunan* of Abū Dāwūd: *kitāb al-luqṭa* (third Hadith in *bāb*).
15. Ibn Qudāma, *al-Mughnī*, 6:348.
16. This judge was Abū al-Muṭarrif 'Abd al-Raḥmān al-Sha'bī (d. 499/1106); al-Nubāhī, *Tārīkh quḍāt al-Andalus*, 140.
17. Al-Juwaynī, *Nihāyat al-maṭlab fī dirāyat al-madhhab*, ed. 'Abd al-'Aẓīm Maḥmūd al-Dīb, 20 vols. (Jeddah: Dār al-Minhāj, 1428/2007), 19:189. For a similar ruling in the Ḥanbalī school for disputes over inheritance, see al-Ḥasan b. Ḥāmid al-Baghdādī al-Ḥanbalī, *Tahdhīb al-ajwiba*, ed. 'Abd al-'Azīz Muḥammad al-Qāyidī, 2 vols. (Medina: Maktabat al-'Ulūm wa'l-Ḥikam, 1425/2005), 1:389.
18. Al-Māwardī, *al-Ḥāwī*, 9:543.
19. Al-Juwaynī compares the judge in this case to a *mujtahid* evaluating different reports; al-Juwaynī, *Nihāyat al-maṭlab*, 19:107–108.
20. Al-Juwaynī, *Nihāyat al-maṭlab*, 19:189.
21. Tāj al-Dīn al-Subkī, *Ṭabaqāt*, 4:363; al-Juwaynī, *Nihāyat al-maṭlab*, 19:135.
22. Cornell Fleischer, *Bureaucrat and Intellectual in the Ottoman Empire* (Princeton: Princeton University Press, 1986), 43; Kınalızade Ali Çelebi, *Ahlâk-ı Alâ'î*, ed. Mustafa Koç (Istanbul: Klasik, 2007), 483–484. See also Baki Tezcan, *The Second Ottoman Empire* (Cambridge: Cambridge University Press, 2010), 52.
23. *yuḥtāju ilā naw' siyāsa*; Abū Shāma al-Maqdisī, *al-Rawḍatayn fī akhbār al-dawlatayn*, 1:60; Ayalon, 125. As Ibn Taymiyya writes, the most comprehensive view is that "the Shariah does not omit any *maṣlaḥa*"; Ibn Taymiyya, *Majmū'at al-fatāwā*, 11:198.
24. Al-Qurṭubī, *Jāmi' li-aḥkām al-Qur'ān*, 3:509–511.
25. Kınalızade, *Ahlâk-ı Alâ'î*, 483–485.

26. "The source of the difficulty is that equity, though just, is not legal justice, but a rectification of legal justice. The reason for this is that law is always a general statement, yet there are cases which it is not possible to cover in a general statement. In matters therefore where, while it is necessary to speak in general terms, it is not possible to do so correctly, the law takes into consideration the majority of cases, although it is not unaware of the error this involves"; Aristotle, *Nicomachean Ethics*, trans. H. Rackham (Cambridge, MA: Harvard University Press, 1926), 5.10.2–6.
27. *Al-sharʿ lā yaʾmuru biʾl-jawr*; al-Sarakhsī, *al-Mabsūṭ*, 9:80. See also Hurvitz, "The Contribution of Early Islamic Rulers to Adjudication," 151. Ibn ʿAbd al-Salām explains that all of God's commands fit under the general command of justice due to the Quranic verse stating that God commands you to do justice (16:90); ʿIzz al-Dīn Ibn ʿAbd al-Salām, *al-Qawāʿid al-kubrā*, ed. Nazīr Kamāl Ḥammād and ʿUthmān Jumʿa, 2 vols. (Damascus: Dār al-Qalam, 1421/2000), 2:315.
28. See Khadduri, *The Islamic Conception of Justice*, 2.
29. Ibn ʿĀbidīn, "Nashr al-ʿarf fī banāʾ baʿḍ al-aḥkām ʿalā al-ʿurf," in *Majmūʿat Rasāʾil Ibn ʿĀbidīn*, 2 vols. (Damascus: [Muḥammad Hāshim al-Kutubī, 1907]), 2:115.
30. *Ṣaḥīḥ al-Bukhārī*: *kitāb al-jihād waʾl-siyar, bāb al-ḥarīr fī al-ḥarb*. For *ʿurf*, see Ayman Shabana, *Custom in Islamic Law and Legal Theory* (London: Palgrave, 2010), 57 and for more examples of important legal rulings defined by custom, see Ibn Ḥajar, *Fatḥ al-bari*, 4:511.
31. For an excellent study on efforts by Muslim jurists to conceptualize and define necessity (*ḍarūra*) and its interaction with legal rulings, see Dana Elizabeth Lee, "At the Limits of Law: Necessity in Islamic Legal History, Second/Eighth through Tenth/Sixteenth Centuries," (PhD dissertation, Princeton University, 2019), particularly p. 78–90 (thanks to Rami Koujah for alerting me to this). Ahmed Fekry Ibrahim observes that jurists made no sustained effort to define necessity or need systematically. This opinion might be reconciled with Lee's extensive study of the topic if we understand that jurists' efforts to define and understand necessity were, as Lee notes, casuistic as opposed to seeking to offer universal definitions; Ahmed Fekry Ibrahim, *Pragmatism in Islamic Law*, 8, 91–92. For efforts to define the related concept of need (*ḥāja*), see ʿAbdallāh Bin Bayyah, *al-Farq bayn al-ḍarūra waʾl-ḥāja taṭbīqan ʿalā baʿḍ aḥwāl al-aqalliyyāt al-muslima*. Al-Suyuṭī offers one taxonomy of need: *ḍarūra* means a situation in which a person will perish, or come close to perishing, if a solution is not found, and it makes the prohibited permissible. *Ḥāja* causes great hardship (*ḥaraj, mashaqqa*) and allows a person to take dispensations like breaking their fast due to fierce hunger; al-Suyūṭī, *al-Ashbāh waʾl-naẓāʾir*, 176. One famous legal maxim, "Need is treated like necessity whether it be specific or general" (*al-ḥāja tunazzalu manzilat al-ḍarūra ʿāmma kānat aw khāṣṣa*) is understood as meaning that, for a group of people (rather than an individual), whether a specific community or people overall, pressing need can have the same licensing effect as necessity. See ʿIzzat ʿUbayd al-Daʿʿās, *al-Qawāʿid al-fiqhiyya* (Beirut: Dār al-Tirmidhī, 1409/1989), 45–46.
32. See, for example, things known with certainty through sense perception; al-Ghazālī, *Miʿyār al-ʿilm* (Cairo: Maṭbaʿat al-ʿArabiyya, n.d.), 122–123.

33. See Alan Watson, trans., "Book One," in *The Digest of Justinian, Volume 1*, 1–39 (Philadelphia: University of Pennsylvania Press, 1998), 2–3.
34. This comes from the formative Ashʿarī theologian Ibn Fūrak (d. 406/1015), who attributes it to Abū al-Ḥasan al-Ashʿarī himself; Abū Bakr Ibn Fūrak, *Maqālāt al-shaykh Abī al-Ḥasan al-Ashʿarī*, ed. Aḥmad ʿAbd al-Raḥīm al-Sāyiḥ (Beirut: Maktabat al-Thaqāfa wa'l-Dīniyya, 2005), 127–128. I thank my most learned friend Rodrigo Adem for this citation. See also Felicitas Opwis, Maṣlaḥa *and the Purpose of the Law* (Leiden: Brill, 2010).
35. Ramon Harvey argues that *qisṭ* and *ʿadl* differ slightly from one another semantically, with *ʿadl* being "an internal quality of equity," while *qisṭ* has the active, transitive connotation of establishing equity, of "justice established concretely within the social sphere." See Ramon Harvey, *The Qur'an and the Just Society* (Edinburgh: Edinburgh University Press, 2018), 19–22. A related term is *inṣāf*, 'fairness' or 'equity,' which comes from the word for portioning in 'half' (*niṣf*). The early Sufi ʿAbd al-Raḥmān al-Dārānī (d. 204/820) is quoted as saying "there is no *ʿadl* like *inṣāf*"; Abū Nuʿaym al-Iṣbahānī, *Ḥilyat al-awliyā'*, 9:270.
36. Muslim scholars were in strong agreement that *qisṭās* (Quran 17:35, 26:182) was borrowed from Greek, though Jeffery and others suggest that it may be from the Aramaic word for 'measure'; Arthur Jeffery, *The Foreign Vocabulary of the Qur'ān* (Leiden: Brill, 2007), 237–239.
37. See, for example, the verse in two famous poems: "And we departed, in the evening, as if we were [date merchants] from Juwāthā, loading some of the oryx meat in saddle bags (*ʿidl*) and some behind" (*wa ruḥnā ka'annā min juwāthā ʿashiyyatan – nuʿālī al-niʿāj bayn ʿidl wa muḥqabi*); *Dīwān Imru' al-Qays*, ed. Ḥasan al-Sundūbī (Cairo: al-Maktaba al-Tijāriyya, 1930), 27. The translation comes from A. Sumi Motoyoshi, *Description in Classical Arabic Poetry* (Leiden: Brill, 2004), 40, 55. For more on the Quranic and early Arabic words for justice, see Khadduri, *The Islamic Conception of Justice*, 6.
38. For equity vs. equality, see Aristotle, *Nicomachean Ethics*, V:1–3. One case offers a fascinating razor for this question. In one Hadith the Prophet instructs parents to be "be just (*iʿdilū*) among your children" when giving them gifts. This has been interpreted in two main ways by jurists. The first position interprets "being just" in light of the Quranic rule (4:11) that daughters receive half the inheritance of sons. Thus, parents should give sons and daughters gifts in a 2:1 proportion. This is the main opinion of the Ḥanbalī school, which views *inter vivos* gifts as analogous to inheritance and also sees the same operative legal cause (*ʿilla*), namely that sons have more duties of care than daughters. It is also the position held by the early Ḥanafī pillar al-Shaybānī. The second position is that "being just" means giving gifts equally to male and female. This is the main position of the Shāfiʿī school, though it noted that some scholars held that the inheritance proportions should be followed. The famous Yemeni scholar Ibn al-Amīr al-Ṣanʿānī explains that equal shares in gifts to male/female children is required, since there is no indication (*dalīl*) that anything but this plain meaning should be taken from the Prophet's command (in fact, one narration of this Hadith quotes the Prophet teaching "Approximate among your children [*qāribū bayn awlādikum*]" and features an explanatory gloss of "Treat them equally [*sawwū*]"). This is also the position of the early Ḥanafīs Abū Yūsuf and al-Ṭaḥāwī (d. 321/932), the latter explaining that the command to "be just" in the Hadith is elucidated as equal treatment by a less well-known

Hadith via Ibn ʿAbbās in which the Prophet tells parents to "be equal (*sawwū*)" in their gifts and another in which the Prophet tells a father to seat his son and daughter equally on his lap. For the main Hadith above, narrated by al-Nuʿmān b. Bashīr, see *Ṣaḥīḥ al-Bukhārī*: *kitāb al-hiba, bāb al-ishhād fī al-hiba*; *Ṣaḥīḥ Muslim*: *kitāb al-hibāt, bāb karāhat tafḍīl baʿḍ al-awlād fī al-hiba*; *Musnad Aḥmad Ibn Ḥanbal*, 4:278; Ibn al-Amīr al-Ṣanʿānī, *Majmūʿ fīhi sabaʿ rasāʾil*, 73. For Ibn ʿAbbās' Hadith, see al-Ḥārith b. Abī Usāma, *Musnad*, apud. Nūr al-Dīn al-Haythamī, *Bughyat al-bāʿith ʿan zawāʾid Musnad al-Ḥārith*, ed. Ḥusayn Aḥmad al-Mubārak (Medina: al-Jāmiʿa al-Islāmiyya, 1413/1992), 512; Saʿīd b. Manṣūr, *Sunan Saʿīd b. Manṣūr*, ed. Ḥabīb al-Raḥmān al-Aʿẓamī, 2 vols. (Bombay: al-Dār al-Salafiyya, 1403/1982), 1:119. For the Hadith of seating the children, see Abū Jaʿfar al-Ṭaḥāwī, *Sharḥ maʿānī al-āthār*, ed. Muḥammad Sayyid Jād al-Ḥaqq, Muḥammad Zuhrī al-Najjār and Yūsuf ʿAbd al-Raḥmān al-Marʿashlī, 4 vols. (Beirut: ʿĀlam al-Kutub, 1414/1994), 4:89. See also Ibn Qudāma, *Mughnī*, 6:263, 268; al-Buhūtī, *Rawḍ*, 327; al-Nawawī, *Minhāj*, 325.

39. Harvey, *The Qur'an and the Just Society*, 20.
40. *Sunan* of Abū Dāwūd: *kitāb al-ijāra, bāb fī taḍmīn al-ʿāriya*; *Ṣaḥīḥ al-Bukhārī*: *kitāb al-ṣawm, bāb man aqsama ʿalā akhīhi li-yufṭira fī al-taṭawwuʿ...*; Aristotle, *Nicomachean Ethics*, 1129a-1132b, 1134a; Plato, *Republic*, 1.332 b-c; Alan Watson, trans., "Book One," in *The Digest of Justinian, Volume 1, 1–39* (Philadelphia: University of Pennsylvania Press, 1998), 2–3. See also Alasdair MacIntyre, *Whose Justice? Which Rationality?* (Notre Dame: University of Notre Dame Press, 1988), 153.
41. Plato, *Republic*, 4.443 b; 4.434 b.
42. Al-Ghazālī, *Iḥyāʾ ʿulūm al-dīn*, 2:911–912; Ibn Ḥajar Haytamī, *Ḥawāshī Tuḥfat al-Muḥtāj*, 5:81; al-Suyūṭī, *al-Ashbāh wa'l-naẓāʾir*, 235; al-Nābulusī, *al-Ḥadīqa al-nadiya*, 1:143.
43. See Khadduri, *Islamic Conception of Justice*, 81–103.
44. Al-Māturīdī, *Taʾwīlāt al-Qurʾān*, 8:104, 177; Qāḍī ʿIyāḍ, *Kitāb al-Shifā*, 363; Saʿd al-Dīn al-Taftāzānī, *Sharḥ al-Arbaʿīn li'l-Nawawī* (Istanbul: Asetane, reprint of the 1316/1898 ʿĀmiriyya print), 77; Aḥmad b. Sulaymān Kamāl Pāshā-zāde, "Fī bayān al-ḥikma li-ʿadam nisbat al-sharr ilayhi taʿālā," in *Rasāʾil Ibn Kamāl* (Istanbul: Asetane, [2015], reprint of Istanbul: Maṭbaʿat Iqdām, 1316/1898), 126; Burhān al-Dīn Ibrāhīm al-Bayjūrī, *Ḥāshiyat al-imām al-Bayjūrī ʿalā Jawharat al-tawḥīd*, ed. ʿAlī Jumʿa (Cairo: Dār al-Salām, 2006), 180; Syed Muhammad Naquib al-Attas, *On Justice and the Nature of Man* (Kuala Lumpur: Ta'dib Intl., 2020), 13–14. Drawing on the Platonic vision of the Virtuous City, political thinkers throughout the Persian and Ottoman lands argued that justice was linked to and predicated upon the notion of cosmic order (or world order, *niẓām-i ʿālam*). This cosmic order is intended to produce the conditions for just conduct. See Gottfried Hagen, "World Order and Legitimacy," in *Legitimizing the Order: The Ottoman Rhetoric of State Power*, ed. Hasan Karateke and Maurus Reinkowski (Leiden: Brill, 2005), 55–83; Shahab Ahmed, *What Is Islam? The Importance of Being Islamic* (Princeton: Princeton University Press, 2015), esp. 462–482. Al-Bayjūrī defines *taḥqīq* as "referring to a thing in its proper and true manner and by establishing it with evidence" (*dhikr al-shayʾ ʿalā wajh al-ḥaqq ʿalā ithbāt al-shayʾ bi-dalīl*); al-Bayjūrī, 79.
45. Al-Māwardī, *Adab*; 87, 195.

46. See Linda T. Darling, "*Mirrors for Princes* in Europe and the Middle East: A Case of Historiographical Incommensurability," in *East Meets West in the Middle Ages and Early Modern Times*, ed. Albrecht Classen (Berlin: De Gruyter, 2013), 223–242; idem, *A History of Social Justice and Political Power in the Middle East* (London: Routledge, 2013).
47. This is clearly stated in the famous *'Ahd Ardishīr* from the late Sassanid period; Beate Dignas and Engelbert Winter, *Rome and Persia in Late Antiquity* (Cambridge: Cambridge University Press, 2007), 211; Iḥsān 'Abbās, ed., *'Ahd Ardishīr* (Beirut: Dār Ṣādir, 1967), 30.
48. Al-Māwardī, *Adab*, 179–198; cf. idem, *Qawānīn al-wizāra*, 122.
49. 'Abbās, ed., *'Ahd Ardishīr*, 30 (according to al-Mas'ūdī, this work was translated into Arabic around 113 AH; see editor's introduction).
50. *Al-mulk yabqā 'alā al-kufr wa lā yabqā 'alā al-ẓulm*; al-Māwardī, *Adab*, 193; idem, *Durar al-sulūk*, 93. This is supposedly the conclusion reached by a conclave of Muslim scholars upon the conquest of Baghdad by the pagan Mongols; Muḥammad b. 'Alī Ibn al-Ṭiqṭaqā (d. 709/1309), *al-Fakhrī fī al-ādāb al-sulṭāniyya* (Beirut: Dār Ṣādir, n.d.), 17; 'Abd al-Raḥmān al-Kawākibī, "Umm al-qurā," in *'Abd al-Raḥmān al-Kawākibī: al-a'māl al-kāmila*, ed. Muḥammad 'Umāra (Cairo: Dār al-Shurūq, 2009), 340. This saying is attributed to the Prophet in the *Naṣīḥat al-mulūk*, attributed to al-Ghazālī, and also by Muḥammad b. Ismā'īl al-Jadhabtī al-Jīzī (fl. 1440 CE); al-Ghazālī, *al-Tibr al-masbūk fī naṣīḥat al-mulūk*, ed. Aḥmad Shams al-Dīn (Beirut: Dār al-Kutub al-'Ilmiyya, 1988), 44; Muḥammad b. Ismā'īl al-Jadhabtī al-Jīzī, *al-Durra al-gharrā' fī naṣā'iḥ al-mulūk wa'l-wuzarā'* (Cairo: Maktabat Nizār Muṣṭafā al-Bāz, 1996), 206. Al-Jadhabtī wrote this book in 843/1439 for the Mamluk sultan, and it was later translated into Turkish for Selim I; Chelebī, *Kashf al-ẓunūn*, 2:89–90. The famous Muslim scholar of Delhi, Shāh 'Abd al-'Azīz (d. 1825 CE), also invoked this saying in light of the loss of Muslim sovereignty in northern India to the relatively good-governing British; Farhan Nizami, "Madrasahs, Scholars and Saints: Muslim Responses to the British Presence in Delhi and the Upper Doab 1803–1857," (PhD dissertation, Oxford University, 1983), 125. This concept is similar to the Medea's statement in Seneca's tragedy, "unjust rule does not last forever" (*iniqua nunquam regna perpetuo manent*); Seneca, *Medea*, 196.
51. Al-Māwardī, *Tashīl al-naẓar*, 338.
52. Ṭāhir b. al-Ḥusayn would later prove the founder of the Ṭāhirid dynasty in Khurasan, under Abbasid nominal sovereignty. He wrote this letter to his son upon the latter's assignment as governor of Diyār Rabī'a; al-Ṭabarī, 5:158.
53. Abū Yūsuf, *Kitāb al-Kharāj* (Beirut: Dār al-Ma'rifa, 1979), 5. Al-Khaṣṣāf wrote that "the judge is put in his position to bring those with claims to rights those rights"; al-Khaṣṣāf, *Adab al-qāḍī*, 245.
54. For example, see Anver Emon, *Religious Pluralism and Islamic Law* (Oxford: Oxford University Press, 2012), 152. For a useful survey and discussion of the notion of *ḥuqūq Allāh* and *ḥuqūq al-'ibād*, see Emon, "*Ḥuqūq Allāh* and *Ḥuqūq al-'Ibād*: A Legal Heuristic for a Natural Rights Regime," *Islamic Law and Society* 13, no. 3 (2006): 325–391; Miriam Hoexter, "*Ḥuqūq Allāh* and *Ḥuqūq al-'Ibād* as Reflected in the *Waqf* Institution," *Jerusalem Studies in Arabic and Islam* 19 (1995): 133–156. Much like I argue here, Emon argues that the notion of the 'rights of God's servants' constitutes a framework for a natural law or

human rights conception of justice and 'the good.' He states, "in their arguments and rationales for certain rules, the jurists engaged in naturalistic reasoning about the individual and the social good"; Emon, "*Ḥuqūq Allāh*," 333.

55. For example, al-Muzanī, *Mukhtaṣar*, ed. 'Abd al-Qādir Shāhīn (Beirut: Dār al-Kutub al-'Ilmiyya, 1998), 133 (transgressing on other's *ḥaqq* to property by damaging it); al-Khaṭṭābī, *Ma'ālim al-sunan*, 3:319, 1:83 (that obligation or responsibility can only be imposed with evidence); al-Shīrāzī, *al-Muhadhdhab*, 2 vols. (Beirut: Dār al-Fikr, n.d.), 1:290 (manslaughter as violation of a *ḥaqq ādamī*) and 1:449 (for a right to debt owed). In the Ḥanafī school, see Abū Ja'far al-Ṭaḥāwī, *Sharḥ mushkil al-āthār*, ed. Shu'ayb al-Arnā'ūṭ, 16 vols. (Beirut: Mu'assasat al-Risāla, 1994), 9: 450; al-Khaṣṣāf, *Adab al-qāḍī*, 333 (on how the Hudud crime of *qadhf* becomes a *ḥaqq ādamī*).
56. See *Ṣaḥīḥ al-Bukhārī: kitāb al-jihād wa'l-siyar, bāb ism al-fars wa'l-ḥimār; Ṣaḥīḥ Muslim: kitāb al-īmān, bāb man laqiya Allāh bi'l-īmān...; kitāb al-zakāt, bāb ithm māni' al-zakāt*. See also *Ṣaḥīḥ al-Bukhārī*: *kitāb al-buyū', bāb al-tijāra fī al-birr*; Baber Johansen, "Secular and religious elements in Hanafite law. Function and limits of the absolute character of government authority," in *Islam et Politique au Maghreb*, ed. E. Gellner et J.C. Vatin (Aix: Table ronde du CRESM, 1979), 300–301.
57. Mu'ayyad-zāde ['Abd al-Raḥmān Efendī, d. 1516], *Risāla* (Bağdat Vehbi, 2052, Süleymaniye Library), 142 a–b; Johansen, "Secular and religious elements in Hanafite law," 300–301.
58. Al-Juwaynī, *al-Burhān fī uṣūl al-fiqh*, ed. 'Abd al-'Aẓīm al-Dīb, 2 vols. (Cairo: Dār al-Anṣār, 1400/1980), 2:747; al-Ghazālī, *al-Mustaṣfā*, ed. Muḥammad 'Abd al-Salām 'Abd al-Shāfī (Beirut: Dār al-Kutub al-'Ilmiyya, 1413/1992), 174, 179. See Opwis, Maṣlaḥa *and the Purpose of the Law*, 67–68.
59. Al-Sarakhsī, *Mabsūṭ*, 10:110. It was a common ruling that, for example, a non-Muslim living under Muslim rule could not claim to have been the victim of the Hudud crime of slander (*qadhf*) if done by a Muslim. But scholars like al-Shīrāzī (d. 476/1083) held that, if a non-Muslim were slandered by a Muslim, they could still seek justice under the rubric of discretionary punishment (*ta'zīr*) or *siyāsa*; Emon, *Religious Pluralism and Islamic Law*, 147, 153. An earlier Ḥanafī legal theorist, al-Dabūsī (d. 430/1039), adds innate freedom as a (derogable) natural right of humans; Abū Zayd al-Dabūsī, *Taqwīm al-adilla*, ed. Khalīl Muḥyī al-Dīn al-Mays (Beirut: Dār al-Kutub al-'Ilmiyya, 2001), 417–418.
60. See, just as one example, Ibn al-Ṣalāḥ, *Fatāwā wa masā'il Ibn al-Ṣalāḥ*, ed. 'Abd al-Mu'ṭī Amīn Qal'ajī, 2 vols. (Beirut: Dār al-Ma'rifa, 1986), 1:83, 277, 290, 302, 2:516.
61. Al-Khaṭṭābī, *Ma'ālim al-sunan*, 3:319.
62. Al-Māwardī, *al-Ḥāwī*, 16:206.
63. Al-Nubāhī, *Tārīkh quḍāt al-Andalus*, 100. Ibn al-Jawzī recalls a chief judge telling him that he would not accept the testimony of the sultan or his close retinue, since they all wore silk; Ibn al-Jawzī, *Ṣayd al-khāṭir*, ed. Ṭāriq 'Awaḍallāh (Riyadh: Madār al-Waṭan, 1437/2016), 372.
64. Ibn Maryam al-Tilimsānī, *al-Bustān fī dhikr al-'ulamā' wa'l-awliyā' bi-tilimsān*, ed. 'Abd al-Qādir al-Būbāya (Beirut: Dār al-Kutub al-'Ilmiyya, 2014), 301.

65. According to one British traveler, this was in practice even before Awrangzīb's decree. See Sarkar, *Mughal Administration*, 109–115; quoting the original *farmān* of Awrangzīb in Khān, *Mirat-i-Ahmadi*, 248–252; Shafaat Ahmad Khan, *John Marshall in India: Notes and Observations in Bengal 1668–1672* (Oxford: Oxford University Press, 1927), 392.
66. Al-Shawkānī, "al-Qawl al-mufīd fī adillat al-ijtihād wa'l-taqlīd," in *al-Rasā'il al-fiqhiyya li'l-imām al-Shawkānī*, ed. Aḥmad Farīd al-Mazīdī (Beirut: Dār al-Kutub al-ʿIlmiyya, 2005), 72. See also al-Munāwī, *Fayḍ al-qadīr sharḥ al-Jāmiʿ al-ṣaghīr*, ed. Ḥamdī al-Damardāsh Muḥammad, 13 vols. (Mecca: Maktabat Nizār Muṣṭafā al-Bāz, 1998), 5:2621; Ulrich Rudolph, *Al-Māturīdī and the Development of Sunnī Theology in Samarqand*, trans. Rodrigo Adem (Leiden: Brill, 2015), 117, 298, 299.
67. Ibn al-Jawzī reports that in 450/1058, the year of al-Māwardī's death, political upheaval in Seljuq Baghdad led to the burning of the house of the chief judge al-Dāmaghānī, with the result that "most of the court records (*sijillāt*) and the legal books (*kutub al-ḥukmiyya*)" perished; Ibn al-Jawzī, *al-Muntaẓam*, 16:32.
68. Al-Māwardī, *al-Ḥāwī*, 16:206.
69. Al-Bayhaqī, *Sunan al-kubrā*, 8:220. But the caliph was reported to 'rectify the wrongs' brought to him by petitioners without demanding 'certain, direct evidence' (*bayyina qāṭiʿa*) due to how oppressive he knew the Umayyad government had been; Ibn ʿAbd al-Ḥakam, *Sīrat ʿUmar b. ʿAbd al-ʿAzīz*, 106–107.
70. See *Ṣaḥīḥ al-Bukhārī*: *kitāb al-diyāt, bāb janīn al-mar'a wa anna al-ʿaql ʿalā al-wālid.*
71. See al-Ḥasan b. Manṣūr Qāḍīkhān, *Fatāwā Qāḍīkhān*, ed. Sālim Muṣṭafā al-Badrī, 3 vols. (Beirut: Dār al-Kutub al-ʿIlmiyya, 1988), 3:357–358; al-Qaffāl al-Shāshī, *Maḥāsin al-sharīʿa*, ed. Muḥammad ʿAlī Samak (Beirut: Dār al-Kutub al-ʿIlmiyya, 2007), 563; Khalīl b. Isḥāq, *Mukhtaṣar Khalīl*, ed. al-Ṭāhir Aḥmad al-Zāwī, 2nd ed. (Beirut: Dār al-Madār al-Islāmī, 2004), 245. Some scholars in Fez/Chefchaouen totally disagreed. Muḥammad b. al-Ḥasan b. ʿArḍūn (d. 1012/1603) insisted the killer should pay the *diya*, since "The blood of a Muslim cannot go uncompensated (*lā yabṭulu dam muslim*)"; al-Wazzānī, *al-Nawāzil al-ṣughrā*, ed. Muḥammad al-Sayyid ʿUthmān, 4 vols. (Beirut: Dār al-Kutub al-ʿIlmiyya, 1435/2014), 4:384.
72. *Sunan* of Abū Dāwūd: *kitāb al-ijāra, bāb al-rajul yabīʿu mā laysa ʿindahu*; *Ṣaḥīḥ al-Bukhārī*: *kitāb al-buyūʿ, bāb bayʿ al-thamar ʿalā ru'ūs al-nakhl bi'l-dhahab wa'l-fiḍḍa.*
73. See al-Bayhaqī, *Sunan al-kubrā*, 10:254, 278–279.
74. See *Sunan* of Abū Dāwūd: *kitāb al-ijāra, bāb fī al-tasʿīr*; Ibn Qayyim al-Jawziyya, *al-Ṭuruq al-ḥukmiyya*, 638–639.
75. In the Ḥanafī school, exceptions could be created for theoretical legal principles and duties out of equitable reasoning (*istiḥsānan*) in light of people's needs (*ḥāja*). See, for example, al-Marghīnānī, *al-Hidāya*, 4:637. For the permissive acceptance of written documents as evidence in court by Mālikī judges out of *istiḥsān*, see al-Nubāhī, *Tārīkh quḍāt al-Andalus*, 247. See also Hassaan Shahawy, "How Subjectivity Became Wrong: Early Hanafism and the Scandal of *Istiḥsān* in the Formative Period of Islamic Law (750–1000 CE)," (PhD dissertation, Oxford, 2019).

76. Al-Suyūṭī, *al-Ashbāh wa'l-naẓā'ir*, 180–181; al-Nawawī, *Minhāj*, 372–374; Ibn Qudāma, *al-Mughnī*, 7:459–460.
77. Ibn Qayyim, *al-Ṭuruq al-ḥukmiyya*, 1:30–32.
78. Others who made this argument include Abū al-Muṭarrif 'Abd al-Raḥmān al-Sha'bī (d. 499/1106) of Andalusia; al-Nubāhī, *Tārīkh quḍāt al-Andalus*, 140.
79. An example of a Shāfi'ī scholar using a *ḥīla* is Muḥammad Sālim al-Sharqāwī (d. 1350/1931), who became well known for helping men who had issued triple, thus final, divorces and who then could not remarry their wives unless the wives first married and divorced other men (Quran 2:229). Since, in the Shāfi'ī school, witnesses to a marriage had to be upstanding (*'adl*), al-Sharqāwī would question whether the witnesses to the men's original marriages had actually met this standard. Declaring the original marriage invalid, the husband would thus be free to (re)marry the wife he had never actually been married to; Aḥmad al-Ghumārī, *al-Baḥr al-'amīq fī marwiyāt Ibn al-Ṣiddīq*, 2 vols. (Cairo: Dār al-Kutubī, 2007), 1:232–233. This same stratagem was used by a woman in Cairo in 1681 CE; Ibrahim, *Pragmatism in Islamic Law*, 153–155.
80. Al-Khaṣṣāf, *Adab al-qāḍī*, 334–335.
81. See Frank Vogel, *Islamic Law and Legal System* (Leiden: Brill, 2000), 82 ff.
82. Al-Jāḥiẓ, *Kitāb al-Ḥayawān*, ed. 'Abd al-Salām Hārūn, 8 vols. (Beirut: Dār al-Jīl, 1996), 1:87; Yaḥyā b. Muḥammad Ibn Hubayra, *Ikhtilāf al-a'imma al-a'lām*, ed. al-Sayyid Yūsuf Aḥmad (Beirut: Dār al-Kutub al-'Ilmiyya, 2002), 2:395; Tāj al-Dīn al-Subkī, *Ṭabaqāt al-shāfi'iyya al-kubrā*, 3:234; Nūr al-Ḥasan Khān, *al-Ṭarīqa al-muthlā fī al-irshād ilā tark al-taqlīd wa ittibā' mā huwa al-awlā*, ed. Sa'īd Mi'shāsha (Beirut: Dār Ibn Ḥazm, 1421/2000), 44–48. See also Ibn 'Aqīl 'Alī al-Ḥanbalī, *Kitāb al-Funūn*, ed. George Makdisi, 2 vols. (Beirut: Dar El-Machreq, 1970), 1:92.
83. Ibn Firkāḥ, *Mas'alat al-ghanā'im*, ed. 'Abd al-Sattār Abū Ghudda (Beirut: Dār al-Bashā'ir al-Islāmiyya, 1427/2006), 39.
84. Al-Buhūtī, *al-Rawḍ al-murbi'*, 502; al-Jāwī, *Qūt al-ḥabīb al-gharīb*, 289; Mullā Hüsrev, *Durar al-ḥukkām*, 2:378; al-Ābī, *al-Thamar al-dānī*, 448.
85. Al-Sha'rānī, *al-Mīzān*, 2:227. For the same explanation of the 'corruption of times' allowing increased flexibility for judges in their procedure and evidence, see al-Qarāfī, *Dhakhīra*, 10:46–47; al-Ṭarābulusī, *Mu'īn al-ḥukkām*, 217.
86. Al-Nubāhī, *Tārīkh quḍāt al-Andalus*, 100. Al-Ru'aynī quotes earlier Mālikī opinions that, if there are no just witnesses due to widespread corruption (*fasād*), then a judge can use the best possible witnesses available (and the magistrate of the *maẓālim* can be even more permissive); Muḥammad b. 'Abd al-Raḥmān al-Ḥaṭṭāb al-Ru'aynī, *Mawāhib al-Jalīl fī sharḥ Mukhtaṣar Khalīl*, 6 vols. (Beirut: Dār al-Fikr, 1398/1977), 6:91.
87. Maitland, *Equity*, 6.
88. Tyan, *Histoire*, 437–438.
89. Maitland, *Equity*, 9–11.
90. Tyan, *Histoire*, 447.
91. Ahmed Cevdet Paşa, *Tezakir*, 1:90.
92. Johansen, "Secular and religious elements in Hanafite law," 300–301.
93. Cited from Davānī's *Akhlāq-e Jalālī* in Shahab Ahmed, *What Is Islam?* 467. The Fez saint Muḥammad b. al-Qāsim al-Qandūsī (d. 1278/1861) said that the person furthest from God is not the one who ceases praying (*tārik al-ṣalāt*) but the one who wrongs people (*ẓālim al-'ibād*); al-Kattānī, *Salwat al-anfās*, 3:54.

94. The Shāfiʿī Mamluk-era jurist Badr al-Dīn Ibn Jamāʿa (d. 733/1333) devotes a section to *ḥuqūq al-ʿibād* in his discussion of the *ḥisba*. He argues that the inspection of scales and the exact measurement units are intended to guarantee that the rights of the servants of God are not breached; Muḥammad b. Ibrāhīm Ibn Jamāʿa, *Taḥrīr al-aḥkām fī tadbīr ahl al-Islām* (Riyadh: Maktabat Dār al-Minhāj, 2012), 413–415.
95. Al-Ṭarābulusī, *Muʿīn al-ḥūkkām*, 212–215.
96. Al-Ṣanʿānī, "al-Masāʾil al-muhimma," 49, 52, 77. The Hadith he refers to is "Whomever you praise as goodly, the Garden is owed them. And whomever you deem evil, the Fire is owed them. You are God's witnesses in the world (*man athnaytum ʿalayhi khayran wajabat lahu al-janna...*)"; *Ṣaḥīḥ Muslim: kitāb al-janāʾiz, bāb fīman yuthnā ʿalayhi khayran*. For a similar conclusion, see al-Nubāhī, *Tārīkh quḍāt al-Andalus*, 100.
97. Though I think this an exaggeration, Schacht argued that, even in the early Abbasid period, much of the subject matter supposedly handled by the *qāḍī* had been taken over by the *maẓālim*; Schacht, *Introduction to Islamic Law*, 51.
98. Schacht, *An Introduction to Islamic Law*, 54.
99. Nielsen, 31. Coulson offers that the *maẓālim*/*qāḍī*-court distinction was as close to secular/religious as one could get given that "all the functions of the Islamic state were theoretically religious in nature"; Coulson, *A History of Islamic Law*, 128.
100. Bernard Weiss, "Qāḍī," in *Encyclopedia of Religion*, ed. Lindsay Jones (Detroit: Thomson Gale, 2005).
101. Khadduri, *Islamic Conception of Justice*, 156–157; Knut Vikør, *Between God and the Sultan*, 190.
102. Nimrod Hurvitz, "The Contribution of Early Islamic Rulers to Adjudication and Legislation," 150, see also 155.
103. Jennings, "Kadi, Court, and Legal Procedure in 17th C. Ottoman Kayseri," 148. A more nuanced assessment that still, inaccurately, in my opinion, reads the *maẓālim* tribunal as secular comes from Rushain Abbasi, "Beyond the Realm of Religion," 554–563.
104. Al-Qarāfī, *al-Dhakhīra*, 10:45–46.
105. Tāj al-Dīn al-Subkī, *Muʿīd al-niʿam wa mubīd al-niqam*, ed. Muḥammad ʿAlī al-Najjār et al. (Cairo: Dār al-Kitāb al-ʿArabī, 1948), 43–44. See also al-Munāwī, *al-Jawāhir al-muḍiyya*, 418.
106. Taqī al-Dīn Aḥmad al-Maqrīzī, *al-Mawāʿiẓ waʾl-iʿtibār bi-dhikr al-khiṭat waʾl-āthar*, ed. Muḥammad Zaynhum and Madīḥat al-Sharqāwī, 3 vols. (Cairo: Maktabat al-Madbūlī, 1997), 3:82–84; Rapoport, "Royal Justice and Religious Law," 95. See also Ayalon, 107–115.
107. Rapoport, "Royal Justice and Religious Law," 82, 86–87. Interestingly, in fifteenth-century England common law justices and lawyers began warning the Chancellor 'off the field' of common law, stating that the equity courts could not handle cases on contracts, torts, etc.; Maitland, *Equity*, 6.
108. Rapoport, "Royal Justice and Religious Law," 94–95. I have altered some of Rapoport's transliteration conventions to match with this present work. See al-Subkī, *Muʿīd al-niʿam*, 41.
109. Ibn al-Jawzī, *Naqd al-ʿilm waʾl-ʿulamāʾ aw Talbīs Iblīs* (Cairo: Maṭbaʿat Muḥammad ʿAlī Ṣubayḥī, n.d.), 81, 128–129, 343. In another work, Ibn al-Jawzī criticizes rulers for terming whatever pigheaded actions they

undertake *siyāsāt*, and he also uses *siyāsāt* neutrally; Ibn al-Jawzī, *Ṣayd al-khāṭir*, 257, 648.

110. Ibn al-Jawzī, *Muntaẓam*, 1:117.
111. Rapoport, "Royal Justice and Religious Law," 95; Nielsen, 33. For the most extensive list of the duties of a ruler, see al-Munāwī, *al-Jawāhir al-muḍiyya fī bayān al-ādāb al-sulṭāniyya*, 65–83.
112. Ibn Farḥūn, *al-Tabṣira*, 2:115.
113. Al-Maqrīzī, *al-Mawāʿiẓ wa'l-iʿtibār bi-dhikr al-khiṭat wa'l-āthar*, 3:82.
114. Tāj al-Dīn al-Subkī, *Ṭabaqāt*, 4:310.
115. Abū Shāma, *al-Rawḍatayn*, 1:40.
116. Ibn Qayyim al-Jawziyya, *al-Ṭuruq al-ḥukmiyya*, 1:29.
117. Ibn ʿĀbidīn, *Ḥāshiyat Ibn ʿĀbidīn*, 6 vols. (Beirut: Dār al-Fikr, 1421/2000, reprint of 1966 Cairo Muṣṭafā al-Bābī al-Ḥalabī edition), 4:15.
118. Al-Māwardī, *Aḥkām*, 114,115.
119. Al-Māwardī, *Aḥkām*, 115; Ibn al-Farrā', 81.
120. Al-Māwardī, *Aḥkām*, 125; Ibn al-Farrā', 89.
121. Al-Māwardī, *al-Ḥāwī*, 14:138, 17:187.
122. For example, Ahmet Akgündüz, *Islamic Public Law* (Rotterdam: IUR Press, 2011), 143–150; idem, "Osmanlı Kanunnâmelerinin Şer'î Sınırları," *Osmanlı* (Ankara: Yeni Türkiye Yayınları, 1999), 6:401–411. The issue of whether Ottoman *kanun* was a normative source outside and at times in tension with the Shariah, or, by contrast, the Ottoman elite/ulama perceived *kanun* to be part of the Shariah/totally in conformity with it has been a scholarly debate for a century, often reflecting the Kemalist/Western-secular or Islamophile leanings of its participants. I side with the harmony/conformity position. The debate was first set forth by Fuat Köprülü, "Orta zaman Türk Hukuki Müesseseleri: İslam amme hukukundan ayrı bir Türk amme hukuku yok mudur?" *Belleten* 2, n. 5–6 (1938): 39–72 and Ömer Lütfi Barkan, "Osmanlı İmparatorluğu teşkilat ve müesseselerinin şeriliği meselesi," *İstanbul Üniversitesi Hukuk Fakültesi Mecmuası* 11, n. 3–4 (1945): 203–224. The harmonious system/conformity position has been argued by: Lauren A. Benton, *Law and Colonial Cultures: Local Regimes in World History, 1400–1900* (Cambridge: Cambridge University Press, 2002); Rhoads Murphey, "Hybridity in Ottoman legal tradition as a source of flexibility in governing the empire: An overview with particular reference to the application of the ruler's executive judicial or *örfi* powers," in *Imperial Lineages and Legacies in the Eastern Mediterranean*, ed. Rhoads Murphey (Oxford: Routledge, 2016), 35–36; Mehmet Âkif Aydın, *Osmanlı Devleti'nde Hukuk ve Adalet* (Istanbul: Klasik, 2014), 15–31; Akgündüz, "Osmanlı Kanunnâmelerinin Şer'î Sınırları," 6:401–411. The *kanun*-and-Shariah in competition/tension side has been argued by: Richard C. Repp, "Qānūn and Sharīʿa in the Ottoman Context," in *Islamic Law: Social and Historical Contexts*, ed. Aziz Al-Azmeh (Oxford: Routledge, 2013, reprint of Repp's 1988 article), 124–125, 128; Şerif Mardin, "The Just and the Unjust," 115 (*kanun* "was secular law determined by sultanic fiat"); Neşet Çağatay, "An Outline of Islamic Law and Different Applications of Some of Its Rules by the Ottomans," *Belleten* 51 (1987): 637–649; Douglas A. Howard, "Historical Scholarship and the Classical Ottoman Kânûnnames," *Archivum Ottomanicum* 14 (1995–6): 81; Colin Imber, "Law and Legislation under Süleymân I," in *The Battle for Central Europe: The Siege of Szigetvár and*

the Death of Süleyman the Magnificent and Nicholas Zrínyi, ed. Pál Fodor (Leiden: Brill, 2018), 112 ("The supposed conformity of *kanun* with *sharia* is... an illusion") (thanks to Guy Burak for pointing out much of this material).

123. For example, Burak, "Between the Kānūn of Qāytbāy," 16.
124. Muḥammad Zāhid al-Kawtharī (Kevsari), *Maqālāt*, 2nd ed. (Cairo: Dār al-Salām, 1428/2007), 79–80.
125. Plato, *Statesman*, 300a-300e.
126. Aristotle, *Nicomachean Ethics*, 5.10.3–6.
127. Translating this line of thinking into a Christian idiom of writing on statecraft, John of Salisbury (d. 1180) urged the prince not to take offense at the failings of his law in the face of God, whose "justice is eternal justice and whose law is equity." Human law can at best be the "interpreter" of this divine justice; John of Salisbury in his *Policratus*, Book 4, 2, paragraphs 1–2; here cited from Oliver and Joan Lockwood O'Donovan, ed., *From Irenaeus to Grotius: a Sourcebook in Christian Political Thought* (Grand Rapids: W.B. Eerdmans, 1999), 283.
128. Khadduri, *Islamic Conception of Justice*, 155–156.
129. Ibn Qudāma, *Taḥrīm al-naẓar fī kutub ahl al-kalām*, ed. George Maqkdisi (London: Luzac, 1962), 65. In one fascinating story of a saint's miracle, one Abū Bakr b. Yūsuf al-Madanī (d. 697/1297–8) has a dream in which God judges the four founders of the Sunni schools of law for breaking the unity of the Shariah. Ibn Ḥanbal, however, uses the details of court procedure to exonerate them all via *fiqh* technicalities; Yūsuf al-Nabhānī, *Jāmiʿ karamāt al-awliyā'*, ed. ʿAbd al-Wārith Muḥammad ʿAlī, 2 vols. (Beirut: Dār al-Kutub al-ʿIlmiyya, 1422/2002), 1:350.
130. Al-Khaṣṣāf, *Adab al-qāḍī*, 338 ff.; Ibn ʿAbd al-Salām, *Fatāwā*, 74 (that judges should honor contracts approved by other *madhhabs*, reminiscent of estoppel concern); al-Laknawī, *al-Fawā'id al-bahiyya*, 50 (that scholars should affirm the validity of prayers said behind imams praying according to different *madhhabs*); Ibrahim, *Pragmatism in Islamic Law*, 116, 129, 130, 135, 152–153 (courts honored other *madhhabs*' rulings in Ottoman Cairo); al-Qarāfī, *The Criterion for Distinguishing Legal Opinions from Judicial Rulings*, 136 ff., 192–197.
131. *Jāmiʿ al-Tirmidhī*: *kitāb al-aḥkām*, *bāb... fī al-qāḍī*; *Sunan* of Abū Dāwūd: *kitāb al-aqḍiya*, *bāb fī al-qāḍī yukhṭi'u*; Ismāʿīl b. Aḥmad al-ʿAjlūnī, *Kashf al-khafā'*, ed. Aḥmad al-Qalāsh, 2 vols. (Cairo: Dār al-Turāth, n.d.), 2:126; Murtaḍa al-Zabīdī, *Itḥāf al-sāda al-muttaqīn bi-sharḥ Iḥyā' ʿulūm al-dīn*, 10 vols. (Beirut: Mu'assasat al-Tārīkh al-ʿArabī, 1414/1994, reprint of 1894 Cairo Maymaniyya print), 1:375–376; 8:316. Ibn Ḥajar apparently devoted a short book to this Hadith; al-Sakhāwī, *al-Maqāṣid al-ḥasana*, ed. Muḥammad ʿUthmān al-Khisht (Beirut: Dār al-Kitāb al-ʿArabī, 1424/2004), 313.
132. *Ṣaḥīḥ al-Bukhārī*: *kitāb al-maẓālim* (yes!), *bāb ithm man khāṣama fī bāṭil wa huwa yaʿlamuhu*; *Ṣaḥīḥ Muslim*: *kitāb al-aqḍiya*, *bāb al-ḥukm bi'l-ẓāhir al-laḥn bi'l-ḥujja*; *Sunan* of Abū Dāwūd: *kitāb al-aqḍiya*, *bāb fī qaḍā' al-qāḍī idhā akhṭa'a*; *Jāmiʿ al-Tirmidhī*: *kitāb al-aḥkām*, *bāb mā jā'a fī al-tashdīd ʿalā man yuqḍā lahu bi-shay' laysa lahu an ya'khudhahu*; *Sunan al-Nasā'ī*: *kitāb ādāb al-quḍāt*, *bāb al-ḥukm bi'l-ẓāhir*; *Sunan Ibn Mājah*: *kitāb al-aḥkām*, *bāb qaḍiyyat al-ḥākim lā tuḥillu ḥarāman wa la tuḥarrimu ḥalālan*. A narration of this Hadith found in a much later and notoriously unreliable collection, the *Firdaws al-akhbār* of Shīrawayh b. Shahrudār al-Daylamī (d. 509/1115),

includes the added wording "I am but a man, and I do not know the unseen (*ghayb*)...," which raises the issues of 1) whether the Prophet knows the Unseen and 2) if he can rule on the basis of such knowledge; Shīrawayh b. Shahrudār al-Daylamī, *al-Firdaws bi-ma'thūr al-khiṭāb*, 2 vols. (Beirut: Dār al-Fikr, 1418/1997), 1:201. Scholars like Qāḍī 'Iyāḍ (d. 544/1149) argued that the Prophet did, in fact, know the truth of such a case but that he acted as if he did not in order to instruct people how to act as judges. Al-Suyūṭī argues that the Prophet actually could and did sometimes rule by such hidden knowledge (*bāṭin*), adducing a number of questionable Hadiths to this effect; Qāḍī 'Iyāḍ, *Kitāb al-Shifā*, 382; al-Suyūṭī, *al-Bāhir fī ḥukm al-Nabī ṣallā Allāhu 'alayhi wa sallama bi'l-bāṭin wa'l-ẓāhir*, 34 ff.

133. Johansen, "Vérité et torture," 159.

134. Lawrence B. Solum, "Procedural Justice," *Southern California Law Review* 78, n. 1 (2004): 184.

135. Al-Qarāfī, *al-Dhakhīra*, 10:45–46. The extent to which the procedural pragmatism of al-Qarāfī and Ibn Qayyim al-Jawziyya found acceptance is clear in the widely-cited *Mu'īn al-ḥukkām* of al-Ṭarābulusī (d. 844/1441), the Ḥanafī judge of Jerusalem. His section on 'Adjudicating on the Basis of Testimony from Non-Upright Witnesses due to Necessity' consists primarily of quotations from al-Qarāfī and Ibn al-Qayyim, and he cites Ibn Qayyim's *Ṭuruq* and al-Qarāfī's *Dhakhīra* by name in his section on ruling by *siyāsa*; 145–46, 212, 216; Kātib Chelebī, *Kashf al-ẓunūn*, 3:307–308. For the influence of the *Mu'īn al-ḥukkām*, see Dede Efendi, *al-Siyāsa al-shar'iyya*, 74, 82, 109, 110, 143, 144, 149, etc.

136. Al-Māwardī, *Aḥkām*, 121.

137. Nielsen's parenthetical acknowledgment (see ibid., 31) that important Mālikī *fiqh* manuals, such as that of Ibn Farḥūn, in fact did devote attention to the *maẓālim* reveals the flaw in his argument. Unlike the other three Sunni schools of law, the Mālikīs considered the application of executive justice on issues like banditry to fall within the *qāḍī's* remit, not strictly that of the ruler. This explains why that school alone included the *maẓālim* amongst the issues covered in *fiqh* manuals.

138. Masud, *Shari'a Today*, 251.

CONCLUSION: DOES THE *MAẒĀLIM* TRIBUNAL MAKE LEGAL REFORMS 'ISLAMIC'?

1. M. Şükrü Hanioğlu, "Garbcılar: Their Attitudes toward Religion and Their Impact on the Official Ideology of the Turkish Republic," *Studia Islamica* 86 (1997): 133–158.

2. Peters, *Crime and Punishment in Islamic Law*, 11; idem, "What Does it Mean to be an Official Madhhab? Hanafism and the Ottoman Empire," in *The Islamic School of Law*, ed. Peri Bearman, R. Peters, and Frank Vogel (Cambridge, MA: Harvard University Press, 2005), 153. Prior to this, the Ḥanafī school had placed different time limits on certain types of claims, and there were regional

variations as well. But this new rule was unprecedented in its breadth. Sultan Süleyman's statute did not apply to land claims.

3. The Mughal emperor in question was Akbar; 'Abd al-Qādir Badā'ūnī, *Muntakhab al-tavārīkh*, ed. Aḥmad 'Alī Ṣāḥeb (Tehran: Anjoman-e Āthār va Mafākher-e Farhangī, 1380/2002), 1:188–189.
4. Umar Shareef, "*Siyāsa* as a Part of the *Sharīʿa*: Tracing the Genealogy of the Ruler's Right to 'Restrict the Permissible' (*Taqyīd al-Mubāḥ*)," (PhD dissertation, Georgetown University, 2025), introduction; idem, "*Taqyīd al-Mubāḥ* and Tobacco: Between Administrative and Legislative Authority," *Islamic Law and Society* 30, n. 3 (2023): 1–30.
5. Iza Hussin, *The Politics of Islamic Law* (Chicago: University of Chicago Press, 2016), 150, 165. The martyred Sufi scholar Muḥammad 'Abd al-Kabīr al-Kattānī (d. 1327/1907) of Fez also encouraged the Moroccan sultan to adopt Ottoman legal reforms instead of European ones; Bazzaz, *Forgotten Saints*, 118. The 1917 Ottoman Family Law Code introduced a law unprecedented in the *madhhab*s: it prohibited marriage completely for a boy under seventeen and a girl under nine (it was permitted for girls under seventeen and boys under eighteen if they were adolescents approved of by the judge). This was justified by going outside all four Sunni *madhhab*s to the opinions of the early Kufan Ibn Shubruma (d. 144/761) and the Muʿtazilite al-Aṣamm (d. 201/817). See *Münâkehât ve Müfârakât Kararnâmesi Esbâb-ı Mucıbe Lâyihası*, found in Ibrahim Alhalalsheh, "Ürdün Ahvâl-i Şahsiyye Kanununun Osmanlı Hukuk-ı Âile Kararnamesi İle Mukayesesi," (PhD dissertation, Marmara University, 2009), 246–247, 273. The 2004 Moroccan *Mudawwanat al-Usra* is based in the Mālikī school but gives an adult woman full agency in contracting a marriage, borrowing an opinion from the Ḥanafī school; al-Ḥusayn al-Mūs, *Mudawwanat al-usra fī ḍaw' taqyīd al-mubāḥ* (Casablanca: Abdulla Abdulghani Foundation, 2015), 71.
6. Mark Cammack and R. Michael Feener, "The Islamic Legal System in Indonesia," *Pacific Rim Law & Policy Journal* 21, n. 1 (2012): 14, 17, 21.
7. Clark Lombardi and Emad Eldin Shahin, "Sanhūrī, 'Abd al-Razzāq al-," in *Oxford Encyclopedia of the Islamic World: Digital Collection*, https://www.oxfordreference.com/view/10.1093/acref/9780197669419.001.0001/acref-9780197669419-e-353. For different perspectives on al-Sanhūrī's landmark contributions, see Ayoub, "A Theory of a State? How Civil Law Ended Legal Pluralism in Modern Egypt," *Journal of Law and Religion* (2022): 1–20 (viewing him more as a committed French comparativist); Lombardi and Nathan Brown, "Do Constitutions Requiring Adherence to *Shariʿa* Threaten Human Rights? How Egypt's Constitutional Court Reconciles Islamic Law with the Liberal Rule of Law," *American University Intl. Law Review* 21, n. 3 (2006): 411–414; Enid Hill, "Al-Sanhuri and Islamic Law," *Arab Law Quarterly* 3, n. 1 (1988): 33–64; idem, "Al-Sanhuri and Islamic Law...Part II," *Arab Law Quarterly* 3, n. 2 (1988): 182–218; and Leonard Wood, *Islamic Legal Revival* (Oxford: Oxford University Press, 2016) (all as an Islamic legal revivalist).
8. For the importance of such 'repugnancy clauses' in Muslim states, including Egypt, Kuwait, Iraq, Iran, Pakistan, and the UAE, see Lombardi, *State Law as Islamic Law in Modern Egypt* (Leiden: Brill, 2006); idem, "Designing Islamic constitutions: Past trends and options for a democratic future," *I-con (International Journal of Constitutional Law)* 11, n. 3 (2013): 615–645.

9. Jonathan Brown, *Slavery & Islam* (London: Oneworld, 2019), 224–227, 254; idem, *Misquoting Muhammad* (London: Oneworld, 2015), 155.
10. Stephen N. Subrin, "How Equity Conquered Common Law: The Federal Rules of Civil Procedure in Historical Perspective," *University of Pennsylvania Law Review* 135 (1987): 918–919.
11. Smith, "Equity as Meta-Law."
12. Alhalalsheh, "Ürdün Ahvâl-i Şahsiyye Kanununun Osmanlı Hukuk-ı Âile Kararnamesi İle Mukayesesi," 246–247, 273.
13. See Ibrahim, *Pragmatism in Islamic Law*. See note 5 above. For Egyptian courts drawing on Ibāḍī law to deal with inheritance claims made by a manumitted slave in 1943, see Ayoub, "After Manumission: Islamic Inheritance Law and the Abolition of Slavery in Modern Egypt," forthcoming. The Indonesian professor of Islamic law and architect of the country's legal system, Hazairin (d. 1395/1975), proposed borrowing an inheritance rule from the Jaʿfarī Shiite school, which allows daughters to inherit more in the presence of agnatic kin and thus accorded better with matrilineal customs in Indonesia (ultimately this was not adopted in the national code); Mark E. Cammack, "Islam and Nationalism in Indonesia: Forging an Indonesian Madhhab," in *The Islamic School of Law*, ed. Peri Bearman, Rudolph Peters, and Frank E. Vogel (Cambridge, MA: Harvard University Press, 2005), 179. See also Euis Nurlaelawati, *Modernization, Tradition and Identity: The Kompilasi Hukum Islam and Legal Practice in the Indonesian Religious Courts* (Amsterdam: Amsterdam University Press, 2010), 98.
14. Leonard Wood notes that, among Islamic legal revivalists like al-Sanhūrī, *siyāsa sharʿiyya* was often used as a synonym for *ijtihād*; Wood, *Islamic Legal Revivalism*, 75, 77, 124; al-Zarqā, *al-Madkhal al-fiqhī al-ʿāmm*, 1:243, 262; Gebril, "Recasting *al-Siyāsa al-Sharʿiyya* in 1920s Egypt."
15. Examples include the law codes of Morocco, Pakistan, Bangladesh, and Indonesia; Cammack, "Islam and Nationalism in Indonesia," 188; idem, "Southeast Asia: Indonesia," in *Oxford Encyclopedia of the Islamic World: Digital Collection*, https://www.oxfordreference.com/view/10.1093/acref/9780197669419.001.0001/acref-9780197669419-e-395); Tarek A. Elgawhary, "Codification of Law," in *Oxford Encyclopedia of the Islamic World: Digital Collection*, https://www.oxfordreference.com/view/10.1093/acref/9780197669419.001.0001/acref-9780197669419-e-90; Haseeb Fatima, "Inheritance Rights of Orphaned Grandchildren under Section 4 of Muslim Family Law Ordinance, 1961 and its Alternative Solutions," *Law and Policy Review* 3, n 2 (2024): 22–42.
16. Gebril, "Recasting *al-Siyāsa al-Sharʿiyya*," 131.
17. Disagreements certainly occur, as with the ongoing refusal of Egypt's state ulama like Shaykh al-Azhar Aḥmad al-Ṭayyib to agree with the dictator ʿAbd al-Fattāḥ al-Sīsī's efforts to require *ṭalāq* to be pronounced in court in order to be registered. See Amīna Khayrī, "Tawthīq al-ṭalāq... ṣirāʿ maktūm bayn al-Azhar wa'l-ri'āsa fī miṣr," *IndependentArabia*, Mar. 24, 2023, https://web.archive.org/web/20250418151117/https://www.independentarabia.com/node/434281/%D8%AA%D8%AD%D9%82%D9%8A%D9%82%D8%A7%D8%AA-%D9%88%D9%85%D8%B7%D9%88%D9%84%D8%A7%D8%AA/%D8%AA%D9%88%D8%AB%D9%8A%D9%82-%D8%A7%D9%84%D8%B7%D9%84%D8%A7%D9%82-%D8%B5%D8%B1%D8%A7%D8%B9-

%D9%85%D9%83%D8%AA%D9%88%D9%85-%D8%A8%D9%8A%D9%86-%D8%A7%D9%84%D8%A3%D8%B2%D9%87%D8%B1-%D9%88%D8%A7%D9%84%D8%B1%D8%A6%D8%A7%D8%B3%D8%A9-%D9%81%D9%8A-%D9%85%D8%B5%D8%B1.

18. See Aria Nakissa, "An Epistemic Shift in Islamic Law: Educational Reform at al-Azhar and Dār al-ʿUlūm," *Islamic Law and Society* 21, n. 3 (2014): 209–251.

19. Wood, *Islamic Legal Revivalism*, 25–28, 32; Peter Mansfield, *The British in Egypt* (New York: Holt, Rinehart & Winston, 1971), 14.

20. Wood, 60; Rashīd Riḍā, "Taqrīr al-ustādh al-imām fī iṣlāḥ al-maḥākim al-sharʿiyya," *al-Manār* 3, n. 11 (1908): 191.

21. Aḥmad Shākir, *Jamharat maqālāt al-ʿallāma al-shaykh Aḥmad Muḥammad Shākir*, ed. ʿAbd al-Raḥmān ʿAbd al-ʿAzīz, 2 vols. (Giza: Dār al-Riyāḍ, 1426/2005), 1:485, 501, 2:595–604, 612; Yāsir Burhāmī, *al-Minna sharḥ iʿtiqād ahl al-sunna*, 2nd ed. (Alexandria: Dār al-Khulafāʾ al-Rāshidīn, 1431/2010), 149–153; ʿAbd al-Ḥalīm Maḥmūd, *Fatāwā al-imām ʿAbd al-Ḥalīm Maḥmūd*, 5th ed., 2 vols. (Cairo: Dār al-Maʿārif, 2002), 2:433; Jakob Skovgaard-Petersen, *Defining Islam for the Egyptian State* (Leiden: Brill, 1997), 259.

22. Wood, 34, 35, 42, 48.

23. Armando Salvatore, "After the State: Islamic reform and the 'implosion' of *shari'a*," in *Muslim Traditions and Modern Techniques of Power*, ed. Armando Salvatore (Münster: Lit, 2001), 133, 135 (thanks to Rachel Scott for alerting me to this source); Wood, 50.

24. *Al-Fatāwā al-islāmiyya min dār al-iftāʾ al-miṣriyya*, ed. Jād al-Ḥaqq ʿAlī Jād al-Ḥaqq et al., 2nd ed. (Cairo: Wizārat al-Awqāf, 1418/1997), 10:3685 (#1321, April 1979). For more recent Dār al-Iftāʾ fatwas, see Fatwa #4139 (Sept. 26, 2005) and an announcement from Jan. 1, 2017; https://web.archive.org/web/20250302200106/https://www.dar-alifta.org/ar/Articles/4880/%D9%85%D9%81%D8%AA%D9%8A-%D8%A7%D9%84%D8%AC%D9%85%D9%87%D9%88%D8%B1%D9%8A%D8%A9-%D9%81%D9%8A-%D8%A8%D8%B1%D9%86%D8%A7%D9%85%D8%AC-%D8%AD%D9%88%D8%A7%D8%B1-%D8%A7%D9%84%D9%85%D9%81%D8%AA%D9%8A-%D9%85%D8%B7%D9%85%D9%8A%D9%86%D9%88%D9%86-%D8%A7%D9%86-%D8%A7%D9%84%D8%B4%D8%B1%D9%8A%D8%B9%D8%A9-%D8%A7%D9%84%D8%A7%D8%B3; https://web.archive.org/web/20250302195615/https://www.dar-alifta.org/ar/fatawa/13999/%D8%A7%D9%84%D9%85%D8%B7%D8%A7%D9%84%D8%A8%D8%A9-%D8%A8%D8%B9%D8%AF%D9%85-%D8%AA%D8%B7%D8%A8%D9%8A%D9%82-%D8%A7%D9%84%D8%B4%D8%B1%D9%8A%D8%B9%D8%A9.

25. ʿAlī Jumʿa, *al-Tajruba al-miṣriyya* (Cairo: Nahḍat Miṣr, 2008), 33–34, 43; idem, *al-Bayān li-mā yashghalu al-adhhān* (Cairo: Muqaṭṭam, 1425/2005), 70.

26. These studies were produced by Shaykh Makhlūf al-Minyāwī (d. 1290/1878) and Muḥammad Ḥilmī ʿĪsā (d. 1372/1953). See Wood, *Islamic Legal Revivalism*, 53, 63. See also John Makdisi, "The Islamic Origins of the Common Law," *North Carolina Law Review* 77, n. 5 (1999): 1635–1740. The claim that French law was based on Mālikī law is still often repeated, as noted by the late Egyptian Mālikī scholar Shaykh Aḥmad al-Rayyān (d. 1442/2021); lecture notes from Mālikī *fiqh* class with Shaykh al-Rayyān, Dardīr mosque in Cairo, June 7, 2011. It was also repeated by Egypt's state Mufti, Shawqī ʿAllām; presentation,

Global Forum for Peace, Abu Dhabi, March 9–10, 2014. Muḥammad Zāhid al-Kawtharī, writing in interwar Cairo, accepts the claim that the French borrowed from Mālikī law but turns it on its head: if they needed to take from us, how can we take law from them?!; al-Kawtharī, *Maqālāt*, 194–195.

27. Shaykh al-Azhar Maḥmūd Shaltūt explained that Egyptian judges applying laws of foreign origin were partially excused because, except for rulings based on explicit texts of the Quran and Sunna, the Shariah was aimed at *maṣlaḥa* and justice even if the actual rulings being applied broke with all the *madhhabs*; Shaltūt, *Fatāwā* (Cairo: Dār al-Shurūq, 1408/1983), 44–45.
28. For example, see Patrick Kinross, *Atatürk: A Biography of Mustafa Kemal* (New York: W. Morrow, 1965); Berkes, *The Development of Secularism in Turkey*, 161; Bernard Lewis, *The Emergence of Modern Turkey*, 120; Erik J. Zürcher, *Turkey: A Modern History* (London: IB Tauris, 1997), 64; and in a new rephrasing, Nurullah Ardıç, *Islam and the Politics of Secularism* (London: Routledge, 2012). For a study of this period, see Bedir, "*Fıkıh* to Law," 378–401.
29. Al-Kattānī, *Salwat al-anfās*, 3:98. The revivalist Sufi of Fez, Aḥmad al-Tijānī (d. 1230/1815), deemed the Ottoman rulers of Algiers unbelievers because they favored their own laws over the Shariah; Zachary Wright, *Realizing Islam: The Tijaniyya in North Africa and the Eighteenth-Century Muslim World* (Chapel Hill: University of North Carolina Press, 2020), 176.
30. Zeghal, *The Making of the Modern Muslim State*, 67, 71.
31. Mehmet Âkif Aydın, "Dîvân-ı Ahkâm-ı Adliyye," in *İslâm Ansiklopedisi* (Istanbul: ISAM, n.d.), 9:388 (https://islamansiklopedisi.org.tr/divan-i-ahkam-i-adliyye) and idem, "İslamcılık: Hukukta," *İslâm Ansiklopedisi*, https://islamansiklopedisi.org.tr/islamcilik#4-hukukta.
32. Al-Kawākibī, "Umm al-qurā," in *ʿAbd al-Raḥmān al-Kawākibī: al-aʿmāl al-kāmila*, 350.
33. Amit Bein, *Ottoman Ulema, Turkish Republic: Agents of Change and Guardians of Tradition* (Palo Alto: Stanford University Press, 2011), 81. See also idem, "ʿUlama' and Political Activism in the Late Ottoman Empire: The Political Career of Şeyhülislâm Mustafa Sabri Efendi (1869–1954)," in *Guardians of Faith in Modern Times: ʿUlama in the Modern Middle East*, ed. Meir Hatina (Leiden: Brill, 2009), 67–90.
34. Butrus Abu-Manneh, "The Islamic Roots of the Gülhane Rescript," *Die Welt des Islams* 34, n. 2 (1994): 173–203; Alp Eren Topal, "Political Reforms as Religious Revival: Conceptual Foundations of *Tanzimat*," *Oriente Moderno* 101 (2021): 153–180; Iris Agmon, *Family & Court: Legal Culture and Modernity in Late Ottoman Palestine* (Syracuse: Syracuse University Press, 2006); Gavin Brockett, *How Happy to Call Oneself a Turk* (Austin: University of Texas Press, 2011), 13–24. As Brian Silverstein has observed, "the genealogy of Turkish secularism is grounded in Ottoman Islamic traditions." See Brian Silverstein, *Islam and Modernity in Turkey* (London: Palgrave Macmillan, 2010), 33.
35. See Ismail Kara, "Turban and fez: Ulema as opposition," in *Late Ottoman Society: The Intellectual Legacy*, ed. Elisabeth Özdolga (London: Routledge Curzon, 2005), 187–188.
36. Ruth A. Miller, *Legislating Authority: Sin and Crime in the Ottoman Empire and Turkey* (New York: Routledge, 2005), 82.
37. See Rubin, *Ottoman* Nizamiye *Courts*; idem, "Modernity as Code: The Ottoman Empire and the Global Movement of Codification," *Journal of the*

Social and Economic History of the Orient 59, n. 5 (2016): 829–856; idem, "Legal borrowing and its impact on Ottoman legal culture in the late nineteenth century," 281, 282, 284.

38. Rubin, *Ottoman* Nizamiye *Courts*, 15; idem, "Legal borrowing," 289.
39. See Rubin, *Ottoman* Nizamiye *Courts*; idem, "Modernity as Code," 829–856; idem, "Legal borrowing," 281, 282, 284; Miller, *Legislating Authority*, 15–16; Frederick F. Anscombe, *State, Faith, and Nation in Ottoman and Post-Ottoman Lands* (Cambridge: Cambridge University Press, 2014), 92–93; Wood, *Islamic Legal Revival*, 1.
40. Jun Akiba, "*Sharīʿa* Judges in the Ottoman *Nizāmiye* Courts, 1864–1908," *Osmanlı Araştırmarları / Journal of Ottoman Studies* 51 (2018): 209–237.
41. Akiba, 218, 233.
42. This critique is anticipated in Salvatore, "After the State," 134. For an example of *sharʿ* and *sharīʿa* used interchangeably, see Muḥammad ʿAbd al-ʿAzīz al-Farhānī, *al-Nibrās sharḥ Sharḥ al-ʿAqāʾid* (Istanbul: Âsitâne, 1430/2009), 722; Ẓahīr al-Dīn al-Rūdhrāwarī, *Dhayl Kitāb Tajārib al-umam*, published in Miskawayh, *Tajārib al-umum*, ed. Abū al-Qāsim Imāmī, 8 vols. (Tehran: Sorūsh, 2001), 7:68; al-Juwaynī, *al-Ghiyāthī: Ghiyāth al-umam fī iltiyāth al-ẓulam*, ed. ʿAbd al-ʿAẓīm Maḥmūd al-Dīb (Beirut: Dār al-Minhāj, 1432/2011), 236–237 (for *sharʿ* and *sharīʿa* both used); Ibn Mufliḥ's *al-Ādāb al-sharʿiyya*, etc. See also some of the earliest papyrus evidence of judicial summons, from the third/ninth century (*al-sharʿ al-sharīf*); Tillier, "The Qadis' Justice according to Papyrological Sources (Seventh to Tenth Centuries CE)," in *Legal Documents as Sources for the History of Muslim Societies: Studies in Honour of Rudolph Peters*, ed. Maaike van Berkel, Léon Buskens and Petra Sijpesteijn (Leiden: Brill, 2017), 51.
43. For a review of the ideological commitments around studies of late Ottoman reforms, see Olivier Bouquet, "Is it Time to Stop Speaking about Ottoman Modernization?" in *Order and Compromise: Government Practices in Turkey from the Late Ottoman Empire to the Early 21st Century*, ed. Marc Aymes, Benjamin Gourisse, and Élise Massicard (Leiden: Brill, 2015), 45–67. Şerif Mardin summarizes the transformation from his perspective: "The Muslim-Ottoman *imaginaire*, which promoted the reproduction of existing social relations, was gradually displaced by the Western reformist *imaginaire*, which was based on a view of society as made of individuals"; Mardin, "The Just and the Unjust," 121.
44. Şükrü Hanioğlu, *A Brief History of the Late Ottoman Empire* (Princeton: Princeton University Press, 2008), 74 (see also ibid., 19). For other examples, see Berkes, 168–169 among many other instances; Lewis, *The Emergence of Modern Turkey*, 260; Erhan Bektaş, *Religious Reform in the Late Ottoman Empire* (London: IB Tauris, 2023), 98; Akiba, "A New School for Qadis: Education of the Shariah Judges in the Late Ottoman Empire," *Turcica* 35 (2003): 125–163. Heyd correctly calls "*maḥkeme-i şerʿīye*" the judges' "law courts"; Heyd, *Studies in Old Ottoman Criminal Law*, 1.
45. Berkes is correct in this; Berkes, 166.
46. Bein, *Ottoman Ulema*, 82.
47. Bein, *Ottoman Ulema*, 44–47, 85–86, 112.
48. Baldwin, *Islamic Law and Empire in Ottoman Cairo*, 4 (based on Hallaq, *Sharīʿa*, 355–499).

49. The state is "the new God" of modernity; Hallaq, *The Impossible State*, 23–33, 57–65, 89.
50. Abdullahi An-Na'im, *Islam and the Secular State* (Cambridge, MA: Harvard University Press, 2007), 7.
51. See, for example, Fadel, "Islamic Law Reform," 44; Gerber, *State, Society, and Law in Islam*, 16.
52. Hallaq, *Sharīʿa*, 368.
53. Ayoub, "The Mecelle, Sharia, and the Ottoman State," *Journal of the Ottoman and Turkish Studies Association* (2015): 121–146. See also Ayoub and Ari Schriber, "A Sense of Justice: Coloniality and the Islamic Legal Tradition," *Die Welt des Islams*, published online to-date (2024): 1–10.
54. Brian Wright, *A Continuity of Shari'a* (Cairo: American University in Cairo Press, 2023); Peters, *Crime and Punishment in Islamic Law*, 129–131; idem, "The Codification of Criminal Law in Nineteenth Century [sic] Egypt: Tradition or Modernization," in *Law, Society, and National Identity in Africa*, ed. J.M. Abu-Nasr, Ulrich Spellenberg and Ulrike Wanitzek (Hamburg: H. Buske, 1990), 211–225; Tobias Heinzelmann, "The Ruler's Monologue: The Rhetoric of the Ottoman Penal Code of 1858," *Die Welt des Islams* 54 (2014): 292–321.
55. Jonathan Brown, "Stoning and Hand Cutting: Understanding the Hudud and the Shariah in Islam," *Yaqeen Institute*, July 12, 2017, https://web.archive.org/web/20250327204224/https://yaqeeninstitute.org/read/paper/stoning-and-hand-cutting-understanding-the-hudud-and-the-shariah-in-islam/.
56. Scott, *Recasting Islamic Law*, 5–6.
57. Jackson, *The Islamic Secular*, 199, 206.
58. Jackson, *The Islamic Secular*, 197, 201, 209.
59. Jackson, *The Islamic Secular*, 115, 132.
60. *Ṣaḥīḥ Muslim: kitāb al-imāra, bāb wujūb ṭāʿat al-umarāʾ...*; al-Albānī, *Fatāwā al-Shaykh al-Albānī*, ed. ʿUkāsha ʿAbd al-Mannān al-Ṭayyibī (Cairo: Maktabat al-Turāth al-Islāmī, 1994), 18, 71; Andrew March, *Islam and Liberal Citizenship* (Oxford: Oxford University Press, 2009), 139–179; Jocelyn Hendrickson, *Leaving Iberia: Islamic Law and Christian Conquest in North West Africa* (Cambridge, MA: Harvard University Press, 2021), 115, 145, 148, 195; Catlos, *Muslims of Medieval Latin Christendom*, 314–317.
61. This general standard can be traced back to medieval Ḥanafīs confronting life under Mongol rule; Edith Chen, "An Unbeliever Can Rule *Dār al-Islām*: Ḥanafī Law in the Wake of the Mongol Invasion," *Islamic Law and Society* 30 (2023): 442–475. The French colonial administration in Algeria and Morocco used an 1893 fatwa they requested from the ulama of Mecca to this effect; Jalila Sbaï, *La politique musalmane de la France* (Paris: CNRS Editions, 2018), 49, 327. Muslim scholars in Delhi from the early 1800s to the 1900s accepted British rule as long as Muslims were allowed to practice their religion; Nizami, "Madrasahs, Scholars and Saints," 166–192; SherAli Tareen, *Perilous Intimacies: Debating Hindu-Muslim Friendship After Empire* (New York: Columbia University Press, 2023), 22, 181–183; Hendrickson, 231–233.
62. Nathan Brown and Clark Lombardi, "The Supreme Constitutional Court of Egypt on Islamic Law, Veiling and Civil Rights," *American University Journal of International Law* 21, n. 3 (2006): 452–453; Jumʿa, *al-Bayān*, 343.

63. Gregory J. Massell, *The Surrogate Proletariat: Moslem Women and Revolutionary Strategies in Soviet Central Asia, 1919–1929* (Princeton: Princeton University Press, 1974), 213–331 (the Soviet state used a variety of direct and indirect methods to combat veiling, the "dark curtain of religion," ibid., 238).
64. Ayah El-Khaldi, "Saudi Arabia: Iggy Azalea triggers backlash for 'blasphemy' song in Riyadh," *Middle East Eye*, Aug. 8, 2023 https://web.archive.org/web/20241127154728/https://www.middleeasteye.net/news/iggy-azalea-saudi-arabia-concert-triggers-backlash-blasphemy, last accessed 11/27/2024.
65. See Usaama Al-Azami, "Legitimising Political Dissent: Islamist Salafi Discourses on Obedience to the Ruler and Rebellion after the Arab Revolutions," in *Salafi Social and Political Movements*, ed. Masooda Bano (Edinburgh: Edinburgh University Press, 2021), 61–85; al-Nawawī, *Sharḥ Ṣaḥīḥ Muslim*, 12:466–470; Muqbil bin Hādī al-Wādiʿī, *al-Makhraj min al-fitna*, 3rd ed. (Ṣaʿda: Maktabat Ṣanʿāʾ al-Athariyya, 2002), 143, 186; al-Albānī, *Fatāwā*, 359–360; ʿAbd al-Mālik Ramaḍānī al-Jazāʾirī, *Mudrik al-naẓar fī al-siyāsa bayn al-taṭbīqāt al-sharʿiyya wa al-infiʿālāt al-ḥamāsiyya*, 9th ed. (Cairo: Dār al-Furqān, 2009), 155–158; Ayman Diyāb al-ʿĀbidīnī, *Manhaj al-salaf al-qawīm fī al-ʿalāqa bayn al-ḥukkām wa'l-maḥkūmīn*, 3rd ed. (Cairo: Mu'assasat Sabīl al-Mu'minīn, 2009), 38–45; Nadeen Ebrahim, "Why the birthplace of Islam is hosting one of the world's biggest raves," *CNN*, Nov. 30, 2022, https://web.archive.org/web/20250307020315/https://www.cnn.com/2022/11/30/middleeast/saudi-arabia-biggest-rave-mime-intl/index.html.
66. Examples of ulama standing up to rulers are legion. Here are a few: Ibn Baṭṭūṭa, 3:693 (judge rules Delhi sultan must pay debt); al-Ghazzī, *al-Kawākib al-sāʾira*, 1:268 (Ottoman state mufti confronts Sultan Selîm over his decision to execute administrators without Shariah grounds, the Sultan relents); Chatterjee, *Negotiating Mughal Law*, 174 (Awrangzīb dismisses chief judge for not convicting his rival Dārā Shikūh of heresy); al-Ḥasanī, *Nuzhat al-khawāṭir*, 6:112 (chief mufti refuses Awrangzīb's request for a fatwa to attack the sultans of the Deccan); Tezcan, *The Second Ottoman Empire*, 42, 62 (in 1621 chief mufti refuses the sultan's demand for a fatwa allowing him to kill his brother; Sultan Süleyman had received this fatwa from his chief mufti, but the claim that Mehmet Fatih did is unsubstantiated); Brown, *Slavery & Islam*, 210 (in the late 1600s, when the Moroccan sultan Mawlay Ismāʿīl ordered the enslavement of all Black African Muslims in the area to fill his military levy, numerous leading ulama opposed this gross violation of the Shariah and were either exiled, imprisoned, or killed for doing so); Afaf Lutfi Marsot, *Women and Men in Late Eighteenth-Century Egypt* (Austin: University of Texas Press, 1995), 64 (ulama stand up to Mehmet Ali in 1804 when he tries to extort money from wealthy woman); Rajāʾ al-Naqqāsh, *al-Imām al-Marāghī: ḥayātuhu wa afkāruhu* (Cairo: Dār al-Shurūq, 2007), 47 (Shaykh al-Azhar Muṣṭafā al-Marāghī refuses King Fārūq's demand that he issue a fatwa that the divorced queen not be allowed to remarry).
67. Taqī al-Dīn al-Subkī, *Fatāwā*, 2:384.
68. This position was fully articulated by Ibn Ḥajar Haytamī, building on fatwas by al-Nawawī and Taqī al-Dīn al-Subkī. Al-Suyūṭī (d. 911/1505) rejected the notion that the ruler's edict could change the ethical or legal valance of an act at all; Shareef, "*Taqyīd al-Mubāḥ* and Tobacco," 23; idem, "*Siyāsa* as a Part of the *Sharīʿa*," chapter 2; Jonathan Brown, *Slavery & Islam*, 254.

69. Jeremy F. Walton, *Muslim Civil Society and the Politics of Religious Freedom in Turkey* (New York: Oxford University Press, 2017); Besnik Sinani, *Sufism in Saudi Arabia Since 1979: The Politics of Orthodoxy in Contemporary Islam* (Leiden: Brill, forthcoming).
70. Fahd Ṣāliḥ al-ʿAjlān, *al-Taḥrīm wa'l-tajrīm fī bayān al-ʿalāqa bayn al-taḥrīm al-sharʿī wa'l-tajrīm al-qānūnī* ([Riyadh]: Markaz al-Bayān li'l-Buḥūth wa'l-Dirāsāt, 2017), 1–210.
71. "*Muftī al-suʿūdiyya: muqāṭaʿat qaṭar fīhā maṣlaḥa li'l-muslimīn...*" *CNN Arabic*, June 11, 2017, https://web.archive.org/web/20250216165622/https://arabic.cnn.com/middle-east/2017/06/11/saudi-mufti-qatar-gcc-rift-muslim-brotherhood.
72. @PPeacenews, "*Muntadā taʿzīz al-silm yadʿū al-ḥukūma al-qaṭariyya ilā taghyīr sulūkihā wa taṣḥīḥ akhṭā'ihā #qaṭʿ al-ʿalāqāt maʿa qaṭar*," X.com, Jun. 7, 2017, 7:29am, https://x.com/PPeacenews/status/872415235512172545. See Usaama al-Azami, "Gulf crisis: How autocrats use religious scholars against Qatar," *Middle East Eye*, Aug. 9, 2017, https://web.archive.org/web/20250216180341/https://www.middleeasteye.net/opinion/gulf-crisis-how-autocrats-use-religious-scholars-against-qatar.
73. Ofir Winter and Yoel Guzansky, "Islam in the Service of Peace: Religious Aspects of the Abraham Accord," *INSS* (Institute for National Security Studies) *Insight* N. 1379, Sept. 6, 2020, https://web.archive.org/web/20250216172736/https://www.inss.org.il/publication/israel-uae-deal-and-islam/; "*Majlis al-imārāt li'l-iftā': al-muʿāhadāt al-dawliyya min ṣalāḥiyyāt walī al-amr al-ḥaṣriyya wa'l-siyāda*," *CNN Arabic*, Aug. 14, 2020, https://web.archive.org/web/20250216202523/https://arabic.cnn.com/middle-east/article/2020/08/15/iftaa-peace-agreement-between-uae-and-israel; David H. Warren, "The Modernist Roots of Islamic Autocracy: Shaykh Abdullah Bin Bayyah and the UAE-Israel Peace Deal," *TheMaydan.com*, Aug. 17, 2020, https://web.archive.org/web/20250216173512/https://themaydan.com/2020/08/the-modernist-roots-of-islamic-autocracy-shaykh-abdullah-bin-bayyah-and-the-uae-israel-peace-deal/.
74. Inalcik, *The Ottoman Empire*, 14; Abudrrahman Atçıl, *Scholars and Sultans in the Early Modern Ottoman Empire* (Cambridge: Cambridge University Press, 2017), 95.
75. P.M. Holt, *The Age of the Crusades* (London: Longman, 1986), 41; Hugh Kennedy, *Muslim Spain and Portugal* (London: Routledge, 1996), 271–272 (thanks to Mohamad Ballan for this).
76. "*Shaykh al-Azhar yarfuḍu tashbīh ustādh fī al-fiqh li'l-sīsī wa ibrāhīm bi'l-anbiyā'*," *Arabic.CNN*, Feb. 9, 2014, https://web.archive.org/web/20250307160429/https://arabic.cnn.com/middleeast/2014/02/09/hilaly-sisi-ibrahim-prophets.
77. Charles Melville, "From Adam to Abaqa: Qāḍī Baiḍāwī's Rearrangement of History," *Studia Iranica* 30, n. 1 (2001): 69, 78–80 (thanks to Ovamir Anjum for this idea); Mona Hassan, *Longing for the Lost Caliphate* (Princeton: Princeton University Press, 2016), 33, 38, 47–50.
78. Here I am exempting tenuous Islamic modernist arguments that the Quran never actually allowed or endorsed slavery; Jonathan Brown, *Slavery & Islam*, 201–239, 254.

79. Muḥammad al-Ṭāhir Ibn ʿĀshūr, *al-Taḥrīr wa'l-tanwīr*, 17 vols. (Tunis: al-Dār al-Tūnisiyya, 1984), 5:43–44.
80. This is the position of the Shāfiʿī, Ḥanafī, and Mālikī schools if the intoxication results from something prohibited like wine; al-Zuḥaylī, *Mawsūʿat al-fiqh al-islāmī*, 10:131, 186.
81. Mūs, 128–129; Mark Cammack, Helen Donovan, and Tim B. Heaton, "Islamic Divorce Law and Practice in Indonesia," in *Islamic Law in Contemporary Indonesia*, ed. R. Michael Feener and Mark E. Cammack (Cambridge, MA: Harvard University Press, 2007), 102; Michael Peletz, "Are Women Getting (More) Justice? Malaysia's *Sharia* Courts in Ethnographic and Historical Perspective," *Law & Society Review* 52, n. 3 (2018): 673. Al-Kawtharī objects that placing *ṭalāq* in a judge's hands is a Western import with no basis in the Shariah; al-Kawtharī, *Maqālāt*, 323–324.

Index